HELLENISTIC POETRY

HELLENISTIC POETRY

G. O. HUTCHINSON

CLARENDON PRESS · OXFORD
1988

Oxford University Press, Walton Street, Oxford OX2 6DP

Oxford New York Toronto
Delhi Bombay Calcutta Madras Karachi
Petaling Jaya Singapore Hong Kong Tokyo
Nairobi Dar es Salaam Cape Town
Melbourne Auckland

and associated companies in
Berlin Ibadan

Oxford is a trade mark of Oxford University Press

Published in the United States
by Oxford University Press, New York

British Library Cataloguing in Publication Data

Hutchinson, G. O.
Hellenistic poetry
1. Greek poetry—History and criticism
I. Title
881'.01'09 PA3092
ISBN 0-19-814040-1

Library of Congress Cataloging in Publication Data
Hutchinson, G. O.
Hellenistic poetry/G. O. Hutchinson.
p.   cm.
Bibliography: p.
Includes indexes.
1. Greek poetry, Hellenistic—History and criticism. 2. Latin
poetry—Greek influences. 3. Callimachus—Criticism and
interpretation. 4. Theocritus—Criticism and interpretation.
5. Appollonius, Rhodius. Argonautica. 6. Argonauts (Greek
mythology) in literature. I. Title.
PA3081.H88 1988   881'.01'09—dc19   87-31517
ISBN 0-19-814040-1

63,806

Printed and bound in
Great Britain by Biddles Ltd,
Guildford and King's Lynn

To my pupils at Exeter

PREFACE

THIS book attempts a literary account of the principal poets writing between c.280 and c.240 BC, and also discusses their impact on Roman poetry. Its potential audience should include both scholars and undergraduates; it could be read by undergraduates who know Latin and not Greek. All classes will have to display tolerance at some points. Greek and Latin in the text is translated: I am guilty of the translations, which aim purely at catching some of the sense, however inelegantly. The work does presuppose a knowledge of such things as the basic literary history of Greece and Rome. The footnotes are intended in the main for my more scholarly readers. The technical apparatus of scholarship has been limited in the book as far as seemed legitimate; however, the interpretation of the poetry frequently depends on matters of detail, and the footnotes are in that regard essential to the work. It should be observed that detailed references are often not given for those opinions of no very fixed origin which are always recurring without much argument in the articles of scholars and the essays of undergraduates. It has not been possible to take account of works appearing in the last part of 1986.

After thought, the quotations from the poets have been kept within stern bounds of length. Experience and inquiry suggest that large quantities of prolonged citation are apt to daunt the less accomplished reader.

The work has been composed in the intervals of a time that might without exaggeration be described as busy. For the many and varied defects which spring from this cause and from others, I can only ask ashamedly for the reader's indulgence. Mr J. Griffin, Professor H. Lloyd-Jones, and Mr R. B. Rutherford were good enough to read a portion of the work in its infancy. I would also like to thank the Press Reader for his vigilance and for his lively remarks. My wife gallantly elected to assist in the construction of the final typescript: a business executed, alas, with such archaic instruments as glue and scissors. She has often dispelled an author's gloom.

Exeter College, Oxford, 1987   G.O.H.

CONTENTS

ABBREVIATIONS

Periodicals are cited more or less according to the system of *L'Année philologique*. The footnotes abbreviate the titles of a few works other than those listed below, but in a fashion readily penetrable; details of most of them will be supplied in the Bibliography.

ARV²	J. D. Beazley, *Attic Red-figure Vase Painters* (2nd edn., Oxford 1963)
CA	J. U. Powell, *Collectanea Alexandrina* (Oxford 1925)
CEG	P. A. Hansen, *Carmina epigraphica Graeca saeculorum VIII–V a. Chr. n.* (Texte und Kommentare XII, Berlin 1983)
CGFP	C. F. L. Austin, *Comicorum Graecorum Fragmenta in papyris reperta* (Berlin 1973)
CHCL	*The Cambridge History of Classical Literature*, i. *Greek Literature*, ed. P. E. Easterling and B. M. W. Knox (Cambridge 1985), ii. *Latin Literature*, ed. E. J. Kenney and W. V. Clausen (Cambridge 1982)
CIL	*Corpus Inscriptionum Latinarum* (Berlin 1863–)
CMG	*Corpus Medicorum Graecorum* (Leipzig 1908–)
FGE	*see* '(Page), *FGE*'
FGrH	F. Jacoby, *Die Fragmente der griechischen Historiker* (Berlin and Leiden 1923–)
Fraser, *PA*	P. M. Fraser, *Ptolemaic Alexandria* (Oxford 1972)
Gow	A. S. F. Gow, *Theocritus* (2nd edn., Cambridge 1952)
(Gow–Page), *Garl. Phil*	A. S. F. Gow and D. L. Page, *The Greek Anthology. The Garland of Philip and Some Contemporary Epigrams* (Cambridge 1968)
(Gow–Page), *HE*	A. S. F. Gow and D. L. Page, *The Greek Anthology. Hellenistic Epigrams* (Cambridge 1965)
GVI	W. Peek, *Griechische Vers-Inschriften*, I (Berlin 1965)
HE	*see* '(Gow–Page), *HE*'
IEG	M. L. West, *Iambi et Elegi Graeci ante Alexandrum Cantati* (Oxford 1971–2)
IG	*Inscriptiones Graecae* (Berlin 1873–)
Kaibel, *CGF* i	G. Kaibel, *Comicorum Graecorum Fragmenta*, i (Berlin 1899)
LSAM	F. Sokolowski, *Lois sacrées de l'Asie Mineure* (Paris 1955)
LSCG	F. Sokolowski, *Lois sacrées des cités grecques* (Paris 1969)
OGIS	W. Dittenberger, *Orientis Graeci inscriptiones selectae* (Leipzig 1903–5)
(Page), *FGE*	D. L. Page, *Further Greek Epigrams: Epigrams Before A.D. 50*, revised by R. D. Dawe and J. Diggle (Cambridge 1981)
Page, *GLP*	D. L. Page, *Select Papyri*, iii. *Literary Papyri: Poetry* (Loeb, London and Cambridge, Mass. 1942)

Pfeiffer	R. Pfeiffer, *Callimachus* (Oxford 1949–53)
Pfeiffer, *HCS* i	R. Pfeiffer, *History of Classical Scholarship: From the Beginnings to the End of the Hellenistic Age* (Oxford 1968)
PMG	D. L. Page, *Poetae Melici Graeci* (Oxford 1962)
P. Mich. Zen.	C. C. Edgar, *Zenon Papyri in the University of Michigan Collection* (Ann Arbor, Mich., 1931)
P. Oxy.	*The Oxyrhynchus Papyri* (London 1898–)
P. Turner	*Papyri Greek and Egyptian, Edited by Various Hands in Honour of Eric Gardner Turner* (Graeco-Roman Memoirs, 68, London 1981)
RE	*Real-Encyclopädie der classischen Altertumswissenschaft* (Stuttgart 1894–)
SH	H. Lloyd-Jones and P. J. Parsons, *Supplementum Hellenisticum* (Texte und Kommentare I, Berlin 1983)
SVF	J. von Arnim, *Stoicorum Veterum Fragmenta* (Leipzig 1905)
Syll.	W. Dittenberger, *Sylloge Inscriptionum Graecarum* (3rd edn., Leipzig 1915–24)
TLL	*Thesaurus linguae Latinae* (Leipzig, 1900–)
TrGF	R. Kannicht, S. Radt, B. Snell, *Tragicorum Graecorum Fragmenta* (Göttingen 1971–)
Vian	F. Vian and E. Delage, *Apollonios de Rhodes* (Budé, Paris 1974–81)
Wilamowitz, *HD*	U. von Wilamowitz–Moellendorff, *Hellenistische Dichtung in der Zeit des Kallimachos* (Berlin 1924)

Epigrams. Capital roman numerals refer to the numbers of poems in Gow–Page, *Hellenistic Epigrams* (save when '*Garl. Phil.*' is prefixed); arabic numerals preceded directly by '*HE*' refer to the numbers of lines in that collection. Capital roman, and arabic, numerals after '*Garl. Phil.*' refer to poems, and lines, in Gow–Page, *Garland of Philip*.

INTRODUCTION

THE celebrated poets of the third century BC have not received much literary treatment; what is sadder, they seem fairly seldom to be read with much enjoyment and understanding. (Theocritus is at any rate enjoyed.) This state of affairs has a number of causes, and involves a number of oddities. Of these one of the most arresting lies in the importance attached to Hellenistic poetry by most critics of Latin poetry.[1] Here stands the great bridge between the literatures of Greece and Rome; yet it seems only rarely to receive more than a swift and very limited inspection. No reproach is intended to Latinists or Hellenists. To Hellenists, indeed, one owes much fine, and some magnificent, work on the text and basic meaning of these poems; by this the approach of the reader is enormously facilitated. And yet the poetry is in itself difficult to discuss and often seems distant from modern enthusiasms. Literary criticism still tends to focus on ideas, and readers (especially young ones) still tend to like their poetry to be in tone and level essentially straightforward. These barriers are greatly strengthened by schematic preconceptions. Crude notions of literary history often lead to ideas of a poetry absolutely different from, or much the same as, the poetry of the classical era, and an obsession with the relationship. Swollen conceptions of the part played in this poetry by learning and still more by theories about literature lead in practice to narrow and dull conceptions of the poems. In consequence, those who are not directly concerned with them are apt to feel tepidly towards what

[1] A necessary note on chronological terms: in this work 'Hellenistic', as used of poetry, will normally denote the time of Callimachus (see p. 5), and will refer in particular to Callimachus, Apollonius, Theocritus, Aratus, Lycophron, Herodas (the poets of whom most is preserved). The use does not imply views about literary history. 'Classical' normally refers to the 5th c., and 'archaic' to the preceding centuries of literature, with Homer included. 'Post-classical' refers to poetry from the 4th c. onwards, and includes 'Hellenistic' poetry.

sounds so arid and unalluring; the tepidity may be tempered by modest respectfulness or active distaste.

This book endeavours to give a literary picture of these poets, and to draw out more of the quality and vitality of their work. The endeavour has many shortcomings, and is very much an experiment. Its object is to do something in awakening a keener interest in this poetry as literature. I hope above all that some readers may seek, and may realize, the same delight that these authors have given me. For others, it may be of interest to have some impression of what these poets are like (in my opinion). Partly to make the book accessible to those, in particular, who read Latin but not Greek, little is said on such important subjects as the level of words or on a poet's general style, seen in narrower terms of language. These subjects have also received greater attention already;[2] there are other aspects of the poetry which require consideration much more urgently, if our conception of these poets is to be expanded as it ought.

The book proceeds in its final chapter from depicting these poets to depicting their influence in Rome. It carries through, and presupposes, the themes and theses of the rest; it also aims to deal with the area which may be most of interest to many of its readers. The treatment there is necessarily selective in the extreme; but it seemed important that the book should attempt to span the chasm of languages.

The attempt implies some idea of literary history, and to this we must now turn. The term may suggest both the viewing of works within the context of their age, and the viewing of them as part of the evolution of literature. For the purposes of this work one must ask how possible it is to achieve such perspectives, and how far they will prove important to the interpretation of the literature. The negative elements in the replies offered here make it desirable to be brief, especially in relation to the contemporary setting. Like the other negative strands and passages in the book, these are intended only to clear the way for positive interpretation, and have been restricted as far as possible. It will be understood that in the present case enormous areas are traversed with the utmost velocity.

The most dubious approach to the relation between this

---

[2] And N. Hopkinson is to produce an anthology of Hellenistic poetry, to which one looks forward eagerly.

literature and its period is to postulate moods of the time, and then simply impose them on the literature and see them as the foundation of our understanding. Thus feelings of nostalgia are held to explain Callimachus' interest in local festivals and Theocritus' in the country. The growth of cities in number and size and the expansion of the Greek world through Alexander's conquests must have caused (it is supposed) a yearning for escape to the country and a homesick preoccupation with the traditions of older Greek communities. However, even if such feelings did really hold sway in men's minds, one ought not to make them the key to the poems, when they are so little to be discerned in the poems themselves, and when to import them is so false to the tone and character of the works.[3]

In other general matters, external evidence may be helpful; but it should hardly generate large a priori principles from which interpretation can begin. As regards religion, for example, it seems impossible to know what the poets believed. To speak broadly, belief in traditional religion shows little indication of decline by our period, for most people. Change in this area of Hellenistic culture, as in many others, consists rather of addition than of substitution, the inherited core retaining the fire of its vitality.[4] On the other hand, philosophy had propounded drastic modifications of traditional conceptions, and any intellectual would have been acquainted with its doctrines. Whether, and how, the existence of such ideas had affected the poets' beliefs, there is little good reason to decide. (The assumptions of their readers are still less accessible.[5]) Where external evidence can assist us here is by showing that many of the religious notions that appear in the poems would have seemed

---

[3] See on Callimachus' *Aetia* pp. 40 ff.; on Theocritus, pp. 145 ff.

[4] Belief is always hard to prove, and the whole notion is difficult; but sufficiently suggestive are such documents as the lead tablets at Dodona (H. W. Parke, *The Oracles of Zeus* (1969), Appendix 1, cf. p. 120), and e.g. *LSAM* 16. 17–27. The behaviour of very powerful individuals shows little; nor should one assume revelations of the heart in the Athenians' hymn to Demetrius (*FGrH* 76 F 13, cf. 75 F 2; cf. e.g. Chr. Habicht, *Gottmenschtum*[2] (1970), 232 f.).

[5] As to familiarity with philosophy, even the references in comedy of the time suggest an audience who knew more than names (e.g. Damoxenus fr. 2 Kock (iii. 349 f.)). For Callimachus' knowledge cf. frr. 191. 9 ff., 393 (epigram, detailed), *Ep.* 23 Pf. (LIII GP); fr. 589 may well not refer to Plato's writings. The comic nature of the epigrams need indicate nothing about Callimachus' real opinions, let alone prove his orthodoxy. His character's disapprobation of the demythologizer Euhemerus in fr. 191 may of course merely make part of Callimachus' archly pious *persona*.

grotesque or outmoded to any sophisticated person: so, in one of the most extreme examples, the notion of beating Pan's statue if there is too little meat at hand (Theocr. 7. 106 ff.). Such a use of the environment by the critic is much more bound up with the careful reading of the text itself. Indeed, the assessment of tone and effect often depends on a feeling not only for literary expression in Greek but for Greek reactions to a particular kind of material. No doubt one's feeling is very fallible; but this is not the same as making the merest conjecture the key to interpreting the poems.

It might be expected that the character of the literature would be illuminated by the visual art of the time. Yet it seems exaggerated to assume that the arts always develop in the same way and always reflect some universal spirit of the age. At any rate, the age we are concerned with presents particular impediments to such a union, and to its fruitfulness for literary criticism. The first impediment lies in the character of the evidence. The poetry that concerns us was mostly written between roughly 280 and roughly 240 by poets all active in the 270s. The period is a particularly obscure one in the history of Greek art, and few works can be dated to it with much certainty.[6] Even if we accept the usual conceptions of how art develops in the last four centuries BC, the trends that it might be easiest to relate to poetry appear mainly in works put later than 240. The second impediment is more fundamental. It is possible to connect with elements or parts of some poems features of some works of art (such as extravagant grandeur). But most of the poems really win their character, according to this book, from combining elements and complicating or distorting them. Such complexities are foreign to the art of this time, and largely depend on the use of features with no real visual equivalent, such as the form of a poem or the tone of the writer. If this is correct, the comparison of poetry with art will not take us far. In any event, it is by no means forced upon us through the whole character of art in the period, as might be the case, say, in the eighteenth century. It could hardly have much weight in

[6] A number of statues once placed there are now dated elsewhere, most notably the Crouching Aphrodite formerly ascribed to 'Doidalsas' (A. Linfert, *MDAI(A)* 84 (1969), 158 ff., D. M. Brinkerhoff, *J. Paul Getty Museum Journal*, 6 (1978), 83 ff.). This dating had been thought secure (and still is, strangely, in J. J. Pollitt, *Art in the Hell. Age* (1986), 56 f.).

initiating or deciding interpretations of the poetry. It could only proceed, and that tentatively, when interpretation had been completed without its aid.

The one respect in which a connection with literature is indeed invited seems essentially a matter of structures and divisions internal to either art. Post-classical literature (it will be argued) can infringe more radically than before the crucial division between high and low. In a way not wholly unrelated, the essentially high form of sculpture admits after the fifth century a more radical invasion of its boundaries. In this form—as opposed to, say, vase-painting—there had been quite severe limitations in the handling of the undignified and the erotic; these limitations come to be much relaxed. We shall return to the matter in literature at a later point; but in Hellenistic poetry such different effects result that the art, so compelling and so various, can do little to help the critic of the literature.

More help may be looked for, and with some reason, from a knowledge of the immediate context within which the poets themselves were placed. All but two of the Greek poets discussed (Aratus and probably Asclepiades) enjoyed the patronage of Ptolemy II Philadelphus, king of Egypt (sole ruler 282–246); all these, it is probable, spent some of their life in Alexandria his capital. Callimachus was writing poetry, and living in Alexandria, by 279–273; he lived there into the reign of Ptolemy III Euergetes (246–221). Apollonius was, in my view, roughly contemporary with Callimachus, and spent a large part of his life in Alexandria; he was tutor to Ptolemy III and lived, it is likely, into his reign. Theocritus, again in my view roughly contemporary with Callimachus, was writing, and probably living in Alexandria, in the 270s; at some time after 265, in my opinion, Theocritus was seeking the patronage of Hieron II of Syracuse. Herodas and Lycophron too were both patronized, probably, by Ptolemy II; both most likely wrote some of their work before c.265. Lycophron, Callimachus, and Apollonius all worked in the massive library of Alexandria: Apollonius was head of it, Callimachus produced from it a catalogue of Greek literature, Lycophron laboured there on texts at the behest of the king.[7]

What can be inferred from all this? In particular, should we

[7] For discussion of dates see pp. 40, 88 f., 190 ff., 214, 236, 258, 264 f.

see this poetry as written for the consumption of a fabulously learned court élite? And does the nature of the audience essentially determine the nature of the poetry? In the first place, it is usually impossible to say for how many readers these poems were designed. The poems which praise the Egyptian royal family were obviously intended to give pleasure to the patrons they will make famous. But the whole notion of such poetry conferring fame demands a wider audience (cf. e.g. Theocr. 16. 98 ff., 17. 116 ff.). One poem of Callimachus', *Iambus* 1 (fr. 191) portrays with gusto the disputes of the learned in Alexandria. Other poems, particularly in the *Iambi*, evoke or allude to controversy in the literary world over Callimachus' own work; these, however, are less promising for attempts to define the audience. In any case, if we see such works and passages as mere weapons in a war of pamphlets, we miss their pretensions to stand aloof in the dignity and distance of great poetry, and to transmute the ephemeral into dramatic scenes and a harmonious presentation of the writer, which will be intelligible and enjoyable beyond the writer's immediate milieu. That milieu does not contain and circumscribe the nature of the poems.[8]

The role of learning in the poems proves less helpful than one might have expected in delimiting their readership. One must separate the resources required of, and the manner employed by, the poets from the difficulty experienced by the reader. The reader of Apollonius and Theocritus finds himself often confronted with allusions to literature and myth, and sometimes with unusual words, as he does in much earlier poetry; yet these authors are not dauntingly inaccessible at the level of verbal comprehension. Callimachus, however, takes more pains to give an air of difficulty with a more regular use of rare words and exacting periphrasis. But the difficulty of reading him has often been grossly exaggerated. His work is infinitely more approachable by the merely educated reader than the unremitting tenebrosities of Lycophron. Indeed, before the end of the

---

[8] Others of the *Iambi* are clearly written for an audience not involved in the situation, e.g. 5 or 3—indeed the situations there may perfectly well be fictitious (Callimachus is unlikely to have been poor then). Only in some of the *Epigrams* does the reader need prior knowledge of literary disputes to comprehend the poems. On the significance of such disputes see below.

century it was being published with elementary elucidation for readers of great ignorance: he had speedily achieved wide circulation and a classic status.[9] Yet uncertainties over the size of poets' audience are quite subsidiary to the fundamental point. One may perfectly well insist that the erudite will have gained more than anyone else from this poetry (as from Aristophanes); but one must not use a conjectural image of the erudite ruthlessly to constrict and distort the poems themselves. There is demonstrably far more to these works than the conduct of scholarly quizzes and polemics; we cannot reduce them to such a compass by conjuring up readers whose concern with erudition drives out all other interests and responses. We must fashion our imaginary readers (if at all) to match the richness of the text, not mould our conception of the poetry to fit our notions of scholarly readers.

Of the authors we know more than of the audience, but our understanding of them as poets must again derive principally from the works they wrote. The Alexandrian library provided Apollonius and Callimachus with recondite sources essential to their creations; but this biographical information does not tell us with what effects that material is deployed in the poems. The milieu does offer something important to us in supplying a certain background for the idea of learning as something dry and abstruse, and the scholar as a pedant of vast erudition and slight sensibility. We have just doubted the propriety of making the reader as reader so limited a figure with such limited interests; the poets, however (Callimachus especially), can play with such conceptions of themselves and their horizons. In doing so they indicate of course that their works and they themselves as poets are larger than the conceptions and values they use in this way. That they do so use them will be argued in the book proper; for the present, we may note features of scholarship at the time which make possible this wry and parodic exploitation.

The literary scholars of this and the preceding generation would appear to have drawn back from the huge range of

---

[9] *SH* 255, 258, 261: see P. J. Parsons, *ZPE* 25 (1977), 4 f. The papyrus seems to be a commercial product; if it was intended for use in schools, the popularity of Callimachus is still more strongly indicated. Of course authors of this period may perfectly well have conceived of being explained by editors.

matters which concerned their predecessors the philosophers of
the fourth century. They would seem to have toiled intensively
in regions more circumscribed, and to have occupied themselves particularly with editing texts and with assembling lists
of rare words and names, explained and discussed.[10] Not that
everything written in Greek made a small field—the Alexandrian library and Callimachus' enormous catalogue of authors
will have given a fresh sense of magnitude. But in manner, so
far as can be gathered, these scholars either cultivated a clipped
dryness in retailing obscure information, or else continued the
aggressiveness of Greek intellectuals in spheres remote from
common interest.[11] This semblance of austerity and of preoccupation with the recondite forms the basis for one delectable
element in the poems. One may note, however, that Aratus (a
scholar, but not of Alexandria) can deploy in a related fashion
the related austerity and abstruseness of science. The primary
thing is the concern with tone.

The question of relations between the poets possesses great
importance, and for this and other reasons is treated within the
book itself. On the one hand, the three chief poets are likely to
have enjoyed a considerable familiarity with each other and
each other's work, even while it was being composed; and this is
likely to have been significant. Not only did they live in the
same city and share the same patrons, but the protégés of the
Ptolemies appear to have been joined into societies. The
Museum, founded by Ptolemy I, seems to have afforded some
degree of communal life for the learned of Alexandria; even in

---

[10] The latter (of especial interest here): Philetas, Γλῶσσαι and ῾Ερμηνεία, frr. 29 ff.
Kuchenm., and note fr. 53 (for the impact on contemporaries cf. Hermesianax *CA*, p.
100. 77 f., Straton *CGFP* 219. 42 ff.); Zenodotus, ᾽Εθνικαὶ Λέξεις (K. Nickau, *RE* xA
(1972), 40); Simias frr. 29 ff. Fränkel (note especially fr. 30 with its quotation); Lycophron, π. κωμῳδίας (C. Strecker, *De Lyc.* etc. (Diss. Greifs. 1884)); Callimachus,
᾽Εθνικαὶ ᾽Ονομασίαι (fr. 406), cf. Pfeiffer, *HCS* i. 135—much of Callimachus' scholarly
work seems to have hovered between the lexicographical and the encyclopaedic. For
the former see Pfeiffer, *HCS* i, S. R. West, in Heubeck–West, edn. of Hom. *Od.*, i, pp.
1 ff., K. Nickau, *Untersuchungen zur textkritischen Methode d. Zenodotos* (Unters. z. ant. Lit.
u. Gesch. 16, 1977).

[11] The dryness is evident in most quotations. For the aggressiveness note especially
Call. fr. 458, and compare and contrast Herodot. 4. 36. 2. The cantankerousness of the
numerous scholars of Alexandria was satirized by Callimachus himself (fr. 191, see
above), and by the hostile Timon (*SH* 786), who speaks of their unending battles in the
narrow confines of the Alexandrian Museum.

the city of Ptolemaïs we find a vigorous society of the Artists of Dionysus and the king and queen, which includes not only tragedians and comedians but epic poets (*OGIS* 51. 31 ff.).[12] We have laid emphasis above on the peculiarly literary nature of the qualities which unite the poets. It can be shown that they all exploited one another's work in many particular ways, and the most satisfying explanation of their affinities lies not in common exposure to the spirit of the age but in deep mutual influence. Even here, however, we must not claim too much; as we shall see, the picture is complicated by our knowledge and our ignorance of earlier poetry.

Certainly the negative side of this matter has no less significance. We should not allow misconceptions about the relationship of the poets to distort our appreciation of their poems. It is mistaken, we shall argue, to find the key to this poetry in a supposed war over aesthetic dogma. One is misguided to conceive of a battle between supporters of long and conventional poems and of short and refined ones, to range the poets into these factions, and to make them embittered antagonists or ardent fellow crusaders—and still more to hold that this is fundamental to an understanding of their works. It is mistaken even to make one a master whom the others follow obediently. The indications suggest that the three poets were roughly of the same age, and they certainly make it probable that each both gave and received. The notion of influence as something overwhelming a poet's individuality and will much obscures the self-contained coherence of each poet's work and the singularity with which it organizes its elements. We can know almost nothing of personal relationships between these authors; figuratively, however, it will be desirable to imagine in their relations as poets, not only a strong affinity as regards their basic concerns, but also a certain sense of pragmatism and independent purpose.

The argument hitherto has been in large part bleak and sceptical. I may stress that I should by inclination be pleased to illuminate the poems through their historical setting. But the character of the evidence, and of the literature and of other as-

---

[12] The numbers of poets are respectively 2, 2, and 3; for the date (Ptolemy II?) see Fraser, *PA* ii. 870. Note too Theocr. 17. 112 ff. On the Museum see Pfeiffer, *HCS* i. 96 ff., Fraser, *PA* i. 312 ff.

pects of the time, seems to discourage attempts to approach the literature by constructing the period. Perhaps, indeed, the very notion of a unified period does not suit a time so heterogeneous and, one might think, so unconscious of itself. We are impelled to seek an understanding of these poems primarily from the poems themselves. This is not at all to say that other material, particularly other literature, will not assist the process of reading; but our approach cannot be directed by the context of history.

We turn now to the second kind of literary history, the attempt to see the Hellenistic poets in the light of the development of Greek literature. Plainly, for our understanding of these poets, as opposed to our understanding of Greek literature as a whole, it will be of great importance to know how new was their approach, and what sort of tradition lay to their hand. Unfortunately, however, our knowledge of Greek poetry is extremely discontinuous. We know very little of poetry in the fourth century, save for the comedies of Menander, which do not assist us greatly.[13] Furthermore, we have little knowledge of non-dramatic poetry in the second half of the fifth century. Comparison between poetry of the third century and of the fifth would certainly look different if what we had from the latter were great quantities of epic and elegy, or if what we had from the former were its large dramatic literature.[14] Finally, we are not even well informed about the first twenty years or so of the third century, and hence about the immediate predecessors of most of our poets. Of the work of some poets (such as Philetas) we know virtually nothing; in other cases where we know more of the poems (such as Alexander Aetolus, Hermesianax, Phanocles, Rhianus), there is little positive reason to make the

---

[13] W. G. Arnott, Loeb edn. of Men., i (1979), pp. xxxviii ff., attempts to show a specifically Hellenistic cleverness in that author; but there seem slender literary grounds for stressing the resemblance. The most promising line of connection would be found in the subtle relations in Menander of comic and serious (see below); but the poetic effects differ too widely to make comparison fruitful. Dover, edn. of Theocr., pp. lxx f., properly stresses our ignorance of poetry in the 4th c.

[14] It will be obvious that we cannot, as a point in literary history, contrast the poetry of 450–400, written chiefly for performance, with the poetry of 280–240, written for reading. Thus the epic of the 5th c. may perfectly well have been designed for reading just as much as that of the 3rd c. (in both periods anecdotes mention recitation, and rhapsodes perform).

poets precede our authors.[15] These obscurities particularly impede a historical view of the Hellenistic poets from the perspective suggested by this book. If one finds fundamental to this poetry complications and subtleties of tone and the related handling of form, then it seems still less practicable to form an opinion of the poetry that preceded it from the scanty material at our disposal.

However, the prospect here is a little less blank than it appears: there is a little of use that can be said with regard to the history of poetry. We do possess from the intervening period some small items of knowledge with a certain utility, and by contemplating a large vista we can perhaps discern significant patterns. For our concerns, it is of relatively little moment that around the turn of the fifth century Antimachus the epic poet and scholar was making much use of rare words from Homer, and Timotheus the composer of advanced lyric was defending his novel art against his critics.[16] Both facts have connections with Hellenistic poetry, and classical antecedents; but it is effect and manner which count. If we look at Hellenistic and at classical poetry with effect and manner as our concern, a general divergence appears, of rather greater significance. It will be shown in this book how Hellenistic poets commonly derive their effects and their impact from piquant combination of, or delicate hovering between, the serious and the unserious, the grand and the less grand. The classical poetry we have in the main upholds a firm and important division between these elements. Hellenistic poets like to cultivate a region which classical poets like to avoid.

In classical, and to a large degree archaic, poetry, the matter is intimately connected with genre. Some types of poetry may be regarded as 'high'. Characteristically, they sustain a marked elevation and intensity; distancing themselves from humdrum realities, they interest themselves in extremes. Much high

---

[15] For the data on Alexander cf. A. Capellmann's edn. (1830), 1 ff.; on Hermesianax see Fraser, *PA* ii. 883 (n. 61); there are no reliable means of dating Phanocles; Jacoby's arguments on Rhianus seem very uncertain (*FGrH* iiiA (Komm.), 89 f., 119 ff., 199). As for Philetas (add *SH* 673 f.), it should be noted that fr. 1 Kuchenm. (Parthenius) does not necessarily summarize an extended narrative: cf. Lloyd-Jones and Parsons on *SH* 413. 12. For likely predecessors better known, including Asclepiades, see below.

[16] Wyss, ed. of Antim., p. 101; Timoth. *PMG* 791. 206 ff. (with Wilamowitz, *D. Perser*, 64 ff.).

poetry presents human greatness and the limits fixed for men by powerful divinities. Low genres (especially comedy) might almost be said to define themselves by contrast with the high. One sees this most pointedly in parody; but in general Old Comedy gains much of its force from defying the limits which prevail in high poetry. They are defied both through the use of unelevated material, whose lowness is comic, and also through the use of fantasy, which dissolves the fixed and ordered world of high poetry (men can even depose the gods). The union of elevation and passion that typifies tragedy, Old Comedy in essence determinedly eschews. This is naturally the very roughest of sketches, and we must consider briefly some authors who complicate the pattern, and display real points of contact with the poets of the third century.

One archaic work must be mentioned, the *Odyssey*. It makes great use of low and homely material, starting from the first scene on earth (1. 106 ff.), and dwelling on it insistently in the second half. The language and conventions of epic suggest a desire in that genre for sustained elevation and grandeur.[17] The poet does not, however, seem to be pursuing mere piquancy as such. These elements are intimately associated with the moral concerns of the poem. Hospitality is essential to the moral design. Eumaeus' poverty touchingly heightens his goodness, Odysseus' humiliations enhance his endurance, the suitors' sordid behaviour and life-style display their coarseness and moral hebetude. The long sequence in Odysseus' palace (Books 17–21) has a heavy sense of suppression; the explosion of heroic violence which destroys its domesticity satisfies deeply in its restoration of grandiose matter and narrative.[18] The poet's exploitation of epic norms is neither playful nor subversive.

Pindar's odes of victory contain not rarely passages of considerable lightness and informality. In particular, he will often write with a certain playfulness about himself.[19] One must

[17] The description of Eumaeus' hut, for example (*Od.* 14. 5 ff.), I would see as making concessions to the genre (so to speak).

[18] Notice the disruption of the idea of feasting at 21. 428–22. 21, 21. 404–13, etc. Here, as with the next two authors, the effects are naturally more complex than I have space to indicate.

[19] Cf. e.g. *Ol.* 6. 87–91, *Nem.* 3. 26–8, 7. 75 f., probably *Ol.* 1. 16 f. Bacchylides has little of such things, though the grace of 3. 95 f. should be noted. In general, D. S. Carne-Ross, *Pindar* (1985), ch. 1, stresses the lighter aspects of Pindar, while not perhaps doing justice to his magnificence.

relate this, however, to the type of the poem, and its explicit inclusion, unlike epic and tragedy, of present people and circumstances as well as the heroic and divine. The poems seek to raise living men into the sphere and the world of high poetry; at the same time, Pindar cultivates the air of a warm and not uneasy relationship with his lofty patrons. The poet occupies a number of roles; and the handling of him is appropriately complex. The exaltation of the poems is not modified, but enriched with a certain geniality. The effects do not truly resemble the disruptive or subtle effects of the Hellenistic poets when they play with their own roles and *personae*. Pindar is often associated with Callimachus in the mannerism with which he designs his narratives; this might be thought relevant here. In both cases, however, the extent of mannerism has been rather overstressed (one must bear Pindar's interests in mind); and Pindar shows here little sense of perversity and play. The two poets' narratives often have in common a boldness of visual imagination and an exciting sense of strangeness; but in Pindar these things are principally the concomitants of elevation.[20]

Euripides comes much nearer to the handling of seriousness in Hellenistic poetry. He often employs bizarreness of incident, and audacity of argument, with a gusto which precludes a simply and intensely serious reaction.[21] In larger terms, however, these modifications of seriousness should be seen as part of a general concern with complicating straightforward reactions, above all in the alignment of the audience's sympathies. The continuity of interest here is seen in the use of the same techniques to achieve complication of different kinds, in particular the techniques of form. Thus the *Orestes* falls into two halves, the second bizarre, the first centred on an action with strong and essentially simple emotional appeal. One may compare the organization of the *Andromache* or the *Hecuba*; yet there the complications in the second half are principally of moral texture.[22]

[20] For an interesting discussion of the resemblances between the two poets, see N. J. Richardson, *Papers of Liv. Lat. Sem.* 5 (1985), 391 ff.

[21] Very obviously e.g. *Orest.* 1369 ff., *El.* 524 ff.; at a nearer remove from such reaction, e.g. *Tro.* 308 ff., 353–405. Note especially B. Seidensticker, *Palintonos Harmonia* (Hypomnemata 72, 1982); however, his concern with *comic* elements leads to some general misplacing of emphasis. The *Helen*, in its arch play and distanced pathos, comes nearest to a Hellenistic quality.

[22] Or Agave's entry at *Bacch.* 1168 ff. has the bizarreness of Cassandra's (n. 21), but a very different force.

Besides this, the action of Euripides' dramas broadly confines its range of reality within the limits observed by tragedy, despite an occasional provocative use of the low or spirited use of the marvellous.[23] In the centre of their artistic concerns, Euripides and the Hellenistic poets widely diverge.

These three somewhat unusual cases help to bring out and define, in the respect we have been considering, the essential character of poetry before the fourth century. They also offer elements through which Hellenistic poets, in their own creations, were to alter that character fundamentally: the sordid, the bizarre, handling of the self, complication through form, and so on. However, one can hardly think of the earlier poets as causing the desire for alteration in the later. This is not simply because their general conceptions of the earlier poets were quite probably more straightforward than those suggested above.[24] Rather, to deploy these elements as they did, they must plainly have developed from elsewhere—from poets of 400–280 or from themselves—a sense of the general area they wished their poetry to occupy and exploit. The difference from the classical poets is the most definite point; but we may consider now to what degree, if any, the intervening period had moved in this direction.

We must begin with one or two general and negative points about literature in the period. Firstly, any movement in such a direction is certainly unlikely to have been universal. Much tragedy continued to be written in the fourth and third centuries; it employed, the evidence suggests, a lavishly grandiose and impassioned manner.[25] It is extremely likely that much epic continued to be written too, although the usual difficulties with post-classical poets make it hard to assign many epics with certitude to the period *c.*400–*c.*280. Of epics on myth (as opposed to the achievements of patrons) we know at least of Antimachus' *Thebaid* around the beginning of the period, and

[23] For the latter cf. Pegasus' flight in the *Bellerophon* (frr. 306–8 Nauck), or the setting of the *Pirithous* (if it is his) in Hades (see P. Oxy. 3531)—but the *PV* is just as weird. The notion of his reducing myth to workaday reality is greatly overplayed: it depends too much on Aristophanes and on a distorted reading of the *Electra*.

[24] In particular, it was the powerfully simple aspect of Euripides that seems to have been best appreciated in the 4th and 3rd cc. Aristotle's *Poetics* makes this especially clear.

[25] Fragments in *TrGF* i and ii. Aristotle's *Poetics* is also suggestive.

Antagoras' around the end.[26] It seems that Antimachus adopted a grand manner and sought extremely grand effects.[27] Later evidence strengthens the suspicion that there had been at this time no simple evaporation of a concern for grandeur. Conversely, however, the time after *c*.240 should also help to keep in our view the possibility that the poetry of the fourth century was a quite disparate affair. Works of simple grandiosity do not cease after Callimachus, but Callimachus and his fellows are popular, and much imitated.[28] One should not expect the literature written between 400 and 280 all to have exhibited a single and uniform line of development.

Secondly, however, the relation of genre and seriousness must not be misunderstood. We noted that in the classical period the divisions of genre were central to the divisions of poetry; but we must beware of seeing the more shifting character of Hellenistic poetry too much in terms of generic categories. In particular, great significance has been attributed to Hellenistic 'crossing of genres', the deliberate and novel conflation of elements from separate genres, so as to use say a dialect abnormal for the metre, or a metre abnormal for the type of poem.[29] It would be tempting to see this development and the development we are investigating as essentially the same, and to look back at the intervening period from this point of view. However, even in the Hellenistic period, as will be seen, significant 'crossing' has a relatively limited role; and the fluctuations and complexities of tone and level are far too subtle and

---

[26] Antagoras: *CA*, pp. 120 f. Fr. 3 (GP II) in my view probably indicates that he was already writing poetry in the late 4th c. (and cf. J. K. Davies, *Athenian Propertied Families*, p. 415). On epic for patrons, see K. Ziegler, *D. hell. Epos*² (1966), 16 ff. (again the evidence is extremely limited). Cf. also Wilamowitz, *HD* i. 104 ff. Choerilus, *SH* 317 (late 5th c.) does not of course prove the demise of mythical epic: one would not use the opening of *Georgics* 3 so naïvely, and Choerilus is in any case not speaking of epic alone. (I leave aside the question of the scholion.)

[27] Test. (Wyss) 25, 27, 28, 29; *SH* 52, 65; R. Kassel in *Catalepton* (Festschrift Wyss, 1985), 69 ff. Antimachus might possibly have suffered some diminution in grandeur after the opening section of his epic; but *Vit. Chis. Dion. Per.* 54 f. (Kassel, p. 72) does not necessarily show this.

[28] Cf. e.g. (for imitators of Callimachus) *CA*, pp. 78 f., *SH* 387 f., 391, etc.; see also above, n. 9. One's view should not be distorted by Callimachus' own pronouncements (see pp. 77 ff.). Ziegler, *D. hell. Epos*², misleadingly presents Callimachus and his supposed allies as an absolute island in the sea of post-classical literature.

[29] Cf. W. Kroll, *Stud. z. Verst. d. röm. Lit.* (1924), ch. 9, L. E. Rossi, *BICS* 18 (1971), 69 ff.

rich to be properly perceived from so restricted an angle. The
period before the Hellenistic in fact presents us with considerations which complicate this whole question of genre. Elaborate
and dignified lyric poetry seems to have faded strikingly in the
course of this period as a form of literature permanent in value
(less so as essentially a form for works sung in rituals).[30] This
fall increases correspondingly the empire of the hexameter and
the elegiac couplet; the range of the latter (in particular) had
always been extremely wide.[31] Hence Erinna, in the fourth
century, writes a lament of 300 lines in hexameters, not lyric,
and in a mixture of Doric and Aeolic, not Ionic (*SH* 400–2). In
literary terms it would be very implausible to see these features
as piquant surprises.[32] The two metres might also invade each
other's territory. Thus Crates (late 4th c.) wrote a parodic
hymn to Parsimony in elegiacs, not hexameters (*SH* 361); the
effect of parody would have been spoiled had the metre seemed
a startling novelty. Ingenious innovation with metre was certainly in vogue from the late fourth century onwards.[33] Less
technical sides of genre are certainly of great importance in the
Hellenistic manipulation of seriousness. But genre forms only
one aspect there; and the evidence from the earlier period suggests that the newness and the force of apparently mixing
genres may easily be misjudged.[34]

One may turn now to the more positive side, beginning with
some items which do not show the subtle combinations of the
later poets, but in various ways provide a background to them.
In the fourth century and early third there seems to have flourished the writing of poems which parodied higher genres
throughout, distorting their language and conventions to fit

[30] Cf. M. L. West, *Greek Metre* (1982), ch. 4, A.

[31] Note e.g. that in the 5th c. Simonides described a battle of the Persian Wars in elegiacs (West, *IEG* ii. 112, cf. 'Adesp.' (but see P. Turner 3) 58, 60). On the range of the
metre in general see West, *Studies in Greek Elegy and Iambus* (1974), ch. 1; Bulloch, ed. of
Call. *H.* 5, pp. 31 ff.

[32] If Erinna is the pretence of a male author (West *ZPE* 25 (1977), 116 ff.), then the
dialect will be mimetic, as part of the pretence. The thesis is possible, but the positive
arguments for it seem weak.

[33] e.g. *SH* 310 (Castorion). It may be observed that the revival of archaic limping
iambics is the work not of Callimachus but of poets in, it seems, the late 4th c. (see ch. 2
n. 47).

[34] Rossi (n. 29) regards Callimachus' approach as 'new and revolutionary' (p. 83):
this is surely exaggerated. Cf. p. 55.

low or topical subjects.[35] The humour is mostly too undiluted
and too straightforward to anticipate Hellenistic poetry; but
the sustained play with poetic convention and level in some sort
prepares for the far more subtle play of the successors. This is
notably the case with Archestratus (later 4th c.). His poem on
delicacies to eat burlesqued the conventions of the didactic
poem.[36] He exploits with great energy the drama of instruction
seen in the prime exemplar for the genre, Hesiod's *Works and
Days*. The vehemence and earnestness with which Hesiod
exhorts his brother, the poet's air of involvement and authority,
Archestratus applies to the two friends he addresses and the fri-
volities of gourmandise.[37] A line runs from this treatment of
the didactic fiction to the much less simple and more delicate
treatment in Aratus' *Phaenomena*.[38]

   The three pattern-poems of Simias (later 4th to early 3rd c.)
do display tensions between serious and unserious elements.[39]
These tensions are essentially far less sophisticated and intriguing than those of the later poets, since they depend so much on
the visible shape of the poems; but even so, the effects sought,
and the very exploitation of form, have for us considerable significance. A sense of distance, artifice, and play is furnished
throughout by the visual evocation of the subject (axe, egg,
wings). The *Axe* concerns the axe used to make the Trojan

---

[35] See in *SH* Archestratus, Crates, Euboeus, Matron, all certainly of this period (for
Arch. Eub. Matr. the notes in P. Brandt, *Corp. Poes. Ep. Gr. Ludib.* i are still useful). The
magnificent work of Timon (*SH* 775 ff.) could be contemporary with that of Callimachus (cf. A. A. Long, *PCPS* ns 24 (1978), 86 n. 28). Note too the φλύακες of
Rhinthon (beginning of 3rd c.): these seem to have been parodies of tragedies. See Test.
1–3 Kaibel (*CGF* i. p. 183). Aristotle regarded the genre of parody as beginning with
Hegemon in the later 5th c. (*Poet.* 1448ᵃ12).

[36] Numerous and often substantial fragments (*SH* 132 ff.) are conserved by
Athenaeus.

[37] Cf. e.g. *SH* 192. 10–18 (cf. Hes. *WD* 682 f. and *SH* 145), 192. 19 ff., 146. 2 ff., 152
(with extreme elements), 167. 5 f. (cf. *WD* 422 with West's note, and for μοι Aratus 413
and *SH* 169. 8). But it is the manner more than the wording of Hesiod that Archestratus
guys.

[38] See pp. 224 ff., 233 ff.

[39] These poems are available in Gow's *Bucolici Gr.*, 172 ff.; for all the fragments cf. H.
Fränkel, *De Simia Rhodio* (1915) (and *CA*, pp. 109 ff). Hephaestion, p. 30, indicates that
Simias was very substantially older than Philicus, who cannot have been younger than
Callimachus (cf. Fränkel, p. 10; Gow–Page, p. 511, are a little misleading). It should be
remembered that the pattern-poem attributed to Theocritus (*Syrinx*) is spurious and
late; the date of Dosiadas' (the *Altar*) is unknown, but I should be surprised if it were at
all early.

Horse, and afterwards dedicated to Athena. It describes in dignified language the fall of Troy; it moves, as the lines grow
smaller, to the lowly status of the maker. It then leaps from
representing the maker's dedication of the object to contemplating his fame in epic, a surprising movement forward in time
and back from event to poetry. It reaches its climax in sense,
praising Athena and dwelling on immortality, as it tapers away
in form, ending with three syllables to a line. The form sometimes enhances, sometimes pulls against, the rhetoric; the stress
on poetry heightens the artifice, but also the rapture. The lines
of the *Wings* (on Eros) first diminish in length and then grow.
The poem opens boldly and grandly, but moves with a conscious air of bizarreness to Eros' facial hair. It achieves the
climax of its sense as the lines, in harmony, reach their greatest
length. There is something exhilarating in the union of the
god's vaunt of his supreme dominion with the pleasing game of
visual symmetry. The *Egg* carries self-reference to its furthest
point. The egg is the poem, the product of the nightingale
Simias. With colourful fantasy, the poem describes itself, and
discourses on its own unusually elaborate metre. Yet the latter
subject carries us away into a simile which engages us in its
autonomous narrative. The world of its animals is tellingly
evoked, and we respond warmly, as in Homer, to their actions.
The appearance in such a place of traditional and emotive
poetry enriches and complicates the impact of the whole. The
poem then returns curtly to itself. These little works possess a
real kinship to the more complex poems of the later generation.

  We may mention at this point the poem *Arai* (Curses) by
Moero: she was probably a generation older than Callimachus.
We know explicitly only that the work mentioned or recounted
an obscure and pathetic legend (*CA*, p. 22).[40] Other examples
of the genre make it evident that the fate of the chief figure in
the legend, among other fates, will have been wished on
Moero's enemy. The genre was popular in the third century;
plainly this example already took the basic theme of cursing,

---

  [40] It is interesting that at least three of Parthenius' stories of love had been used by
poets of this time, not later; the present case, Philetas fr. 1 Kuchenm., Simias fr. 16
Fränk. But in this connection the thing to observe is not a Hellenistic interest in
amatory material as such—the subject has always interested—but rather its role in
literature which is in some respects elevated.

which implied strong passion, and modified the effect of such passion on the reader through the inventive and recherché use of myth.[41]

Now we arrive at works which more decidedly belong with Hellenistic poetry in the complexity with which they handle material serious and dignified, and the reverse. The poetess Erinna (4th c., probably middle) wrote a poem of 300 lines lamenting the death of her friend Baucis (see above); a substantial but lacunose papyrus survives (*SH* 401).[42] In this fragment she refers in detail to features of their lives as young girls, describing their play together at the game of Tortoise, and the hideous figment Mormo with whom children were threatened. Such things, in a poem, have a very different resonance from Sappho's depiction of maidens' parties, when speaking of her farewell to a girl, or from Andromache's depiction of other children's behaviour to her son, when lamenting her husband.[43] Children's bogies and their ritualized games had been more or less confined in literature to the lowness of comedy and the unconventionalities of Plato.[44] One cannot simply ignore the strangeness of this material in a passionate work on the grounds that the writer is female: she is plainly conscious of the poetic tradition. In part the childish elements heighten the lament by contrast.

$$\text{``}a\emph{i}]\alpha\hat{\imath}\ \emph{ἐγώ}\text{''}, \mu\emph{έγ'}\ \emph{ἄϋσα}. \tag{16}$$

'Alas! Alas!', I cried out loudly.

Erinna's cry in the happy game contrasts with the laments she utters now in earnest. (To these she refers in the next line but one; *αἰαῖ* 'alas' she uses at l. 54.) The game of Tortoise itself involved a play with bereavement (*PMG* 876(c)). But Erinna's

---

[41] *SH* 970 shows the same kind of poem. J. W. B. Barns and H. Lloyd-Jones (*SIFC* 35 (1963), 205 ff.) incline for stylistic reasons to place it in or near this period; but we know too little of the general history of elegy in the 3rd c. to repose a very solid assurance in the linear progression their argument would postulate.

[42] Asclepiades XXVIII in my view places Erinna in the 4th c. (on Asclepiades' own date see pp. 264 ff.). Eusebius has her flourish in the 350s.

[43] Sappho fr. 94 Voigt, Hom. *Il.* 22. 496 ff. The treatment of Astyanax is meant to stand at a lower level than the treatment in Andromache's second lament (*Il.* 24. 732 ff.).

[44] Many references were collected in an ancient work of scholarship on games in general (by Didymus?): see Pollux 9. 94 ff., Sueton. π. παιδιῶν (ed. Taillardat). On Plato cf. R. K. Sprague, in *Gk. Poetry and Philos.* (Festschrift Woodbury, 1984), 275 ff.

attitude as speaker involves both a sense of the distance of childhood from herself and from Baucis (20 (f.); 28 ff.) and a love
which consciously transvalues these humble trivialities. Yet the
reader familiar with Greek poetry will also receive from these
detailed renderings of lowly and strange material a certain
pleasurable and piquant charm, tinged with a feeling of detachment and almost of amusement. One must hesitate with so
isolated and so broken a fragment; but it seems to treat its
material with complexity, and to produce a response com-
pounded of different elements, which cannot be simply resolved
into strong and straightforward emotion. However, the author
is felt to stand closer to her subject than in most Hellenistic
works. That is partly in the nature of the poem, but it does
create a significant difference in flavour.

It is with the epigram that we feel most nearly in the same
tonal sphere as Callimachus and his coevals. The epigrams of
Asclepiades and Posidippus are the first to occupy this region at
all insistently. They were active in the third century, and very
probably began to be so well before Callimachus (cf. p. 265).
Posidippus was patronized by the royal family of Egypt; Asclepiades is not known to have been, but was admired by Theocritus and Callimachus. Asclepiades will be treated at length in
ch. 5; the affinity with later poets will there emerge clearly. At
present we must place them on one side, and outline from our
point of view the general development of the early epigram.

The genre in effect began in the period we are considering. It
was very likely only in the later fourth century that authors collected and even composed their epigrams for the delectation of
a reader.[45] The earliest writers known to have cultivated the
genre will not have been writing before the last part of that century. Indeed, the number of poems and poetical careers that

---

[45] On the early history of the epigram see R. Reitzenstein, *Epigramm u. Skolion*
(1893), Wilamowitz, *HD* i. 119 ff., W. Ludwig, *GRBS* 4 (1963), 59 ff., and *Entr. Hardt*
14 (1967), especially 342 ff., West, *Studies in Gk. El. and Iamb.* 20 f. Of the two kinds mentioned below, the quasi-inscriptional epigram may well have received an impetus from
the collection of epigrams ascribed to Simonides; the amatory and symposiastic epigram may perhaps have received an impetus from the collection of epigram-like
extracts ascribed to Theognis. The former collection had probably arisen before the
early 3rd c. (see Page, *FGE*, pp. 207 ff., 119 ff.); the latter may belong to the 3rd c. or
later 4th (cf. West, 57 f., and that whole chapter—perhaps his *terminus post* is fixed too
dogmatically).

can with any confidence be taken back to the fourth century is very small indeed: perhaps one poem.[46] The early epigrammatists took as their formal models or their inspiration poems actually inscribed, notably the most common kinds, those written on tombs and on objects dedicated to a god. Some of their own poems might have been inscribed as well as collected. Probably it was a little later that poets engaged themselves with epigrams on love and wine, drawing on archaic elegy and lyric. There survives hardly any such poetry from this period save for that of the two closely related poets Asclepiades and Posidippus. There are some grounds for contending that, had many such epigrams been composed at this time or indeed earlier, we might have expected to have some.[47]

The epigram, then, probably owes to Asclepiades and Posidippus a fundamental expansion in its areas of principal concern; it probably owes to them also a very important delimitation of its normal manner and style. In other early epigram there is no dominating tendency to movement, density, and the striking close, and no extensive concern with play, wry irony, or the deft modification of emotive material. The two developments clearly go together, although they are quite distinct. The theme of love allows a wider range to poets concerned with complications of tone, particularly through the opportunities it offers for an elaborate handling of the self. Such concerns appear too, however, in quasi-inscriptional poems (e.g. Asclep. XXVII, Posid. XV). Similar tones are heard as well, now and then, in the work of other poets of this time.

Perses VIII is supposedly written for the statue of a very minor divinity:

[46] The poets with the best title are Antagoras, Duris, Moero, Perses, Phalaecus, Philetas, Simias; only with Antagoras and Philetas is the claim fairly certain rather than possible. The epigrams attributed to Philetas may well be spurious (and late), and he may not have written any epigrams, despite *Suda* Φ 332. Of Antagoras' two epigrams, one probably belongs in the 4th c., one does belong in the 3rd. The epigrams ascribed to Plato are clearly spurious (see Ludwig, *GRBS* (n. 45), Page, *FGE*, pp. 125 ff.); those ascribed to Erinna are likely to be so (thus Page, p. 155, West, *ZPE* 25 (1977), 114 ff.).

[47] Cf. Ludwig in *Entr. Hardt*, 14, 343. The date of Nossis is uncertain, though she probably belongs to this period; only one amatory epigram by her survives (I). Meleager's statement that 'Love melted the wax on her writing-tablet' (*HE* 3935) need not be confined to her epigrams (cf. *HE* 3974). Note also Phalaecus I (dedicatory in form, but symposiastic in subject).

κἀμὲ τὸν ἐν σμικροῖς ὀλίγον θεὸν ἦν ἐπιβώσῃ
  εὐκαίρως, τεύξῃ, μὴ μεγάλων δὲ γλίχου·
ὡς ὅ τι δημοτέρων δύναται θεὸς ἀνδρὶ πενέστῃ
  δωρεῖσθαι, τούτων κύριός εἰμι Τύχων.

> Even among the little gods I am a small one; but if you
> call on me with prayers of suitable compass, you will gain
> your wish—do not, though, long for mighty things. What-
> ever a god of the ordinary people can give to a poor man,
> over that I possess authority—I, Tychon.[48]

The poem delectably interweaves the god's potentially proud
assertion of his power to aid and his disarmingly depreciatory
account of his own limitations. In the first couplet ('Even ...
things') Tychon's ability to help is conveyed in the single word
τεύξῃ 'you will gain your wish'. The rest emphasizes his littleness, and the assertion of τεύξῃ is instantly followed by the
warning to limit one's desires (in homely language). The
second couplet reinforces the idea of his humble role, but it ends
stating simultaneously his restrictions and his mastery. It is the
use of the first person which gives subtlety and charm to this
piquant handling of a god (his recherché name is suspended
until the last word). The poet exploits the convention of inscriptions which has objects speak about themselves, and produces a winning treatment of voice and the self.

Antagoras II commemorates Xenocles' erection of a bridge
in Attica to rescue the great procession of Eleusinian initiates
from the difficulties of floods. The poem begins with the dramatic evocation of a ritual call:

ὦ ἴτε Δήμητρος πρὸς ἀνάκτορον, ὦ ἴτε, μύσται.

> Go, initiates, go, to the Shrine of Demeter![49]

It proceeds (in essence): 'And do not fear the floods: so safe is
the bridge which Xenocles has built for you here.' The apparent intensity and solemnity of the opening gesture are modified.
One recognizes the cleverness of the poet's praise and feels the
transition to decorous eulogy and the primary subject of the

---

[48] On Tychon cf. H. Herter, *De dis Atticis Priapi similibus* (1921), ch. 4. He was
blurred with Priapus, the rustic god whose statues defended gardens ('interque cunctos
ultimum deos numen' *Priapea* 63. 11).

[49] Cf. Eur. *Bacch.* 152 f. ὦ ἴτε βάκχαι, ἴτε βάκχαι, *Phaeth.* 112 with Diggle's n., Call. *H.*
5. 13 with Bulloch's.

bridge before us (in imagination at least). Moero I, with more
radical play, hints at motifs from sepulchral epigram while
dedicating a bunch of grapes to Aphrodite. It opens κεῖσαι
'here you lie', and the second couplet of the quatrain runs:

οὐδ᾽ ἔτι τοι μάτηρ ἐρατὸν περὶ κλῆμα βαλοῦσα
φύσει ὑπὲρ κρατὸς νεκτάρεον πέταλον.

No longer will your mother (the vine) cast her lovely
tendrils around you and bring forth above your head the
fragrant leaves.[50]

The effect is not one of hearty parody. One receives a fantastic
sense of transmuted pathos; the language creates a rich sense of
loveliness interrupted. But the basic subject prevents one from
responding with strong emotion to the emotional form: the
poem feels light, and is tinged with a consciousness of absurdity.

It would appear, then, that the early epigram displays
sporadically the kinds of effect which are crucial to the work of
Callimachus, Apollonius, and Theocritus; but that attention
was concentrated on such effects only by Asclepiades and Posidippus (and conceivably others of whom little is preserved). It
seems evident that this concentration is a secondary development and not an intrinsic feature of the genre from the beginning. The development is of great interest in itself for the poetry
which followed shortly; but we can scarcely assume it to have
been matched in other sorts of poem. For poetry of this period,
we are comparatively well informed about the epigram.
Thanks to the Byzantine Palatine Anthology (drawing on
Meleager's anthology of around the early first century BC), and
thanks too to the brevity of the epigram, we possess perhaps
around 120 complete poems from this time by a variety of
hands. However, the brevity of the poems, and the want of a
literary tradition for the genre, might make this an entirely
special case. Certainly complication and play on so small a
scale stand at a great distance from the elaborate creations of
the succeeding poets. It is intriguing that when Posidippus
writes about himself in an introductory elegy, he should employ

---

[50] Cf. for κεῖσαι e.g. Perses IV. 4 (also giving the place), *CEG* 95 (opening). For the
second couplet cf. *GVI* 1827. 1 f. (Alexandria, 3rd c. BC) οὐκέτι δὴ μάτηρ σε, Φιλόξενε,
δέξατο χερσὶν | τὰν ἐρατὰν χρονίως ἀμφιβαλοῦσα δέρην, Perses VI; Simias I, etc. For the
vine as parent in poetry add to Gow–Page's note Ion fr. 26. 4 ff. West.

a dignified and lofty manner, and make no play with tone or with himself (*SH* 705).[51] Whether before Callimachus and his colleagues any poets showed a sustained concern with such regions of art in a sizeable *œuvre* of substantial works—of that we must acknowledge our ignorance.

Yet something has been gained for our understanding of the Hellenistic poets in terms of literary history, and this does something to sharpen our perceptions. On the one hand, we see the imposing basis provided by poetry before the fourth century (particularly the classical). Its aesthetic principles and its essentially firm divisions continue to govern the character and the aspirations of much poetry in the fourth century, and beyond. For the poets of the Hellenistic period who concern us most, these presuppositions form a vital point of reference: they need them to give full force to the strangeness and boldness of their own divergent approach.[52]

That approach, however, does not arise out of nothing. The period intervening shows interest in the sustained though straightforward distortion of grand poetry; it provides examples of interplay between serious and unserious which have some kinship with Hellenistic poetry; finally, it contains part of the careers of two writers of epigram who, in that tiny genre, display a recurring concern with effects markedly related to those of their younger contemporaries.

Of that period, where so very little is known, one cannot make negative generalizations; and hence no final view can be achieved on the originality of Apollonius, Callimachus, and Theocritus. But the distinctiveness of their work is emphasized when one compares poets of their time closely related in milieu or in artistic concerns. Even Aratus does not attain—or seek—the vigour and audacity with which tone and level are handled by these three poets; Lycophron does not approach their delicacy. One is still, then, inclined to imagine that their influence on each other was of great importance in forming these central concerns of their art. Certainly no amount of ignorance

---

[51] Cf. Lloyd-Jones, *JHS* 83 (1963), 98.

[52] It is interesting that in *Ia.* 13 (fr. 203 *Dieg.*, and ll. 43 ff.) Callimachus should defend the diversity of his *œuvre* with a poet of the 5th c., Ion: various later poets could have served. Even if the argument is purely *ad homines*, it suggests particularly clearly a contemporary attitude to poetry before the 4th c. as possessed of a classic and even normative status. (There is much evidence which points in the same direction.)

about their predecessors should make us anxious as to the individuality of each of the three: poets who make a strong impression are always individual.

These aspects of poetry in the intermediary time have been
sketched with relative amplitude, despite the obscurity of the
period. This has been done principally because it was felt to set
our authors in a context to some degree helpful and illuminat-
ing. Yet clearly such a picture as this can only be drawn in the
light of conceptions formed from the poetry of the third century
and of the fifth, and earlier. No attempt can be made to recover
the totality of literary history at that time: one must either look
for things which connect, positively or negatively, with one's
notions of the surrounding periods, or else present a heap of
random fragments. The former of these alternatives is perfectly
legitimate, and its answers are not merely an arbitrary imposition, so long as one makes no claims to be depicting the whole
of that vanished assortment of verse. The answers, and the
whole scheme into which they fit, do enhance the conceptions
of our poets to be derived from reading them; but those conceptions are altogether primary, and to them most of the book is
devoted.

Even interpretations which are based firmly on careful reading are naturally never certain. Yet I feel, however temerari-
ously, that it is possible to acquire some sort of instinct for
ancient poetry which is not solely reflected preconception.
Proper brooding on syntax, style, resonance, design can then
bring one in principle to an appreciation of passage or poem
which possesses some measure of historical validity. Not that
one enjoys a boundless confidence in one's own judgement; but
without some aspiration to read appropriately, literary criticism would (for me) have little point. One's appreciations will
inevitably be incomplete. The business of expression and communication is no less daunting. For the sake of clarity, I have
generally simplified to some degree my impression of the passages and works I speak of: to my mind, they are still more complex and elusive than I have depicted them. But for all the
inadequacies of both perception and description, I hope the
reader may find here some lines of approach which are not devoid of a certain value.

CALLIMACHUS

THIS chapter will seek to accumulate an impression of Callimachus through considering in turn his various, and consciously various, works. But to establish a sense of direction, it will be best to begin from the general conception of Callimachus which many nurse who are less familiar with his poetry. They tend to think of him as a frivolous pedant, obsessed with the abstrusest details of mythology and cult, and uninterested in serious human emotions. In attempting to remove this obstacle, we shall be taking up paths already prepared in the first chapter; by following them, we shall arrive in central areas of Callimachus' art.

We may begin with the question of pedantry. Clearly it would be naïve to find objectionable any poetry in which conspicuous erudition played an important part: one would have to find objectionable *The Divine Comedy*, *Paradise Lost*, and the second part of *Faust*. The objection to Callimachus would have to be that erudition encloses his poetry within a dry and uninteresting world, where only learning matters. Such a charge, however, would be entirely superficial.

Even a poem where the author's interest seems most ruthlessly confined gains its force from the things it appears to exclude. In his sixth *Iambus* (fr. 196) Callimachus describes Phidias' statue of Zeus at Olympia to a friend who is travelling specially to see it. The statue was widely regarded as the greatest achievement of sculpture and the most sublime representation of a deity.[1] It seems from the fragmentary papyrus of the poem, and from an ancient summary of it, that Callimachus made no aesthetic comment.[2] He simply stated the detailed

---

[1] J. Overbeck, *Die antiken Schriftquellen der Geschichte der Bildenden Künste* (1868), 125 ff. For later depictions of the work see G. Becatti, *Problemi fidiaci* (1951), pls. 71–3, J. Leigle, *Der Zeus des Phidias* (1952). (Archaeologists seem unfamiliar with Callimachus' poem.)

[2] On the summaries (*Diegeseis*), and the state in which the various works are preserved, see p. 40.

measurements of the work, and gave its cost, and the identity of the artist. The perversity of the scholar is much enjoyed by the poet. When he comes to the particularly low topic of the cost, he says:

τὸ δ᾽ ὦν ἀναισίμωμα (λίχνος ἐσσὶ [γὰρ
καὶ τό μευ πυθέσθαι)   (45 f.)

As for the expenditure (I know you are greedy to learn this too from me) ...

The device of the parenthesis makes as light as possible in outward form this clear intimation of humour and absurdity in the entire conception of the poem. The strong word λίχνος 'greedy' with obvious but graceful comedy shows the contrast between the friend, actually eager for aesthetic experience, and the speaker, bent on retailing facts. This play with personality is used to stress that for its total effect the poem depends on what lies outside its pretended boundaries.[3]

That poem is unusual in the uniformity of its apparent tenor and tone. Much more commonly, the poetry openly contains elements with which the pedantry stands in forceful contrast. Fr. 178 describes most elaborately how Callimachus met at a feast in Egypt a native of the island Icus. The two show an affinity to each other in the refinement of their approach to drink. The talk proceeds, and Callimachus begins a speech with a lengthy and involved preamble; this exalts the dignity of conversation above the triviality of drinking. He ends his sentence, and begins a couplet, with the Ician's name (21): the effect of personal warmth is striking. 'Tell me', asks Callimachus, 'what my heart yearns to hear from you':

ὅσσ[α] δ᾽ ἐμεῖο σ[έ]θεν πάρα θυμὸς ἀκοῦσαι
ἰχαίνει, τάδε μοι λ[έ]ξον [(21 f.)[4]

'Why do the inhabitants of Icus hold rites in honour of Peleus from distant Thessaly?' The comic anticlimax disrupts the suggestion of human intimacy with the intrusion of the

---

[3] Pfeiffer, *Ausgew. Schr.* 79, recognizes that there is irony in the poem, but thinks that Callimachus is avoiding 'flabby rhetoric' and showing his love of true knowledge. The irony is more radical. C. M. Dawson, *YCS* 11 (1950), 72, and D. L. Clayman, *Callimachus' Iambi* (1980), 34 f., seem a little puzzled.

[4] Note the expressive juxtaposition of the personal pronouns, and the placing of ἰχαίνει.

scholar's recondite concerns. Again the language of vehement
desire brings out the oddity of the things which arouse his
strongest passions. The humour springs from a jolting contrast;
but the conjunction of differing elements in this passage is not
simply a matter of amusing deflation. The Ician doubtless went
on, beyond the confines of the fragment, to tell of Peleus' grim
death; but even the non-mythological scene moves on to
another, and a complicating, change of register. Callimachus
had claimed to possess no first-hand knowledge of Ician cult
(27 ff.), having never been at sea. The Ician begins:

> τρίσμακαρ, ἦ παύρων ὄλβιός ἐσσι μέτα
> ναυτιλίης εἰ νῆϊν ἔχεις βίον· ἀλλ᾽ ἐμὸς αἰὼν
> κύμασιν⁵ αἰθυίης μᾶλλον ἐσῳκίσατο.   (32–4)

Ah, you are thrice happy, and your felicity is rare, to have
a life without knowledge of seafaring. My own life has
made its home more in the waves than does a seagull.

Here the two people are used for an expressive contrast and an
emotional utterance; the reality of the man's existence is evoked
with vigorous yet haunting poetry. By reapplying the language
of knowledge which Callimachus had used, the author delicately underlines the contrast of tone. The pedantry of the
dramatic character makes one ingredient in a richer mixture.

Particularly rich is the mixture we see in fr. 75. This comes
from Book 3 of the *Aetia*, a poem dealing principally with the
events which explain particular religious customs; it gives us
the last 77 lines of the story of Acontius' love for Cydippe.⁶ As it
begins, Callimachus is in the course of telling how Cydippe's
imminent marriage to another man is abruptly prevented by
illness. He is elaborating the idea, in typically concrete manner,
by mentioning a pre-nuptial rite of the locality. He is about to
give its *aition*, the myth which explains it. This would echo the
principle of the *Aetia*, whereas the love-story itself, which does
not explain a ritual or the like, does not really answer the criteria of the work. But the poet breaks off in mid-sentence, abusing himself with grotesque violence: it would be a gross impiety

⁵ κύμασί μ᾽? κύμασιν comes only from the quotations; and they would suggest that
with ἐσῳκίσατο the sense was complete.
⁶ On the *Aetia* see p. 40 (ff.). We can form some idea of the earlier parts of this
narrative from frr. 67–74 and from Aristaenetus 1. 10, which is based on this poem.

to recount this particular myth (of Hera's sleeping with Zeus before marriage). The poet pushes to a wild and comic extreme a device of Pindar's.[7] The comedy is directed against himself as the poet of the present learned work. He speaks of singing (ἀείσῃ 5), and of an account of rites (ἱστορίην 7), and closes with a denunciation of incontinent learning:

> ἦ πολυιδρείη χαλεπὸν κακόν, ὅστις ἀκαρτεῖ
> γλώσσης· ὡς ἐτεὸν παῖς ὅδε μαῦλιν ἔχει.   (8 f.)

Much learning is a dangerous evil when a man has no control over his tongue. He is in truth like the child with a knife in the proverb.[8]

The irony of course brings out the poet's real control over the narrator's obsessive erudition. None the less, there is startling paradox in the complete disruption of the narrative precisely through the procedures and stance which supposedly organize and justify the work.

The account of Acontius' love seems to have possessed a real force of narrative and emotion, despite the repeated intrusion of unemotional elements. The tale reaches its climax in the bridal night of Acontius and Cydippe. The note of rapture is achieved through the personal declaration of the poet: 'I do not think (οὐ ... δοκέω, 44) that you, Acontius, would have changed that night for the swiftness of Iphiclus or the wealth of Midas. And all would bear witness to my verdict who are not ignorant of the harsh god of love':

> ψήφου δ' ἂν ἐμῆς ἐπιμάρτυρες εἶεν
> οἵτινες οὐ χαλεποῦ νήϊδές εἰσι θεοῦ.   (48 f.)

The opening declaration on Acontius' happiness is strong and satisfying in essence, though lightly modified by the involved expression.[9] The narrator's personal engagement there heightens the emotion, and contrasts strikingly with his earlier pose. When he reinforces his judgement in the couplet quoted, the term 'ignorant', and its hint of scorn for the uninitiated, show the language of knowledge reapplied to mark the disjunction from the mere scholar. We are, however, moved slightly away from the story to the poet's light intimation of his experience.

---

[7] See especially *Ol.* 9. 35 ff., *Nem.* 3. 26 ff., and cf. pp. 12 f.

[8] P. Oxy. 666. 156, 3699(*d*) 6 show the currency of the saying.

[9] Cf. e.g. the lover's passionate outburst at Plaut. *Curc.* 178 ff.

The unexpected epithet chosen for the god runs wistfully counter to the sense of a triumphant ending.

Three lines on the descendants of the couple serve both to round out the completed narrative, and to prepare a sense of distance in time between narrator and subject (δὴ γὰρ ἔθ' (51) 'even to this day'). A surprising appendix ensues. Callimachus begins:

> Κεῖε, τεὸν δ' ἡμεῖς ἵμερον ἐκλύομεν
> τόνδε παρ' ἀρχαίου Ξενομήδεος, ὅς ποτε πᾶσαν
> νῆσον ἐνὶ μνήμῃ κάτθετο μυθολόγῳ.   (53–5)

Acontius of Ceos, I myself heard of this passion of yours from Xenomedes of old, who once set down the whole island of Ceos in his account with its tales.

He then devotes nineteen lines to a résumé of this work, a fifth-century local history of Ceos. The relation between Callimachus and Acontius, emphasized by the placing of personal pronouns in the Greek, becomes no longer the sympathetic and emotional relation of fellow lovers, but rather that of scholar and subject-matter. The abstruse source, evoked at length, interposes between the two men. Xenomedes himself is a distant figure ('of old', 'once'). The word μυθολόγῳ 'with its tales' often has the sense 'fabulous', and hints that the story is a fiction; this hint is strengthened by the first item mentioned from the history, how the island was first inhabited by nymphs chased from Mount Parnassus by a lion. We feel also, however, that Callimachus has as much in common with the dusty Xenomedes as with the passionate Acontius.[10] This feeling, and our general sense of distance from the story, are increased as Callimachus recapitulates the historian's work. The tale is now seen in a strange perspective.

Finally Callimachus lists the four cities of Ceos and their founders, and then closes:

> εἶπε δέ, Κεῖε,
> ξυγκραθέντ' αὐταῖς ὀξὺν ἔρωτα σέθεν
> πρέσβυς ἐτητυμίῃ μεμελημένος, ἔνθεν ὁ πα[ι]δὸς
> μῦθος ἐς ἡμετέρην ἔδραμε Καλλιόπην.   (74–7)

---

[10] Pfeiffer notes the parallel between ἐν μνήμῃ κάτθετο . . . ἄρχμενος ὡς used of Xenomedes here, and μ]νήμῃ κάτθεο . . . ἄρχμενος ὡς fr. 7. 24 f., which is used of Callimachus himself in the early part of *Aetia* i.

Mixed in with these cities, your fierce passion, Acontius of
Ceos, was told by that old man devoted to truth; from
there the lad's story came down to my Muse.

Here the poet brings out directly the difference in quality
between the dryness of local history and the emotion of his
story.[11] He makes almost explicit the object of the appendix, to
provide a piquant contrast in flavour, and to set the story at a
distance. It is certainly not its real object to assure us that the
story is true.[12] The reference to truth carries considerable irony
from the opening of the appendix, here resumed; and Callimachus' language here separates himself as a poet from Xenomedes the historian, his far-off source. He separates himself also
from Acontius: he forcefully changes the address to Acontius for
a designation of him as 'the lad'. The contrasted figures of 'the
lad' and 'the old man' are referred to with a sense of indulgent
affection; this only marks out the poet's real remoteness from
either.

One must clearly reject the notion of Callimachus' poetry as
actually confined within the circumscribed interests of scholarship. The force of this extract (fr. 75) springs from the interaction of conscious pedantry with quite different elements. The
difference is made salient through vigorous contrasts and extravagant surprises. By dramatizing himself and playing with
his character, Callimachus makes it as clear as possible that his
professed involvements as scholar are treated in the poetry with
the keenest awareness and the easiest detachment. We are
obliged to allow that Callimachus regarded the concerns of his
poetry as distinct from those of his learned books of reference.[13]
The matter and manner of scholarship are subjected completely to the transforming imagination of the creative writer.

[11] I incline to think that συγκραθέντ' αὐταῖς is sound, despite Maas (Pfeiffer i. 501). It
is a little unexpected that the anaphoric pronoun should be used to take up the cities,
but the continuity of syntax slightly sharpens the point. The use of μιν at fr. 191. 64 is
decidedly more striking, as of σφε at *H*. 3. 80; the referent, as here, is generally in mind.
(Callimachus is not averse to αὐτόν.) Even if the phrase were corrupt, the difference in
colour would emerge clearly from the sentence.

[12] Thus Pfeiffer, *HCS* i. 125.

[13] On Callimachus' scholarly activity, see above, pp. 7 f., and Pfeiffer, *HCS* i. 123 ff.
(the *Pinakes* are more realistically described in K. J. Dover, *Lysias and the Corpus Lysi-*
acum (1968), ch. 2); R. Blum, *Kall. und die Literaturverzeichnung bei den Griechen* (1977),
169 ff.

Yet the elements of pretended pedantry do not comfortably consort with the emotive elements in an interesting patchwork. They cause bold disruptions. The poet's play with himself in the fragment serves to heighten, though entertainingly, the paradox and strangeness of such subversions. The effect is not, however, to undermine completely and destroy the serious and romantic elements in the narrative: the impact of the poetry is not so simple. The poet uses himself to enhance as well as to dissipate emotion, and this complexity in the treatment of the poet brings out the complexity of his work. The appeal of the story is not simply dissolved even when we have reached the ending. The lingering remembrance of that appeal is what makes the last lines piquant; ὀξὺν ἔρωτα σέθεν 'your fierce passion' reinforces that awareness. The emotional elements in the fragment are not cancelled, but modified, complicated, and placed at a distance.

It will be seen that the question of frivolity has already been approached. Callimachus is not a writer unconcerned by strong human feeling, and its expression in poetry. He makes abundant use of emotion and emotional language; but he normally contrives to avert a simple and straightforward response to them. His work characteristically explores the effects which lie between absolute seriousness and entire deflation. One must not seek, therefore, to resolve the poetry into either extreme—nor even rest content with asserting that it belongs to neither. Rather one should endeavour to perceive more exactly what sort of position or positions between the extremes are occupied by the poem or the passage before one. Callimachus varies greatly the degree and the manner in which the serious is modified; but modification is essential to the poetry.[14] From some modern readers such writing may demand an expansion of their own aesthetic. This work may perhaps suggest the interest of the literary experience which such expansion lays open. Certainly the continuous contact of the poetry with

[14] Scholars do of course sometimes acknowledge that Callimachus' poetry is not wholly serious or wholly the reverse in its effect (this question often being confused with others); but unfortunately the nature of that effect, or effects, is seldom explored much further. For an interesting general statement, deliberately eschewing more definite analysis, cf. Hopkinson, commentary on *H.* 6, pp. 11 ff. (in the first place on *H.* 6 itself); cf. also P. Veyne, *L'Élégie érotique romaine* (1983), ch. 2.

human emotion makes it anything but a chilly waste of mono-
tonous triviality. It is irrepressibly alive.

These aspects of Callimachus may be illustrated by a brief
discussion of two narrative *Hymns*. In the fifth *Hymn* Callimachus tells the story of the blinding of Teiresias. The story,
however, occupies only half the poem; the proportion is far
smaller than in Callimachus' formal models, the narrative
hymns ascribed to Homer. In the rest (1–56, 137–42), the
poet's voice portrays dramatically an Argive ceremony; he
eventually tells the story to the girls who are celebrating it. So
enormous a 'frame' would in any case place the story at a certain distance; but the content here is particularly strange. At
each recurrence of the festival Athena herself is supposed to
appear in her chariot to take a bath prepared by the Argive
maidens. This regular and predictable arrival is placed by the
hymn not in the world of myth but in what looks to present
itself as a sort of contemporary reality. Such a notion would
have seemed to the poet's readers archaic and grotesque. Hero-
dotus regards the Athenians of the sixth century as exceedingly
naïve and backward to have credited the arrival of Athena in
her chariot at Athens to restore the tyrant Peisistratus (1.60).
Yet that would have been an intervention in a crisis of the
state.[15]

One cannot simply accept the appearance as part of the
unquestioned world of the poem. Callimachus plays with the
epiphany. He announces in the third line that the goddess is
ready to come (3, cf. 15); as the poem proceeds, he calls on her
twice to come forth (ἔξιθ' 33, 43). So far this seems acceptable;
but finally he says:

> πότνι' Ἀθαναία, σὺ μὲν ἔξιθι· μέσφα δ' ἐγώ τι
> ταῖσδ' ἐρέω· μῦθος δ' οὐκ ἐμὸς ἀλλ' ἑτέρων.   (55 f.)

---

[15] Bulloch normalizes the ritual by regarding Athena as in fact merely a statue, identified with the goddess for religious purposes (commentary, p. 3, *al.*; contrast Wilamowitz, *HD* ii. 14 f.). But the goddess is never referred to in the ceremony as a statue, and
such lines as 17, 31 f., 53 f. demand the living body of the heavenly deity. (The argument on p. 111 seems very questionable: note for the article *H.* 2. 1, 9, 13, 30, fr. 194.
71, etc. Ll. 38–42 do not make an equation for the ceremony of the poem, though they
suggest to the reader the original cult.) At all events, the point to which the identification is pushed would still seem bizarre; Bulloch sees only the exciting evocation of religious fervour.

> Lady Athena, do you come forth; in the meantime, I will
> tell something to these maidens. The story is not my own:
> it comes from others.

One can only see here an unexpected delay, which the poet will
fill by improvising a narrative. The setting for the tale of Teiresias, which follows, could scarcely be more awkward. The play
also underlines the strangeness of the conception in what seems
to present itself as the normal world; and it even toys covertly
and teasingly with its truth. This is confirmed by the declaration when the goddess does finally arrive: ἔρχετ' Ἀθαναία νῦν
ἀτρεκές (137) 'now Athena comes in truth'.[16] The emphasis
enhances the awkwardness of the earlier moment; and the word
ἀτρεκές 'in truth' ironically separates the world of the poem
from reality. The cultic first half of the poem shows considerable complexities itself in tone and colour (cf. p. 64); but its
basic conception and structure clearly serve to distance the passionate and tragic story of Teiresias by placing it in a weird environment.

That effect is felt in a reading of the entire poem. However,
such a mode of distancing the emotional would permit the emotion to conserve its purity within the narrative section. Yet even
within that section, Callimachus lightly complicates the impact
on the reader. The story tells how Teiresias while hunting on
Mount Helicon saw Athena bathe, and was blinded. The
blinding is witnessed by his mother the nymph Chariclo, the intimate friend of Athena. She turns with passion on the goddess
who had seemed to be her friend. The goddess defends herself,
appealing to the laws which bind the gods, and promising a
rich compensation. This dramatic exchange is the heart of the
story as Callimachus presents it.

The narrative which leads up to the dialogue develops a
powerful momentum. It engages the reader strongly through
its potent movement between the grimness of the narrator in
archaic epic and an opulence of atmospheric description.[17]
The speeches are more complicated in effect. To take first
Chariclo's:

---

[16] On ἀτρεκές cf. Bulloch's n.
[17] Cf. with 68 f. Hom. *Od.* 15. 245–7, and on 78 see Bulloch.

ἁ νύμφα δ' ἐβόασε "τί μοι τὸν κῶρον ἔρεξας,
πότνια; τοιαῦται, δαίμονες, ἐστὲ φίλαι;
ὄμματά μοι τῶ παιδὸς ἀφείλεο. τέκνον ἄλαστε,
εἶδες Ἀθαναίας στήθεα καὶ λαγόνας,
ἀλλ' οὐκ ἀέλιον πάλιν ὄψεαι. ὦ ἐμὲ δειλάν,
ὦ ὄρος, ὦ Ἑλικὼν οὐκέτι μοι παριτέ,
ἦ μεγάλ' ἀντ' ὀλίγων ἐπράξαο· δόρκας ὀλέσσας
καὶ πρόκας οὐ πολλὰς φάεα παιδὸς ἔχεις."   (85–92)

The nymph cried out, 'What have you done to my child,
lady? Is this the sort of friend you goddesses are? You have
taken away the eyes of my son. Wretched child, you have
seen the bosom and loins of Athena, but you will never
again see the sun. Oh misery! Oh Helicon, the mountain I
shall never pass again! For a little injury you have exacted
a penalty great indeed: you lost a few deer, and you have
taken the eyes of my son.'

The opening three sentences (85–7, 'What … son') display a
simplicity of wording which matches the primal force of their
emotion. Callimachus has altered his source so as to make
Chariclo, not beg Athena to restore Teiresias' sight, but rupture their friendship in maternal anger and pain. With great
tragic impetus, female emotion surges through the structures
which ensure the gods respect.[18] The address to Teiresias,
however, introduces a more devious thought: '*but* you will
never see the sun' implies that the sight of Athena's body was in
itself desirable. The ingenuity and the hinted sensuality complicate and distance a little the sense of simple pathos. A passionate directness returns in the exclamation of lament ('Oh …
again').[19] But a fresh conceit appears, audaciously far-fetched;
the dismissive οὐ πολλὰς 'a few' adds to its somewhat distancing
effect. The indictment of the mountain closes similarly to the
indictment of Athena ('you have taken the eyes of my son'; 'you
have taken away the eyes of my son'); but the resemblance
brings out the artificiality of the gesture and the anger here.
Callimachus is subtly and slightly modifying a straightforward
response.

---

[18] Compare for the effect Helen at Hom. *Il.* 3. 406 ff., Creusa at Eur. *Ion* 881 ff. The source: cf. Pherecydes, *FGrH* 3 F 92.

[19] Bulloch on 90 notes the resonant echo of Agave's lamentation, Eur. *Bacch.* 1383 ff.

The following speech of Athena reinforces this approach: it shows similar movements from powerful simplicity to complicating cleverness. It displays overall an imposing union of warmth and control; we see the divine order both in its sternness and in its harmonizing generosity. However, after the noble first section (97–106) Athena contrasts the fate of Teiresias with the worse fate of Actaeon, who will be torn by his own dogs for beholding Artemis bathe. The argument, emotionally acceptable in itself, is presented with the frame of a devastating conceit. How many sacrifices the parents of Actaeon will offer to see their son blind (that is, not dead) (107 ff.)! His mother will call Chariclo most happy to have received her son back blind (117 f.). The extravagance and artificiality again tinge somewhat the sense of noble tragedy; they do not at all destroy it. The ritual setting distances lavishly; the writing within the narrative complicates discreetly and delicately. The differences, and the similarities, to fr. 75 will be obvious (the last part of *Acontius and Cydippe*, with its distancing appendix, and its internal disruptions). The combination here is distinctive, the compound effect convincingly itself.

Our general response to the fourth *Hymn* bears a very different relation again to the serious and the straightforwardly emotional. Here the distancing springs primarily from the basic situation of the plot. The *Hymn to Delos* is based on the Delian half of the Homeric Hymn to Apollo (3. 1–181). In that work Leto, pregnant with Apollo, traverses the Aegean, but all places fear to bear so mighty a god. The island Delos is willing; but until Leto swears an oath, even Delos is afraid that Apollo will destroy her in disgust when he is born. Callimachus makes the situation more grandiose and more fantastic. Leto wanders round the whole of Greece. As she comes, each place actually rushes away in terror. They fear not the pride of Apollo but the jealousy of Hera: Zeus had fathered him. The only place both willing and able to accept her is Delos, at this time still wandering widely about the sea, unfixed. One might have some difficulty in accepting places as protagonists; but the wild conception of them all in flight makes it impossible to feel involved in the story with simple seriousness. None the less, the story is told emotionally, and makes many appeals to our sympathies. The appeals can be answered only within the framework of a preposterous situation; but even so the nature of our response is not uniform.

We are touched most by Leto: she is anthropomorphic, and we can readily understand her physical sufferings. These are brought out, for example, within a speech of hers, with a forceful combination of emotive rhetoric and poignant physicality.

> ὦ ἐμὸν ἄχθος,
> ποῖ σε φέρω; μέλεοι γὰρ ἀπειρήκασι τένοντες.

(116f.)

My burden, Apollo, where can I bear you to? My poor sinews fail me.

Yet this outburst comes in the middle of a passionate appeal to the features of Thessaly as they fly. The directness of effect forms one element within a weirder whole. Even the address to Apollo here, as when Leto is giving birth (212 ff.), reminds us that this particular child is fully conscious of his situation, and has indeed delivered speeches on it.

Delos was a diplomatist in the archaic poem: she was allured by Leto's offers, but first exacted an oath (*Hom. H.* 3. 42–90). In Callimachus she acts with spontaneous generosity. She defies the violence of Hera in the briefest of speeches.

> Ἥρη, τοῦτό με ῥέξον ὅ τοι φίλον· οὐ γὰρ ἀπειλὰς
> ὑμετέρας ἐφύλαξα. πέρα, πέρα εἰς ἐμέ, Λητοῖ.   (203 f.)

Hera, do what you like to me: I have not conformed to your threats. Leto, come over, come over to me.

The moment is of course theatrical, but, within the framework, the theatricality is not ludicrous. This is partly because this scene is contrasted with an earlier one, more directly humorous (see below); and partly because we had followed the career of Delos from the beginning of the poem. The wandering Delos had not been a distinguished figure. We feel a naïve delight when the lowly heroine reappears and surpasses her fellows in nobility and daring.

She is transfigured when Apollo is born. All parts of her turn gold, and the huge anaphora of words for 'gold' and 'golden' is not merely a cerebral game (260–4): the feeling of climax and the visual images evoked give a wild and incantatory richness.[20] She bursts into an extravagant but affecting speech of triumph (266 ff.). The moment has a magic and a lyricism only heightened by the unreality. For the first time in the poem, she appears in human form as well as in the form of the island.[21] The effect in the context is paradoxical, for her identity as a place is dwelt on here. But we sympathize the more warmly with her exultation.

Before Leto reaches Delos, she asks the river Peneius to accommodate her. At first he regretfully declines, but then suddenly he makes a magnanimous decision:

$$τί μήσομαι; ἢ ἀπολέσθαι$$
$$ἡδύ τί τοι Πηνειόν;—ἴτω πεπρωμένον ἧμαρ·$$
$$τλήσομαι εἴνεκα σεῖο \dots$$
$$ἠνίδ' ἐγώ· τί περισσά; κάλει μόνον Εἰλήθυιαν.$$

(127–9, 132)

> What else can I do? Would it give you pleasure that Peneius should perish? But let the day of destiny come upon me! For your sake I will endure ... Here I stand. What more is needed? Do but summon the goddess of childbirth.

Such ostentatious heroism, and even the sudden choice, may have accorded well enough with the spirit of post-classical tragedy.[22] But the abruptness of this complete reversal (in mid-line, with no connection) has something absurd about it, even within the framework of the story. The narrative that ensues sustains the note of grandiosity deliciously overdone.

When Leto arrives at the island of Cos, Apollo says that she must leave this island to be the birthplace of Ptolemy (Ptolemy II, Callimachus' present patron). He prophesies, from within his mother's womb, the glory of the dynasty. He unites his own triumph over the invading Gauls at Delphi with Ptolemy's triumph over the Gauls in Egypt (that is, Ptolemy's destruction of some rebellious Gallic mercenaries of his own). This passage, unlike the passage on Peneius which precedes it, has the auth-

---

[20] For antecedents and parallels see Mineur on 260 ff.; the effect of this passage is quite distinct.

[21] This identification of the place and its presiding nymph is approached in Pindar, but not with the intention of paradox. See especially *Isth.* 8. 17–26.

[22] Cf. (probably) Aesch. *Theb.* [1026 ff.], [1066 ff.], *TrGF* 60 F 1 i.

entic tone of grandeur. But the poet avoids the obviousness of panegyric through the strangeness of the situation and the novel perspective of time. The close brings out both these weird elements, in the midst of magnificence:

ἐσσόμενε Πτολεμαῖε, τά τοι μαντήϊα Φοίβου·
αἰνήσεις μέγα δή τι τὸν εἰσέτι γαστέρι μάντιν
ὕστερον ἤματα πάντα. (188–90)

O Ptolemy who will one day exist, these are Apollo's prophecies to you. In time to come you will give high praise
all your life to the prophet who is still in the womb as he
speaks.

Even the praise which would sound perfectly straightforward if delivered by the poet in the present here acquires freshness and distance.[23] The chief part of the speech, however, adds its own touch of the oblique. The poet dwells mainly on Apollo's victory, in a gigantic sentence of over fifteen lines (171 ff.), and then tacks on Ptolemy's in an appendage of less than three (185–7). In fact this is not unflattering to Ptolemy. But the con-nection between the two 'victories' is tenuous, and the develop-ment is unexpected.[24] The mode of narrative is also indirect. Much is presented as sights seen by others; these others include the shields of the Gauls.[25] The anonymous third-century frag-ment *SH* 958 appears to touch on the same act of Ptolemy's. At any rate, that crude narrative, probably panegyrical, shows what Callimachus has gained. In this place we are actually awed and impressed, and the weirdness of the setting at once rarefies the feeling and saves it from the death of triteness. Such

---

[23] Ll. 166–70, on the extent of the Ptolemaic dominions, should be compared with Theocr. 17. 77–94, a more straightforward treatment of a very similar theme.

[24] The scholion on 175–87 claims that Ptolemy's mercenaries were recruited from the remains of Brennus' army, which invaded Greece. Even this is hard to reconcile with Pausanias' account (1. 7) and with the historical situation. I suppose the notion to have been fabricated in order to make the link less strained. On the epiphany of Apollo in 278 BC see *Syll.*³ 398. If Call. fr. 379, two lines on Brennus' Gauls, comes from the poem *Galateia*, that poem would seem to have approached the invasion from at least an unusual angle.

[25] ἰδοῦσαι 186, taking up ἴδωσι 179, ἀπαυγάζοιντο 181. For the problems of the sub-ject at 177a ff., cf. Mineur, *Mnemosyne* 4th Ser. 32 (1979), 119 f. (he does not wholly con-vince me that Pfeiffer must be wrong). στήσονται at 185 must be corrupt: the word could hardly be used in this way.

is the mobility with which Callimachus ranges within the field of tone he has created for this poem.

Something has now been suggested of the preoccupations in Callimachus' poetry. With this in view, let us turn to consider the individual works. Those we know most of are the *Aetia*, the *Iambi*, the *Hecale*; six *Hymns*, and perhaps sixty-one complete *Epigrams*. The *Hymns* are transmitted entire by medieval manuscripts; the *Epigrams* appear mostly in the Byzantine anthologies, though some are only quoted by other writers. For our knowledge of the remaining works we depend on papyrus fragments of texts and commentaries, many extremely substantial, quotations in later authors, and a set of prose summaries (*Diegeseis*), also preserved, incomplete, on papyrus. We have sizable fragments too of a lyric poem, *The Apotheosis of Queen Arsinoe* (fr. 228), and an elegiac poem, *The Victory of Sosibius* (fr. 384). Most of these works we have little good means of dating. Callimachus' earliest datable poem belongs in 279(6?)–3 (fr. 392), his latest in or after 246/5 (fr. 110; *SH* 254 ff., probably fr. 384).[26] The only probable surmise regarding the main works is that Books 1 and 2 of the *Aetia* precede by a considerable interval Books 3 and 4; the final form, and the first and last poems, of Books 3 and 4 are certainly very late, as is the prologue to the whole *Aetia*.[27] Yet no significant differences of style appear between the earlier and later portions. No general evolution can be traced in Callimachus' manner: the only important boundaries are those of the different works.

The *Aetia* presents a series of expositions, mostly narrative and nearly all explanatory.[28] They explain, as a rule, religious customs, sometimes features of sacred statues, once a place-

[26] Fr. 392: cf. E. E. Rice, *The Grand Procession of Ptolemy Philadelphus* (1983), 41, Fraser, *PA* ii. 367. Coinage can hardly supply a date for *Ep.* 20 (XXXII). Fr. 228 belongs in or shortly after 270. On fr. 384 cf. Maas, *Kl. Schr.* 100 ff., Fraser, ii. 1004 f.

[27] See Parsons, *ZPE* 25 (1977), 44 ff.; Bulloch, commentary on *H.* 5, p. 42 n. 1. A difference of time between the two halves feels much the most plausible way of accounting for the data, particularly in regard to the Muses. It would seem that *Aetia* 1–2 in some sense precede the *Argonautica*, at some point imitated by Theocritus (pp. 88, 192 f.): it would be very awkward to date the whole *Aetia* to the time of the *Coma* and the *Victoria* (fr. 110, *SH* 254 ff.).

[28] On Acontius and Cydippe see above. What fr. 96 (The Hunter) and fr. 107 (Gaius) explain we are not told by the *Diegeseis* or by Diod. 4. 22; we are not told either for fr. 102 (Pasicles), but here it is easier to imagine possibilities. Fr. 64 (Simonides' Tomb) is also puzzling.

name (frr. 94–5). The stories were deeply obscure. By contrast with the stories in the *Hymns*, not one story known to be treated in the *Aetia* is known to occur in previous poetry, save for Heracles' fight with the Nemean lion.[29] That appears in a poem composed for a special occasion. For the rest, Callimachus' sources, whenever they are known, or can be conjectured with some probability, were local historians.[30] It seems likely that local historians are his sources throughout. Every tale would accord with their interests. One may consider for example *FGrH* 315 F 1 (an explanation of why the Arcadians send to Eleutherae those who enter the Lycaeum through ignorance);[31] 432 F 5 (an explanation of why the Mariandyni call on Bormos); 472 F 1 (the myth of Zeus' being suckled by a sow, which explains why the Praesians offer sacrifice to one). All these subjects are the sort of thing one finds in the *Aetia*. The last two fragments are quoted directly; they show the dryness and simplicity of style which one would expect in this genre, and which one finds in a fragment of Agias and Dercylus that we know Callimachus to have used (*FGrH* 305 F 4). The recondite character of the material was important for Callimachus, as we shall see.[32] From the bareness of his sources, Callimachus produced poetry of particularly dense and startling complexity.

One important element which this material provided was that of the bizarre and the barbaric. The notion that Callimachus was motivated by nostalgia for dying tradition is hard

---

[29] Bacch. 13. 44 ff. Bacchylides may actually be Callimachus' chief source for the main plot, though not of course for the individual sub-plot of Molorchus. Cf. Parsons, *ZPE* 25 (1977), 41, H. Maehler, *Die Lieder des Bakch.* i/2 (1982), 252.

[30] Known: Agias and Dercylus of Argos (frr. 3–7. 14, Graces; frr. 26–31*a*, Linus and Coroebus; frr. 65–6, Springs of Argos); Xenomedes of Ceos (frr. 67–75, Acontius); Leandrus of Miletus or another local historian in -andrus (frr. 91–2, Melicertes). Probable: Aethlius of Samos (fr. 100, Statue of Hera); Timaeus of Tauromenium (fr. 96, Hunter); Antiochus of Syracuse or another historian of Sicily (fr. 43, Zancle).

[31] It is probable that Plutarch in his *Greek Questions* drew on local historians for other material reminiscent of the *Aetia*, as from Question 45 to the end. Similarly P. Oxy. 2688–9.

[32] We do not know whether local historians were quarried much by poets before Callimachus. The most interesting author is Polycritus of Mende, who wrote a verse *Sicelica* which contained a *paradoxon*. He belonged to the 4th c., and would seem to have been used by Callimachus in his own paradoxography (*FGrH* 599 F 2, 4; *SH* 696, 697). On Rhianus see ch. 1 n. 15.

to reconcile with stories of human sacrifice (frr. 91–2, 93), appalling punishments (frr. 94–5), and the ritual deflowering of virgins (frr. 98–9), all now abolished; or of the pelting with stones of a human scapegoat at Abdera (fr. 90). The proximity of these stories in Book 4 suggests that they were intended to have a cumulative effect. It is also difficult to believe that, for example, the abusive language used in various rituals (frr. 7–25) affected Callimachus with sentimental regrets. Rather, the element of the bizarre is sought for the sake of piquancy and of contrast. Some measure of opposition is intrinsic to the material: the customs tend to strike the reader as odd or outlandish, the stories which explain them tend to employ the familiar patterns, and often persons, of Greek mythology. Callimachus exploits this; but he also positively cultivates divergences of tone.

The poem on the sacrifice of Theodotus began with four lines describing some food sweeter than nectar or ambrosia (fr. 93. 1 ff.).[33] The appearance of human sacrifice was to be a shock. In fr. 43 the account of the colonization of Zancle contains nothing at all startling; Callimachus throws in a mention of Cronus' castrating his father with a sickle (70 f.), but marks it off by using a parenthesis and a different perspective of time. The two founders of the city ignore a bird of ill omen, quarrel, consult Apollo's oracle, and learn that the city is to belong to neither of them. The founding of cities in general is described in familiar and practical terms (64 f.). However, this simple story produces a ritual which is odder than we expected. It is not merely that the founder is called on without a name (54 f., 79). The prayer of the officials of Zancle runs:

> ἵ]λαος ἡμετέρην ὅστις ἔδειμε [πόλ]ιν
> ἐρ]χέσθω μετὰ δαῖτα. πάρεστι δὲ καὶ δύ' ἄγεσθαι
> κ]αὶ πλέας· οὐκ ὀλ[ί]γως α[ἷ]μα βοὸς κέχυ[τ]αι.
>
> (81–3)

May he come to this feast of sacrifice with favour towards us, whoever it was that built our city. But indeed two

---

[33] Was the victim supposed to eat some special food? Cf. 'purioribus cibis' in Servius, *Aen.* 3. 57 (Petronius fr. 1).

heroes may be brought, or more: no small quantity of
bull's blood has been shed.[34]

The speech ends the action, and the structure requires something curious here. And in fact the officials' sequence of diplo-
matic opening and nervous expansion gives an entertaining
unseriousness to this peculiar situation.

In Book 1 it is told how Heracles killed and feasted on a bull
appropriated from a peasant, who stood there cursing him furiously; the Lindians therefore sacrifice bulls to Heracles with
curses. The cursing at the sacrifice was obviously described in
the defective lines fr. 23. 9–17. With this must be contrasted the
dignified and (outwardly) respectful address to the god in 19 f.,
which is probably uttered by the poet to close.[35]

χαῖρε, βαρυσκίπων, ἐπίτακτα μὲν ἑξάκι δοιά,
    ἐκ δ' αὐταγρεσίης πολλάκι πολλὰ καμών.

Hail, god of the heavy club: you performed twelve labours
at Eurystheus' command, but many, many labours of
your own will.

The poet, while decorously heightening the hero's whole
achievement, points slyly at the unelevated greed which has
produced this action. The last phrase of the peasant's furious
abuse is preserved in fr. 23. 1: ναὶ κεραῶν ῥῆξιν ἄριστε βοῶν 'Ah!
You are truly valiant and admirable at smashing horned bulls.'
This vehement and heavy sarcasm contrasts with the urbane
and gentle mockery of the god by the author (5 f., see below).
The bizarre elements stand in delectable opposition to others.
Such elements in general play a major part in creating the
polychromatic surface of the *Aetia*.

In the first two books of the *Aetia*, Callimachus exploited the
obscurity of the material to fashion an elaborate framework for
the stories, which complicates the whole effect. Callimachus is
transported to Mount Helicon; there he asks the Muses learned
questions, and they tell in reply the explanatory tales that form

---

[34] ἄγεσθαι should not be middle: one would then expect ἕτερον.

[35] *Pace* Pfeiffer. The tone is quite unsuited to the cursing invocation of the Lindians,
and it is implausible that this, as well as the original words of the peasant, would have
been quoted in *oratio recta*. The χαῖρε is a typical close for the poet, in the style of a
hymn, cf. fr. 66. 8, fr. 112. 8, and all the *Hymns*; for the utterance of the poet in Book 1
compare the close of the *aition* on the Graces, fr. 7. 13 f. Cf. also Prop. 4. 9. 71 f.

the body of the work.[36] The effect of this arrangement was not straightforwardly solemn. Certainly archaic poets bid the Muses instruct them on questions of fact. When the Muses met Hesiod on Helicon—the model for this encounter—they seem to have inspired him with knowledge as well as ability.[37] But these poets owe everything to the teaching of the Muses. When Hesiod meets them, or when Homer invokes them, contrasting their knowledge as gods with the ignorance of men, we feel strongly the awe, and the inferiority, of mortals in the face of the divine (Hom. *Il.* 2. 485 f.). Callimachus appears as an erudite scholar seeking from superior authority the solution of some recondite problems about anomalies and curiosities. In this encounter between gods and mortal we see (in what is preserved) only voluble learning from the mortal, and from the gods business-like concentration on the facts. In the first sequence of the work Callimachus stated three conflicting genealogies for the Graces, and asked the Muses for the true version (Sch. Flor. 32–5, Pfeiffer i. 13; fr. 3.) In Book 2, shortly after an eloquent statement of the value of learning to him (fr. 43. 12–17), Callimachus asks the Muses why the founder of Zancle in Sicily is invoked without a name. In asking this, he explains that he knows the founders of all the other cities in Sicily, and retails them indefatigably, stressing his knowledge. The Muse explains, as elsewhere, without preamble, and simply closes with the prayer that was quoted above. Callimachus feels wonder, θάμβος (fr. 43. 85), but only at hearing the answer to so obscure a question. He desires yet further information (ἐπὶ καὶ [τὸ πυ]θέσθαι), and launches us into another *aition*. One can

---

[36] See Lloyd-Jones and Parsons on *SH* 238 (p. 90). One would naturally suppose that all the *aitia* in these books were included in the framework. Fr. 26. 5–8 καὶ τὸν ἐπὶ ῥάβδῳ μῦθον ὑφαινόμενον ... ἠνεκὲς ἀείδω δειδεγμένος cannot mean that the story of Linus and Coroebus was narrated in the poem by Callimachus: we know that it was narrated by a Muse, no doubt in a different version from that mentioned here (fr. 31b, Pfeiffer ii. 108 ff.). Fr. 114 (The Statue of Delian Apollo) and frr. 178–85 (The Ician) cannot be accommodated in the colloquium with the Muses; but there is probably sufficient room for them both after the proem of Book 3. It is true that if frr. 178–85 preceded fr. 43 in Book 2, fr. 43. 12–17 would refer to the instruction imparted at the feast by the stranger, and ἠρίον fr. 43. 4 and]ειθετιςενπ[6 would refer to Peleus. (The second point is made by H. Herter, Bursians *Jahresb.* 255 (1937), 125, 129, the first is almost made by J. E. G. Zetzel, *ZPE* 42 (1981), 31 ff.). Yet there are other possibilities with fr. 43, and it would be imprudent to accept the combination.

[36] Hes. *Theog.* 22 ff. (cf. p. 278). On the concept of inspiration in archaic poetry see P. Murray, *JHS* 101 (1981), 87 ff.

scarcely miss the quaint and amusing element in the pictured situation, where learning predominates so absolutely, and in Callimachus' use of his scholarly *persona*.[38]

This framework plainly increases the complexity of Books 1–2. The stories are distanced by being placed on a different narrative level, and made formally to subserve a strange dialogue, which dramatizes their abstruseness. The contrasts in feeling between frame and stories are important, and various. The most significant strand is the opposition between the strong emotion and vigorous action of the characters in the stories and, in the frame, the preoccupation with mere learning, and the static, unflurried dialogue. But this opposition wears a very different appearance when the story has the drama and grandeur found in the episode on the Argonauts (cf. fr. 7. 30 ff., fr. 18, *SH* 250), and when it has the undignified comedy and the charming pathos found in the companion episodes on Heracles (frr. 23–4). Clearly the richness of the books in tone and colour is much enhanced by the handling of form.

The third and fourth books do not use the framework. They form a collection of distinct and separate poems. The poems are connected to each other only implicitly, through the principle of the *aition*, and through arrangement: most obviously, the third book probably began and the fourth ended with poems in praise of Queen Berenice.[39] The first two books are presupposed: plainly those books are in some sense prior, and the epilogue at the end of Book 4 looks back to the beginning of the colloquy in Books 1–2 (fr. 112, cf. fr. 2). (The four books were finally published together, it seems, with a prologue apparently written then.) The poet sometimes plays with the difference between the two halves. Part of the effect with the excursus on Xenomedes comes from its undoing of the fiction in the earlier books. The final reference to 'my Muse', ἡμετέρην ... Καλλιόπην (above, p. 30), only stresses that Callimachus' real source is not a Muse but a historian. (Cf. also fr. 92.) The excursus here, and, if it came in this half, the encounter with the Ician, perform for two individual poems something of the

---

[38] Such an approach is confirmed by the little exchanges with goddesses in *H.* 3. 183 ff., 4. 82 ff.

[39] See Parsons (above, n. 27). The chronology to which this difference is probably related historically has only a secondary significance for us.

function that the framework had supplied for the whole design in Books 1–2. The later books inherit and share, not only the basic conception of the earlier, but their poetic interests. In the *Aetia*, Callimachus goes still farther than elsewhere in his weaving of diverse and conflicting elements into a rich and discordant texture; this procedure is apparent in every part of the work.

The victory-ode for Berenice which seems to have opened Book 3 (*SH* 254–69) might originally have been written, in some form, for separate publication; but it can of course be regarded as an integral part of the *Aetia*, and it suits its present environment exceedingly well.[40] It has a far wider and more discordant range of tone than the victory-ode for Sosibius (fr. 384). It shows not a little in common with the *Hecale* in its use of lowly rusticity and in its bringing to the fore of a little-known character. Molorchus the peasant entertains Heracles before he fights the Nemean lion, as Hecale the old woman entertains Theseus before he fights the Marathonian bull. But the *Hecale* was a much longer poem; here everything is compressed into (say) 200 lines. The *Hecale* did not contain anything so audacious as the parody of Heracles' lion-hunt in the mouse-hunt of Molorchus.[41] The account of Molorchus and his mice itself juxtaposes lines of the most elevated style with lines of the most humble subject-matter. Its discordances are perhaps further heightened and complicated by inversions of the *Odyssey*.[42] In Molorchus' speech to Heracles (*SH* 257) the description of the lowly and trivial depravations brought on countrymen by the lion (21 ff.) is to be contrasted with the account of its awesome origin (33 ff.). The opening declaration

---

[40] Even originally the work might have been written for separate consumption, but with *Aetia* in mind. Such a possibility would be quite plausible for the victory-ode written in the form of an Ionic iambus, now *Ia.* 8 (fr. 198, with *Diegesis*).

[41] *SH* 259, with n. See E. Livrea, *ZPE* 34 (1979), 37 ff., 40 (1980), 21 ff. Note, however, on the *Hecale* below, p. 000. In the *Victory of Berenice*, R. F. Thomas suggests that the story of Heracles and Molorchus was told as an ἔκφρασις of a tapestry woven for Berenice (*CQ* ns 33 (1983), 92 ff.). But the argument seems very tenuous, and the conclusion improbable: note especially *SH* 264. Catullus 64 does *not* provide a parallel to the narrative style of the supposed ἔκφρασις: see p. 301 f.

[42] The suitors destroy and eat up Odysseus' home (*Od.* 22. 36, 2. 237, etc.): cf. *SH* 259. 13, 31. But at first the owner of the house in Callimachus is terrified of his enemies (contrast the simile in 10 f. with *Od.* 4. 335 ff.). His denunciation is whispered and ineffectual, and his trickery and the hidden death he plans for them are at first overcome by superior cunning.

of Berenice's triumph at Nemea (*SH* 254) is grand and splendid in style. Near the end of the story, Heracles prophesies that the Isthmian Games will change the plant used for victors' garlands in emulation of the Nemean Games (*SH* 265. 5 ff.). Here, by contrast with the opening, the praise of the Nemean Games is mingled with the pedantry of archaic ritual, seen from a curious perspective of time. The piquant richness of the poem is made salient both through its larger structure and in the detail of its writing.

The diversity of colour even within short passages of the *Aetia* may be illustrated by some places where Callimachus elaborates a theme. In fr. 23 we have Heracles ignoring the curses of the peasant.

> ὡς ὁ μὲν ἔνθ' ἠρᾶτο, σὺ δ' ὡς ἁλὸς ἦχον ἀκούει
> Σελλὸς ἐνὶ Τμαρίοις οὔρεσιν Ἰκαρίης,
> ἠϊθέων ὡς μάχλα φιλήτορος ὦτα πενιχροῦ,
> ὡς ἄδικοι πατέρων υἱέες, ὡς σὺ λύρης
> ([ἐσσὶ] γὰρ οὐ μάλ' ἐλαφρός ...)
> λυγρῶν ὡς ἐπέων οὐδὲν ὀπιζόμενος ...   (2–7)

So he cursed, but as for you, exactly as much as the native of Dodona hears in the Tmarian mountains the sound of the sea, or as much as the wanton ears of boys listen to an impoverished lover, or as immoral sons listen to their fathers, or you listen to the lyre (you are not outstanding for your delicacy ...)—just so you paid his baneful words no regard whatever.

Each member, shorter than its predecessor, strikes a new and surprising tone. The first is elevated, the second knowing but wry in manner, the third is more plainly moral, the last delectably comic. We move giddily between different spheres of reality. The lovers and sons suggest the contemporary world, the lovers perhaps Callimachus' own *persona*; the return to mythology is doubly startling, as it occurs within the simile and it brings not dignity but stronger humour.[43]

At the beginning of the story of Acontius and Cydippe, the hero and the heroine are described in a beautiful line as καλοί

---

[43] For Callimachus' poverty, etc., cf. Pfeiffer's note and perhaps, within these books of the *Aetia*, *SH* 239, 253.

νησάων ἀστέρες ἀμφότεροι 'both the fair stars of their islands' (fr. 67. 8). The theme is then expanded.

πολλαὶ Κυδίππην ὀλ[ί]γην ἔτι μητέρες υἱοῖς
ἑδνῆστιν κεραῶν ἤτεον ἀντὶ βοῶν·
κείνης ο[ὐ]χ ἑτέρη γὰρ ἐπὶ λασίοιο γέροντος
Σιληνοῦ νοτίην ἵκετο πιδυλίδα
ἠοῖ εἰδομένη μάλιον ῥέθος, οὐδ' Ἀριήδης
ἐς χ]ορὸν εὐδούσης ἁβρὸν ἔθηκε πόδα.   (67. 9–14)

While Cydippe was still a child, many were the mothers who used to seek her as a fiancée for their sons in exchange for horned bulls. For no other girl of Naxos who went to the gushing rock of shaggy old Silenus had a face more like the dawn; nor did any who set her soft foot in the dance of Ariadne sleeping.

We have first a reminder of well-known archaic practices, made to sound strange. Then local topography and custom are deployed; the references are recherché in themselves, but full of direct appeal. The mythical figures of Silenus and Ariadne are contrasted, but so are Silenus and Cydippe. His ugliness and age are set against the girl's beauty and youthfulness (the dawn suggests both); the attractive natural spring forms, in the order of the Greek, an exquisite intermediary. Later Callimachus turned, with parallel phrasing, to the loveliness of the young Acontius: many dedicated to him their throws in the game of kottabos (fr. 69). The custom is much more modern and familiar, and the tone is again quite different.[44]

To an extent, the *Aetia* differs from Callimachus' other productions more in degree than in kind. In some ways it may be regarded as the most Callimachean of the works of Callimachus.

The book of *Iambi* belongs to a lowly genre, and tends to restrict the level of its poetry. Within its own terms, however, it aims at a subtle handling of tone, and an intriguing use of form and contrast. All these things are closely related, and are apt to find their scope in the fields provided, not by the range of poetic level, but by personality and individual manner.

The genre was eminently personal. The *Iambi* look back explicitly to the sixth-century poet Hipponax (fr. 191, 1 ff., 203.

---

[44] On kottabos see B. A. Sparkes, *Archaeology*, 13 (1960), 202 ff.

12 ff., 64 ff.), who was thought to have invented the 'limping iambic' used in poems 1–5 and 13. Hipponax in his poems abused others and pitied himself, and retailed disgusting stories about both. The poems seem to have proceeded not so much from moral indignation as from a desire to insult and entertain.[45] Later Greeks were much struck by his abuse, as by that of his predecessor Archilochus. His personal aggressiveness is stressed in various mock-epitaphs, though one of them gives it a moral slant.[46] The genre seems to have been taken up by poets before Callimachus.[47] They emphasize the element of personality, and can denounce others with the most passionate hatred and graphic vituperation. They are distinguished by their enthusiasm for moral censure of the times. These poets too are important for Callimachus.[48]

The *Iambi* of Callimachus value a very different ethos from their predecessors. This ethos, cool, smiling, rational, is brought out by contrasts. In the last of the *Iambi* (13, fr. 203) the poet himself replies to a critic. The critic attacks Callimachus with an unbridled invective, culminating in the charge of insanity.

> τ[ε]ῦ μέχρι τολμᾶς; οἱ φίλοι σε δήσ[ουσι ...
> ὑγιείης οὐδὲ τὠνυχι ψαύεις.   (19, 22)

How far will your shocking acts proceed? Your friends will strait-jacket you ... You can't touch sanity even with the very tips of your fingers.

Callimachus answers with urbanity and with argument, forcibly expressed. ὦ λῷστε, he begins: 'my good friend'. His manner alone ensures our support for his case. Within the speech

---

[45] This statement would have to be modified if Hipponax wrote the Strasburg Epode (Hipp. fr. 115 West). There the poet complains of treachery in the tones of an Archilochus.

[46] *HE* 76 ff. (Alcaeus), 2325 ff. (Leon. Tar.), 3430 ff. (Theocr.), *Garl. Phil.* 2861 ff. (Philip). His abuse directed at wickedness: Theocr. loc. cit.

[47] Paus. 1. 9. 7 indicates that Phoenix wrote of the fall of Colophon as a contemporary event (or so Pausanias thought). This occurred most likely in 302, perhaps in 294, not after 289. On the history of choliambic poetry in general see G. A. Gerhard, *Phoinix von Kolophon* (1909), 202 ff., who makes too much of Cynicism; on Herodas see ch. 5.

[48] Cf. for personality *CA*, p. 214. 27 ff., 217. 6 ff., 218. 36 ff.; for abuse, notably col. iv of the Heidelberg papyrus (Gerhard, *Phoinix v. Kol.*, 6 f.)—not an attack on pederasty in particular. For moral censure see *CA*, pp. 213 ff. (wealth, cf. Call. *Ia.* 3 (fr. 193), and compare *CA*, p. 214. 31 ff. with *Ia.* 12 (fr. 202. 57–70, Pfeiffer ii. 118f.); contrast Ananius frr. 2–3 West); 217 (with stress on own virtue, cf. *Ia.* 3), 235 f.

itself he portrays the crude abuse to which fellow poets subject
him (and perhaps others).[49] In the fourth *Iambus* (fr. 194) the
same contrast appears in fiction. The laurel and the olive are
debating which is superior. The laurel is forthright and graphic
in abusing her opponent. ὤφρων ἐλαίη, she begins, 'senseless
olive' (18); she uses the words as a refrain. She derides the
olive's appearance with extravagant colour (22 f.); she dwells
with harsh physicality on the association of the olive with
funerals (40–3). She herself stands aloof from death and suffering, almost like a Greek god: πῆμα δ' οὐχὶ γινώσκω ... ἀγνὴ γάρ
εἰμι (37, 39) 'I know nothing of pain ... I am holy'. The
language pretends to an elevated simplicity, which clashes
bizarrely with the coarseness of the abuse: the laurel alienates
us by her excess in both invective and self-praise.[50] The olive's
opening address is unexpectedly flattering: ὦ πάντα καλή (46)
'you who are lovely in everything'. The poet has just stressed
her self-possession (45), and the irony we suspect is formidable
through its control. The olive neatly and movingly converts
into praise of herself her association with death; but she soon
breaks off her arguments and affects to report the speech of two
birds in her branches. These champion her case with forthright
argument—though without scurrility. The olive herself pretends to be appalled at their loquacity (81 f.). Narrative level is
exploited in this arrangement to achieve an elaborate obliquity
of approach. The sly indirectness of the olive is more effective
than the crudity of her antagonist. It is also to seem attractive,
and its appeal conjoins the aesthetic and the personal.

In the first *Iambus* (fr. 191) Hipponax himself takes on this
new tone; the paradox is deliberate and striking.[51] He has
returned from the dead in order to rebuke the scholars of Alexandria for their jealous quarrels. He does so by means of a fable,
which illustrates the behaviour he approves of. This oblique
and circumspect approach is itself contrasted with the inflam-

[49] Fr. 203. 52 ff. 60–3 I take to describe the weakness of poetry when the Muses are
put to flight. καὐταί in 59 prevents us from referring the lines to the weakness of poets'
abuse.

[50] Perhaps κοὐ ... ἰρὴ γάρ εἰμι is spurious? If not, the absurdity of the laurel is mirrored in an absurdity of style. For ancient sensibility to tactless self-praise see e.g.
Plutarch's essay, *Mor.* 539 ff.

[51] Fr. 191. 3f. οὐ μάχην ἀείδοντα | τὴν Βουπάλειον must mark the paradox for the
reader, even if such a point was not part of the rhetorical surface.

mability of the Alexandrians. He interrupts his tale after its first
three words to address a disgusted member of his audience:

> οὐ μακρὴν ἄξω,
> ὦ λῶστε, μὴ σίμαινε· καὶ γὰρ οὐδ' αὐτὸς
> μέγα σχολάζ[ω·] δ[ε]ῖ με γὰρ μέσον δινεῖν
>]ευ Ἀχέρο[ντ]ος.   (32–5)

I won't be long, my good friend; don't wrinkle up your
nose. I have no great leisure myself: I must soon be whirl-
ing in the midst of Acheron.

Here the relaxed humour at the opening is set against the bad
temper of the addressee; the grimmer humour and the sudden
pathos of what follows bring out the triviality and the excess of
the scholar's irritation. After telling the fable, Hipponax gives a
picture of the vehement and naïve attacks of the Alexandrians
on each other (78 ff.). This passage makes us sharply aware of
the difference in ethos; it serves the same purpose as the picture
of the poets' attacks within the speech of Callimachus in *Ia.* 13
(fr. 203. 52 ff.). The targets of the first *Iambus* are so closely
related to Callimachus himself that we are forced to reflect on
his own strategy too. He does not present this picture of the
scholars (78 ff.) in his own person, but assigns it to a dramatic
character, as the olive assigns her reply to the birds. He is indirect and aloof, where his colleagues are fierce and crude. The
intricacies of the form are again significant. In the fifth *Iambus*
(fr. 195) Callimachus marks his distance from the manner of
the historical Hipponax by adapting the opening of an epode of
his.[52] That opening was vigorously insulting; Callimachus,
addressing a pederastic schoolmaster, studiously avoids
throughout the poem any overt obscenity. His metaphors are
less obscure than he pretends (32 f.): Callimachus is playing
with indirectness. But we are intended to savour his divergence
from the spirit of his model.

A basic element in the creation of the *Iambi* is the fable.
Actual fables appear in *Ia.* 2 (fr. 192: Zeus gives the voices of
animals to men), *Ia.* 4 (fr. 194: the contest of the laurel and the
olive),[53] and *Ia.* 12 (fr. 202: the rivalry among the gods in

---

[52] Fr. 118 West. The resemblance is noted by R. Kassel, *RhM* NF 101 (1958), 235f.

[53] See H. Diels, *Intern. Woch. f. Wiss. Kunst u. Technik*, 4 (1910), 993 ff., B. E. Perry,
Babrius and Phaedrus (1965), p. xxvii.

giving presents to Hebe).[54] The story in the first *Iambus* of the
Seven Wise Men and the gold cup also has the character of a
fable. It is also notable that two *Iambi*, 7 and 9 (frr. 197, 199),
should have for their subject statues of Hermes, the theme of
several fables in the collections that have come down to us.[55]
Ia. 9 ended with a crushing speech by Hermes, the second
speech of two; the form is reminiscent of Babrius 30 and 117.
The use of fables in the *Iambi* must to some degree recall their
tradition. We do not know that Hipponax employed fables, but
other early iambographers did so, Archilochus in epodes and
Semonides in iambics.[56] Besides this, Semonides fr. 7 describes
Zeus' creation of various kinds of women from different animals: clearly it bears a relation both to the fable and to Callimachus' *Ia.* 2. The story of *Ia.* 1 seems to be anticipated in
Phoenix fr. 4 (*CA*, p. 234); another of Phoenix' poems (*CA*, pp.
231 f.) presents a narrative reminiscent of fable, and of *Ia.* 11
(fr. 201).[57] The role of these elements of fable seems to have
been, in the archaic poets, to add force and colour to condemnation and ridicule: tact and indirectness were not in question
with Archilochus or Semonides.[58] In Phoenix one seems to find
the strong and heavy communication of a message about existence. It is of course for its potential indirectness that Callimachus values the form; but in his use of it we see him enjoying
not merely obliqueness but play with obliqueness and the self.

The fable in Hipponax' speech in *Ia.* 1 is employed, as we
have seen, to show Hipponax' tact and discretion. The use of
the fable in *Ia.* 2 (fr. 192) is more complicated. The poet seems

[54] Compare for this type of story Aesop 46 Perry, Babrius 68. No doubt the type was
more common in the collection of Demetrius (4th c. BC) than in our late collections.
The latter seem to have reduced the element of the divine: cf. B. E. Perry, *TAPA* 93
(1962), 287 ff.

[55] Babrius 30, 48, 119, Aesop 88, 99 Perry. There are a number of other fables
involving the god. He also appears with great frequency in Hipponax.

[56] Archil. frr. 172–84, 185–7 West; Semon. fr. 9 West, noted by W. Bühler, *Entr.
Hardt*, 10 (1964), 232. The whole essay, on Archilochus and Callimachus, is illuminat-
ing.

[57] Cf. Clayman, *Callimachus' Iambi*, 67 f. Phoenix' story expands the famous epitaph
of Sardanapallus (*SH* 335).

[58] It is not certain that Archil. frr. 172–3 West come from the same poem as 174–81.
But it is probable, and 172–3 would in any case indicate the tone of the fable, which
was certainly directed against Lycambes. The fable of the fox and the ape had a personal point (fr. 185), and fr. 187 does not suggest that it aimed at tactful restraint. On
the early functions and history of fable see West, *Entr. Hardt*, 30 (1983), 105 ff.

simply to be relating the tale of how the animals forfeited their voices to men. But at the end he suddenly elaborates the basic notion with insulting, and modern, particularities: Eudemus was given the voice of the dog, and so on (10 ff.). Narrative abruptly turns into blunt satire and personal declaration. Callimachus ends his account with a vocative, thereby addressing it to a contemporary friend. He proceeds:

> ταῦτα δ' Αἴσωπος
> ὁ Σαρδιηνὸς εἶπεν, ὅντιν' οἱ Δελφοὶ
> ᾄδοντα μῦθον οὐ καλῶς ἐδέξαντο.   (15–17)

So said Aesop of Sardis—he to whose performance the people of Delphi gave no kind reception.

The fable is ascribed to Aesop of old, and Callimachus affects now to evade responsibility for his words; but the mode of ascription, and the juxtaposition of modern and ancient, produce a startling impression of discrepancy and paradox. We are then reminded how the creator of fable caused his own death through his incautious mockery. Callimachus, while withdrawing from his utterance, yet emphasizes by implication its directness. The sudden dryness and reserve of tone mark at once a decided movement away from his own world, and a grim glance at his own probable reception. The very grimness, however, contains a self-mocking exaggeration and melodrama: Callimachus is unlikely to be slain for his poem. In *Iambus* 2, then, the poet is playing disconcertingly with the tactful and the outspoken, with the narrated and the personal.

We have already seen how in *Iambus* 4 (fr. 194) the indirectness of the olive triumphs within the fable. The fable itself clearly bore a relation, and a more elaborate relation, to the indirectness and directness of the narrator; but the beginning and end of the poem are ill preserved, and we can have no precise understanding. The contest of laurel and olive is interrupted by a bush who attempts to placate them, speaking as if it were their equal; it meets with a furious rebuke from the laurel. The story was told, as the *Diegesis* reveals, to a man who intruded with similar pretension in a dispute between Callimachus and a rival. The laurel, whose pride has been wounded in the contest, shows to the bush an extreme of rudeness and vehemence (101 ff.). The telling of the fable suggests a contrasting indirectness and self-control in the poet. But the fable was most likely preceded by some forthright insults of the poet's own (*Dieg.* 5 f.). The laurel's attack opens, ὦ κακὴ λώβη, | ὡς δὴ μί᾽ ἡμέων καὶ σύ; 'So you too, you foul plague, are one of us?'; the poet begins the poem with the ironical Εἷς—οὐ γάρ;— ἡμέων, παῖ Χαριτάδεω, καὶ σύ 'You too are one of us—are you not?—son of Charitades.' One sees here both a contrast in tone and a forceful connection. One can go no further. The narrative of the contest absorbs us in its own right after the poet's direct address to the intruder, which occupies only the first five lines of the poem. The appearance and humiliation of the bush produce a striking interruption of the line of narrative and a startling recurrence from narrative to the poet's own concerns. The poet is evidently exploiting narrative level and personality in a fashion less than straightforward.

Still less clear to us is the handling of the fable in *Iambus* 12 (fr. 202, with addenda at Pfeiffer ii. 118 f.). Callimachus' poem is written for the daughter of a friend, just born, and tells how when Hebe was born her best gift was Apollo's song to her. Formally at least Callimachus will be displaying the seemly indirectness of his own self-praise: it is Apollo who says ἡ δ᾽ ἐμὴ τῇ παιδὶ καλλίστη δόσις (Pfeiffer ii. 119, l. 68) 'my most lovely gift to the child' will last for ever.[59]

Apollo disparages Hephaestus' gift by a moralizing attack on gold (Pfeiffer ii. 118 f.). One is to recall the attacks made by recent choliambic poets in their own voices (above, p. 49). But here Apollo speaks, and of what has not yet occurred (gold not yet having been discovered by men); and all serves to praise poetry and the present poem. The moralizing on the present age in *Ia.* 3 (fr. 193) again looks to convention, but takes a personal turn of an unexpected kind: Callimachus resents his treatment at the hands of a wealthy boy he is in love with. He dwells on his own virtue, but then moves in a bizarre conclusion to lamenting his own folly in becoming a poet. The straightforward use of the poet's personality in the tradition diverges into distance and strangeness in the passage from *Ia.* 12, and, in that from *Ia.* 3, into strongly personal writing, but such as to dissolve seriousness and pride into inglorious humour. The

---

[59] The point is not affected by the uncertainties of construction or text.

Iambi are much interested in good manners; on basic morality they seek to avoid any simple involvement.

In *Ia.* 1–5 (frr. 191–5), and 12–13 (frr. 202–3), the poet's pre-occupations arise from the nature of this particular class of poetry. The genre is fundamental to the effects. The poet startles his readers, however, by placing after *Ia.* 5 six poems in which genre is deliberately flouted. Unfortunately, the fragments of *Ia.* 7–11 (frr. 197–201) are exceedingly slight, and our knowledge of their matter comes principally from the outlines of the *Diegeseis*. One can only observe the bare externals. *Ia.* 7, 9, and 11, as we saw, have connections with the fable and the choliambographers; but they flirt with the forms of the epigram: 8 is a victory-ode, 10 gives an aetiological myth (as do 8 and 7).[60] The first in the group describes Phidias' statue of Zeus (6, discussed above); the subject is intended to surprise us. So too is the dialect. The proper dialect for choliambi was Hipponax' dialect, Ionic. This poem, like 9 and 11, is in Doric; 7 is intended to be in Aeolic (despite certain Doricisms). In the case of 6, 7, and 11, the dialect is meant to be appropriate, in a general way, to the locale.[61] But it is none the less meant to startle, and in *Ia.* 13 Callimachus' critic seizes on this feature (fr. 203. 18). His ἀρχαῖον 'ancient' two lines before may refer to the weaving into the book (ἐμπέπλεκται) of aetiological mythis. This section of the book is meant to diverge from our expectations. The genre was defined particularly sharply in its range and its regional associations: we do not find elsewhere in Callimachus so audacious a transgression of the limits of genre.[62] *Ia.* 13 defends, and advertises, both the startling diversity in his handling of genre within this single book of *Iambi*, and the diversity of genres in his work as a whole. The conception of that

---

[60] Aetiological elements occur outside the *Aetia* in Callimachus, but only rarely do they explain not a name but a practice, as in the *Aetia* and *Ia.* 8 (fr. 198) and especially 10 (fr. 200: ritual). Cf., most notably, the brief passage *H.* 5. 35–42; *H.* 3. 200–3 are appended to the explanation of a name, *H.* 2. 97–104 explain a name and a cry. Callimachus may be playing not only with the established genre but with the divisions of his own work.

[61] Cf. *H.* 5, where the generalized Doric suits Argos (so rightly Bulloch, commentary, p. 26); compare also perhaps *Ep.* 46 Pf. (III).

[62] See p. 16 on this question, and particularly on the width of elegiacs. On *H.* 5 (Doric and elegiac) see Bulloch there cited. Callimachus' use of elegiacs for two epinician poems, not one, would seem to weaken the notion of a great piquancy with those works (*SH* 254–69, fr. 384), as opposed to *Ia.* 8.

poem invites us to see the movement in the second half of the book as fundamental to its effect, not as mere wandering. It also invites us to connect the character of that book with the character of Callimachus' whole *œuvre*, both alike unpredictable and various. The terms in which it invites this connection are very formal and limited; but we should certainly be justified in relating the concerns of the *Iambi* to the concerns of Callimachus' poetry in general. The book of *Iambi* shows strikingly both the continuity of his interests and the novelty of conception in which those interests can appear.

In his *Hecale* Callimachus composed a continuous narrative on a substantial scale. It was certainly much longer than the longest of the *Hymns* (326 lines); the possible limits are perhaps 700 lines and 1,800.[63] Although the narrative was of unusual size, its basic story was of no great intricacy. Theseus goes from the city of Athens to Marathon on the coast of Attica, in order to fight the Marathonian bull. On the way a storm breaks out, and he takes shelter with the old woman Hecale. When he returns victorious from fighting the bull, he finds that she has died. To repay her hospitality he founds the deme of Hecale and the cult of Zeus Hecaleius. The whole story (apart from the storm) is probably derived from Philochorus the historian of Attica.[64] What Callimachus built on this slender base, we may see best by considering three of his figures: Hecale, Theseus, and the crow.

The poem began with Hecale, and described her hospitality (frr. 230, 231, 342). But her character was developed primarily, it would seem, in the long scene where she entertained Theseus. We have little text for this scene that is continuous and com-

---

[63] A length of *c.* 950 lines would be suggested by the approach I hazard in Appendix III of A. S. Hollis's forthcoming edn.—a work one awaits eagerly. (In the light of it many details in what follows will no doubt need to be modified.)

[64] It is not clear exactly what Plutarch ascribes to Philochorus in *Thes.* 14. But Philochorus certainly associated the institution of the cult with Theseus and probably he mentioned the hospitality. Wherever exactly the deme of Hecale was situated, the connection with the expedition to Marathon seems inevitable. It is unlikely that either Plutarch or his source for this Life, if he had one, based his account of Hecale on Callimachus. The Life refers often to historians, never to Hellenistic poets (even if *SH* 1155 is Hellenistic, it is taken from the historian cited). Plutarch himself seldom quotes Callimachus, and only the Prologue to the *Aetia* and epigrams, save at *Quaest. Conviv.* 5. 3 (*Mor.* 677 A–B), where the erudition is probably not his own (note the Euphorion which precedes).

plete; but our knowledge of it is not inconsiderable. The scene was modelled, as is well known, on the fourteenth and fifteenth books of the *Odyssey*, where the swineherd Eumaeus entertains Odysseus, disguised as a beggar. Callimachus takes up a part of Homer particularly bold in its positive treatment of humble material (cf. p. 12). Homer emphasizes the lowliness of hospitality in the swineherd's hut, forcefully contrasting it with the lordliness of the hospitality in Menelaus' palace; but Callimachus appears to have depicted the poverty of Hecale much more harshly. Eumaeus gets a skin from his own bed for his guest to sit on; it is big and thick (*Od.* 14. 51). Hecale gets from her bed ὀλίγον ῥάκος, 'a little rag' (fr. 241). Her fare is αὐχμηρός, rough, poor (fr. 252, cf. *SH* 284). The material realities of poverty formed a low and sordid subject for Greek poets; the picturesque and recherché elements in Callimachus' description (cf. fr. 251 and *SH* 283) suggest that he relished its flavour here. The passage stood in strong contrast with the grandeur and violence of the passage just before it, which depicted the storm encountered by Theseus (fr. 238).[65] However, the bitter poverty of Hecale also constitutes the final stage in her half-tragic experience, which the scene will go on to narrate. The account of the meal thus served a double function, dwelling on the low and preparing the emotional.

The scene seems then to have progressed to a dialogue; in this Hecale told at length of her life and how she came to be poor. The figure of Hecale appears now to acquire new seriousness and depth from the exposition of her past, and from her emotions. We may reasonably conjecture that there lay before Callimachus no tradition on the life of Hecale. His primary model was Eumaeus' account of how he passed from the life of a prince to slavery (*Od.* 15. 390 ff.). Eumaeus was abducted as a small boy by Phoenicians. Although his misfortune arouses the distress of his listener, he himself can now contemplate it with detachment (*Od.* 15. 400 f.). He has experienced much kindness from the royal family of Ithaca, to whom he is devoted. Hecale's calamities, and her attitudes to them, have much more the shape of tragedy. Her prosperity lasted long. She came of a wealthy family (fr. 254, *SH* 285. 7); she married a de-

---

[65] Fr. 238. 19 f. only heighten the contrast: the device serves to mark out the abnormal, as in Homer (*Od.* 12. 439 ff., etc.).

sirable husband (*SH* 285. 8ff. seem to describe her first sight of him); she bore him two fine sons (*SH* 287. 1 ff.). An accumulation of disasters destroyed all three of her family and reduced her to poverty. This pattern in a sense resembles the life of Hecuba, who lost her husband and all her sons, and fell from her queenly state. Within her narrative Hecale stresses the series of deaths. She addresses one of her perished family directly:

> ἠρνεόμην Θανάτοιο πάλαι καλέοντος ἀκοῦσαι
> μὴ μετὰ δὴν ἵνα καὶ σοὶ ἐπιρρήξαιμι χιτῶνα;

(*SH* 287. 12 f.)

Was it for this that I refused to heed Death, who had long been summoning me—that I might rend my dress, after no long interval, for you as well?

The gesture is rich in tragic associations, the form strong and essentially convincing in its pathos.

Yet the female exemplars of suffering whom Hecale evokes from epic and tragedy differ from her fundamentally in the grandeur of their experience. Hecale's prosperity was a very local affair: her glorious husband came from nearby Aphidnae (*SH* 285. 8 ff.). The fates of her menfolk do not have the same resonance as death in the Trojan War. One, indeed, was killed by the loathsome Cercyon killed by Theseus, who forced strangers to wrestle with him: even this has a touch of the grotesque, and we are conscious of the ingenuity of the poet in interweaving his plots and accommodating legend. Hecale's language simultaneously assimilates her to great figures of the *Iliad* and tragedy and marks her distance from them. When she says that her sons shot up like trees (*SH* 287. 7), the words echo Thetis' lament for her own doomed son (Hom. *Il.* 18. 56); but this is not a goddess lamenting for an Achilles. She says of Cercyon,

> ζώοντος ἀναιδέσιν ἐμπήξαιμι
> σκώλους ὀφθαλμοῖσι καί, εἰ θέμις, ὠμὰ πασαίμην.

(*SH* 287. 24 f.)

May I stick thorns into his wicked eyes while he is still alive, and may I—if it is lawful—eat his flesh raw!

The cry recalls Hecuba, who wished that she could eat the liver

of Achilles, the slayer of her great son Hector, and in truth had
pins thrust into the eyes of Polymestor, the murderer of her last
son Polydorus (Hom. *Il.* 24. 212 f.; Eur. *Hec.* 1169 ff.). Yet,
situation apart, the conjunction of desired atrocities gives the
utterance a bizarre and exaggerated quality. The caution of εἰ
θέμις 'if it is lawful', a phrase deliberately incongruous in this
abandoned imprecation, only heightens the air of grotesqueness in the whole.[66] Callimachus creates a heroine with a tragic
aspect to her suffering and her passion; but he eschews with her
a sense of continuous elevation.

Hecale must die knowing that the son killed by Cercyon has
been avenged, but ignorant of Theseus' triumph. Her epitaph
is spoken by dwellers in the neighbourhood or by travellers.

> ἴθι, πρηεῖα γυναικῶν,
> τὴν ὁδὸν ἣν ἀνίαι θυμαλγέες οὐ περόωσι.
> πολλάκι †σεῖο†, μαῖα, φιλοξείνοιο καλιῆς
> μνησόμεθα· ξυνὸν γὰρ ἐπαύλιον ἔσκεν ἅπασιν.   (fr. 263)

> Go, most kindly woman, along that way which is un
> traversed by pain and anguish. We shall often remember,
> dear, your hut and its hospitality: your little house was
> shared by all.

We recur to the description of her hospitality to travellers that
was given probably at the start of the poem (fr. 231). But her
figure has now been enriched by the weight of her suffering.
The first sentence does not merely transfer the idea of travel
with poignant elegance; it acquires from her story a sonorous
fullness of meaning and a satisfying air of quasi-tragic conclusion. Yet the second sentence is still more touching. The
warmth and simplicity of its unglamorous praise assert the
value of Hecale precisely in her own humble terms. Callimachus gives a fresh turn to the lowliness of his heroine.

Hecale, then, presents a striking combination of elements,
and calls forth a complicated response. The character of combination and response are brought out further by Theseus and

[66] εἰ θέμις at Soph. *Trach.* 809 is obviously quite different: the wish does not have the
crude savagery of Hecale's, and Hyllus is cursing his own mother. The phrase is used
there for the sake of a movement to assurance in the following line. Hecale's formula at
SH 286. 10 f., with regard to the fatal voyage of husband or son, is likewise deliberately
incongruous in the distance it suggests.

by the crow. Shortly after Theseus' splendid triumph with the bull, we find a crow talking at length of how she or her family fell from Athena's favour (*SH* 288).[67] The crow may be telling this story to deter the other bird from carrying to Theseus the news of Hecale's death.[68] The crow offers us a kind of parody of Hecale. She traces the unhappy history of herself and her family, from her early position as a protégée of Athena to her penurious old age, perhaps as Hecale's pet (*SH* 288. 44–6). This narration is surely linked with Hecale's. The lines that follow the conversation (63 f.) echo most strikingly the lines that follow the conversation of Odysseus and Eumaeus in *Odyssey* 15 (494 f.); that conversation, as we saw, provided the model for Hecale's narrative. The crow's very description of herself as γρηῦ[ν] ... κορών[ην (50) 'the old crow' suggests in Greek a correspondence to the 'old woman' Hecale.[69] This delightful counterpart helps to define the seriousness of Hecale.

The theme of a fall from felicity is reinforced at the conclusion of the crow's speech: she prophesies that the day will come when Apollo will change the raven from white to black.

> ναὶ μὰ τ[όν]—οὐ γάρ [π]ῳ πάντ᾽ ἤματα—ναὶ
> [μ]ὰ τὸ ῥικνὸν
> σῦφαρ ἐμόν, ναὶ το[ῦτ]ο τὸ δένδ[ρ]εον αὖον
> ἐόν περ—
> οὐκ ἤδη ῥυμόν τε κ[α]ὶ ἄξονα κανάξαντες
> ἠέλιοι δυ[σ]μέων εἴσω πόδα πάντες ἔχουσι,
> δ]είελος ἀλλ᾽ ἢ νὺξ ἢ ἔνδιος ἢ ἔσετ᾽ ἠὼς
> εὖτε κόραξ, ὃς νῦν γε καὶ ἂν κύκνοισιν ἐρίζοι
> καὶ γάλακι χροιὴν καὶ κύματος ἄκρῳ ἀώτῳ,
> κυάνεον φὴ πίσσαν ἐπὶ πτερὸν οὐλοὸν ἕξει ...
>
> (*SH* 288. 51–8)

By goodness I swear—the whole of time has not yet

---

[67] Perhaps the crow who speaks was not herself the culprit: *SH* 288. 42 αὐτὰρ ἐγὼ τυτθὸς παρέη[ν] γόνο[ς seems otherwise hard to account for. (Note the plurality of crows at 35.) *SH* 289 (cf. *FGrH* 330 F 1) would then have to be a speech reported by the present bird, and Ovid's imitation (*Met.* 2. 549 ff.) would have to simplify. The extreme old age of the crow would sort well enough with the notion of Aegeus as the eighth king after Cecrops (as e.g. on the Parian Marble).

[68] Cf. B. Gentili, *Gnomon*, 33 (1961), 32 f.

[69] Elsewhere Callimachus never uses γραῦς or even γέρων save of old persons or gods. The phrase may distort γραῦς γυνή, ἀνὴρ γέρων. γρηῦς is used of Hecale at *SH* 285. 5, and most likely, at fr. 310, by Hecale (perhaps both old females are to be seen as garrulous, cf. *SH* 285. 4).

passed—by my shrivelled skin, by this tree, withered
though it is, the suns of successive days have not yet all
broken the poles and axles of their chariots and set their
feet in the west, at an end: no, there will come an evening,
or a night, or a noon, or a dawn, when the raven, who
now might vie with swans in his colour, or with milk, or
with the topmost bloom of the wave, will show an ugly
wing as dark as pitch . . .

The poetry here becomes completely wild. One strand is seen in
the extravagant grandiosity with which the course of all time is
described, and in the portentous list of possible moments for the
catastrophe. Such pomp is to seem absurd for the fate of the
raven. The list outdoes, to ludicrous effect, the line which
Achilles uses of his coming death ('a dawn will come, or an
evening or a noon', Hom. *Il.* 21. 111). The relation to heroic
material is here one of untrammelled parody. At the start the
grandeur is mixed in extraordinary confusion with grotesque
images of old age. The description of the raven's present hue—
paradoxical to the reader, self-evident at the time of the
speech—brings the mind to rest in the luxuriance of its weirdness and beauty. All this is then destroyed abruptly in the ugliness of the event. The prodigious sentence is still not closed.
Thus the treatment of calamity disappears completely from
seriousness into the wildest fantasy and burlesque.

Theseus, on the other hand, seems to have provided an undiluted heroism, to set against the lowness which complicates
our response to Hecale. Callimachus did not begrudge space to
the hero and his story, though famous. Theseus' initial arrival
in Athens appears to have been narrated with dramatic force
(frr. 232–6). The father's recognizing his son, and rescuing him
at the last moment from the death that was planned for him,
provided, one supposes, a crisis characteristic of tragedy.[70]

The son's subsequent relations with his father were used to
display his spirit. The poet depicted a scene in which Theseus
besought Aegeus to let him fight the bull (fr. 238, *SH* 281); this

[70] Euripides' *Aegeus* evidently handled this subject. It may have treated both this
and the fight with the bull of Marathon: cf. P. Oxy. 3530. For the conjunction of the
events before Callimachus, cf. F. Brommer, *JDAI Arch. Anz.* 1979, 504 f. (P. Oxy. 3434
is, I think, describing the *Hecale*, Ἐ]κάλη in 6 being the work, not the character.) Callimachus was of course under no obligation to treat the story of Aegeus so fully.

must have shown his valour.[71] The anxious father persisted in his refusal; the son's boldness made him defy his parent and leave secretly (*Diegesis* 26 f., Pfeiffer i. 227). But when he has overcome the bull, Theseus' first concern is to send a messenger to his father so as to 'relieve him from much solicitude' (*SH* 288. 7). The humane and dutiful feeling is strikingly combined in this scene with formidable heroism. As Theseus appears dragging the bull, the rustics fear to look not only on the 'vast beast' but on the 'massy man' (ἄνδρα μέγαν καὶ θῆρα πελώριον, *SH* 288. 3).[72] Yet his heroism is not a matter of physical prowess alone: his message to his father exhibits a noble brevity and a proud restraint.

> Θησεὺς οὐχ ἑκὰς οὗτος, ἀπ᾽ εὐύδρου Μαραθῶνος
> ζωὸν ἄγων τὸν ταῦρον.   (*SH* 288. 8 f.)

Theseus is here, close at hand; from watery Marathon he is leading the bull alive.

Only the name of the place receives the least decoration. The hero is no dull foil: his character is vigorously and attractively imagined and conveyed.

Theseus' scene with Hecale clearly confronted and contrasted the active young hero's and the passive old woman's accounts of themselves and their deeds. *SH* 285 shows Theseus telling of himself in answer to Hecale's inquiries, and then asking Hecale about herself in turn. It is also probable that Hecale's narrative of helpless suffering was followed by Theseus' account of slaying the vainly detested Cercyon, and quite likely other villains too.[73] In *SH* 285 we seem to see Theseus speaking of his own intentions with impressive con-

---

[71] I would guess that fr. 238. 2 f. may have run something like: my grandfather (cf. fr. 237) used to bid me never shame my family, but to endure all labours (e.g. μέ]νει⟨ν⟩{η} δ᾽ ὑπό (for the order cf. e.g. *SH* 264. 1) πάντας ἀέθλου[ς). On the reading of the papyrus see Hollis, *CQ* NS 32 (1982), 470 n. 2; the caesura, δ᾽, and τῷ (4) make νείη very implausible. Hollis takes line 3 differently.

[72] The fight itself was probably compressed or omitted in the narrative (cf. *SH* 288. 1, despite fr. 258); but Callimachus' purpose was clearly not to diminish the stature of Theseus. If P. Oxy. 3530 gives Euripides' narrative of this encounter, it might throw further light on Callimachus' mannerist treatment.

[73] Cf. *SH* p. 127. Theseus must have enlightened Hecale about Cercyon; fr. 328 (speech) might perhaps be thought to suit this account better than Hecale's. It seems likely that there was a full narrative on Sciron (cf. Hollis, *CR* NS 15 (1969), 259), and at any rate that would be implausible in Theseus' first speech to Hecale.

cision, and then addressing Hecale with warmth and interest. It is sad that the fragments do not show us more of the personal relationship between the two characters, a relationship touching for its strangeness and the interval between the participants (one should contrast Theseus' relationship with Aegeus). Theseus was returning to Hecale after his victory when he came on the men digging her tomb. He lamented in bitter disappointment (fr. 262; *Diegesis* XI, Pfeiffer i. 227). The scene must have exploited the poignant contact between these divergent figures. We can at least see the divergence, and perceive something of how the elevation of Theseus' heroism stands against the lowly element in Hecale's pathos, and goes to make up the tonal structure of the poem. In this lavish work, Callimachus' poetic concerns organize an arrangement broad in conception and amply satisfying in effect.

The *Hymns* were not designed for performance in ritual. With *Hymn* 5, for example (pp. 33 f.), the professed, and deliberately awkward, improvisation would be absurd in a premeditated performance—to say nothing of the expected epiphany. There is no reason to allow that they were not performed in the circumstances they evoke, but yet make them a part of religious celebration. If one does so, one fails to perceive the complication of the poetry.[74] The poems take as their models the archaic narrative hymns which were by convention ascribed to Homer. Callimachus chose to imitate works which pretended to Homeric authorship, but ones which were obscure and short: these little-read poems were thought of as being 'preludes' to the performance of the great epics.[75] Callimachus' *Hymns* may well constitute a set designed, at some point, by the author.[76] But the collection would not make the same claims to form an entity as the *Aetia* or the *Iambi*; and the six poems show greater differences from each other even than the large Homeric

---

[74] Against e.g. Fraser, *PA* ii. 16, see e.g. Hopkinson, commentary on *H.* 6, pp. 37 ff.

[75] The continuing obscurity of the works may be seen by contrasting Thuc. 3. 104 with 1. 9. 4, and the vast quantity of papyri of the *Iliad* and *Odyssey* with the single fragment from the text of a Homeric Hymn (P. Oxy. 2379). The questionable notion of προοίμια will derive from 5th-c. attempts to sort out the huge corpus of 'Homer'. Scepticism about authorship is less vocal for the Hymns than for the Cycle, and it is interesting that Callimachus should seem to accept the *Margites* (fr. 397); but it is the convention that matters for our purposes.

[76] Cf. Hopkinson, commentary on *H.* 6, p. 13.

Hymns. It will naturally be more fruitful to pursue a single line of thought which illuminates some of the poems than to concentrate on generalizations which embrace the whole group. *Hymns* 4 and 5 have been spoken of above (pp. 33 ff.); here attention will be given chiefly to *Hymns* 1, 2, and 3.

The figures of the gods themselves form a primary focus, most especially in the poems where a single story is less predominant (1–3; 5). They are treated in no straightforward manner. Firstly, Callimachus seeks, almost as an artist, to convey the quality of the gods he depicts, the flavour of their being. The opening of *H.* 5, for example, presents two contrasted pictures of Athena (5–12, 13–32). One shows her as warlike, with great arms and with equipment bespattered with gore; the other shows her as beautiful, with an exquisite redness running up her body. The contrast itself suggests her nature with force, but the context complicates and enriches. In the first passage, the poet is stressing Athena's loving care for her horses, whom she always cleans before herself: the devotion and the practicality enhance her manliness, but they are also subtly tinged by her femininity. In the second passage, the poet is stressing her scorn for the female apparatus of beauty, and for female interests: her own beauty is coloured, and made piquant, by this virile indifference. The fusion of sexes in Athena seems not merely paradoxical but convincing.

The author is plainly enjoying the clarity and power of the figures he recreates; but such descriptions are not delivered in a neutral or connoisseur-like voice. They are presented in terms of the extreme and the surprising, and these qualities are made to serve the rhetoric of religious praise. The speaker's voice, when talking of the god, is characteristically enthusiastic and animated. However, the magnificence of the gods and the decorous vigour of the speaker suffer various complications in order to produce more elaborate and devious poems. Let us consider the complications of these aspects themselves in the first three *Hymns*.

Hymn 1 divides essentially into two parts; the first treats of Zeus principally at his birth and shortly after, the second treats of him principally as lord of the world. The structure insinuates a piquant contrast between supreme god and baby, which the first half itself brings out. The birth and infancy of gods had been important in the Homeric Hymns (1, 3, 4); Callimachus uses this element from his tradition precisely to modify and startle.[77] Here the mere physicalities of babyhood are used to disconcert. 'When the Nymph was carrying you from Thenae, Father Zeus (Ζεῦ πάτερ),'

τουτάκι τοι πέσε, δαῖμον, ἀπ' ὀμφαλός· ἔνθεν ἐκεῖνο
'Ομφάλιον μετέπειτα πέδον καλέουσι Κύδωνες.   (44 f.)

Then there fell away from you, O god, your umbilical cord. Hence ever after the Cretans have called that the Plain of the Navel.

The juxtaposition of divine address with the crudities of after-birth[78] feels positively jarring in its harshness. The poet steps swiftly aside into the mock-pedantry of tidily registering an *aition*; but the change of voice only produces a different sort of distance. The section ends σέο κουρίζοντος (54) 'you making your babyish cries'; again it is a piquant way to be addressing the highest god. In between the poet describes the nurture which the baby enjoyed (46–9) in a warmer and richer manner; but we are still far from exaltation and reverence.[79]

In other places the speaker's voice is pleasingly modified, as the forms of praise disclose the lurking scholar. At the start, sonorous laudation turns into a discussion of Zeus' birthplace. The poet moves amid the armoury of praise. As in the Homeric Hymns, he asks how to sing the god, and mentions rival traditions as to his birth (cf. Hom. *H.* 3. 19, 1. 1 ff.); he eventually clinches his ingenious argumentation by asserting the god's immortality. But the play with scholarly controversy emerges palpably, and again address points the audacity.

Ζεῦ, σὲ μὲν Ἰδαίοισιν ἐν οὔρεσί φασι γενέσθαι,
Ζεῦ, σὲ δ' ἐν Ἀρκαδίῃ· πότεροι, πάτερ, ἐψεύσαντο;   (6 f.)

---

[77] On divine children in Callimachus see G. T. Huber, *Lebensschilderung u. Klein-malerei im hell. Epos* (Diss. Basel, 1926), Herter, *Kl. Schr.* 378 ff. (too simple and too sentimental). A. W. Bulloch, *MH* 41 (1984), 209 ff., takes a psychologizing approach oddly remote from the tone of the poetry.

[78] Cf. N. Hopkinson, *CQ* NS 34 (1984), 143.

[79] It is instructive to compare the passage that will have inspired Callimachus, Hom. *H.* 3. 120–30. There the addresses only heighten the rapt and solemn tone.

They say, Zeus, you were born in the mountains of Crete,
they say you were born in Arcadia—which, Father, have
told a lie?

Startlingly, the supreme deity is appealed to for a solution himself. The pose is that adopted in the *Aetia*, and exploited elsewhere in the *Hymns*.[80] In the question, ἐψεύσαντο 'have told a
lie' rings very differently from the resonant ψευδόμενοι 'they lie'
with which the poet of Hom. *H*. 1 ends the list of false birth-
places for Dionysus (6). It suggests a scorn for falsehood as such
which is academic as well as religious. This scorn appears with
sharpened edge when Callimachus denies the story in the *Iliad*
(15. 187 ff.) that Zeus, Poseidon, and Hades cast lots for the
sky, the sea, and the underworld. Given the model for Callimachus' *Hymns*, the refutation of Homer has particular
piquancy; the oblique reference to him with δηναιοί ... ἀοιδοί
(60) 'singers of old' only enhances the distancing feeling of play
within the genre. Callimachus' argument is one of common
sense (hell and heaven are not equal options to cast lots for); his
tone is robustly polemical.[81] He ends:

ψευδοίμην ἀίοντος ἅ κεν πεπίθοιεν ἀκουήν.   (65)

May I tell lies that would at least convince my hearer!

The scorn is obviously an intellectual's, but couched in so
extreme and paradoxical a form that it cannot itself be taken
seriously. Yet he proceeds at once:

οὔ σε θεῶν ἐσσῆνα πάλοι θέσαν, ἔργα δὲ χειρῶν,
σή τε βίη τό τε κάρτος, ὃ καὶ πέλας εἷσαο δίφρου.

(66 f.)

No, it was not lots that made you lord of the gods, but the
deeds of your hands and your might and strength—
Strength, indeed, you seated by your throne.

The poet suddenly rises into splendid and imposing praise. This
is only lightly modified by the abstruse word for 'lord' and by
the final clause, which busily reinforces the argument with

---

[80] See above, n. 38. I take it that in l. 8 we do not actually hear Zeus' voice in
answer: the continuation would be too awkward.

[81] In 60 it is much more suitable to take οὐ πάμπαν ἀληθέες ἦσαν as a vehement 'were
utterly untruthful' than as an ironical 'were not altogether truthful'. Cf. e.g. Hom. *Il*.
21. 338 f. (μηδὲ ... πάμπαν), Herodot. 7. 152. 3 (οὐ ... παντάπασιν, usually misunderstood), AR 4. 1356 (οὐ πάγχυ).

mythology, and reminds us that Callimachus is following Hesiod instead of Homer (cf. Hes. *Theog.* 386–8). The grandeur and enthusiasm in the poem are most decidedly not destroyed by the presence of other elements. They do not merely sit side by side with such elements, however, in a varied sequence: their impact is to a certain degree limited by them and distanced. It could not be otherwise when the speaker's own voice becomes the medium and the subject of play, and the author exploits for play the magnificence of the god himself. The compound feels strange, a little disquieting, and highly exhilarating.

The second *Hymn* gives less sense of play, and more of weirdness. The figure of the god, Apollo, possesses an awesomeness and a beauty which remain as the reader's predominant impression. Yet there are not a few touches by which the impact is, not so much limited, as delicately complicated with a certain strangeness. At 47 ff. the god is hymned, first as a god of shepherds, then as a god of the founding of cities. The first passage (47–54) begins with his time of pastoral servitude to Admetus; it ascribes this, abnormally, to his being in love with that mortal. Erotic slavery, a commonplace metaphor with humans, is a curious actual state for a god; but the poet moves to the supernatural fertility and abundance that are brought by the favour of the deity.[82] The second passage (55–64) begins with stately and insistent anaphora; but it moves to the bizarre picture of the four-year-old Apollo building a temple of goats' horns.

The roles of Callimachus in the poem are, until the end, striking for the absence of play with personality. Callimachus appears as the bard, excitedly directing the chorus at the thrilling and fantastic epiphany of the god. He appears also as a subject of Ptolemy (26 f.), and, more prominently, as a representative of his native city Cyrene (71 ff.).[83] At the close, however, we have a short and surprising section which presents obliquely a different aspect of the poet. The personification Phthonos (Envy, Calumny) once attempted to make Apollo dislike any poem that was not long. Apollo kicked Phthonos

---

[82] Metaphorical slavery for lovers: e.g. Plat. *Smp.* 184 B–C, *CA* 178. 27 f. (Grenfell Fragment).

[83] ἐμῷ βασιλῆϊ (26, 27) has a somewhat less personal air than we might think: cf. τοῖς ἐμοῖς βασιλεῦσι in Appian, *Praef.* 10.

away and praised, allusively, poetry that was short and refined.
Callimachus adds his own curse on Censure (Momos), who
takes over the part of Phthonos.[84] The poet's own feeling
emerges boldly at this point, though mixed with the formulae of
hymns. In what precedes the writer is using the authority of the
god and the impersonality of narrative, firstly, to defend the
poem itself: the genre is marked out by brevity, and Phthonos'
words relate to the hymning of Apollo. He also makes us look
outside the poem itself to the historical realities of the poet's
reputation: this notion other evidence confirms (see p. 82).[85]
All this considerably distances the rest of the poem (1–104) as
an ardent hymn. Particularly weighty in this respect is the shift
of Callimachus himself from excited bard and worshipper to
maligned writer. The effect has something in common with the
end of *Acontius and Cydippe*.

The long third *Hymn*, to Artemis, is especially complex. The
first part of the poem (1–109) essentially presents a single line of
narrative, relatively uniform in effect, though that effect is a
compound of elements; the second part (110–268) is much less
obvious in design, and moves much more giddily in tone. The
first part shows Artemis in her infancy. The fourth Homeric
Hymn had shown Hermes as a baby, amusingly unlike one in
everything save physical appearance; a hymn probably by
Sappho (44A Voigt), which Callimachus is using here, had
shown Artemis as a child, briefly asking Zeus' assent to her
choice of life. Callimachus' Artemis mixes divinity and childhood more radically. Her speech to Zeus is irrepressible, imperious, assured: we hear both the girl and the goddess. The
poet's accent at the start is strongly on the childish note in the
discordant combination:

> δός μοι παρθενίην αἰώνιον, ἄππα, φυλάσσειν,
> καὶ πολυωνυμίην, ἵνα μή μοι Φοῖβος ἐρίζῃ.   (6 f.)

Give me perpetual virginity, Daddy, and many titles, so
that Apollo does not vie with me.

---

[84] One should read ἵν' ὁ φθόρος, ἔνθα νέοιτο, a decorous paraphrase of ἴτω ἐς φθόρον.
The usual reading Φθόνος is inferior in rhetoric, attestation, and intrinsic probability;
nor is ἵνα (with indicative) then very clear or forceful.

[85] Cf. on the passage E. L. Bundy, *CSCA* 5 (1972), 39 ff., who stresses the reference to
the poem, though exclusively; similarly A. Köhnken, *AJP* 102 (1981), 411 ff. Williams's understanding of the lines (commentary, pp. 85 ff.), is I fear impossibly devious,
and rests in part on a reading probably corrupt (οὐδ' ὅσα 106: οὐχ Scaliger).

The proud declarations as the speech proceeds sound stranger and stranger in the girl's mouth; she ends with the circumstances of her own birth. Zeus' reaction articulates the reader's: it mixes indulgent amusement and admiration. The source of this articulation (the adult god) enhances the curious quality of the reader's double perspective, as grown-up and as mortal. Later the poet vaunts the astounding courage of the young goddess with a still earlier scene (72 ff.). But the courage is expressed in the action of an infant: she pulls a handful of hair from a Cyclops' chest, as, in the *Aetia*, Heracles' infant son pulls hair from his father's (76 f., cf. fr. 24. 1 ff.). The action is comic (cf. fr. 24. 3), and the consequences for the poor Cyclops' chest grotesque.

In the second part, the poet begins by asking the goddess recondite questions about her deeds, and reporting the answers (113 ff.). We have moved from easy narrative into a rigid, discontinuous form, and a scholarly mode. The poet is playing too with Homer's questions to his Muses; but such interchange with Artemis rings much more oddly. The poem suddenly moves, with exciting power, to Artemis' punishment of the wicked and the prosperity of those she favours (121 ff.). The passage is impressive in the concrete force with which it conveys its moral and traditional theme. This elevation is matched as the poet comes back to himself; he seeks for prosperity and then sweeps on:

μέλοι δέ μοι αἰὲν ἀοιδή.
τῇ ἔνι μὲν Λητοῦς γάμος ἔσσεται, ἐν δὲ σὺ πολλή,
ἐν δὲ καὶ Ἀπόλλων, ἐν δ' οἵ σεο πάντες ἄεθλοι.

(137–39)

And, goddess, may song always be mine! There, in my singing, will appear Leto's lying with Zeus, there you yourself will appear often, there Apollo too will be, there all your labours ...

The poet's voice attains an intoxicating rapture, which blends joy in his art with joy in the goddess. We soon descend, abruptly, to a comic though charming scene with Heracles and food.

Later in the poem the form of questions recurs (183 ff.), its oddities brought out more strongly. We have six questions in a row, most of them to be answered with the same dispatch. The distortion of poets' manner and relationship with their Muse is taken further than before in the request to Artemis:

εἰπέ, θεή, σὺ μὲν ἄμμιν, ἐγὼ δ' ἑτέροισιν ἀείσω.

(186)

Do you tell me, goddess, and I shall sing the replies to the others.[86]

The relation of poet and god now has a quite different atmosphere and effect to that in the lyrical passage quoted just above.

The poem ends depicting Artemis' punishment of those who offend her. A dark and powerful passage on the Cimmerian army that attacked her city of Ephesus (251 ff.) leads on to an accumulation of warnings against angering the goddess. Each warning is followed by a parenthesis containing a mythical deterrent. The static and repetitive form of this extended series falls very strangely in so nervous a writer. On the one hand we are made to feel the extraordinary ferocity of the goddess; on the other, the passage is distanced by the bizarreness of its manner from absolute seriousness. The harshness of Artemis forms part of Callimachus' general conception of her elsewhere.[87] But the effect is striking at the end of a hymn to her, and the passage hovers near the limits set by the decorum of eager praise. One contrasts the feeling of the earlier passage on her treatment of the unjust, and also of the first part on her childhood: that indomitable spirit now appears in a more terrible light.[88]

The hymn then ends:

χαῖρε μέγα, κρείουσα, καὶ εὐάντησον ἀοιδῇ.

Hail, hail, O queen, and be favourable to my song.

The preceding examples insinuate the thought that the poet

---

[86] For the poet's special position as oracle of the Muses cf. Bornmann ad loc. and e.g. C. M. Bowra, *Pindar*, 3 f. (Plat. *Ion* 534 E does not really belong here, and follows a quite individual line of thought).

[87] See especially fr. 96, with Pfeiffer's n.; add *H.* 5. 107 ff., where Athena's clemency is brought out through a contrast with Artemis.

[88] Cf. Wilamowitz, *HD* ii. 61.

feels some anxiety about the fierce goddess's reception of his hymn. One looks back to the parenthesis at the very opening:

Ἄρτεμιν (οὐ γὰρ ἐλαφρὸν ἀειδόντεσσι λαθέσθαι)
ὑμνέομεν.

I sing of Artemis (to forget her when singing is a hard matter).

The Greek had suggested both the difficulty of forgetting so memorable, and the danger of forgetting so formidable, a divinity as Artemis. The warmth, and the odd familiarity, seen earlier in the relationship between god and poet now recede, with a slight touch of irony, in the hinted nervousness of this close.[89] Again from the connected handling of these two figures Callimachus has built up the complication of his poem.

Callimachus' *Epigrams* are strongly connected with the brief tradition of literary epigram, and show many links with Asclepiades in particular. But they also look behind, to the conventions and concepts of the inscriptional poems and the love-poetry from which literary epigram derives. (Cf. above, p. 20.) With these conventions Callimachus plays more continually and more disconcertingly than his predecessors and contemporaries. The play is made possible by the genre; but the effects fit the nature of the poet.

We may look at the handling of conventions in the poems dedicatory and sepulchral. The most important conventions relate to speech. On inscriptions the dedicated object was often made to speak of itself as 'I'; so too the tombstone, or the person buried.[90] To play with the unreality of this device was congenial to an author who liked subversions, and peculiar speakers. *Ep.* 56 Pf. (XXV GP) records the dedication of a bronze cock, which stands for the cock with which its owner won a victory. It begins:

---

[89] Bornmann on 268 rightly notes that the last line refers back to the first, but mistakenly makes it optimistic. The structure of 259–68 renders that supposition very improbable.

[90] These conventions are common enough, not only in the 6th and 5th cc., but in the century before Callimachus. Some examples from the latter period: dedication, *IG* ii/iii². 4320, 4658, iv/1². 236, xii. 8 67; tomb, *GVI* 111, 172, 1174; deceased, 328, 931, 1061. They are common later too, but here influence is possible from the literary epigram.

φησὶν ὅ με στήσας Εὐαίνετος (οὐ γὰρ ἔγωγε
γινώσκω) νίκης ἀντί με τῆς ἰδίης
ἀγκεῖσθαι ...

Euaenetus, who set me here, says (I am ignorant of the
matter myself) that I have been dedicated on account of
my own victory ...

The opening is innocent enough (cf. *CEG* 270. 4, Ebert, *Gr. Epigramme auf Sieger* 33. 3). But the parenthesis suddenly turns
standard procedures into a weird situation: the bird speaks and
presents itself as a personality, yet being a metal object knows
nothing of its 'own' actions. The poem ends with the cock
expressing its confidence in Euaenetus' veracity (πιστεύω 'I
trust his word'). It politely settles any suggestion of awkward
disagreement; this only highlights the strangeness of the situation. A parenthesis is used in a related fashion in 4 Pf. (LI).[91]
The couplet, an exchange with Timon on death, begins: Τίμων,
οὐ γὰρ ἔτ᾽ ἐσσί, 'Timon, since you exist no more, tell me ...'.
The choice of expression jauntily stresses the impossibility of the
conversation before it begins.

Ep. 54 (XXIV) is addressed to the god of healing Asclepius.
The offering—the tablet on which the poem is inscribed—
fulfils a vow. εὐξάμενος 'having vowed' is used of the man who
makes the dedication; this is the stock word in inscriptions of
this kind.[92] However, the language dwells on the notion of the
offering as discharging a debt to the god. The poem ends: φησὶ
παρέξεσθαι μαρτυρίην ὁ πίναξ, 'the tablet says it will bear
witness' if the god forgets that the debt has been paid. The tablet, in a distanced form of words, shows a dogged concern for its
owner's interests, and a correspondingly suspicious attitude towards the god it addresses. The practice of cult is again
involved in the preposterous situation; the situation is adumbrated lightly through the handling of speech.

Personifying speech leads to other surprises, as when a
pseudo-Homeric poem talks of itself in the first person, and
then itself exclaims with an oath on its author's undeserved
good fortune (6 Pf., LV).[93] But still more elaborate effects are

[91] Cf. also 5. 9 Pf. (XIV), if the MS reading ἄπνους should be correct.
[92] Cf. e.g. *IG* iv. 1² 199 (4th c.), 259 (2nd c.), from the shrine of Asclepius at Epi-
daurus, and *CEG* 190–280 *passim*. Addresses to the god are ubiquitous in dedications.
[93] On the oath and the ostensible type of the poem cf. Wilamowitz, *HD* i. 124 f.

obtained from dialogue. Dialogue between the beholder and the object had appeared in inscriptions and in quasi-inscriptional epigram; dialogue had appeared on inscriptions even between dead and living. The form is generally one of questions and answers about facts. Callimachus often transposes it into strange communication between personalities.

In the couplet 34 (XXII) the object offered is questioned about the identity of the dedicator by the god himself.

τίν με, λεοντάγχ' ὦνα συοκτόνε, φήγινον ὄζον
θῆκε—"τίς;" Ἀρχῖνος. "ποῖος;" ὁ Κρής. "δέχομαι."

To you, lion-throttling, boar-slaying lord, I, a branch of oak, was dedicated by—'By whom?' Archinus. 'Where from?' Crete. 'I accept it.'

The questions intrude with rough curtness in the second line, and they suit the nature of Heracles. This nature had been suggested already in the violent epithets of the object's more ample address. In 61 (XLII) Callimachus talks with a friend Menecrates who has died through drink. The poem alludes not only to epigrams where the dead man tells of his death but to the more naturalistic conversation in Homer between Odysseus and his dead comrade Elpenor.[94] Callimachus asks, 'What destroyed you, best of friends?'

"ἦ ῥα τὸ καὶ Κένταυρον;" "ὅ μοι πεπρωμένος ὕπνος
ἦλθεν, ὁ δὲ τλήμων οἶνος ἔχει πρόφασιν."

'Was it what destroyed the Centaur too?' 'My destined sleep came upon me; accursed wine was merely the immediate cause.'[95]

The poet's inquiry alludes to drink with tactful indirectness and elliptical erudition; both suit his *persona*. Menecrates is indeed sensitive to the disreputable appearance of his decease. He begins his reply with emphatic dignity. But he speaks with natural though unexpected vehemence of the wine that has killed him (however secondary the causation) and has also

---

[94] *Od.* 11. 51 ff. Elpenor's opening ἆσέ με δαίμονος αἶσα κακὴ καὶ ἀθέσφατος οἶνος (60) 'my mind was driven astray by fate and much wine' matches Menecrates' statement here.

[95] 'Is merely supposed the cause' would give τλήμων much less force and point, for the epithet would be occasioned only by Menecrates' ill repute.

injured his fame. Through this sudden human touch in the dead man's utterance the whole exchange becomes lightly and wryly humorous.

The form can also lead to more haunting exploitations of convention. Thus in 15 (XL) Callimachus reads a tombstone of common type which merely states the names of the deceased, her father, her husband, and her city. His reading takes the form of a lively and personal address to the dead woman. He ends, 'Your widowed husband Euthymenes grieves much indeed, I declare', ἦ μέγα φημὶ | χῆρον ἀνιᾶσθαι σὸν πόσιν Εὐθυμένη. Here the thought enters of great emotion, but only through Callimachus' inference, prompted by a name. The prominence of the speaker's voice heightens the strange sense of distance.[96]

Even when these poems are at their most moving, they often derive their poignancy from their relation to customary treatments. So with 16 (XXXVII):

Κρηθίδα τὴν πολύμυθον, ἐπισταμένην καλὰ παίζειν,
    δίζηνται Σαμίων πολλάκι θυγατέρες,
ἡδίστην συνέριθον ἀείλαλον· ἡ δ' ἀποβρίζει
    ἐνθάδε τὸν πάσαις ὕπνον ὀφειλόμενον.

Talkative Crethis, who could joke and sport so well, the daughters of the Samians often wish for: their delightful fellow worker, always chattering. But she, in this tomb, sleeps the sleep which is owing to all women alike.

The epitaph avoids lauding the woman's merits in the vague terms of inscriptions;[97] it dwells on a quite undignified quality, but one which gave pleasure and won affection. An answering feeling is aroused in the reader; its strength springs from the unlooked-for vividness of the depiction and the unpretentiousness of its values. Against the animation of Crethis' volubility, which begins and ends the description, Callimachus sets the quietness and solemnity of death. The vigorous sense of

---

[96] G. Kaibel, *Hermes*, 31 (1896), 264, well implies the contrast between Callimachus' words and the tomb's. His note on Soph. *El.* 1296 seems to suggest that Callimachus did not know Timonoe before—and this is surely more plausible (cf. also Theocr. 3. 15 νῦν ἔγνων τὸν Ἔρωτα, etc.). At any rate, the sequence of the first line would indicate that he did not know her well.

[97] For these cf. J. Pircher, *D. Lob d. Frau im vorchristlichen Grabepigramm d. Griechen* (1979).

life in what precedes makes the antithesis more forceful, and less grandiose. The standard devices of tragic contrast and grave commonplace take on a gentler yet more concrete existence.

Fundamental to Callimachus' epigrams is the brevity which almost defines the genre.[98] The smallness of their compass makes particularly sharp and devastating their sudden changes of register, subject, or speaker, the sudden revelations and surprises in their movement. Callimachus elsewhere tends to develop far more amply the material on which he concentrates. Abruptness is not rarely deployed, but it gains its effect from contrast. Here we enter so to speak a self-consciously miniature world; brevity indeed is sometimes played with explicitly (52 (VI), 11 (XXXV), *al*.). The smallness of proportion has striking effects in the poems where Callimachus' love is presented, or emerges, as the centre of concern. The concentration of their drastic but elegant movements both intensifies the semblance of emotion and enhances the detachment of the reader: so much of our attention is captured by the author's neatness.

Ep. 41 (IV) may serve to illustrate these features.

> ἥμισύ μευ ψυχῆς ἔτι τὸ πνέον, ἥμισυ δ' οὐκ οἶδ'
> εἴτ' Ἔρος εἴτ' Ἀΐδης ἥρπασε, πλὴν ἀφανές.
> ἦ ῥά τιν' ἐς παίδων πάλιν ᾤχετο; καὶ μὲν ἀπεῖπον
> πολλάκι "τὴν δρῆστιν μὴ ἀναδέχεσθε, νέοι."
> †ουκισυνιφησον† ἐκεῖσε γὰρ ἡ λιθόλευστος
> κείνη καὶ δύσερως οἶδ' ὅτι που στρέφεται.

I still have half my soul here breathing; half I don't know whether Love or Death has snatched away, but it has vanished. [ll. 1–2] Has it gone to one of the boys again? Indeed, I have often had to call out, 'Don't put up that

---

[98] It would be awkward to argue that both brevity and definition are the artificial result of selection by later anthologists with more decided notions of the epigram. The starting-point of inscriptions implies a rough presupposition about size, and early anthologies (some 3rd-c.) imply a related conception. Antigonus of Carystus (late 3rd c.) accords, and incidentally extends the notion of epigram beyond the quasi-inscriptional (*SH* 125, 126, 129; the diminutive in the last is not significant). The only real doubt arises from the title σύμμεικτα ἐπιγράμματα in *SH* 961; the first poem of the volume (probably) seems longer than normal. There special factors may very well be involved. Meleager's anthology certainly did not exclude poems of over fifteen lines. Even if we had a misleadingly high proportion of short epigrams, and even if the line between epigram and elegy were fluid, yet brevity was certainly associated with the epigram, and only common there.

runaway, lads!'[99] [ll. 3–4] ... I know that that is where
that accursed creature has gone with her wretched love; it
is somewhere there she is moving.'

The poem plays boisterously with the notion that the soul may
leave the body in an extremity of love (cf. e.g. AR 3. 1151). The
opening couplet, with its dramatic urgency and its impressive
phrase on Love and Death, half invites us to take it seriously
within the framework of its situation; the close of it, however,
already intimates burlesque. With the next couplet the extravagant gestures are abruptly displaced. We have on the one
hand the bathos of the poet's familiarity with this experience
('again', 'often')—a device employed by the archaic lyric
poets.[100] On the other hand, the separation of lover and soul is
pushed to the extreme of a ludicrous fantasy; this is based on
the humdrum topic of the escape of slaves.[101] The speech from
the past is colourful, prosaic, absurd. The final couplet brings
us closer to mental experience. Callimachus' abuse of his soul
dramatizes one's loathing of impulses one always fails to resist.
The dramatization is both wry and comic. The poem is ex-
citingly volatile and unstable; its movements are vigorous and
startling. But in them all a single line of thought is developed
persistently. The whole poem is given a firm sequence by its
progression from bewildered ignorance to moral certainty: οὐκ
οἶδ' 'I don't know' appears in the first line, οἶδ' 'I know' in the
last. The modulations are thus bold but purposeful; the abrupt
strokes surprisingly cohere into a harmonious design. We feel a
delicious distance between Callimachus the lover, who has not
the least control over his feeling, and Callimachus the poet,
who so exquisitely orders his little artefact. Even in these short
poems the structure plays a great part in creating the richness
and abnormality of the effects.

   We have now seen something of the different ways in which
Callimachus' works realize his large concerns in poetry. We

---

[99] The general sense is clear. For the makeshift conjecture ἀναδέχεσθε (for ὑποχεσθε)
cf. *OGIS* 339. 20 (2nd c. BC). In the next half-line Gow's conjecture διφήσω gives
unusual prosody, cf. Gow–Page, *Garl. Phil.*, p. xl n. 1.

[100] Anacreon in particular uses δηὖτε 'once more' to deflate the description of wild
emotion: fr. 358. 1 Page, 376. 1, 413. 1, 428. 1.

[101] Actual procedure with runaway slaves was of course more elaborate: cf. Rea on
P. Oxy. 3616; P. Turner 41.

have seen also how, to achieve this realization, certain features often recur: play with genre and with personality, the exploitation of scholarship and of religion, the handling of different levels of poetry and different levels of narrative. Form is of quite fundamental importance here. 'Concerns' was essentially a metaphor for things which dominate the poetry, and give it its basic quality, things to which more limited features may be seen as contributing. Talk of the author (as of the reader) has been meant primarily as a way of describing what I think to be present in the works. In historical terms, one need not necessarily suppose more than that Callimachus aimed by instinct to achieve the sorts of effects that appealed to him. There is no need to see here an articulated 'programme', which the works were consciously written to fulfil. It may be doubted whether Callimachus had any 'programme' of that kind, and very much doubted whether it would greatly illuminate the poetry if he did. Callimachus' general remarks on his own work have on the whole served merely to hinder and distort interpretation.

These remarks are both poetry and rhetoric. In so far as Callimachus means to influence the reader's views, he wishes to make him admire his own work; the aim is not to write full descriptive criticism or to aid our understanding, still less to win converts to a theory for its own sake. In mentioning some passages, we shall now be compelled to throw emphasis on this aspect of influencing the reader, rather than achieving a fully balanced account of their impact, internal and external.

The last of the *Iambi*, it will be remembered (fr. 203), seems to deal with two objections, which it relates: Callimachus writes many different types of poem, and in one of these types, the *Iambi*, he has mingled many different elements. The point of the second and straightforward objection is obviously one of genre, and local to the work just read. The underlying point of the first appears to be that Callimachus is a dabbler. He has not established himself as a great epic poet, or a great tragedian, or the like, but has attempted a little in many fields. Callimachus treats the objection as again a formal one: there is no reason, he argues, why one poet should not write many different kinds of poem. This is shown by the example of the fifth-century author Ion of Chios; earlier Callimachus has rebutted his critic more generally.

τίς εἶπεν ...
"σὺ πεντάμετρα συντίθει, σὺ δ᾽ ἠ[ρῷο]ν,
σὺ δὲ τραγῳδε[ῖν] ἐκ θεῶν ἐκληρώσω";
δοκέω μὲν οὐδείς·   (fr. 203. 30–3)

Who is it that has said ... 'You must compose elegiacs,
and you hexameters; as for you, writing tragedy is the lot
the gods have assigned'? No one, I think.

Absurd invented speech is used with a Horatian air of vigorous
rationality. We have effective rhetoric and effective drama,
which accord with the preoccupations of the *Iambi*. The passage
would have been much less effective as drama and rhetoric, but
more satisfying as an answer and as literary criticism, had
Callimachus shown the cohesion of his work in subtler terms
than those of genre.

The end of *H.* 2 was described above in relation to the whole
poem (p. 67 f.). As regards the issue of Callimachus' poetry, the
form creates distance, and avoids the tones of self-praise. But
through the medium of the god's speech, generalizing and
metaphorical, Callimachus communicates an image which
lauds his own work deliciously. It excites us about that work
through its sensuous attractiveness as an image; through its
vividness it prevents us from questioning the necessity of the
association that it embodies between smallness of scale and refinement of technique. In opposition to the mud and rubbish of
the huge river, we see

ἥτις καθαρή τε καὶ ἀχράαντος ἀνέρπει
πίδακος ἐξ ἱερῆς ὀλίγη λιβάς, ἄκρον ἄωτον.   (111 f.)

Whatever small drop of water rises pure and undefiled
from the sacred spring—water in choice perfection.[102]

The eloquence of Apollo's language gives him dramatically a
triumph of style over Phthonos.

The prologue to the *Aetia* (fr. 1) treats the question of brevity
more elaborately. It begins with the familiar form of a dramatic
confrontation. The poet gives in reported speech the charge of
those he calls Telchines (malignant sorcerers of mythology).

---

[102] Given ἀνέρπει ἐκ πίδακος it seems difficult to refer ἄκρον ἄωτον primarily to the
top of a surface of water: *flumina summa* in Virg. *Georg.* 4. 54 f. is different (cf. Pfeiffer,
HCS i. 284). It is not inconceivable that there may be some corruption in 109–11; the
lines do not feel completely right.

Callimachus, they say, has not written a single continuous poem in many thousands of lines dealing with monarchs or heroes. This language suggests an epic, grandiose in style (see below) and conception: that type of production was very probably standard and well worn at the time. Callimachus puts the matter thus in order to commend by contrast his own originality. The point at issue is not the value of epic as such, as we shall see, and as *Ia.* 13 indicates. (It is unnatural not to connect the debates in the two poems.)[103] There is little sign, indeed, that the contemporary emulation of Homer, and its folly, was the crucial matter for Callimachus that it is often supposed.[104]

Callimachus' reply is made more vivid than the charge by being presented in direct speech. He argues, it seems, that the small scale is not merely more suitable for certain poets but more attractive absolutely. He also deprecates the 'loud-sounding', thundering style which the Telchines are taken to desiderate. Length and pomp of style are made to go together, and the concreteness of the foolish charge makes this more plausible. Callimachus' speech is vehement in its abuse of the half-mythologized opponents, but it is not distastefully arrogant in its claims for the poet. He appeals again to precedent: his two great predecessors in the elegiac genre, to which the *Aetia* belongs, had excelled in their shorter poems.[105] He declines to thunder: that is the province of Zeus (βροντᾶν οὐκ ἐμὸν ἀλλὰ Διός, 20). The freedom of metaphor in the poetry here comically but cunningly associates a stylistic choice with the prudent avoidance of *hybris*.[106] Callimachus has indeed insinuated the suggestion that this small scale has made possible

---

[103] On such epics cf. p. 14 f.; cf. also, in particular, *SH* 946–7 (Rhianus?). Alan Cameron is apparently to argue (M. S. Santirocco, *Unity and Design in Horace's Odes* (1986), 190 n. 71) that Callimachus is not here rejecting epic. As a foil to his own choice, however, epic in particular is pointed at here, one would have thought: the terms of 3 ff. must be taken together to form a single notion. The size is crucial to the argument and must apply throughout the clause; but the *Aetia* itself, which has thousands of lines, suggests that size alone is not in question, and ἐν ἄεισμα διηνεκές is placed emphatically at the beginning and must also apply throughout.

[104] *Ep.* 6 Pf. (LV) does not give much ground for that view. Whether τὸ ποίημα τὸ κυκλικόν (*Ep.* 28. 1 (II)) denotes poems of the Epic Cycle or any banal or commonplace poem, it would be unnatural to make the point this. (The second view of κυκλικόν best suits the style and the sentence.) As to *Ep.* 27 (LVI), I agree with Gow–Page: Hesiod is not compared with Homer. On Theocr. 7. 43 ff., see pp. 201 ff.

[105] Cf. p. 280; pp. 278 ff. deal with some further aspects of this prologue.

[106] Contrast the infatuated Philocleon at Arist. *Wasps* 619–27.

his striking originality. But he reserves more positive assertion for the speech which Apollo made to him when he first began to write.

The god commanded the poet to cultivate a slender Muse and thus to tread paths which others had not frequented. The poet merely conformed. The narrative device saves the poet from explicit boasting. At the same time, the friendly, though superior, tone of Apollo's speech to Callimachus stands in marked contrast to the scorn of Callimachus' speech to the Telchines. This prepares us for the notion that Callimachus, unlike the Telchines, has always been a friend of the Muses (37 f., cf. 2). After Apollo's speech Callimachus implies that his verse is not loud and ugly like a donkey's bray, but clear and elegant like the cicada's song. What he actually expresses is a preference for the cicada and a wish that he might become one:

> ἐγ]ὼ δ' εἴην οὐλ[α]χύς, ὁ πτερόεις,
> ἇ πάντως ... (32 f.)

As for me, may I be the little creature, the winged one—
oh! indeed may I be he ...

We ascend into a delectable lyricism and fantasy, and at the same time a sympathetic presentation of personality: by becoming a cicada Callimachus would escape the heavy burden of his old age.[107] Even when Callimachus comes to speak of the Muses' favour towards himself, he says:

> Μοῦσαι γὰρ ὅσους ἴδον ὄθματι παῖδας
> μὴ λοξῷ, πολιοὺς οὐκ ἀπέθεντο φίλους. (37 f.)

Those on whom as children the Muses have looked with
eye not askance, they do not discard from their love when
they grow old.

The designation is discreetly and attractively general and negative in form.

Although the poem gives the impression of being a reasoned and sustained defence of his poetry, that impression is contrived. Callimachus is employing the insidious devices of poetical rhetoric which he manipulates so consciously elsewhere. In

---

[107] Plat. *Ion* 534 B suggests how the fantasy feels fitting as well as strange: κοῦφον γὰρ χρῆμα ποιητής ἐστιν καὶ πτηνὸν καὶ ἱερόν (like a bee).

accordance with these, and with his handling of himself elsewhere, he does not describe directly his own poetry and its
merits. One may contrast the statements of Pindar or Aristophanes, or Callimachus' own brief praise of Aratus (*Ep.* 27 Pf.,
LVI). He does indeed imply that his poetry is elegant, and
above all original; but this does not take the modern critic of his
work very far.

The claim to originality is itself conventional.[108] The theoretical and general quality of Callimachus' own speech is also
dictated by his strategy (as in *Ia.* 13). Dramatically, the poet
must seem to be rational and intelligent in contrast to his un-
reasonable interlocutors. It would be naïve to infer that Callimachus wrote his poems in order to obey or enforce an absolute
principle: that with poems the smaller scale is always superior.

Why do the Telchines dislike the smaller scale? The poem
itself (the prologue) invites us to see the account of the
Telchines' charge as a version rhetorically pointed by Callimachus. It would be fantastic to imagine a poem defending
Callimachus purely against the incredible proposition that
solemn epic is the only legitimate form. Rather, there is the
underlying thought that Callimachus' reputation can be
detracted from if one stresses that he has not produced a work
of grand design. The thought relates partly to the *Aetia*: that is
shown by the references to great authors of the genre, as well as
by the function of the poem and its smooth transition to the
Aetia proper.[109] The second half of the *Aetia* in particular
might be assailed as a series of small separate poems, not part of
a great continuous whole. The thought may also be referred to
Callimachus' whole *œuvre*. Callimachus from the end of his
career tells of the instructions he received at its beginning; the
Telchines close by remarking on his age (6). His entire *œuvre*

---

[108] In 25 ff. the imagery echoes Pind. *Pae.* 7b. 10 ff. Cf. also e.g. Pind. *Ol.* 3. 4 ff.,
Arist. *Clouds* 545–8.

[109] In a papyrus commentary a coronis separated this prologue (or part of the prologue), on Callimachus' poetry, from the second prologue (or second part of the prologue), on his encounter with the Muses (Pfeiffer ii. 101). This first section seems to
have ended with a transition to the dream: e.g. 'remind me', Muses, of your 'answers'
then, so that others 'may learn of them'. To the second section Callimachus returns at
the end of the whole work (fr. 112, end of *Aetia* 4). It is very uncertain whether the first
also forms a prologue to a collected edition of Callimachus' works. On fr. 112. 9 cf. P. E.
Knox, *GRBS* 26 (1985), 59 ff. (though his positive theory seems uninviting).

might be represented as a meagre assemblage of slight productions. Such a notion would fit well enough with the general indictment in *Ia.* 13. The charge in *H.* 2, that what the poet sings
is not 'as much as the sea', makes better sense, in its general aspect, if applied rather to the scale on which Callimachus is
accustomed to work than simply to the raw total of lines he has
ever composed. It is notable that Phthonos whispers secretly to
Apollo, and the Telchines mutter secretly against Callimachus.
This does not fit a staunch and traditionalist defence of the epic
as the only form permissible. The speakers are seen as slyly
diminishing the stature of a single poet.

Whether criticisms of something like this kind had actually
been voiced cannot be determined with certainty. (Naturally,
one would not have to believe that the particular application to
Iambi and *Aetia* was more than the poet's fiction.) Jealous de-
traction of great poets had long been a standard theme (in
poets who thought themselves great). Yet the satire in *Ia.* 13 on
poets' abuse of poets refers to Callimachus' own milieu (fr. 203.
52 ff.; cf. also the *Diegesis* to *Ia.* 4, fr. 194). It seems most natural
to suppose that it had for its basis some real point of reference.
Ep. 8 Pf. (LVIII), to be spoken of in a moment, presupposes a
knowledge of the general criticism. The poem works far better
if the unstated criticism is taken to be real, not merely an extension of fictions from other poems. This is not to say that we can
identify Callimachus' detractors, and still less to say that they
represented an orthodox majority.[110] The matter makes much
more sense if we think more of personal denigration than of a
debate about traditional aesthetics. Callimachus himself thinks
primarily of his personal fame; the generalities are weapons of
his rhetoric.

Two epigrams are of interest here. Their different mode
brings out still more sharply the primacy of the personal element. *Ep.* 8 (LVIII) contrasts the brevity of the victorious
(dramatic) poet, who says νικῶ 'Success!', and the loquacity of
the defeated poet, who says σκληρὰ τά γινόμενα 'I've had very
tough luck.' It concludes:

---

[110] The Florentine scholia (Pfeiffer i. 3) give a list, probably without authentic basis.
Praxiphanes, one may note, is not likely to have been alive for some time; nor is Asclepiades, whom Callimachus actually imitates. On Apollonius see ch. 3.

τῷ μερμηρίξαντι τὰ μὴ ἔνδικα τοῦτο γένοιτο
τοὔπος, ἐμοὶ δ᾽, ὦναξ, ἡ βραχυσυλλαβίη.

May the man who has contrived wicked deeds get the
long speech; may I, Lord Dionysus, have that brevity!

The epigram only has point if we think of the charge we have
discussed.[111] Callimachus is associating brevity with poetical
success, but he whimsically reverses the connection: he pretends
to pray for brevity because it is the fruit, not the cause, of triumph. Formally the 'I' of the final prayer has a typical quality,
as the mock-solemn contrast with sinners suggests. But the note
of personal excitement is sounded strongly, and we see the poet
concerned with achieving victory for himself, with the acclama-
tion of his own supremacy. It is his brevity that is in question.

Ep. 28 (II) describes Callimachus' distaste for everything
common, in literature and in love: ἐχθαίρω 'I detest', οὐ χαίρω
'I do not take pleasure in', μισέω 'I hate', σικχαίνω 'I feel sick
at' (an unliterary word). The description implies, as it were by
the way, Callimachus' own originality; but it is striking that he
should now present his feeling as a matter of personal and peculiar temperament, not as a categorical imperative. Callimachus
has turned the authoritative 'I hate' of classical poets into a
statement of admirable but individual predilection.[112] What
he is inviting us to contemplate is not the aesthetic principle but
himself.[113]

Since Callimachus wrote of his own poetry to defend and
exalt what he had achieved, it would be idle to seek in these
utterances the foundation of principle on which the poetry was
actually erected. As an account of the poetry, they do not tell us
much. Indeed, if one made them the basis for one's picture of
Callimachus, one would be positively led astray. In the first
place, it suits Callimachus' position to oppose the grand and
thundering style which he associates with the large poem and
the delicacy and lightness which is peculiar to the small. This
simple opposition obscures the importance in his work of grandeur and the grandiose, and the complexity and variety with

---

[111] Gow and Page, who somehow fail to, are puzzled.

[112] Cf. Theogn. 579 ff., and e.g. Soph. *Ant.* 495 f.

[113] The interesting treatment in J. C. Bramble, *Persius and the Programmatic Satire*
(1974), 59 ff., thus goes somewhat awry in its emphasis.

which they are exploited. If we imagine applying the notion he gives us to the *Hecale*, or any of the *Hymns*, we can see at once how crudely we should flatten the poems.[114]

Still more gravely, in his own speech to the Telchines, and in Apollo's speech to Phthonos, Callimachus might make one think that the primary interest of his work lay in its verbal technique. A wider perspective is suggested by the intimation of originality in the Prologue; and the language he uses is far from precise (for these purposes). Yet the metaphor of purity (*H.* 2. 111), the emphasis on the 'sweetness' of poetry (fr. 1. 11, 16), and the insistence that poetic skill ($\sigma o \phi i \eta$) should be assessed $\tau \acute{\epsilon} \chi \nu \eta$ 'by art, craftsmanship' (fr. 1. 17 f.), tend to leave the impression that Callimachus is thinking principally of refinement and finish in the choice and arrangement of words.[115] One sees such an outlook very definitely in the epigram which praises Aratus and his $\lambda \epsilon \pi \tau a \grave{\iota}$ $\dot{\rho}\acute{\eta}\sigma\iota\epsilon\varsigma$, his 'delicate utterances' (27, LVI).[116] At any rate, such a notion of Callimachus' poetry has done much damage to its appreciation. Readers have often narrowed their gaze to words and lines, seeking the infinite fastidiousness and refinement they expect. They have tended rather to neglect the wider features which give the elegant vitality of the writing its point and force. Something of those features this chapter has attempted to convey.

[114] Another very striking case is provided by the extraordinary fragment from the ’Εκθέωσις ’Αρσινόης (fr. 228), which there has not been space to describe.

[115] γλυκύς of Mimnermus (fr. 1. 11), μελιχρός of poetry (16, whatever the supplement), could in principle suggest simply the giving of pleasure (compare the sections π. γλυκύτητος in Hermogenes and Aristides, *Rhet. Gr.* ii. 357 ff., 499). But contemporary evidence, especially *Ep.* 26. 2 (LVI), does favour understanding them of style. τέχνη is a wide word, and its syntax in fr. 1. 17 f. is not straightforward; but the sentence does invite the notion of technique, and the context sets one's thoughts on smaller aspects of poetry.

[116] Callimachus uses λεπτός purely as a description of style in *Ep.* 27 alone. The discussion of the word by E. Reitzenstein, *Festschrift R. Reitzenstein* (1931), 25 ff., makes rather too much of it.

3

APOLLONIUS

THE understanding of Apollonius' epic tends to be vexed by presuppositions related to its imagined environment, literary and historical. These presuppositions between them now inform the bulk of scholarly writing; ultimately they contribute to the general impression of Apollonius in the minds of those relatively unfamiliar with his work. That impression, however, seems to be much less definite and decided than in the case of Callimachus. It will be best to begin from these presuppositions as such, and proceed to an account of the poem which may suggest its interest and appeal.

The epic is considered to have been at this time a problematic form. Callimachus is taken to have campaigned against it; some sources tell of a quarrel between Callimachus and Apollonius, which has traditionally been related to a dispute over the genre. Epic is thought to have been intrinsically out of place, both in its art and in its values. In its art, it by nature exacted a tired reworking of Homer, and overwhelmed elegance and precision in its unwieldy pomposity. Apollonius is thought either not fully to have realized the force of Callimachus' views, or else to have reformed the epic radically in order to comply with them. The matter of values brings in presuppositions about heroism. Heroism itself is held to have been a problematic notion in that supposedly jaded period. Jason, the leader of the Argonauts, displays the contrary of heroism, in his weakness and his diplomacy: he is the Hellenistic 'answer' to the archaic hero, whether Apollonius admires him or detests him. It is less common to think that Apollonius is simply offering up again the heroic world of Homer; he is sometimes supposed to be making the attempt but failing, as was inevitable in that decadent age.

These approaches to heroism, though not absolutely out of contact with elements in the poem, yet depend on dubious assumptions and rather crude exaggerations. Thus in Greek

poetry the heroic world is never a simple embodiment of the
author's world, but rather is marked out as separate and distant, very plainly so in Homer. Nor are Homer's characters
simply 'heroic': even in the *Iliad*, the leader Agamemnon is a
much less acceptable person than Jason, being not only readily
despondent but also tactless and brutal.[1] There is little concrete reason to think the Hellenistic period world-weary, or to
think poems always a conscious and didactic reflection of their
age. But above all, such views demand distortions of the *Argonautica*. It is not merely that one has to make crude and heavy
something as delicate, hovering, and often playful as the depiction of Jason. The whole structure of the poem seems to be lost
from view. The role and the utility of males and of valour
change, and not simply, within the movement of the poem: the
poem does not assign them a fixed position as axioms of its
universe. Indeed, the structure of the poem, rarely appreciated,
is absolutely primary to its impact; the chapter will seek to
explain its character and effect.

Still less secure is the conception of epic as an especially
problematic genre. The pronouncements of Callimachus have
been considered above, and the lines of Theocritus (7. 45 ff.)
which are generally connected with them will be considered
below (pp. 77 ff.; 201 ff.). Neither, it is argued, show us contemporary warfare over the epic.[2] Without their support, there
seems nothing intractable in the idea of Apollonius' relation to
Homer. Between them, the genre had continued to be written
in (cf. pp. 14 f.); Homer was thought of as essentially its
founder, and the prime source of its basic language and conventions. Apollonius very often looks back to him; but one sees
little in this tangible relationship to suggest either slavishness or
anxiety. The same holds of Apollonius' relationship with Callimachus, to which we now turn.

The story of the quarrel does not appear until the very latest
and most worthless stages of the tradition about these poets: a
probable interpolation in the *Suda*, the Byzantine poem pre-

---

[1] Bulloch rightly makes much of this point (in *CHCL* i. 591).

[2] *SH* 339A is taken by J. S. Rusten to portray Apollonius as a verbose traditionalist
(*Dionysius Scytobrachion* (1982), ch. 3); but such an interpretation is far from necessary
(see Lloyd-Jones and Parsons ad loc.). The point seems to be that Apollonius' digressions are concise (as indeed they are).

fixed to the MSS of the *Hymns* of Callimachus, a marginale in the Palatine Anthology.[3] It was unknown, it seems, to the ancient scholia on the prologue to the *Aetia* (Pfeiffer i.3), and also to the two *Lives* of Apollonius. One needs no great measure of scepticism to reject it.[4]

The poems themselves show a relationship of influence. The clearest instance of all is provided by Book 1 of the *Aetia*, one part of which dealt with some events in the return of the Argonauts, the subject of Apollonius' fourth book. Near the end of the Argonauts' journey sudden darkness assails them; Jason prays to Apollo, and he appears bearing light.

$$\pi o \lambda \lambda \grave{a} \; \delta' \; \dot{a}\pi\epsilon\acute{\iota}\lambda\epsilon\iota$$
$$\dot{\epsilon}s \; \Pi v\theta\grave{\omega} \; \pi\acute{\epsilon}]\mu\psi\epsilon\iota\nu, \; \pi o\lambda\lambda\grave{a} \; \delta' \; \dot{\epsilon}s \; {}^{\prime}O\rho\tau\upsilon\gamma\acute{\iota}\eta\nu.$$

(Call. fr. 18. 6 f.)

Jason was promising to send many gifts to Delphi, many to Delos.

Jason goes on to refer to Apollo's guidance at the start of the expedition. Apollonius' account both of the incident itself and of the start of the expedition contains many close correspondences of language with Callimachus, especially at 4. 1704 f. and the very similar passage at 1. 418 f.

$$\pi o\lambda\lambda\grave{a} \; \delta\grave{\epsilon} \; \Pi v\theta o\hat{\iota} \; \dot{\upsilon}\pi\acute{\epsilon}\sigma\chi\epsilon\tau o, \; \pi o\lambda\lambda\grave{a} \; \delta' \; {}^{\prime}A\mu\acute{\upsilon}\kappa\lambda\alpha\iota s,$$
$$\pi o\lambda\lambda\grave{a} \; \delta' \; \dot{\epsilon}s \; {}^{\prime}O\rho\tau\upsilon\gamma\acute{\iota}\eta\nu \; \dot{a}\pi\epsilon\rho\epsilon\acute{\iota}\sigma\iota\alpha \; \delta\hat{\omega}\rho\alpha \; \kappa o\mu\acute{\iota}\sigma\sigma\epsilon\iota\nu.$$

(AR 4. 1704 f.)

Jason promised to bring many offerings to Delphi of innumerable gifts, many to Amyclae, many to Delos.

Other elements in this *aition* are strikingly matched in Apollonius, as we shall see presently. It would be implausible, as well as unnecessary, to postulate a common source. One poet is imitating the other. In this particular case Callimachus will

---

[3] The first three items appear in Pfeiffer (ii, pp. xcv ff.) as *Testimonia* 1. 14 f., 23. 8, 25 (cf. *FGE*, p. 17, though Page is credulous here). The scholion of Marsus (AD 1472) on Ovid, *Ibis* 447 (b 1 in La Penna's edn.) naturally has no authority. The target of Callimachus' *Ibis* was clearly given no other name than Ibis; for the attempt at identification cf. the *Diegesis* to *Ia*. 5 (fr. 195), Pfeiffer i. 185 (the Apollonius here cannot be the poet).

[4] If one inserted a reference to a quarrel—still more to a poetic quarrel—in l. 8 of the first *Life* (Sch. p. 1 Wendel) one would produce an unlikely sentence or sequence. The quarrel is now meeting with increasing suspicion. Cf. especially M. R. Lefkowitz, *Lives of the Greek Poets* (1981), ch. 11.

precede. We saw that in the *Aetia* Callimachus most likely confined himself to stories told not by poets but by local historians (pp. 40 f.). The character of the sources was important to the effect of the poem. It is scarcely probable that in the second *aition* of his first book Callimachus should choose to follow, and sedulously, a poem recently produced by a colleague in Alexandria.[5]

There are many other striking connections between the poets; but on the whole these elude attempts to order them. So we should expect with craftsmen of such address.[6] What matters is the fact of connection.

The two poets should be thought of as colleagues and contemporaries. The statement that Apollonius was Callimachus' pupil is unreliable, as such statements always are, and we should concentrate on more promising evidence.[7] Those poems of Callimachus which can be dated indicate that he resided in Alexandria between the 270s and the 240s (p. 40). Apollonius is likely to have been in Alexandria, as an adult, for some or all of this period. He was succeeded as chief librarian by Eratosthenes (P. Oxy. 1241 ii 5 f.), and this occurred in the reign of Ptolemy III (246–221) (*Suda E* 2898). We know of no predecessor but Zenodotus, who is said to have 'flourished' in the reign of Ptolemy I (305–282) (*Suda Z* 74). It follows that Apollonius is likely to have been chief librarian for part at least of the period in question. That he was a grown man at this period

---

[5] The same argument applies, though a little less strongly, to frr. 108–9 (*Aetia* 4): there Callimachus narrated an incident narrated briefly by Apollonius (1. 955–60). Callimachus' opening rather suggests that his story is obscure. That instance would tend to favour the notion of fluid chronology supported below. Note also fr. 24, in the same section of *Aetia* 1 (the story of Theiodamas, told briefly at AR 1. 1213 ff.): the juxtaposition would make still less plausible the adaptation of Apollonius in the part on the Argonauts.

[6] E. Eichgrün, *Kallimachos u. AR* (Diss. Berlin 1961) fails to convince on these matters. In particular, he judges that AR 1. 742 ff. derive from Call. *H.* 3. 212 ff., because the adjective θοός is suitable to arrows but not to a shield (AR 1. 743). Cf., however, AR 4. 201 ἀσπίδας ... θοòν ἔχμα βολάων, *Et. Magn.* s.v. θοή, etc. Bulloch, *AJP* 98 (1977), 121 f., makes an interesting case for having Call. *H.* 5. 103 imitate AR 2. 445, on the grounds that the unusual handling of the metre is matched in three other places of Apollonius and none of Callimachus. One must bear in mind, however, that there are between 3 and 4 times the number of hexameters in Apollonius available for comparison.

[7] The statement is made clearly in the two unsatisfactory *Lives* attached to the MSS (Sch. pp. 1 f. Wendel), and in the *Suda, A* 3419; Καλλιμάχου γνώριμος in P. Oxy. 1241 ii. 2 f. probably means the same.

is suggested also by two poems of Theocritus (13 and 22) which are probably based on Apollonius rather than vice versa (pp. 192 f.). Theocritus' only datable poems belong in the 270s (15, 17, Alexandria) and probably in 264 or later (16, Syracuse); he is most likely imitated by Callimachus (p. 197). It follows that the three poets are likely to have been roughly contemporary. In theory we might accept this and then arrange elaborate chronologies to accommodate the intricate circles of imitation, reckoning with single dates of publication for each work. It seems much easier to postulate that the poets had seen one another's work before it was published in its final shape. The ancient commentaries on Apollonius, indeed, refer to a first or preliminary edition (προέκδοσις), differing from the text we possess; but the value and significance of this information is uncertain.[8] We may grant, then, the basic notion, that Callichamus and Apollonius are contemporary and connected. But even if it is most often fruitless to inquire which influenced which, we still need to be more precise about the relation of their poetry. The danger now is not so much that we should create an unreal opposition as that we should miss the difference. The poets were no antagonists; but Apollonius' work cannot be seen as a mere docile echo of Callimachus'.

Certainly the association between them is deep. This may be illustrated from two passages where connections between the poets seem obvious. We do not find, however, the mere superficial appropriation of material or of a device; we perceive a much more fundamental relationship. In Book 2 of Apollonius the Argonauts sing in praise of Apollo (701 ff.). Apollonius gives an account of how the ritual cry originated which they use: the account, and an obscure detail within it, are plainly linked with Callimachus (*H.* 2. 97 ff., fr. 88).[9] But Apollonius also inserts a parenthesis very similar in manner to Callimachus, in which the author nervously retracts the apparent suggestion that Apollo's locks are ever shorn:

[8] The notion may be generated by the dubious story of Apollonius' early failure and retirement to Rhodes; or it may have helped to generate that story. If the notion is correct, one may perhaps compare the statement about Posidippus in Sch. Hom. *Il.* 11. 101a.

[9] The name of the Serpent of Delphi (Call. fr. 88, AR 2. 706) comes ultimately from a local historian, used elsewhere by Callimachus (Diog. Laert. 1. 28); cf. also fr. 92 and *FGrH* 491 F 3 (Apollonius).

—ἱλήκοις, αἰεί τοι, ἄναξ, ἄτμητοι ἔθειραι,
αἰὲν ἀδήλητοι ...   (708 f.)

Oh be gracious, forgive! Your hair, lord, is always uncut,
always unspoiled ...[10]

The intrusiveness of the poet's prayer is heightened by parody
of a prayer just uttered by a character. Apollo has appeared to
the Argonauts, and after his epiphany Orpheus has addressed
the god with the language traditional at such moments:

ἀλλ' ἴληθι, ἄναξ, ἴληθι φαανθείς.   (693)

Be gracious, be gracious, lord, now you have appeared to
us.[11]

The parody points the whole contrast of tone between the
numinous epiphany, with its powerful directness of effect, and
this scholarly passage with its delicious disruption. Immediately after it, the Argonauts swear eternal loyalty to one
another (715 ff.): the moment is solemn and weighty, and we
feel another striking contrast in tone. The whole design here exhibits concerns akin to those that preoccupy Callimachus.

Similarly, in Book 3 of Apollonius we have a crow in a tree
that rebukes the prophet Mopsus (he comprehends the speech
of birds). Mopsus and another Argonaut are accompanying
Jason to meet Medea, who is in love with him: they should let
Jason meet her alone, as anyone not ignorant of love would
realize. The device of the crow speaking in the tree recalls Callimachus' fourth *Iambus* and the *Hecale* (fr. 194. 61 ff., *SH* 288.
17 ff.; pp. 50, 60 f.). But the actual tone of the speech is very
reminiscent of Callimachus too. It ends:

ἔρροις, ὦ κακόμαντι, κακοφραδές· οὔτε σε Κύπρις
οὔτ' ἀγανοὶ φιλέοντες ἐπιπνείουσιν Ἔρωτες.   (3. 936 f.)

Begone, you bad prophet, with your bad sense! Aphrodite
and the gentle Erotes do not love you and breathe inspiration upon you.

The exaggerated vehemence and the approach to love feel
highly 'Callimachean'. The reader's response is guided by the

---

[10] On these lines cf. R. L. Hunter, *MH* 43 (1986), 56 ff. For such an effect elsewhere
in Apollonius cf. notably 4. 984–6. Imitation of Aratus 637 would not account for the
tone of 2. 708–10.
[11] Cf. particularly Hom. *Od.* 3. 380.

character's: he smiles (938). The lines are preceded by a description of Jason's beauty (919 ff.) and followed by a description of the overwhelming effect which that beauty has on Medea. There we find, admixed with other elements, writing much warmer and more intently engaged in emotional experience. This moment, both in its fantasy and in its light and knowing tone, breaks in on and complicates the poet's evocation of love. Again we see at work poetic concerns connected with Callimachus' at a fundamental level.

Yet by isolating these passages we limit artificially their full effect. They have their force within a large poetic and narrative design, which helps to make their total impact quite distinct from that of Callimachus' poetry. The combined scale and continuity of Apollonius' work (5,835 lines) are profoundly important to its nature. Despite many 'Callimachean' moments and elements throughout its course, the essence of the work as a whole is that it realizes on a huge scale, in its entire structure, a great process of modifying and complicating the straightforward. The primary concern here obviously involves a deep affinity with the poetry of Callimachus; but the conception and the impact are altogether different, and make the poem radically individual.

We can perceive the importance of form, and the difference it makes, even in places were Apollonius is most strongly joined to Callimachus, and is probably his debtor. So with the section of the *Aetia* on the return of the Argonauts. The chief fragments of that section deal with: the angry speech of Aeetes, king of the Colchians, when he discovered that his daughter Medea had enabled Jason to perform the tasks he had imposed on him and to escape with the Golden Fleece—and with her (Call. fr. 7. 23 ff.); the foundation of cities by the Colchians who pursued the Argonauts, but in vain (frr. 11 and 12); the darkness which fell on the Argo and Jason's prayer to Apollo (*SH* 250, and fr. 18); Apollo's epiphany, (frr. 19 and 20); the jocular improprieties that passed between the Argonauts and Medea's maids (fr. 21).

In Apollonius the utterance of Aeetes (4. 228 ff.) takes up an earlier utterance (3. 579 ff.), which also makes use of Callimachus fr. 7. Both are in reported speech, unlike Call. fr. 7. 29 ff., and unlike most of the speeches in Apollonius. In the earlier place the device suits the hidden treachery of Aeetes, suddenly revealed to the reader. In this, it makes still more sinister the violent and furious father and tyrant. Apollonius has produced a connection which embraces all the decisive events in Colchis, and which presses home the danger still posed to the Argonauts by the terrifying figure of the king. The accounts of the Colchians' subsequent activities are used by Apollonius to make a dry ending to two central and emotional incidents: the killing of Medea's brother Apsyrtus and the marriage of Jason and Medea (4. 507 ff., 1206 ff.). In Callimachus the murder of Apsyrtus had occurred before the Argonauts left Colchis (fr. 8). The dryness gains its force from our involvement in the developing narrative.

Jason's prayer in Apollonius (4. 1704 ff.) looks back, as we saw, to his prayer at the start of the poem (1. 411 ff.). The link, reinforced by the reminiscence of Callimachus, spans the whole action of the work. It also lends especial force to this final deliverance from peril, virtually at the end of the voyage. Apollonius compresses the elaborate narrative of Callimachus so as to give predominance to strong emotion and strange extravagance. Thus the hellish darkness was so terrible that:

> εἴτ' Ἀΐδῃ εἴθ' ὕδασιν ἐμφορέοντο
> ἠείδειν οὐδ' ὅσσον· ἐπέτρεψαν δὲ θαλάσσῃ
> νόστον, ἀμηχανέοντες ὅπῃ φέροι.   (4. 1699–1701)

Whether they were being borne along in Hades or on the sea they had no notion. They entrusted to the sea their return home, in despair of knowing where it was carrying them.

The idea of the return has dominated the poem. The perverted use of ἐπέτρεψαν 'entrusted' brings out the poignancy of such despair at such a point. The reference to Hades seems to invest this last trial with the concrete horror of death. Yet the conceit and expression there are fantastic, and the next sentence cancels them out ('they entrusted to the *sea* ...'); we feel a slight sense of detachment from the danger, which again wins its force from our knowledge of the real end in sight for the Argonauts.

With the maids, Apollonius again creates strong internal connections. They had been given to Medea by Alcinous, when she and the Argonauts were on Phaeacia (Call. fr. 21. 6 f.).

Apollonius makes from this a very emphatic connection between the end of the present episode (4. 1722–4) and the end of an earlier section (4. 1221 f.), which marks out an important division in the narrative (between the travels before, and after, Phaeacia). The moment also reverses an earlier one. When the Argonauts had been stranded in Libya, the maids, in a place apart from the men, had mourned aloud the certain destruction which the men were lamenting silently (1296 ff.). Now men and women, rescued by Apollo, engage with delight in mutual badinage. Both incidents play a part in those changing oppositions between male and female which form an important ingredient of the poem as a whole.

The poetic role of *aitia* in the *Argonautica* bears a strong relation to their role in the *Aetia*; but the importance of the whole in fact appears here too, though in very different ways from those just considered. The poem gives a very prominent place to *aitia*, to connections pointed between (principally) things in the story and names, rituals, and so forth which survive to Apollonius' own day.[12] An *aition* appears in the first item of the opening catalogue (1. 28 ff.); the poem ends in a flurry of *aitia*. There are about forty *aitia* in the books of voyaging (1, 2, 4); they are normally placed at the very end of the episode in question. Although in fact they are sparse in some stretches and densely clustered in others, the reader feels them to have some sort of significant structural function, as they overtly have in Callimachus. They are handled in such a way as to distance us from the story, and to obtrude on our attention with recondite lore. For its mythology Apollonius' poem draws throughout on a very wide range of sources, in both poetry and prose; but here in particular the reader is apt to be made suddenly and sharply aware of the scholarly narrator. The treatment of erudition and the author, though necessarily less open in this formally impersonal genre, yet suggests notable resemblances to the treatment in Callimachus' poem. For example, in 2. 841–54 the treatment of the *aitia* is bound up with a playful and disconcerting treatment of poet and Muses. In closing the pathetic account of Idmon's death and burial, Apollonius so handles the mention

---

[12] On *aitia* in the poem cf. the commendable discussion of M. Fusillo, *Il tempo delle Argonautiche* (1985), 116 ff.

of his tomb, which stands to the poet's day, as to avoid any harsh disruption of the feeling. But he then proceeds abruptly in mid-line to a further *aition*:

$$εἰ δέ με καὶ τὸ$$
$$χρειὼ ἀπηλεγέως Μουσέων ὕπο γηρύσασθαι \ldots \qquad (2.844\,f.)$$

And, since I seem compelled by the Muses to declare this too, forthrightly, . . .[13]

The poet affects a kind of reluctance to dissolve his narrative by this additional information; with deliberate incongruity he associates the movement with the inspiration of the goddesses. After the *aition*, he toys further with his stance. He proceeds, again abruptly, to a second death, with a question, τίς γὰρ δὴ θάνεν ἄλλος; (851) 'who also died?'. He thus affects to deploy an imposing gesture of the Homeric narrator; but then he explains the reason for his asking, the existence of a second tomb, a second object inviting aetiology.[14] He cautiously ascribes his answer, not to the Muses or his own authority, but to φάτις 'the story men tell'. The poet is playing delicately with his role and his erudition, and so breaks up an atmosphere.

The force of such effects, however, is very different within an epic poem. Here the poem is formally a pure narrative. When we are moved forward from the time of the myth to the time of Apollonius—and the movement is generally stressed by Apollonius' phraseology—we feel a stranger sense of intrusion and interruption. This is partly a question of our emotional involvement in the story: we look for it to be sustained, and the *aitia* characteristically dispel and frustrate it. One of the first episodes using *aitia* establishes this function in a spectacular manner (1.1015 ff.). The Argonauts have been entertained by the Doliones; they are swept back to their country unawares by

---

[13] Μουσέων ὕπο does not go very effectively with γηρύσασθαι alone, 'under the Muses' guidance'. Cf. for ὑπό as I take it 4.643. However, the essential point would not be invalidated by the other view.

[14] For the device of the question cf. *Il.* 1.8, *al.* I incline to think that such questions are always addressed to the Muse, and that Apollonius is actually feinting here at the notion of the scholarly poet seeking enlightenment from the all-knowing divinities. Apollonius was not obliged by tradition to place the two deaths together: see Sch. 2. 854 (Herodorus, *FGrH* 31 F 54), *SH* 250. 9.

night; they fight with their unrecognized hosts and Jason kills
their ruler, young and newly married. The narrative powerfully deploys the grandeur and pathos of epic; in shape it offers
a tragic accumulation of disaster, the king's bride hanging herself for grief. It seems to engage our responses with a new intensity and elevation; but as it proceeds, the effect is again and
again dispersed—and eventually destroyed—by information
on rituals, names, and monuments derived from the local historian Deiochus. This function of dissolving or diluting involvement continues throughout the voyage to Colchis (Books 1–2).
Apollonius is particularly eager thus to interrupt the flow of his
narrative where by doing so he will most damage continuity
and cohesion: between one episode and the next. We come to
feel these interruptions, we saw, almost as a structural principle
of the poem. Apollonius is not disguising but deliberately high-
lighting the disjointedness of his narrative. Even within Books
1–2 this disjointedness only makes its impact as an aspect of a
large unit (the narrative of the two books) and of a work in this
particular genre. But the relation between this aspect and the
whole poem is not merely a negative one, with the discontinuity
simply pulling against the presupposition of unity on which its
effect depends. Rather, the discontinuity has itself an essential
role to play within the extraordinary structure of the poem.

In Book 4 the *aitia* are again used to emphasize disjointedness, but the effect and force are more complicated: in that
book a sort of cohesion develops precisely out of disruption.
How this is so will be explained presently; here we may simply
note one or two surprising uses which accompany the different
place of the book in the structure. Thus *aitia* can here be
employed, on occasion, to strengthen the narrative as well as to
disrupt it. An *aition* ends the description of Jason and Medea's
murder of her brother Apsyrtus:

> ὑγρὸν δ᾿ ἐν γαίῃ κρύψεν νέκυν, ἔνθ᾿ ἔτι νῦν περ
> κείαται ὀστέα κεῖνα μετ᾿ ἀνδράσιν Ἀψυρτεῦσιν.　　　(4. 480 f.)

Jason hid the wet corpse in the ground; in that spot those
bones lie even today, in the land of the Apsyrtes.

Here too there is some movement of feeling: we are brought forward to the present after a ghastly account of murderers' prac-

tices which had set us in a distant environment.[15] But the
continued existence of the bones (like the name Apsyrtes)
heightens the horror of the crime in another way: its results
abide. By the change from the wet corpse to bones the horror is
only enhanced. When that whole appalling episode seem firmly
set behind us, Apollonius moves abruptly to a new part of the
voyage (4. 552 ff.). He asks a question of the Muses, developing
lavishly the grand device. That effect, however, is interwoven
with muted play: in a certain region there are various monuments said, and said truly, to derive from the Argonauts, and
the scholarly author would like them explained. Aetiology
seems to be disrupting the narrative and stressing discontinuity.
But in fact the answer introduces continuity of the grimmest
kind: Zeus is angry at the killing of Apsyrtus. The appearance
of discontinuity had served only as a foil.[16]

   In dealing with these two aspects of connection with Callimachus (Callimachus' treatment of the Argonauts; Apollonius'
treatment of *aitia*), we have approached two different and divergent aspects of the poem viewed as a whole. On the one
hand, we have seen the poet binding the work together; on the
other, we have seen him breaking it apart. Both aspects, it was
claimed, bear a positive relation to the total design. Complaints
have often been registered as to the unity of the poem; but the
matter is commonly approached in a misleading way. It seems
almost as if lack of unity were a damaging charge against the
poet, whose guilt or innocence must be established. Those prosecuting, so to speak, will often talk as if only one sort of unity
will be truly acceptable, mostly an Aristotelian singleness of
action or plot.[17] The defence, by contrast, appear to feel that

---

[15] The arch ᾗ θέμις αὐθέντῃσι 'as is the custom for murderers' only heightens the
sense of distance. The Homeric sense of θέμις (cf. especially *Il.* 9. 134) is intended to
conflict harshly with its usual sense, 'law, right'; ᾗ τε δίκη is used in the same way at 4.
694.

[16] The answer seems to derive not from the Muses but from the poet's conjecture: so
the second word που suggests (557). 1. 996 and 1. 1140 and the use of the particle in
Aratus do not really make against this. The play, then, would actually continue into
the sombre answer itself.

[17] Cf. notably Wilamowitz, *HD* i. 208 f., consciously echoing the pronouncements of
Aristotle (*Poet.* 1459ᵃ17–ᵇ7); cf. also ibid. ii. 217 ff., and, on the first book, Vian i. 119 f.
For more bibliography on the unity of the poem see Herter, *RE* Supp. xiii (1973), 27 ff.
J. Preininger, *D. Aufbau d. Argonautika d. AR* (Diss. Graz, 1976) unfortunately adopts an
elaborately numerological approach.

any one type of unity will suffice to repel the indictment, in particular a unity of theme.[18] A broader viewpoint seems preferable. Disunity can often be sought and relished by poets; and there are various kinds and areas of unity, which are compatible, and often combined, with various kinds and areas of disunity. Apollonius' design is particularly bold and strange.

The *Argonautica* offers a basic, loose unity of action: this serves as a framework to hold more complicated types of unity and disunity. We shall deal first with this fairly straightforward sort of unity; even this, however, acquires complications in the later parts of the work. The single action of the poem is the voyage of the Argonauts to and from Colchis to gain the Golden Fleece. The separate incidents which make up such an action cannot all be connected causally, but it is perfectly possible for the writer to make the reader aware of the action as a whole. Apollonius does this by concentrating our foremost attention on the return to home which is the end and goal, actual and desired, of the entire expedition.[19] Throughout the poem we are made to look forward, not simply to the taking of the Golden Fleece, but to the safe arrival of the Argonauts back in their own land. Even before they reach Colchis, the latter is much more prominent a concern than the former. The safe return, the νόστος, is not just mentioned frequently. It acquires a heavy weight of emotion, not least through its association with the leader Jason. In concentrating on Jason's desires and despairs in this respect, the poet is not primarily concerned with showing him as more feeble-spirited than his companions. Even before Colchis is reached, they too are (of course) concerned with their return (cf. especially 2. 859–63). Rather, the concentration on this individual concentrates and intensifies our own involvement in the issue.

At the very beginning of the poem we learn that Pelias, Jason's uncle, is sending Jason on the expedition so that he νόστον ὀλέσσῃ 'may lose his return', perish far from home (1. 17, the close of a section). Jason's mother and father, and his mother's maids, treat the event as a disaster, almost as if he

---

[18] So much recent criticism, by implication.

[19] It is interesting to see the weight given to the return in a new fragment of archaic epic on the voyage, P. Oxy. 3698. 15 (perhaps not part of an account both full and lengthy, cf. P. Oxy. 2513).

were going to die (1. 247–93).[20] Jason conducts himself here
with self-control; but as the Argo leaves his native land, he
weeps.

εἵλκετο δ' ἤδη
πείσματα καὶ μέθυ λεῖβον ὕπερθ' ἁλός· αὐτὰρ Ἰήσων
δακρυόεις γαίης ἀπὸ πατρίδος ὄμματ' ἔνεικεν.

(1. 533–5)

Now already they were drawing up the ropes and pouring
their libations upon the sea. Jason, weeping, took his eyes
away from his native land.

The privacy and simplicity of the act is set poignantly against
the busy movement about him. A simile follows, which invests
with cheerfulness the activity of his comrades.

When he is leaving Hypsipyle, with whom he has dallied on
Lemnos, Jason indicates that all he wishes is to dwell in his own
country (1. 903 f.); but if he is fated not to return to Greece, and
Hypsipyle bears him a son, she is to send him to assuage his
parents' anguish (δύης ἄκος, 1. 907). In the light of the earlier
scene with his parents, this utterance has strong pathos. There
is pathos too (as well as irony) when at the beginning of his
dalliance he rebuts Hypsipyle's suggestions that he should take
up rule on the island: ἀλλά με λυγροὶ ἐπισπέρχουσιν ἄεθλοι (1.
841) 'fearful trials urge me on'. ἄεθλοι 'trials' is also an important word in the poem, often heavy with gloom. In Book 2 the
blind seer Phineus tells the Argonauts in detail how to reach
Colchis. They are all alarmed at the prospect; but it is Jason,
ἀμηχανέων κακότητι 'despairing at his troubles', who inquires
whether, and how, they will return to Greece (2. 413 ff.). His
concern is not merely practical. Shortly afterwards he says that
he would be as happy if Phineus' sight were restored as he
would be if he himself were to return home (2. 441 f.). The passage movingly displays together both the warmth of Jason's
sympathy and the intensity of his desire to return.

Tiphys the helmsman dies, 'far from his homeland' (2. 856).
All the Argonauts are overcome with ἀμηχανίαι 'despair' and
with grief, for themselves: they have lost all hope of returning
(863). Hera inspires Ancaeus to take over the helm: he speaks

[20] 292 f. echo the description in the *Iliad* of the laments for the dead Hector (24. 745).

to Peleus, and Peleus addresses to the company in general a rousing speech of exhortation, reminiscent of Archilochus (fr. 13 West). He begins:

δαιμόνιοι, τί νυ πένθος ἐτώσιον ἴσχομεν αὔτως;
οἱ μὲν γάρ ποθι τοῦτον ὃν ἔλλαχον οἶτον ὄλοντο·
ἡμῖν δ᾽ . . .   (2. 880–2)

My friends, why are we continuing this useless grief? As for Tiphys and Idmon, this doom that they have suffered was allotted them, I suppose. But as for us . . .

Jason responds with a speech of bitter hopelessness, and ends with bleak reapplication of Peleus' words:

καταυτόθι δ᾽ ἄμμε καλύψει
ἀκλειῶς κακὸς οἶτος, ἐτώσια γηράσκοντας.   (892 f.)

In this very place we shall be buried, without glory, by a wretched doom, as we grow old uselessly.

The order of words and the rhythm enhance the black finality. ἐτώσια 'uselessly' answers to Peleus' πένθος ἐτώσιον 'useless grief'; the preceding clause answers to his οἱ μὲν . . . ὄλοντο 'as for Tiphys . . . suppose'. Jason is of course in earnest.[21] He assumes that his feelings are shared by all (cf. 887 f.), not knowing that Ancaeus will volunteer, under the influence of heaven (895), and that others will be inspired to follow his example. Nonetheless, the design of this scene has the effect of marking out his own despondency and distress. We sympathize with his feelings, and their object, while seeing that they are misplaced (and a little unvalorous). The pathos of the theme is now distanced somewhat by the situation, but the theme itself does not lose its weight. The focus of the dramatic irony is the return, and the irony presupposes and confirms the emotional importance of that event.

In the second half of the poem the idea of the return is complicated and enriched in resonance through its association with Medea. Medea, the daughter of King Aeetes, falls in love with

---

[21] H. Fränkel attempts to deny this, on quite inadequate grounds (*Noten z. d. Argonautika d. Apollonios* (1961), 240 ff.); he is obliged to contend that ἀμηχανέων 'despairing' in the introduction to the speech is corrupt (2. 885). Still more strangely, Vian follows Fränkel's view, but holds the text to be sound (*Gnomon* 46 (1974), 349). The following sequence of events is misunderstood by D. N. Levin, *Apollonius'* Argonautica *Re-examined*, i. (1971), 190, in a different way from Fränkel.

Jason, and it is on her and her sorcery that hopes of returning now rest. Her feelings are presented as a conflict between her loyalty to her father and her love for 'the foreigner'.[22] Her love compels her to leave her home and her parents and to travel back with the Argonauts to Greece—for them home, for her, a place as distant as Colchis is to them.[23] In two of his speeches to Medea, Jason explicitly links the return of the Argonauts to Greece with Medea's coming there to marry him (3. 1128 ff., 4. 95 ff.). Medea's passion here finds triumphant satisfaction; but in both places the following lines indicate the anguish for the maiden who loves her home and her parents. After the second speech, the Argo leaves the shore, with loud din from the hastening Argonauts.

$$\text{ἡ δ' ἔμπαλιν ἀΐσσουσα}$$
$$\text{γαίη χεῖρας ἔτεινεν, ἀμήχανος· αὐτὰρ Ἰήσων}$$
$$\text{θάρσυνεν τ' ἐπέεσσι ...} \qquad (4.106-8)$$

But Medea, darting her body back, stretched out her arms
to the land in despair. Jason endeavoured to hearten her
...

We witness the same scene as when Jason left Thessaly, but in a more passionate and almost tragic form; the role of Jason as comforter lends edge to the irony of the reversal. After the first speech, the poet stresses that Medea's coming to Greece will result from the grim politics of Hera (she wishes to punish Jason's uncle Pelias). The close of the passage conveys the extremity and the pathos of Medea's experience:

$$\text{ὄφρα κακὸν Πελίη ἱερὴν ἐς Ἰωλκὸν ἵκηται}$$
$$\text{Αἰαίη Μήδεια, λιποῦσ' ἀπὸ πατρίδα γαῖαν.} \qquad (3. 1136 f.)$$

... so that Medea from Colchis might come to sacred
Iolcus as the destruction of Pelias, leaving her native land.

The two place-names are expressively opposed, and the final phrase has a Homeric weight and poignancy.[24]

---

[22] Cf. e.g. 3. 616 ff.; note the juxtaposition of 'father' and 'foreigner' or the like in 3. 628, 630, 743.

[23] See the pointed inversion in the words of Medea's sister Chalciope at 3. 679 f. 'The ends of the earth' means Greece (or the like) from a Colchian viewpoint. M. Campbell seems to mistake the meaning, *Studies in the Third Book of AR's Arg.* (1983), 43. Cf. also 3. 1060 ff., 1071 ff., etc.

[24] Note the explicit pathos and paradox of *Od.* 4. 261 ὅτε μ' ἤγαγε κεῖσε φίλης ἀπὸ πατρίδος αἴης, of Helen taken to Troy.

The Argonauts' return and Medea's exile are brought elsewhere into a more direct opposition. When Medea fears that the Argonauts will give her up to her brother, she uses the most forcible rhetoric to contrast her own loss of home, parents, and country with the Argonauts' return to them (4. 1036 ff.). Under similar circumstances she prays that Hera will not let Jason obtain his return while she is punished, that her own curse will drive Jason from his country, like her (4. 379 ff., cf. 360 ff.). When she actually leaves her home and her family she wishes that the foreigner had been destroyed by the sea (4. 30 ff.). The Argonauts' return, then, means the opposite of return for Medea, an opposite full of terror and suffering, bitter and not unresented.[25] This neat and disquieting irony makes deeper and more complex the impact of the unifying event.

In Book 4, Apollonius also complicates in other ways the notion of return and our sense of the relation between the return and the incidents of the voyage. He does this in particular through a continuous interplay between his poem and the *Odyssey* of Homer. His attention is fixed primarily on Odysseus' own voyage of return. It need not have been significant that Odysseus and the Argonauts should encounter many of the same figures. Each of the two myths had long been affected by the other. The Sirens and the Phaeacians had been associated with the Argonauts before Apollonius.[26] Circe is not known to have played a part earlier in the return of the Argonauts, but she is the sister of Aeetes, and it is more likely her place in the story of Odysseus that comes second.[27] Thrinakie, the island of Helios, had already been identified with Sicily;[28] the Argonauts would naturally pass it, given other localizations of their itinerary. However, the standard account of all these figures and places was Homer's, and Apollonius' descriptions and

---

[25] When Circe has purified Jason and Medea from the murder of Medea's brother, she says to Medea σχετλίη, ἦ ῥα κακὸν καὶ ἀεικέα μήσαο νόστον (4. 739). The use of νόστος is poignantly unexpected—we should contrast 4. 822. Livrea, ad loc., and Vian, *RÉA* 75 (1973), 92 f., are wrong to deny that νόστος is connected with 'home' here: Medea has joined her lot with a foreigner and helped him back to a home that is not her own. See also Fränkel, *Noten*, 524 ff.

[26] Herodorus *FGrH* 31 F 436, West, *The Orphic Poems* (1983), pl. 4; Timaeus, *FGrH* 566 F 87, 88 (probably).

[27] Cf. K. Meuli, *Ges. Schr.* ii. 626 ff., 649 ff. Hom. *Od.* 10. 137 ff., like 12. 59–72, characteristically draw attention to the relations between the two myths.

[28] Cf. Dover on Thuc. 6. 2. 1.

expressions make it clear enough that we are intended to compare the passages in question with the *Odyssey*. Homer himself
constantly relates the 'adventures' of Odysseus to his return: it
is natural enough that this element should stand at the centre of
the play between the two texts.

The interplay begins in 557 ff., with a point of resemblance.
Zeus is angry at Jason and Medea's murder of Apsyrtus,
Medea's brother; he ordains that the Argonauts shall return
home only after suffering innumerable calamities, πρό τε μυρία
πημανθέντας (560 f.). We should probably recall how Odysseus
and his men arouse the anger of Poseidon, and of Helios, and so
cause the calamities they will suffer from Poseidon and Zeus.
Odysseus will now return home only ὀψὲ κακῶς (late, with
suffering and humiliation).[29] And yet for a long time hereafter
the relation between the two stories, as regards the return, is
one of unexpected contrast. The Argonauts' progress towards
home is made to seem, in relation to the voyage of Odysseus,
strangely secure. The Argonauts pass through the Odyssean
territory, but with quite different results. The isle of Calypso,
where Odysseus was long detained, is 'far away' from the Argonauts as they pass it (573). The point is made more strongly in
the episode of Circe, to whom Jason and Medea must turn to be
purified from the murder of Apsyrtus. Circe attempts to beguile
the Argonauts as she beguiled the men of Odysseus, but they
withstand (686 ff., cf. *Od.* 10. 230–2). Jason and Medea's sup-
plication of Circe, and Medea's kinship to her, ensure their
safety after she has purified them (743 f.). Before, the pollution
of their act undid the power of Circe's transforming potions.[30]
Apollonius' characters are secure; but here their security is
most disturbing.

Aeolus arranged for the west wind to blow Odysseus home
(*Od.* 10. 17 ff.), but the arrangement ended in calamity when
home was in sight; Aeolus inferred that the gods detested
Odysseus (*Od.* 10. 64, 72 ff.). Hera has Aeolus make the same
arrangement (AR 4. 764 ff.), but there is no calamity. On the

---

[29] Cf. *Od.* 9. 532 ff., 11. 110 ff., 12. 137 ff. For the anger of Poseidon and Helios cf. 1.
68 f., 77, etc., 12. 376 ff., for Zeus' part, 9. 551 ff., 12. 387 f., 415 ff. Note the use of τεκ-
μαίρομαι in AR 4. 559 and in *Od.* 11. 112 = 12. 140.

[30] So her dream implies (665 ff.). αἵματι in 665 is the blood of the murder, αἵματι in
668 is the blood of purification: on the importance of purifying blood by blood cf.
R. C. T. Parker, *Miasma* (1983), 371 ff.

contrary, the west wind sweeps the Argonauts past the Sirens (910 f.), where for Odysseus the δαίμων had produced a sudden calm (*Od.* 12. 168 f.). Divine aid—including the west wind— enables the Argonauts to make a safe return (AR 4. 822) through the Planctae; Odysseus, unaided, had lost his best six men when he followed the alternative path and passed between Scylla and Charybdis. The two paths are contrasted in *Od.* 12. 55 ff., where the Argo and Hera's aid are mentioned explicitly. Apollonius echoes this passage (4. 924 f., cf. *Od.* 12. 59 f., 69; 4. 922, cf. *Od.* 12. 79); and he has Hera refer to the fate actually suffered by Odysseus' crew but avoided by the Argonauts (830 f., cf. *Od.* 12. 245 ff., 11 f.). The Argonauts pass swiftly by the cattle of the Sun (964 ff.), the slaughter of which caused Odysseus' men to lose their return (*Od.* 1. 9, and 12. 419, a tremendous climax). The island, the cattle, and the daughters of the Sun who herd them, are described with a sense of placidity, beauty, and physical separation which the memory of Homer makes haunting.[31]

This relation between the return of Odysseus and the return of the Argonauts is altered abruptly when the Argonauts reach Phaeacia. The trials of Odysseus' travels were to reach an end when he landed on that island (*Od.* 5. 30 ff., cf. 344 f., 386 f.). Apollonius plays at first with the notion of the Argonauts' arriving home. The Phaeacians welcome the Argonauts with delight:

> φαίης κεν ἑοῖς περὶ παισὶ γάνυσθαι.
> καὶ δ᾽ αὐτοὶ ἥρωες ἀνὰ πληθὺν κεχάροντο,
> τῷ ἴκελοι οἷόν τε μεσαιτάτῃ ἐμβεβαῶτες
> Αἱμονίῃ. μέλλον δὲ βοῇ ἔπι θωρήξεσθαι.   (4. 997–1000)

> You would have thought it was their own sons that were making them glad. The heroes themselves rejoiced in their midst; it was as if they had arrived in the middle of their own land Thessaly. But they were shortly to arm for war.

Αἱμονίη 'Thessaly' ends the sentence with force; but immediately, in mid-line, the joy and the play is broken with war and the reappearance of the Colchians on the track of Medea.

Odysseus is transported from Phaeacia to his homeland with

---

[31] For the daughters cf. *Od.* 12. 131 ff., 374 f.

the greatest ease and swiftness: the passage which describes the journey beautifully conjoins these two aspects and contrasts his previous toils (*Od.* 13. 70 ff., 90 ff.). The Argonauts too sail swiftly when they leave Phaeacia, but when the Peloponnese is just appearing to view, a northerly gale sweeps them towards Africa (4. 1228 ff.). The moment recalls most emphatically the moment earlier in the *Odyssey* when Ithaca appears to view and Odysseus' companions untie the bag of winds, so that a gale sweeps them away (*Od.* 10. 29 f., 49 f.).[32] The Argonauts arrive at the desolate shallows of the Syrtis, 'from which ships have no return' (4. 1235 f.). They believe this to be the end of their return home (1272 f., 1275 f.). Their first speech of despair (1251 ff.) recalls very markedly the speech made by Odysseus when he has actually arrived home in Ithaca, though he does not know it (*Od.* 13. 200 ff.). Homer's own humorous play with the actual return has been made serious here: the Argonauts are truly in a foreign land, and their emotion befits the strangest and direst impediment to their homecoming. The weirdness and hopelessness of this new turn is heightened by the inversion of the *Odyssey.*

The use of Odysseus', and Menelaus', travels does not end here. Enough has been said, however, to intimate how through them the idea of return, while strengthening its force still further, becomes now the object of greater play and surprise, and accompanies what is made to feel an odder sequence of voyaging. Strangeness is felt both when the Argonauts' progress seems easy and when it seems hopeless. The poem moves away from the straightforward.

This brings us to the more complicated aspects of the design. Books 1–2, it will be remembered, offer us a series of separate events as the Argonauts voyage to Colchis. Book 3 shows us how in Colchis the king's daughter Medea falls in love with Jason, and is persuaded to use her witchcraft to help him; he thus accomplishes the trials that Aeetes has imposed as an obstacle to the taking of the Fleece. In Book 4 Jason and the Argonauts depart, abducting from the furious Aeetes Medea and the Fleece; the book describes their voyage home, complicated by

---

[32] AR 4. 1231 κατεφαίνετο echoes *Od.* 10. 29 ἀνεφαίνετο, AR 4. 1232 ff. ἀναρπάγδην ... θύελλα ... πελαγόσδε ... φέρ' scatters *Od.* 10. 48 ἁρπάξασα φέρεν πόντονδε θύελλα. Cf. also *Od.* 9. 79–84.

the pursuit of the Colchians and its consequences. Book 4 has obvious affinities with both Book 3 and Books 1–2: it shows a voyage, in a sequence of distinct episodes, and also continues the story of Medea.

The poem deliberately plays on the reader's conception of its unity as it develops. On a first reading Books 1–2 seem far from possessing a tight or radical unity; attempts to eliminate this impression are misguided. The author highlights the discontinuity of his narrative. As for a unity created by themes, the reader is not, on a first reading of these books, given sufficient directive to organize the text into a firm and sustained thematic structure. Certainly it would be unacceptable to take the books (at any reading) as a continuous presentation of the anti-heroic: one would distort many episodes intolerably, for example the battle with the Bebryces (2. 98 ff.) or the passage through the Symplegades (2. 531 ff.). It is retrospectively that the first two books are incorporated into the whole, and that, as a consequence, one sees their narrative as embodying significant and unifying themes. Any kind of literary structure emerges more clearly as the work progresses, but here the concealment is extreme. As one first reads the books, one has the sense of a fairly loose, relaxed cohesion, frequently disrupted; but this impression of them changes when in Book 3 (in particular) one seems to see negated what had there mattered most, and when in Book 4 (in particular) actual incidents from the books are reworked.

Book 3 as we read it appears to join the whole poem into a bold but simple kind of unity through contrast: love, cunning, woman, now have superiority over courage and men. The virile element has of course been much to the fore in the first two books; but it acquires a more distinctive existence now that it forms one side of an antithesis, and not simply an aspect of heroic narrative. We seem to find a unity through pointed reversal and forceful opposition. The radical contrast in ethos is strengthened by a radical contrast in narrative, as disjointedness seemingly gives way to a sweeping continuity. But this relatively simple notion of unity proves in turn to be incomplete, and our impression to have been in some degree misleading.

The fourth book takes both sides of the antithesis between

male and female, valour and guile, and so forth, and causes them to undergo a whole variety of mutations, grim, playful, and fantastic, in a disruptive series of episodes. It reworks not only themes but events and scenes. Through this unresting transformation and distortion the whole poem finally comes to feel strongly and satisfyingly cohesive, in the midst of wild volatility. Furthermore, we now see the whole development of the work, not as a mere series of false leads, but as a pattern aesthetically delightful. Firstly, we have the movement from disjointedness to continuity and then to an extraordinary combination; this movement appears too with ethos and other aspects of the work. Secondly, we have the large progression from the relatively straightforward to the complicated, above all in tone and effect. It is with the fourth book that the great shift takes place; but we should not of course suppose that the earlier books are devoid of play with tone, say, or striking modification of serious elements. Examples enough have appeared already to make that evident. The larger and more drastic complication of the fourth book finds a certain foreshadowing in the lesser complications found earlier in the poem: it is for this reason that the development does not seem mere extrinsic addition. The movement feels satisfying and as it were convincing: but it is none the less startling and exciting for that.

The design suggested might be looked at as an arbitrary imposition on a poem which has simply been constructed without care or forethought. Such a conception does not seem inviting. The artistry and deliberation of Apollonius are apparent at every level. It becomes particularly hard to think him indifferent to his poem as a whole when we consider the numerous and very pointed links that he makes across the work, and the very plain anticipations of themes that appear by retrospect in the first two books. Some of these last will be mentioned at the end; the space available must largely be devoted to elaborating the development of the poem in Books 3 and 4. By doing this we shall give some colour and substance to the scheme baldly outlined.

In considering Book 3, we may look first at Jason, and then at Medea. In this book Jason is first seen making a speech to the Argonauts on a problem which has already presented itself: the best means of tackling King Aeetes, who possesses the Golden

Fleece. Jason suggests that they should try persuasion first, and only then resort to war, or a plan if war is prevented; he stresses that words are often more effective than courage (177 ff.). He thus gives weight to the medium in which he is particularly adept: the reader has been shown the value of Jason's soft, tactful, and persuasive speech. Thus in 2. 620 ff. he puts the morale of his men successfully to the test: one is to contrast the half-comic failure of the parallel attempt by Homer's Agamemnon (*Il.* 2. 110 ff.).[33] Warfare as such is not in the least alien to his nature (cf. e.g. 2. 122 ἀρήϊος ... 'Ιήσων 'warlike Jason', 1. 1032 ff.); but he takes a more prudent attitude to it here than had the valiant Peleus. The Argonauts had lately been joined by the sons of Phrixus (who had been given the hand in marriage of Aeetes' daughter Chalciope, having arrived in Colchis on the Golden Ram). They actually knew Aeetes, and had described his fearsomeness in war (2. 1204 ff.); Peleus had replied with impressive but obviously misplaced confidence that the Argonauts were a match for Aeetes in arms (2. 1219 ff.). Yet persuasion too, as the reader has seen, is most unlikely to succeed with this ferocious personage.[34] Jason's only plausible argument—that Aeetes had been persuaded to treat Phrixus hospitably (3. 190–2)—is later refuted directly (584 ff.). The opposition of words and deeds seems to be leading nowhere.

The actual confrontation with Aeetes appears to be a dismal failure. The tact of Jason is set, as earlier, against the impetuous irascibility of the Argonaut Telamon (cf. 1. 1289 ff., 1336 ff.). Telamon would answer Aeetes' fury with fury, but Jason answers with soft words (3. 382 ff.). The softness is stressed again at the end of his speech:

ἴσκεν ὑποσσαίνων ἀγανῇ ὀπί. (396)

He spoke fawning insidiously with gentle voice.

But the softness has no effect on the Oriental tyrant. Aeetes lays down seemingly impossible tasks which are to be accomplished before the Fleece can be taken. Jason despairs, and eventually accepts in a spirit of hopeless pessimism (422 ff.). His feelings

---

[33] Cf. also 1. 294, 494, 1336, *al.* Softness of speech is in question with Aeetes, as appears from 2. 1279, 3. 15, and the encounter itself.

[34] Note 2. 1197, 1202 f. (the sons of Phrixus), 3. 14 ff. (Hera).

are made quite clear by the phrase after the speech, ἀμηχανίη
βεβολημένος 'stricken with despair' (432), by the account he
later gives to the other Argonauts, and by their depressed reaction, which answers his own (502 ff.).[35] He closes his speech
to the Argonauts:

> ὃ δή νύ οἱ—οὔ τι γὰρ ἄλλο
> βέλτερον ἦν φράσσασθαι—ἀπηλεγέως ὑποέστην.
>
> (500 f.)

These trials of Aeetes'—there was no better course one
could think of—I engaged firmly to undertake.

The parenthesis expressively undercuts any appearance of
heroism in the statement or the action. Peleus, on the other
hand, asserts boldly—but not tactlessly—that he would be
ready to take on the trials himself. He closes saying that the
worst that will befall him is merely death (514). He thus transposes into the mode of magnificence Jason's declaration to
Aeetes: Jason will endure the trials

> εἰ καί μοι θανέειν μόρος. οὐ γὰρ ἔτ' ἄλλο
> ῥίγιον ἀνθρώποισι κακῆς ἐπίκειται ἀνάγκης.
>
> (429 f.)

as it seems in truth my fate to die. Loathsome necessity is
the most terrible thing that weighs on mortal men.

The pessimism and bitter gloom are very characteristic.[36]
Jason's attitude is in no respect contemptible or low-spirited.
Yet the contrast with Peleus must be intended, as in the scene
after Tiphys' death (pp. 98 f.), to show Jason as not achieving
the highest boldness. The contrast both enhances the pathos of
his present situation, and tinges it with a suspicion of humour.
Here, however, Peleus' vigour is misguided. He emphatically

---

[35] κερδαλέοισι in 426 remains problematic: Hom. *Il.* 10. 44 hardly helps. If the text is
sound, Apollonius might possibly intend the sense 'tactful', having in mind *Od.* 6. 148.
σμερδαλέοις 433 would be a possible source of corruption.

[36] L's ἐπικείσετ' cannot be right in 430: Vian's interpretation (*Studi in on. di A.
Ardizzoni* (1978), ii. 1032) does not fit ἀνθρώποισι. But even his interpretation does not,
as he suggests, make Jason as heroic as Peleus, and eliminate the contrast. At the opposite extreme to Vian's view of Jason stands G. Lawall's depiction of him as an 'anti-
hero', *YCS* 19 (1966), 121 ff. For further bibliography on Jason's character see Herter,
RE Supp. XIII (1973), 35 ff., add T. M. Klein, *QU* 13 (1983) 115 ff.; other works are
mentioned below.

exalts κάρτεϊ χειρῶν 'the might of our hands' against βουλῆς 'planning, deliberation' (506 f.). κάρτος 'might' has been of great significance in the first two books. The statement here echoes particularly closely 2. 333 f.: there the prophet Phineus declares that, as the Argonauts encounter the Clashing Rocks, even prayer will be of less value than 'the might of your hands'.[37] But here physical strength will be unavailing, as the poet has already made clear. Apollonius also pointedly models Peleus' volunteering on the rash volunteering of Menelaus to fight Hector (*Il.* 7. 92 ff.). Again as in the scene following Tiphys' death (and as in Homer), there are now other volunteers, inspired by passion (Telamon), self-confidence (Idas), and valour (Meleager). The poet is stressing as firmly as possible the idea of physical power, and so marking the altered situation. Neither tact nor might appears to be of the slightest use.

Yet, while Jason's gloomy interpretation of the meeting with Aeetes seems obviously just, and is indeed more appropriate than the attitudes of Peleus, nonetheless that interpretation is quite wrong. The crucial event of that scene naturally escaped him, that is, his effect on the king's daughter Medea. The poet, however, gives it the greatest emphasis. The extended description of Eros' shooting of Medea and her falling in love with Jason is placed directly after the entry of Aeetes (275 ff.); directly after the colloquy with Aeetes the impact of Jason on Medea is described at length (439 ff.). The framing stresses the importance, now, of the element which Jason does not perceive; and the juxtaposition of apparent failure with real success emphasizes the change that is taking place in the poem. Medea is overcome, not only by the appearance of Jason, but by Jason's αὐδή τε μῦθοί τε μελίφρονες οὓς ἀγόρευσεν (458) 'his voice and the sweet words he spoke'. These win her as they so failed to win Aeetes, at whom they were aimed.

The strangeness of the significance acquired by a woman, and by love, is brought out in a different mode through the dialogue that follows. As the party walks back from Aeetes' palace,

---

[37] 2. 333 f. οὐ ... ὅσον τ᾿ ἐνὶ κάρτεϊ χειρῶν, 3. 506 f. οὐ ... ὅσον τ᾿ ἐπὶ κάρτεϊ χειρῶν. 2. 335 is taken up in the incident itself, the passage through the Symplegades, 2. 559 κάρτεϊ ᾧ πίσυνοι. Note also κάρτεϊ χειρῶν at 1. 1162, of Heracles, the supreme exemplar of vigour and might in the poem.

Argus the son of Phrixus—who had been made to show the truth about Aeetes in advance—now raises the notion of Medea's aid. He begins with the crucial word μῆτις 'cunning plan' (475). He deprecates Jason's disapproval, which Jason actually goes on to voice:

$$μελέη γε μὲν ἧμιν ὄρωρεν$$
$$ἐλπωρὴ ὅτε νόστον ἐπετραπόμεσθα γυναιξίν. \qquad (487\,f.)$$

But it is a wretched hope indeed, entrusting our return to women.

The contemptuous γυναιξίν 'women' closes Jason's reply; the word is set in forceful opposition to the resonant νόστον 'return'. The idea seems as unlikely to Jason as to anyone.[38]

Argus raises the suggestion more forcefully in the general debate, after several Argonauts have volunteered to take Jason's place (see above). This arrangement opposes Argus' speech to the positive desire of those heroes to undertake the trials (522). Response is prevented by an omen, which the seer Mopsus interprets. He refers back to the prophecy of Phineus that their return would depend on the goddess Aphrodite, θεῇ ἐνὶ Κυπρίδι νόστον ... ἔσσεσθαι (549 f.). In Phineus' original speech it had been the accomplishment of the trials that so depended, ἐν γὰρ τῇ κλυτὰ πείρατα κεῖται ἀέθλων (2. 424).[39] With the new wording the poet provides an explicit answer to Jason's dismissal quoted above. It is the recollection of Phineus that determines the Argonauts (3. 555 f.): an event earlier in the poem is not only bound up with this moment but causes it. There is also a connection with an earlier occasion when the Argonauts remembered the bidding of Phineus: they accordingly employed μῆτις 'a cunning plan' in dealing with the birds of Ares.[40] That episode in a sense blurs the antithesis between the first two books and the third (it comes near the end of the

---

[38] 485, where αὐτῷ is important, shows that Jason is not rejecting an attractive offer through moral scruples (thus Campbell, *Studies*, 35).

[39] Reading ἀέθλων with the MSS, not ἀέθλου with Sch. 3. 946a.

[40] μῆτι παντοίῃ at 3. 548 echoes the use of the same phrase by Phineus at 2. 383; cf. also 3. 555 f. with 2. 1051. Compare too 3. 183 f. εἴτε τις ἄλλη | μῆτις ἐπίρροθος ἔσται (looking forward to the present μῆτις for us) with 2. 1049 f. ἀλλά τιν' ἄλλην | μῆτιν πορσύνωμεν ἐπίρροθον.

second); yet in a sense it sharpens it. There the μῆτις was still related to warfare (they used their shields) and was justified by the action of Heracles himself in a very similar situation (2. 1052 ff.). Quite different is the total reversal here.

Prophecy and omen do not persuade the impious Idas. Jason has a number of foils in the poem, who arouse very different responses.[41] The valiant Peleus always awakes admiration; Telamon's rash but generous wrath is more ambivalent; Idas, rough and blasphemously self-confident, appears in a bad light when he conflicts with Jason. He speaks here μεγάλῃ ὀπί 'in a loud voice' (3. 557); the phrase recalls to us his abuse of Jason before the start of the expedition as a whole (1. 462). His scorn for omens and prophets recalls his treatment of the seer Idmon in the ensuing altercation (1. 487 ff.). This character is particularly well suited to bring out the extremity of the change for these men.

> ὦ πόποι, ἦ ῥα γυναιξὶν ὁμόστολοι ἐνθάδ' ἔβημεν,
> οἳ Κύπριν καλέουσιν ἐπίρροθον ἄμμι πέλεσθαι,
> οὐκέτ' Ἐννυαλίοιο μέγα σθένος.   (558–60)

Oh shame! We have sailed here, it seems, with women, who call on Aphrodite to be our helper instead of the mighty Ares.

The feeling of the utterance strengthens the irony and surprise of its pregnant statement on the gods. With Idas' crude application of the word 'women', Jason's earlier attitude (487 f., see above) is transposed into another mode, as with Peleus. Idas' speech also reminds us of Heracles' speech when Jason is postponing the expedition for pleasure with Hypsipyle (1. 865 ff.): there love, and Aphrodite, were indeed a diversion from the expedition, not its salvation. Although the folly and crudity of Idas is made clear to the reader, he represents a true element in the feeling, and nature, of his fellows. Many murmur, as after his speech in Book 1 (1. 474, cf. 3. 564), but all are too ashamed to oppose out loud his decrying of the feminine (3. 565). Jason astutely ignores Idas' speech, but suggests another action which

---

[41] A point not properly noticed in Fränkel's discussion of Idas (*MH* 17 (1960), 1 ff.).

will show that the Argonauts are not afraid of war (571). He thus overmasters and acknowledges the values innate in these heroes.

Jason, though a tactful leader, had never been in the earlier books supremely and uniquely well fitted to save the expedition. His various foils had made his limitations clear, and we had been drawn to view him with subtle and shifting combinations of sympathy and amusement, admiration and pity, liking and bewilderment. Here, in this special and surprising situation, he is indeed so fitted. This is partly because of his beauty. Before he meets Medea, Hera so enhances it that he excels all heroes that have ever been—in this respect (3. 919 ff.). He approaches Medea like the star Sirius (956 ff.). The passage recalls the comparison of Jason to a star at 1. 774 ff., when he approaches the palace of Hypsipyle;[42] but here his beauty will save, not delay, the expedition. The simile here echoes Hom. *Il.* 22. 25 ff., where Achilles approaches Hector, not only in order to suggest the destructiveness of Jason's charms (3. 959), but also to stress by contrast with the *Iliad* the unmartial nature of the crucial event.

No less important than beauty, however, is the very tact, softness, and shrewdness that were so unsuccessful when applied directly against the antagonist. Hera, in the passage mentioned, makes Jason still more attractive 'both to look at face to face and also to speak with', ἠμὲν ἐσάντα ἰδεῖν ἠδὲ προτιμυθήσασθαι (923). By the end of the interview Medea delights ὁμῶς μορφῆ τε καὶ αἱμυλίοισι λόγοισιν 'in his beauty and his cunning words alike' (1141). αἱμυλίοισι ('cunning', almost 'wily') is a striking word to use, particularly since Jason has now fallen in love with Medea himself. The moment of his falling in love (1077 f.) does not affect the continuity and the control with which he manipulates Medea's emotions. His strategy is emphasized throughout. He perceives at once that Medea is in love with him, and begins speaking ὑποσσαίνων (974) 'fawning insidiously', the same word that was used when he spoke with Aeetes (396). In this speech he suggests the possibility of love only obliquely, with the parallel of Ariadne's help for Theseus, which he mentions formally for a different reason.

---

[42] Campbell notes the connection, *Studies*, 61.

Even after he has fallen in love, and Medea has pointedly asked him to elaborate on the story of Ariadne, he carefully dwells at great length on the history of his homeland, casually slipping onto the story of Ariadne at the end, and stopping short of an explicit statement of his wish for her hand (1097 ff.). In his words he is 'caressing' her with the 'gentleness' so characteristic of his speech (1102). His control of his feelings leads Medea into a passionate vehemence (1105 ff.); he can then reassure the emotion he has drawn forth, and proceed to promise marriage and love until death. While Medea returns home unconscious of her surroundings and oblivious of her sister, Jason unfolds to his companions the success of his diplomacy. Idas, and he alone, is overcome with rage at the triumph of Jason through love (1169 f.).

Jason's accomplishment of the trials imposed by Aeetes is presented as a splendid heroic deed, which yet is only made possible through Medea's witchcraft. Love has produced an act of prowess that prowess itself could not produce. Thus in the last part of Book 3, the two contrasted elements appear to be brought together and married, though uneasily; this seems to seal the unity which Book 3 has apparently imparted to the poem. The diverging aspects of the splendour of the deed and its dependence on Medea are held in balance by the structure. In order to secure the aid of magic, Jason (in Apollonius' account) must perform a nocturnal rite which will win the favour of Hecate. This impressive event is given great weight. Medea describes the procedure fully (1026 ff.), the happening itself is recounted at some length (1191 ff.), and the narrative of the trials is made to follow on immediately. The element of magic is thus as firmly implanted in our minds as possible; and the account of the preliminaries to the trials at first strengthens the suggestion. Aeetes arms himself; his spear, we are told, no Argonaut could have withstood save Heracles, whom the Argonauts had left behind in Mysia (1232 ff.). Aeetes had made it clear that to perform the tasks Jason would need to be the equal of himself (403, 420 f., 437 f.); what is said here indicates very forcibly that none of the Argonauts is in fact Aeetes' equal. The force lies in the role of Heracles in the first two books, to which the mention of the desertion refers us back explicitly (the incident is narrated at 1. 1273 ff.). Heracles had been presented as

the 'best' of the Argonauts, and, in particular, as better than
Jason.[43]

The description of the magnificent Aeetes arming and arriving is matched by an account of Jason. It starts:

τόφρα δὲ Μηδείης ὑποθημοσύνῃσιν Ἰήσων
φάρμακα μυδήνας ἠμὲν σάκος ἀμφεπάλυνεν
ἠδὲ δόρυ βριαρόν, περὶ δὲ ξίφος.   (1246–8)

Then, following Medea's instructions, Jason moistened
the magic drugs and sprinkled, all over, his shield, his
weighty spear, and his sword.

Medea's name begins. The sentence proceeds to present the
magic, and closes with the weapons; the series of weapons has a
very different ring in such a context to the grandiose series in
Aeetes' heroic scene of arming (1225 ff.). This series is un-
glamorously brief; the epithet 'weighty', with its Homeric air,
deftly enhances the distortion. Idas, raging once more,
attempts to break Jason's now unbreakable spear (1252 ff.). His
appearance, following shortly on his appearance in 1169 f., reminds us of the detestation for the means of love which he
embodies, while the incident sets his principles in a ludicrous
light. Jason then anoints himself and ἀλκή 'valour, might'
enters him (1256 f.). On the one hand this reminds us of heroes
in the *Iliad* (cf. especially 17. 210 ff.); on the other, the passage
recalls what Medea predicted at 3. 1043 ff., and so stresses still
further the source of the effect. From this point on the presentation of Jason's actions becomes as resplendent and heroic as
possible. But it will by now be clear that we cannot simply forget the stress on Medea and magic while we read on,[44] the less
so when the narrative has been prefigured in Medea's advice
(1047 ff.). Rather, the memory of what has preceded must
colour our reading of what follows. At the same time, the movement of emphasis allows the element of glory to have its place
(within the limits prescribed to it).

Various features are used to emphasize the heroic in this

---

[43] For the former aspect cf. 1. 338 ff., 1158 ff., 1285 f., and also 2. 145 ff. (a striking
moment); note too 2. 774 f. For the latter cf. 1. 341 ff., 1290 ff. Valerius Flaccus, as suits
his portrayal of Jason, wishes to draw him and Hercules together: cf. 7. 623 f.; 8. 125 f.,
230 f.

[44] So it might be inferred from Campbell, *Studies*, 78.

passage. The extraordinary number of similes produces a kind of hyper-Iliadic effect.[45] Especially significant among the similes is the comparison of Jason rushing on the Earth-born men to an ascending star (1377 ff.): this both recalls, and contrasts with, the comparison of Jason to a star when he approached Medea (956 ff., see above). Another prominent aspect of the passage is the recurrence of the word Ἄρης (the god of war, and war itself). Ares had been presented in opposition to Aphrodite by Idas (559 f., see above), and is of course particularly well suited to convey the martial quality of the action. When Jason advances to the trials, he is

$$\text{ἄλλα μὲν Ἄρει}$$
$$\text{εἴκελος, ἄλλα δέ που χρυσαόρῳ Ἀπόλλωνι.} \qquad (1282 \text{ f.})$$

in some regards like Ares, in others not unlike Apollo of the golden sword.

Jason is shown, with elegant deliberation, to appear outstanding in both youthful beauty and martial power. When he advanced to begin the whole expedition, he had been compared only to the beautiful Apollo (1. 307 ff.).[46] Other mentions of Ares are deliberately heightened. At 1357 Ἄρεος τέμενος φθισιμβρότου 'the sacred land of Ares, slayer of men', the epithet reminds us pointedly of the destructive deity. At 1366 δεινὸν Ἐνυαλίου σόλον Ἄρεος 'a terrible throwing-weight of Enyalius Ares' (of the rock which Jason throws), the addition of the title Enyalius prevents us from seeing the name as merely metonymous for 'war'. Even where the stem is indeed wholly metonymous, the stress on war makes the action seem more glorious. Homer had compared Paris and Hector coming to battle with a horse on the meadow (*Il.* 6. 507 ff. = 15. 263 ff.); Apollonius adapts the simile for Jason coming to the trials, but makes the horse ἀρήϊος ἵππος, ἐελδόμενος πολέμοιο 'a war-horse longing for battle' (1259). A simile from the *Iliad* is now made not less but more warlike. It is at this point that the change of

---

[45] C. R. Beye stresses the number of similes, *GRBS* 10 (1969), 150. Several of them are discussed by Campbell, *Studies,*.78.

[46] The passages are linked by a common association with Pind. *Pyth.* 4. 87 f. There Jason is compared to Apollo and Ares, but the comparison is made at the beginning of the story. It seems excessively reductive to limit the point of comparison with Ares to Jason's equipment, and this does not really suit the phrasing (cf. Vian ii. 104 n. 2).

atmosphere in the narrative begins: the use of the *Iliad* holds great significance.

In the earlier part of the book Apollonius often distorts Iliadic imagery and language to apply to love rather than war. In this way he elegantly heightens the reversal that has occurred in the poem.[47] The centre of this distortion is Medea (to whom we now turn). A resonant instance is 761 ff.:

$$\text{ἔνδοθι δ' αἰεὶ}$$
τεῖρ' ὀδύνη, σμύχουσα διὰ χροὸς ἀμφί τ' ἀραιὰς
ἶνας καὶ κεφαλῆς ὑπὸ νείατον ἰνίον ἄχρις,
ἔνθ' ἀλεγεινότατον δύνει ἄχος, ὁππότ' ἀνίας
ἀκάματοι πραπίδεσσιν ἐνισκίμψωσιν Ἔρωτες.

Within her, a pain was oppressing her continually. It smouldered, through her skin, about her fine sinews, right up to beneath the base of her skull—that is where the pain enters at its most agonizing, whenever the tireless Erotes press anguish upon the spirit.

The description is closely linked to an erotic tradition; but it is full of echoes of the *Iliad*.[48] Its anatomical precision at once pushes the physicality of the erotic tradition to an extreme, and piquantly recalls Homer's description of a wound: 'he struck him between the genitals and the navel; that is where 'Ares' (i.e. a wound in war) is most painful to wretched mortals'— ἔνθα μάλιστα | γίνετ' Ἄρης ἀλεγεινὸς ὀϊζυροῖσι βροτοῖσιν (*Il.* 13. 568 f.). The Erotes significantly take the place of Ares. Again, the arrow with which Eros shoots Medea (279) resembles arrows in the *Iliad*: it too has not been used before and brings much distress (πολύστονον), in a different fashion.[49] Examples of such reworking could readily be multiplied.

Memorable scenes in the *Iliad* are also reworked. Medea spends a sleepless night in her anxiety for the man she loves (744 ff.). Although there are other Homeric models, the whole

---

[47] On love in the work cf. G. Zanker, *WS* NF 13 (1979), 52 ff. He does not see that it is first with Book 3 that love really comes to be felt as a theme in the work. One finds a little exaggerated his contention that love had no importance in earlier epic. Even in the *Iliad*, love for Briseis is a crucial element in Achilles' feelings (cf. especially 9. 336–43).

[48] For the tradition cf. Sappho fr. 31. 9f. Voigt, Theocr. 3. 17, etc.; for the echoes, see Campbell, *Echoes and Imitations of Early Epic in AR* (1981), 54 (he does not mention *Iliad* 13).

[49] Cf. e.g. Vian's note (ii. 121).

structure of the section 751–60 and much of its phrasing recall *Il.* 10. 3–10.[50] There Homer (or a later archaic poet) describes the sleepless night spent by Agamemnon as he fears for the destruction of his host. The contrast in ethos is marked; Apollonius substitutes for the grandiose imagery of the *Iliad* (thunder, storm, and snow from Zeus, 10. 5 ff.) a much homelier simile (sunlight in a household vessel, 756 ff.). There follows the passage on the pains of love that we have just considered. When Medea's elder sister Chalciope sees her weeping through the dilemma of her passion, she asks the cause. Is it some illness? Has Medea learnt of some rebuke to Chalciope and her children from their father (674 ff.)? This reminds us of Achilles' similar speech when he sees Patroclus weeping at the plight of the Greek army (*Il.* 16. 7 ff.). The cause of Medea's sorrow is not so grand, and there is a further irony. Chalciope's tone is highly agitated, but Achilles mocks Patroclus, comparing him to a little girl pestering her mother (he satirizes their relationship). Now Achilles adopts this tone because he knows that Patroclus is weeping for the disaster which Achilles himself is causing.[51] None the less, it is effective that the tears scorned as feminine in the martial epic should be regarded with such extreme earnestness in the feminine situation here. The difference in tone embodies the difference in ethos.

It was another aspect of the change in the poem, we saw, that the Argonauts should now win success not by strength but by trickery. The term δόλος 'trickery, trick' is closely linked in this connection with the more favourable term μῆτις 'cleverness, plan' (cf. pp. 110 f.). In this book both ideas find a centre in Medea, but her various associations with trickery are particularly important. Medea the witch has trickery and cunning to some degree by nature. Jason deals with the Earth-born men by the instructions of Μηδείης πολυκερδέος 'cunning Medea' (1364). Hera maintaining that with Medea's help Jason will easily take the Fleece, and return home: ἐπεὶ δολόεσσα τέτυκται (89) 'for Medea is full of trickery'. But it is love that brings this

---

[50] One must reject Fränkel's transposition of 761–5 to follow 754: cf. H. Erbse, *Ausgew. Schr.* 464 ff. However, a full stop should not be placed after ἔθυιεν with Vian: the asyndeton is most displeasing. The simile in part takes up πυκνά (755), cf. *Il.* 10. 9.

[51] Patroclus has been sent to the other Greeks (*Il.* 11. 602 ff.), and their distress— which Achilles mentions last—would be the most obvious reason for his tears.

element to a higher pitch. Love makes the modest girl capable of trickery so dangerous and so contrary to her natural feeling as the deceit of her formidable parent. And through love she is not only the agent but the vehicle and object of trickery and cunning. In the speech of Hera just referred to the Argonauts' return home is strikingly connected with trickery, but not Medea's alone. Hera is speaking to Aphrodite, whose aid she and Athena have come to seek. She begins that speech:

οὔτι βίης χατέουσαι ἱκάνομεν οὐδέ τι χειρῶν.   (84)

It is not in any need of might that we come, or the strength of hands.

In this delicate encounter she naturally does not call it a trick that she requires from Aphrodite; but in her earlier conversation with Athena the plan of making Medea fall in love has been considered in just such terms (δόλον 'trick', 12, 20). Here the opposition with physical strength is striking, and shows the antithesis at work on the level of the gods. It was the 'help through trickery of the goddess Aphrodite' that Phineus bade the Argonauts seek, θεᾶς δολόεσσαν ἀρωγὴν | Κύπριδος (2. 423): θεᾶς 'goddess' makes it clear that this is no metonymy. Aphrodite and Eros are conventionally styled 'full of trickery' or the like; in the present episode this character is gently suggested even in their handling of other divinities (51, 130).[52]

The impact of love on Medea's behaviour is seen strikingly in her dialogue with her sister. When Chalciope asks her why she is crying, Medea is for a long time held back from speaking by αἰδὼς παρθενίη 'her maiden's modesty and sense of shame' (681 f.).

ὀψὲ δ' ἔειπεν
τοῖα δόλῳ, θρασέες γὰρ ἐπικλονέεσκον Ἔρωτες.   (686 f.)

But at last she spoke as follows, with trickery and deceit, for the bold Erotes were forcing her on.

The trickery is part of the effect of love, as the word-order

<hr />

[52] Cf. e.g. Sapph. fr. 1. 2, Thgn. 1386, Simon. fr. 575. 1, Bacch. 17. 116, Eur. *IA* 1300, Plat. *Smp.* 205 D (poetic quotation?), Theocr. 30. 25. The scene is discussed by P. G. Lennox, *Hermes*, 108 (1980), 45 ff.

suggests.[53] Although Medea is still filled with emotion, she
controls her feelings and cunningly manipulates her sister's.
She pretends that her concern is only for her sister and her sister's sons (the sons of Phrixus), who have cast their lot in with
the Argonauts. She brings Chalciope to suggest that she,
Medea, should devise for Jason 'some trick or plan', ἢ δόλον ἤ
τινα μῆτιν (720). The two levels of trickery, the deceit which
Medea is now practising on Chalciope, and the deceit which
Medea is going to perform for Jason, again lend richness and a
certain irony to the theme. Medea's handling of Chalciope, in
turn, decidedly resembles Jason's handling of Medea, although
that is cunning rather than deceitful (Idas regards it as deceitful, 563). Like Jason, Medea draws forth a wild and threaten-
ing expression of emotion, which she then placates.

> δαιμονίη, ... οἷ' ἀγορεύεις,
> ἀράς τε στυγερὰς καὶ Ἐρινύας.　　　　　　　　　(711 f.)

My good sister, ... what talk, of terrible curses and
Erinyes!

She mocks and reuses Chalciope's own words (704), with an air
of surprised good sense. Jason will deploy the same technique,
still more smoothly (1120 f., cf. 1114 and 1112). Love gives
Medea weapons, but utterly disarms her to the man she loves
(Jason retains the finer weapons he always possessed).

The point is stressed further by the speech Medea makes to
her maidservants while waiting for Jason. She pretends to them
that she is deceiving both Chalciope and Jason, and extracting
presents which she will share with the maids if they keep her
secret (902 ff.). They are delighted with the deceitful plan
(ἐπίκλοπος ... μῆτις, 912); but Medea is actually tricking them.
This elaborate complex of deceit is contrasted with Medea's
part in the next conversation. And we know that she will not, as
she claims to the maids, be tricking presents from Jason, and
then giving him a fatal drug (910 f.). She gives him the drug
which will preserve him, and she would gladly have given him
all her life and soul as well (1015 f.).

The interweaving of different strands of trickery and

---

[53] For the thought cf. e.g. Call. fr. 67. 1 ff.: Eros instructed Acontius, who was not
wily by nature (πολύκροτος).

cunning becomes particularly elaborate and forceful in relation to Aeetes himself. He is the primary object of deceit for the Argonauts. After the embassy has left him, and the Argonauts have decided to approach Medea, Aeetes holds an assembly of the Colchians (576 ff., see pp. 91 f.). He, who has the better of the Argonauts in force, suddenly plans treachery against them (δόλους, 578). He suspects them of 'secret trickery' against himself (592); in fact this will now be true, although the tyrant's suspicion is unduly inflammable. The real danger, however, to this powerful ruler comes from an utterly unexpected source. A prophecy of his father Helios has actually warned him to beware 'the crafty trickery, the plans, and the ruinous cunning of his own family', πυκινόν τε δόλον βουλάς τε γενεθλῆς | σφωϊτέρης ἄτην τε πολύτροπον (599 f.).[54] Yet he is not, he says, in the least afraid of his daughters (602 ff.). It is the sons of Chalciope and the Greek Phrixus that he fears. But his own daughter, a girl, will defeat him, prompted by love.

A few lines later, indeed, we learn that Chalciope, his other daughter, had been planning to enlist Medea's aid before her son approached her on the Argonauts' behalf. The language points the irony of Aeetes' suppositions (μητιάασκε (612) 'was planning', μῆτιν (603) 'plan'). But fear of her father's wrath had restrained her. Medea herself, when she has agreed to devise 'some trick or plan' for Jason (ἢ δόλον ἤ τινα μῆτιν, 720), feels the strongest terror of Aeetes.

τίς δὲ δόλος, τίς μῆτις ἐπίκλοπος ἔσσετ' ἀρωγῆς;   (781)

What trick, what plan, could conceal my aid from him?

The question hovers between hopelessness and pondering; the heightened language stresses her emotion. The fear and shame of Medea are much emphasized throughout; the violent fluctuations of her monologues and her actions convey dramatically the strangeness of Medea's all-important intervention, the foreignness of the behaviour exacted by love.

The figure of Medea, then, is used to express and embody the great movement in the work. In 616–912 our attention is

---

[54] The device of the prophecy lends weight to the fact and increases its surprise. A somewhat different oracle had appeared in Herodorus (*FGrH* 31 F 9). Cf. A. C. Pearson, *The Fragments of Sophocles* (1917), ii. 15.

focused primarily on her, not on the Argonauts, and so sustained and intense a diversion of interest has a striking effect after the first two books. The most salient movement of scene away from the Argonauts had been the mere fifty-six lines describing Hypsipyle's assembly (1. 653–708). That movement had strengthened the feeling that the dalliance in Lemnos was an interruption of the expedition. Here the sense of diversion stresses the opposite point: the most important thing for the expedition is now—of all things—the emotions of a girl. I do not at all imply that we are not interested in Medea from her own point of view. On the contrary, the two viewpoints interact, with pointed and poignant results; we have seen several instances of this, the most forceful perhaps in the scene with Medea and Jason alone. Indeed, there the poet even plays with our interest in the two aspects of his narrative. The long speech in which Medea instructs Jason how to succeed in the trials (1026 ff.) is of central importance in the story of the expedition. Yet it is not mere romanticism to feel it as something of an interruption to the story of Medea's passion. The dry tone stands apart very sharply from the warmth of what precedes, and the sudden faltering at the very end (1061 f.) must stir and almost please us. But the poet is able to sport with us in this way precisely because he is so conscious of the pregnant interrelations and conflicts which his design has evoked from his material.

The fourth book will be best considered by surveying most of its episodes in turn. This book, like the third, begins with an invocation of the Muse; the second book has no invocation, and follows on very smoothly from the first; the first has a prelude of a different kind.[55] The invocation of the fourth book is not logically on a level with the invocation of the third;[56] formally, however, the two invocations are felt as parallel, and reinforce the structure of the work. They mark out very plainly the division between each of the last two books and all that precedes it. In manner the prelude to Book 4 well suits its book.

---

[55] The division of books is discussed by Campbell, *Mnemosyne*, 4th ser. 36 (1983), 154 f., somewhat cursorily perhaps.

[56] That in the third strictly covers the action of the next two books, that in the fourth only a small part of the action in that book. Cf. H. Faerber, *Zur dichterischen Kunst in ARs Arg.* (Diss. Berlin 1928), 89.

Now that Jason has succeeded, Medea's position is perilous, and she must make terrible choices. The poet opens by bidding the Muse tell of Medea's suffering and her plans; but he proceeds at once to his own mental uncertainties. Should he tell of her anguish or her flight?[57] His mind whirls round within him in speechless bewilderment (ἔμοιγε | ἀμφασίῃ νόος ἔνδον ἑλίσσεται, 2 f.). The intensity of the opening is dissolved as the poet makes his own emotion a ludicrous parody of his character's.

The first event in the book is Medea's flight from her home to the Argonauts. The passage looks back to the third book, especially to 3. 744–824, where Medea ponders her course of action, and decides not to kill herself, but to help Jason. That moment has led to this. The broad pace of that passage is changed for a suitably rapid tempo. There Medea did not see how she would prevent Aeetes' knowing of her help (3. 779 ff.); now he realizes (4. 9 f., 14 f.), and Medea is terrified. Suicide is again envisaged (4. 20 f., a mere two lines). Hera's control of Medea's emotions is emphasized much more bluntly now (4. 11, 22; contrast 3. 818); this emphasis makes the pathos starker. Medea must now leave the whole world of her maiden's life (4. 28 ff.): it was the thought of that which had earlier kept her from suicide (3. 813 f.).[58] Then she wished she had died before seeing Jason (3. 773 ff.); now, with great bitterness, she wishes that Jason had died before reaching Colchis (4. 32 f.). A simile intensifies the poignancy of Medea's experience, and hints that her troubles have only begun (37 ff.). The episode conveys, with impetuous force, the suffering which now results from Medea's passion. The third book had looked forward to this (3. 836 f., *al.*), but the event is left for the fourth. Its form was chosen or invented by Apollonius.[59]

Yet the poet suddenly distances the pathos and the excitement: he introduces a malicious speech by the Moon (57 ff.). The witch Medea has often for her own purposes frustrated the Moon's visits to her beloved Endymion with her charms of trickery (δολίῃσιν ἀοιδαῖς). The Moon rejoices in the suffering

[57] The lines are now commonly referred to Medea's motivation; but this seems implausible Greek. Maas's μὲν for μιν seems desirable.
[58] It has ironic significance that in 3. 948 ff. the delights of a girl's life fail to interest Medea as she waits for Jason.
[59] Cf. Sch. 4. 66, 86: Medea did not make her solitary flight in the *Naupactica* (frr. 7–8 Kink.) or Herodorus (*FGrH* 31 F 53).

Medea will endure. It is a wonderful moment. The novel perspective is stunning, and ingenious; there is delectable piquancy in the past discomfiture of the goddess and in her present unexalted emotion. The sentence that introduces the Moon is so arranged as to heighten the bizarreness and the surprise.

τὴν δὲ νέον Τιτηνὶς ἀνερχομένη περάτηθεν
φοιταλέην ἐσιδοῦσα θεὰ ἐπεχήρατο Μήνη
ἁρπαλέως.   (53–6)

The Titaness, rising newly from the horizon, the goddess Selene, saw Medea's roaming and snatched greedily her malicious pleasure.

The poet has wildly disrupted a tragic development with a deliciously fantastic and unserious intrusion.[60]

The capture of the Golden Fleece, which Medea promises to the Argonauts, naturally belongs with the performance of the trials; Apollonius strengthens the parallelism of the two deeds. Yet they are divided by the end of Book 3, and the parallels only bring out the differences. In both events the magic of Medea is essential: her invocation of Hecate in 4.147 f. recalls that in 3. 862.[61] The trials take place in the field, the capture in the grove, of Ares (the connection is brought out at 2. 1268 f.). Here the name makes a forceful appearance when the deed is accomplished (4. 166).[62] But there is no manly action here; Jason does not even kill the serpent that guards the Fleece.[63] All depends on Medea. She makes the spell, elaborately evoked by the poet;

[60] Critics either think the absurdity unintended (thus Wilamowitz, *HD* ii. 213 n. 3) or non-existent (thus A. Hurst, *AR: Manière et cohérence* (1967), 104; Fränkel, *Noten*, 459: the passage is intended to further the reader's emotional involvement!). Zanker (n. 47), 64, thinks the passage 'curious'; Fusillo, *Il tempo delle Arg.* (1985), 43 f., is more sympathetic.

[61] νυκτιπόλον χθονίην appears in both places. The *Naupactica* certainly, and Herodorus probably, seem to have eschewed here the witchery of Medea; note also perhaps the absence of Medea from *ARV²* 524. 28. For the other version cf. Pind. *Pyth.* 4. 249, Eur. *Med.* 482.

[62] The Fleece lay in the grove of Zeus, according to Pherecydes (*FGrH* 4 F 129). It is perhaps notable that Sch. 2. 404–5a mentions no authority of the grove of Ares, given the second sentence of the scholion. But cf. Jacoby's note on Pherecydes, loc. cit. The *Naupactica* had a different version again (fr. 9).

[63] Apollonius chooses to follow Antimachus, fr. 63 Wyss (Sch. 4. 156–66a); the serpent is killed by Jason in Pind. *Pyth* 4. 249, Pherecydes, *FGrH* 3 F 31, Herodorus, *FGrH* 31 F 52.

εἵπετο δ' Αἰσονίδης πεφοβημένος.   (149)

Jason was with her, terrified.

The brevity is inglorious. At last Jason takes the Fleece, κούρης
κεκλομένης (163) 'at the girl's bidding': the appended clause
makes her the decisive figure. Valour and female craft are no
longer permitted to coalesce, as in the triumph at the end of the
third book.

Jason's speech to the Argonauts on his return contains a
weightier paradox than he intends:

ἤδη γὰρ χρειὼ τῆς εἵνεκα τήνδ' ἀλεγεινὴν
ναυτιλίην ἔτλημεν, ὀϊζύϊ μοχθίζοντες,
εὐπαλέως κούρης ὑπὸ δήνεσι κεκράανται.   (191–3)

Now, at last, the purpose for which we have endured this
painful voyage and laboured with distress has been
achieved, and with ease, thanks to this girl's craft.

The heavily spondaic μοχθίζοντες 'labouring' at the end of one
line is set against εὐπαλέως 'with ease' at the start of the next; it
is also set against the finality of the spondaic κεκράανται 'has
been achieved'. The same speech, however, abruptly moves us
to a virile and martial atmosphere. Aeetes will pursue: the
Argonauts must defend their return through physical prowess.
Jason uses the language conventional in exhortations before
battle (202 ff.).[64] He shows a vigorous commanding spirit
which he has not been allowed to display before, and at the end
of his speech he dons 'the arms of war' (τεύχε' ἀρήϊα, 206). It
seems as though, with the return journey, we have come back
to the sphere of uncomplicated courage and strength.

A brief scene with Aeetes (see pp. 91 f.) shows the terrifying
might of the king and of the force he sends out (he is too late
now for trickery, cf. 4. 7). The Argonauts decide to take a
different route home. The scene of decision (241 ff.) recalls the
scene in Book 3 where the Argonauts decided to seek the help of
Medea (3. 521 ff.). Again the advice of Phineus in Book 2 is
remembered (4. 253 ff.), again it is Argus the son of Phrixus
who suggests the right course of action, again this is confirmed
by a sign (294 ff.). The sign here is much grander. But with
Argus' speech the poet deliberately dissolves the excitement he

[64] Cf. e.g. Aesch. *Pers.* 402 ff.

has been building up. With a dizzying sweep of time and place, we are introduced, obliquely, to Egypt at the beginning of time, to the Pharaoh Sesostris, to the foundation of Aea in Colchis, and at last to a map—a surprising item—which contains the route that the Argonauts should follow.[65] The speech ends with the Greek river Achelous, which to Argus is only the far-off object of hearsay (292 f.). The speech distances us much more unexpectedly than a digression by the poet (and most of Apollonius' digressions are brief): we expect the speech to be pertinent.

The pursuit of the Argonauts and Medea is led, not by Medea's father Aeetes, as in other accounts, but by her brother Apsyrtus. The Argonauts fail to escape. They agree to submit the case of Medea to external arbitration; they are to keep the Golden Fleece themselves. But Medea persuades Jason to kill Apsyrtus by means of her treachery, and have the Argonauts take his army by surprise. The usual version of the story was that Medea herself killed Apsyrtus, who was still a child; after, she cut his body into pieces and threw them forth, to delay pursuit.[66] Apollonius eschews this story in order to maintain the continuity of his work, and to pursue and darken its themes. Medea does not perform an act of horrific wickedness, snapping the threads of her character and our sympathy; she and Jason are entangled in a fresh imbroglio of deceit, much more disquieting than those of Book 3.

Medea accuses Jason furiously of breaking his oath that he would take her to Greece (355 ff.). Jason's speech intimates that the arrangement just made with the Colchians is to serve as cover for trickery against Apsyrtus (δόλον, 404). Apollonius archly omits to tell us whether Jason had had this in mind all along; he leads us to suppose, however, that Jason is placating Medea with adroit improvisation. Jason makes his speech ὑποδδείσας, 'in terror' (394); it would be strange if he had not

---

[65] Eratosthenes supposed the first map of the world to have been produced by Anaximander: see H. Berger, *D. geographischen Fragmente d. Eratosthenes* (1880), 41 f.

[66] Thus Pherecydes, *FrGH* 3 F 32a (see Sch. AR 4. 223–30a and d), Roman poets, and even Apollodorus (1. 9. 24), who mostly follows Apollonius. Medea kills him: Eur. *Med.* 167, 1334, *SH* 964. 15, *al.* He is killed in Colchis: Eur. *Med.* 1334, Call. fr. 8, Soph. fr. 343 Radt (who kills him in Callimachus and Sophocles is unknown). Jason kills him in Hygin. *Fab.* 23 (a jumbled version of Apollonius' account). See Wilamowitz, *HD* ii. 191 ff. (perhaps too confident that Apollonius has invented his version).

thought to inform Medea before, or consulted her on the mode
of treachery, which it is she who suggests. He 'fawns' once more
(ὑποσσαίνων, 410), his words are once more 'gentle' (μειλιχίοις,
394). Again Jason's tact and persuasiveness have rescued him,
but the predicament and the solution are alike discreditable.
Medea has forced Jason to treachery, and she is now forced to
take up his suggestion: she will 'gently persuade' Apsyrtus to
come into Jason's hands (μειλίξω, 416). Medea and Jason set
about their 'enormity of deceit' (μέγαν δόλον, 421). Medea pretends to Apsyrtus that she will devise a trick (438) to secure the
Golden Fleece for Apsyrtus. Although Apsyrtus had seemed extremely just in his agreement with the Argonauts, he now reveals a propensity for trickery himself (462). But Medea's
proposal is itself a trick, and Jason ambushes their victim. The
description of the killing that follows shows the theme of trickery brought to a hideous issue.

The contrasting element of manly valour also undergoes disturbing modulations. The Argonauts, we are told, would have
been defeated in war by the larger force of Apsyrtus (338 ff., cf.
401 f.). This Homeric device of telling us what would have been
is much exploited in the book, usually to undermine the self-
sufficiency of the characters.[67] The Argonauts do not show the
imprudent and splendid spirit which Peleus had earlier exhibited towards war with the Colchians (2. 1219 ff.); they strike
an agreement with them. Jason claims unconvincingly to
Medea that the Argonauts are only postponing warfare (396),
and stresses his own bellicosity (408 f.); this only strengthens the
feeling of disquiet raised by Medea's speech. The valour of the
Argonauts appears a little tarnished, however necessary the
treaty. The Argonauts' destruction of the Colchians after
Apsyrtus' death is endued with grandeur; the simile of hawks
and doves used at 485 f. recalls the simile used when the Argonauts fought the Doliones (1. 1049 f.; note too 3. 541 ff.). But
the act is stained, in moral and even military terms, by its
dependence on, and its close association with, Jason's slaying of
Apsyrtus himself. The end of Medea's last speech to Jason
couples the acts in a chilling pair of lines:

---

[67] Cf. 4. 20, 639, 1305, 1651. For the device in Homer cf. *Il.* 2. 155, 3. 373, 5. 388, 16.
698 f., etc.; G. P. Shipp, *Studies in the Language of Homer*[2] (1972), 367.

ἔνθ', εἴ τοι τόδε ἔργον ἐφανδάνει, οὔτι μεγαίρω·
κτεῖνέ τε καὶ Κόλχοισιν ἀείρεο δηϊοτῆτα.　　　　　(419 f.)

Then, if the act suits your wishes, I make no objection—
kill Apsyrtus and begin warfare with the Colchians, too.

The term ἥρωες 'heroes' is used emphatically of the Argonauts
when they destroy the Colchians (485); but eight lines before it
had been used of Jason as he cut off the extremities of Apsyrtus'
body in order to hinder his ghost. There the appellation has a
hint of irony. Six lines earlier again it had been used of Apsyrtus.[68] Jason's act was martial; but stress is laid on its
cunning.[69]

The murder is invested with crudity, archaism, and horror;
but the horrors are finely judged. Apsyrtus is killed only in the
vestibule of the temple (471);[70] his corpse is hideously treated,
but by Jason, not Medea, and from primitive belief and custom, not in cruel exploitation of Aeetes' feelings as a father.
Apsyrtus himself is crude in his retaliation: he stains his sister's
raiment with his blood, in order to pollute her. She has turned
away from the killing of her brother (465 ff.). The event is
appalling, but it is credible that Apollonius' characters should
be forced to perform it.

The idea of continuity, and degeneration, is most important
with Medea. She starts thus the speech in which she gives
instructions for the murder:

φράζεο νῦν—χρειὼ γὰρ ἀεικελίοισιν ἐπ' ἔργοις
καὶ τόδε μητίσασθαι, ἐπεὶ τὸ πρῶτον ἀάσθην
ἀμπλακίη ...　　　　　　　　　　　　　　　(411–13)

Now attend.—I am compelled to contrive this act to add
to my wicked deeds, having once come to madness and
error.

---

[68] There is, not irony, but a certain richness in some other uses of ἥρως of Jason
(2. 410, 3. 509, 4. 750; less likely, 1. 781; very unlikely, 4. 784 f., 1528).

[69] 465 presents dramatically the drawing of Jason's sword, as he leaps from his
πυκινοῦ ... λόχοιο (464). Ambushes on a grander scale were thought courageous in the
epic (Hom. *Il.* 13. 276 ff.), but they are all but completely excluded from the heroic
action of the *Iliad* (Paris, *Il.* 11. 379). The Homeric πυκινοῦ must be intended to suggest
craft here; ὀπιπεύσας in 469 is meant to recall *Il.* 7. 243 (in a contrast with more open
and honourable warfare).

[70] Contrast Sch. Eur. *Med.* 1334, 'on the altar of Artemis, as Apollonius says'. Does
the καί before Ἀπολλώνιος (deleted in Schwartz) indicate the loss of another author's
name?

With the same phrase, 'now attend', she opened her instructions to Jason on deceiving her father (3. 1026). She turns away her discourse to register bitterly and justify hollowly the progress of her fall. The poet himself rounds on Eros with impassioned and impressive rhetoric (445 ff.); but the effect is brusquely deflated as he turns to the murder: 'that was to be the next subject in my song', he explains, τὸ γὰρ ἦμιν ἐπισχερὸν ἦεν ἀοιδῆς (451). In attacking Love he affects a personal mode that connects him with his characters; then he distances himself nonchalantly: they are a part of his poem.

Deterioration also appears in the relationship between Jason and Medea. It will already be evident that the interchange here distorts their interchange in Book 3. The theme of remembrance, so important there, receives a bitter twist in Medea's (legitimate) reproaches (355 ff.). The vehemence she displayed in 3. 1111 ff. on the possibility of Jason's forgetting her is here intensified and inverted: she prays that Jason will remember her, not with gratitude as his preserver, but with self-reproach as his destroyer (4. 383 f.). The relationship is restored for the present, but after the conversation the poet reminds us of Jason's eventual desertion of Medea. He describes the cloak given to Jason by Hypsipyle, whom he had left on Lemnos. This had been mentioned after the conversation with Medea as a μνημήϊον εὐνῆς, a gift given in remembrance of Hypsipyle's embraces (3. 1206); the hint is developed further here. The cloak is connected with Ariadne, deserted by Theseus (4. 433 f.): the poet leads to its end the story with which Jason beguiled Medea.

The Argonauts, and Medea, take counsel after the defeat of the Colchians. It is Peleus, somewhat unexpectedly, who suggests a stratagem (494 ff.). In fact, it is through the action of Hera that they are preserved from the enemy (509 f.). Peleus (501 f.) and the Argonauts in general (522) think the return will now be easy; but Zeus, as we saw, is angry at the murder of Apsyrtus (557 f., cf. p. 102). The poet allows a brief passage of straightforward voyaging (562–76); the type recalls the first two books (cf. e.g. 1. 592 ff., 922 ff., 2. 930 ff.). Even here the Odyssean elements just begin their complication (574 f.); but we shall not mention these again. This relative straightforwardness is soon disrupted. Hera, aware of Zeus' wrath, send gales to drive the Argonauts back and the Argo itself cries to them of the anger of Zeus and the need to be purified by Circe (576 ff., 580 ff.). At the very commencement of the expedition, at the break of day, the Argo had cried encouragement (1. 524–7). Here, at nightfall (4. 592), it warns the Argonauts of pollution and divine displeasure. The link between the two passages is probably reinforced by the repetition of a whole verse, and a third, (4. 582 τό ῥ'–583 = 1. 526 τό ῥ'–527): such repetition is highly unusual in Apollonius.[71] This passage dwells more on the extraordinary nature of the occurrence, and the Argo's words are now reported (though in indirect speech); this heightening only strengthens the distortion.

Further travelling follows (592 ff.). The region is associated with myths of grief and deprivation (the mourning of Phaethon's sisters, the exile of Apollo): these furnish a disturbed and uneasy atmosphere. The tone is modified, and the effect made weirder, by prolonged description set in Apollonius' own day (599 ff.), and by the intellectual citation of a variant story (611 ff.). The episode with Circe has already been spoken of. The ritual and the imagery of pollution bring to a point the horror of the killing. It is emphasized that Circe is a member of Medea's family (684, 725 ff., 743, cf. 697, 731 f.); this relation is used to heighten the wrongness and strangeness of what Medea has done. Circe pities Medea (738, 744), but condemns her actions (746 f.). She tells Medea to leave her house together with Jason; he is for us a hero (750, cf. 733), for Circe

ξείνῳ ...
ὅντινα τοῦτον ἄϊστον ἀνεύραο πατρὸς ἄνευθεν. (745 f.)

the foreigner, whoever this unknown man may be that
you have found yourself without your father's consent.

'Foreigner' had once been Medea's term for him. Jason takes Medea's hand, and leads her, crying and trembling, from the house of her relative (750 ff.). Medea had boldly taken Jason's hand at their first meeting, and they had joined hands solemnly when he had sworn to marry her (3. 1067 f., 4. 99 f.).[72] Now,

---

[71] It is doubted by some: see especially G. Wiegel, *Hermes*, 86 (1958), 255 f.; on the other side, Vian, *RÉA* 72 (1970), 88, 75 (1973), 98. Note also G. W. Elderkin *AJP* 34 (1913), 199 ff.

[72] Note also the significance of the gesture at Pind. *Pyth.* 9. 122.

the action marks concretely how joining with him disjoins her, and terribly, from her family and from tranquility. Such are the pain, guilt, and peril that love has brought her.

With extraordinary abruptness we move to an episode as different as possible in its total mood. It begins with a scene on Olympus, the second in the poem. In the first Hera persuaded Aphrodite to persuade Eros to make Medea fall in love; here she has in view a deed potentially of the greatest valour. The Argonauts have to pass through the Planctae, the Wandering Rocks, a task self-evidently parallel to their passage through the Symplegades, the Clashing Rocks, in Book 2. There divine intervention had played a part; here it dominates the narrative completely, and gives the episode a quite different flavour.[73] Before the Argonauts had arrived at the Symplegades, the flight of Athena to the spot had been described, in twelve lines (2. 537–48). Here we have eighty-nine lines in which Hera elaborately arranges for the Argonaut's safety. It is characteristic of the second half of the poem that Hera should be helping the Argonauts instead of Athena.[74] As at the beginning of Book 3 the queen of the gods uses other deities to accomplish her ends (and her manner is still more queenly). We have here a more complex divine machinery than the physical intervention of one goddess, and Hera's account of her (supposed) benefits to Thetis presents at length the intricacies of divine society (790 ff.). That speech is touched with a, mostly rather rarefied, suggestion of humour;[75] we are distanced directly from the tragedy of Medea by the ingenious revelation of her surprising future—she is to marry in the Elysian Fields Thetis' still infant son Achilles.

Thetis is sent to her husband Peleus to bid the Argonauts proceed. She had left him when he cried out at her strange treatment of Achilles their son; her anger is stressed both in her speech to Peleus and in the digression which follows it.[76] Peleus, ever sanguine, had exhorted and encouraged his despairing companions before (2. 880 ff., 1216 ff.); here Thetis'

---

[73] Cf. Herter, *Kl. Schr.*, 439, Vian i. 150; but they seem to see the difference from the earlier episode as simply a matter of avoiding monotony.

[74] Cf. Faerber (above, n. 56), 82 ff.

[75] Less rarefied at 794 f. At 815 the περ is ambiguous for the reader.

[76] 863, 864, the ends of the last and penultimate lines of the speech; 868, 879, at the beginning and end of the narrative.

speech of exhortation and encouragement fills him with personal grief, and ἀμηχανίη δῆσεν φρένας 'depression, despair
fettered his spirit' (880). The moment is not quite an inversion,
but a sad alteration, of Peleus' usual role.[77]

The passage through the Planctae itself only gains its full
point when compared with the passage through the Symplegades (2. 549 ff.).[78] There, the emphasis falls on the Argonauts.
The peril of rocks and waves, lavishly described, is presented
through their eyes, and we are shown the alarm and the vigorous action with which they respond. The sound of the Clashing
Rocks 'was striking their ears unceasingly' (553 f.); they see the
rocks open, and they are overcome (559 ff.); they watch the
dove going through, lifting their heads (562 f.), and they shout
when it succeeds (573);[79] as they go through themselves, with
terror (575, 577), they behold the open sea from between the
rocks (579); they see a huge wave coming and turn their heads
away (581 f.). They have been told that their safety depends on
the might of their hands (κάρτεϊ, 332 ff., see above), and they
prepare to rely on their might (κάρτεϊ, 559). The helmsman
Tiphys bids them row with might (κρατερῶς, 574); Euphemus
bids them row with all their strength (ὅσον σθένος, 589). The
oars are bent against the wave like bows as the heroes attempt
to force their way through (βιαζομένων ἡρώων, 592—a splendid
spondaic close).[80] In the end a whirlpool seizes the ship, and
Athena intervenes with a grandiose gesture: seizing a rock with
one hand she thrusts the Argo through with the other. With
that single act, of which the Argonauts remain ignorant, she
departs. She has not obscured the prowess of the heroes.

In the passage through the Planctae the Argonauts disappear from our view.[81] The poet passes to this episode by

[77] At the beginning of the expedition Chiron's wife showed Peleus his son Achilles
from the shore (1. 557 f.); that joyful action is here given a darker background (cf. also
4. 812 f.). All this is only made possible by Apollonius' adoption of an unusual chronology for the marriage of Peleus and Thetis: cf. Vian i. 254 (there is no reason to think
that the sarcophagus which he mentions draws on a source independent of Apollonius.

[78] For actual assimilation of the two sets of rocks cf. Sch. Eur. *Med.* 2 (οἱ νεώτεροι),
Rusten, *ZPE* 36 (1979), 63 f., *SH* 944.

[79] The evident parallel between the passage of the dove and the passage of the Argo
is stressed by Levin (above, n. 21), 169 ff.

[80] The excitement of the sequence 561–75 is enhanced by the large number of pauses
at the bucolic diaeresis, which lends great energy to the rhythm.

[81] This contrast is noted, broadly, by Vian, iii. 181.

mentioning their emotion at the episode preceding (4. 920); but here their feelings and even their perceptions are virtually omitted. The fear that we are told of is the hysterical fear of Hera (959 f.). Apart from the initial statement that Scylla's rock προυφαίνετο (922) 'was appearing in front', there is no word of the Argonauts' perceiving the things described. The Argonauts' reaction to the Nereids that surround the Argo may naturally be suggested in the comparison of the nymphs to dolphins, 'a joy to the sailors' (936); but the failure to mention this reaction in the narrative becomes the more noticeable.[82] The Argonauts do not act; indeed, it is the Argo, not they, that is acted on. In Book 2 a single goddess gave the ship a single push. Here the number of the Nereids is constantly stressed with phrases like 'some from this point, some from that' (930, 934 ff., 937, 942, 951, 954); they push the ship through by turns, labouring for the length of a spring day (961 ff.). They are compared to girls throwing a ball from one to the other (948 ff.); we surely think of the games of Medea and her maids (3. 897 ff., 948 ff.).[83] At any rate, the virile prowess of the Argonauts, exhibited so memorably at the Symplegades,[84] is here displaced not merely by divine intervention but by an intervention markedly feminine in quality. The stress on the female attire of the girls in the simile (4. 949) echoes the stress on the female attire of the Nereids (940). This scene dissolves the earlier one in a delicious extravagance of fantasy, grace, and playfulness.

The Argonauts reach Phaeacia (Corcyra), and the mood is changed no less abruptly than before (1000, see p. 103). The Colchians catch up, and we return to the situation we thought we had left. The Colchians want Medea back, and threaten war (1004 ff.). But the Argonauts do not escape by a dubious agreement; it is Alcinous, the king of Phaeacia, who desires a settlement without force (1008 ff.). Medea begs the aid of the queen, Arete, and addresses to the Argonauts a speech (1031 ff.) that matches her speech to Jason in the earlier episode (335 ff.); it is linked not only by its subject but by the

[82] The nymphs will presumably be visible to the Argonauts, unlike Athena, cf. 862 f.

[83] They are further linked by the connection of both scenes with Nausicaa (Hom. *Od.* 6. 99 ff.).

[84] Note the retrospective speeches 2. 615 ff., 641 ff.; these are significantly misguided about the future.

extremity of its rhetoric. However, while Medea accuses the Argonauts of being cowardly now—they would have fought for the Golden Fleece—the Argonauts shake spears and swords and assure Medea they will defend her, if defence should be needed (1055 ff.). We have here no awkward avoidance of war, and no devious trickery and cunning, but manly valour and frank loyalty. The speech is not addressed to Jason: this is emphasized by the ascription, in the first sentence, of Jason's achievement in the trials of Aeetes to the Argonauts in general (1033 f.). We have no rift in the relationship of Jason and Medea. Rather, the story which seemed to find so grim an ending with the episode of Circe will now move towards a happy conclusion.

Medea passes a sleepless night, as in 3. 744 ff., but her anxiety is now for herself (4. 1058 ff.). She is compared to a woman in the distress of widowhood and of poverty. As elsewhere with Medea, the simile has a tragic quality (cf. 3. 656 ff., a bride who loses her husband-to-be; 4. 35 ff., a captive girl sent into slavery). Yet as well as making her situation poignant, it indicates how that situation in fact diverges from tragedy (it falls short in 3. 656 ff.). Medea has not lost a husband, she will gain one. Meanwhile Arete talks with Alcinous in bed.[85] Alcinous suggests a plan which is clever (πυκινόν, 1111, 1200), and avoids war (1098 f.), but he does so from a regard for justice (1100). If Medea marries Jason, it would be wrong for Alcinous to separate her from her husband and return her to her father. Arete tells this to Jason—at the instigation of the all-pervasive Hera, as we learn at the end of the wedding festivities (1199 f.). The marriage is prepared for, and takes place, that same night.

Apollonius' description of the marriage contains beautiful and numinous elements, such as the nymphs bringing flowers in their white bosoms (1144 ff.); recherché myth and aetiology complicate the tone (1131 ff., 1153 f.); ingredients of the story are ingeniously redeployed. The Golden Fleece covers the pair that won it (1141 f.); the description of it here (1145–8) recalls the description of it when it had just been secured (173, 178, 185 f.). The Argonauts, wearing garlands, sing to the accompaniment of Orpheus' lyre (1158 ff.); so they did after fighting

[85] Cf. Herodot. 3. 133 f. (Darius and Atossa).

the Bebryces (2. 159 ff.). But we do not have a simple antithesis between war and love: the Argonauts wield 'spears of war' (δούρατα ... ἀρήϊα, 1156), to ward off any attack by the Colchians. We look back to the passage where they brandish them to assure Medea they will fight for her (1055 ff.). The poet is not merely combining antithetical themes in a different way: at the end of the passage, he strengthens the sense of danger, so that he can distort abruptly the sense of a happy ending. The scene has essentially felt rich, delicate, and fulfilled; the bridal night, that supreme conclusion, has been exquisitely trans-figured. But Apollonius first makes that conclusion imperfect by separating it from the true conclusion of the poem: Jason and Medea had intended to wed on Jason's homecoming, τότ' αὖ χρεὼ ἦγε μιγῆναι (1164) 'but necessity was driving them to sleep together then'. The unexpected conjunction of necessity and an earlier union is presented with strong concision. The poet proceeds:

> ἀλλὰ γὰρ οὔποτε φῦλα δυηπαθέων ἀνθρώπων
> τερπωλῆς ἐπέβημεν ὅλῳ ποδί, σὺν δέ τις αἰεὶ
> πικρὴ παρμέμβλωκεν ἐϋφροσύνῃσιν ἀνίη.
> τῷ καὶ τούς, γλυκερῇ περ ἰαινομένους φιλότητι,
> δεῖμ' ἔχον εἰ τελέοιτο διάκρισις Ἀλκινόοιο.

(1165–9)

Never do we, the race of wretched mortals, stand with our whole feet on delight: always some bitter pain has joined our felicity. Hence Jason and Medea, though delighting in the sweetness of their union, were gripped all along by fear as to whether Alcinous' decision would be effectual.

The ending and the former mood are here dissolved, in the second sentence, with specific detail; but the generality of the first sentence, rather than intensifying the narrative, distances us from it in the sombre vision itself. The language is emphatic, pungent, and almost vehement; the thought, in contrast, strikes us as subtle and resigned. It is a haunting counterpoint.[86]

---

[86] Cf. above, pp. 29 f., on Call. fr. 75. 43 ff. for a quite different complication of the bridal night as the happy ending. More akin is the end of *Vanity Fair*; cf. also for the sense of subtlety Corneille, *Le Cid* 3. 5. 1 ff. (ancient parallels for the thought in Bömer on Ovid, *Met.* 7. 453). Apollonius follows Timaeus (*FGrH* 566 F 87) in having the marriage on Corcyra, in the cave (Sch. 4. 1153–4, cf. Sch. 4. 1141). Antimachus had the pair sleep together in Colchis (fr. 64 Wyss); that would give an utterly different story.

The Argonauts leave Phaeacia, and there is yet another sudden change to a section of utterly different atmosphere (1225 ff., see p. 104). The wanderings of the Argonauts in Libya were a particularly well-established part of the saga; but Apollonius makes them embody singularly striking developments of themes in his poem.

The Argonauts are stranded in the desolate shallows of the Syrtis. In describing the place the poet employs rhetorical figures more liberally than he is wont in order to make the prospect seem as hopeless, and as extraordinary, as possible (1237, 1239 f., 1246, 1247 f.). The despair of the Argonauts reminds us of their despair at the death of their former helmsman Tiphys (2. 858 ff.). They are overcome with ἀμηχανίη 'despair' (4. 1259, 1308, 1318, cf. 2. 860, 885); they believe they will die an inglorious death in this remote place (4. 1254 f., 1261 ff., cf. 2. 892 f.). The poet himself reinforces this thought strongly at 4. 1305 ff.: these greatest of heroes (ἡρώων οἱ ἄριστοι) would all have died in obscurity, their task unaccomplished. At 2. 864 he says merely 'they would have stayed grieving still longer'. As before, the Argonauts cover themselves in their cloaks and neither eat nor drink (4. 1294 f., cf. 2. 861 f.). But here the description grows far more extravagant: the simile at 4. 1280 ff. piles up disasters and passes to perversions of nature. In Book 2 all was solved when Ancaeus took over the helm; and there were other knowledgeable mariners too (2. 874 ff., 896 ff.). Here it is Ancaeus who pronounces that hope is gone (4. 1261 ff.), and the other experts agree (1277 f.). Medea, and her Phaeacian maids, lament no less than the men (1296 ff.). In Pindar it is Medea who suggests that the Argonauts should carry the Argo (*Pyth.* 4. 27); here feminine ingenuity is of no avail.

Help comes from deities: not from Hera, who is absent from the whole Libyan section, but from 'heroines of Libya'.[87] In the sentence mentioned above (1305–11), ἡρώων (the greatest of 'heroes') is set against the ἡρώσσαι, the 'heroines', without whose pity the masculine heroes would have perished (1307 *init.*, 1309 *init.*). The femininity of the goddesses is emphasized by their dress (1314, 1348 f. ἠΰτε κοῦραι 'like girls'). Menelaus is

---

[87] These rare beings are found also in Call. fr. 602, Nicaenetus *HE* 2689 ff.

saved on Pharos by a local goddess who pities him (Hom. *Od.* 4.
364 ff., cf. AR 4. 1308); but these deities are much more mysterious and indirect. They give riddling instructions, and disappear; understanding and fulfilment depend on a divine
apparition (1364 ff.).

It is Peleus who understands; he addresses his comrades,
filled with joy, as in the episode in Book 2 (2. 878, 4. 1369).
After the sadness of the scene with Thetis, Peleus again announces deliverance. The Argonauts carry the Argo across the
waste. For this action the form of narrative is interrupted.

> Μουσάων ὅδε μῦθος, ἐγὼ δ' ὑπακουὸς ἀείδω
> Πιερίδων, καὶ τήνδε πανατρεκὲς ἔκλυον ὀμφήν,
> ὑμέας, ὦ πέρι δὴ μέγα φέρτατοι υἷες ἀνάκτων,
> ᾗ βίῃ, ᾗ ἀρετῇ Λιβύης ἀνὰ θῖνας ἐρήμους
> νῆα μεταχρονίην ὅσα τ' ἔνδοθι νηὸς ἄγεσθε[88]
> ἀνθεμένους ὤμοισι φέρειν δυοκαίδεκα πάντα
> ἤμαθ' ὁμοῦ νύκτας τε.   (1381–7)

This is the discourse of the Muses; it is by giving ear to
them that I sing. I have heard from them this report, in
absolute truth: that you, you far the greatest among the
sons of kings, in the desolate sand-dunes of Libya, by your
own strength, your own excellence, set high on your
shoulders the ship and all you had been transporting
within the ship, and bore it on them for twelve whole days
and twelve whole nights.

We have here the poet's own enraptured address to the
heroes—reusing a character's address earlier (Medea, 1031).
The exultant anaphora of ᾗ βίῃ, ᾗ ἀρετῇ (1384) 'your own
strength, your own excellence' heats with personal emotion the
theme of manly prowess. That theme appears to find its climax
in the triumphant rhetoric of the sentence. However, the figure
of the poet also distances and modifies. The elaborate and extravagant emphasis on the poet's relationship to the Muses and
on the truth, or faithfulness, of his account, sets the narrative
statement in a frame which places it apart. We do not simply
accept the narrative on its own terms, but are made to think of
the author and of historicity. The device of reported speech
enhances the effect, and conflicts with the directness of the

---

[88] Stephanus: ἄγεσθαι MSS. Surely ἄγοντο would be better, the infinitive being suggested to a scribe by the syntactical environment? For the plural cf. e.g. 3. 813, 1. 679.

apostrophe. The action is too strange. The riddle given by the heroines brings out the paradox: the Argonauts are paying a return to the mother that bore them in her womb, the Argo (1327 ff., *al.*). The mention of the cargo increases the element of the bizarre through its solid practicality. But the splendour is modified, not simply subverted.

The task accomplished, a grotesque image suddenly supervenes: the heroes rush about searching for water like dogs with rabies (1393 ff.). Help comes again from the pity of local deities, still more mysterious. The Argonauts come on the Hesperides, who have been lamenting; they change into dust (1408 ff.). When prayed to they turn into trees, and then into their true form (1423–30). Their apparition is made parallel to that of Apollo in Book 2 (674 ff.): again it is Orpheus who prays for their favour; again he promises sacrifice if they should return to Greece, and uses a similar syntactical structure (4. 1418 ff., cf. 2. 689 ff.). The link brings out the contrast between the magnificent and yet standardized epiphany of Apollo and this weird scene.

The chief object, however, of the episode with the Hesperides is to confront us with Heracles, who the day before slew the snake which guarded their apples. The sudden re-entry of Heracles, the prime embodiment of might in the first two books, is an extraordinary surprise in the poem; it is perfectly conceivable that Apollonius invented this link between the Labour of Hesperides and the Argonauts.[89] The re-entry is oblique: the Argonauts hear of him from the resentful Hesperides, who do not know his name. Several go in pursuit, but only the sharp-eyed Lynceus catches a far-off sight of him, as of a hazy new moon (1477 ff.). The Argonauts' supreme exemplar remains intangible, and the poet reminds us of the circumstances in which they lost him (1469 ff., cf. 1. 1240 ff., 1321 ff.). We should contrast his destruction of the Hesperides' snake by force with the Argonauts' evasion of Aeetes' snake by Medea's witchcraft.[90] However, even he now appears in a somewhat altered light. In Book 1, Heracles had been pointedly removed

---

[89] *ARV*² 1313. 5 shows nothing to the contrary, as will be seen if one considers all the other subjects on the vase.

[90] Both creatures are called φρουρὸν ὄφιν 4. 88, 1434. Heracles' actions had paralleled those of the Argonauts in 2. 1052 ff.; note also the parallel of their drinking here.

from the tradition which had him governed primarily by physical appetites. While the others feasted, he went to find a tree to
make an oar from (1. 1187 ff.); he had demanded Theiodamas'
bull, not from hunger, but from the highest motives
(1. 1219 ff.).[91] Here the account of Aegle shows him driven by
parching thirst. The language of the final description, the more
amusing for its hostility, presents vividly and earthily a huge
and violent appetite; the tradition is to some extent revived.[92]

αὐτὰρ ὅγ᾽, ἄμφω χεῖρε πέδῳ καὶ στέρνον ἐρείσας,
ῥωγάδος ἐκ πέτρης πίεν ἄσπετον, ὄφρα βαθεῖαν
νηδὺν φορβάδι ἶσος ἐπιπροπεσὼν ἐκορέσθη.   (1447–9)

He rested his chest and both his hands on the ground, and
drank prodigiously from the cleft in the rock, falling forward in the posture of an animal, until he had sated his
great stomach.

It is the grotesqueness of great thirst that here joins him with
the Argonauts, likened earlier to rabid dogs, and now to
swarming ants and flies (1425 ff.).

Two Argonauts now die in succession. Their deaths had been
prepared at the start of the work (1. 77 ff.), with stress on the
geographical paradox of their dying in Libya, not in Colchis.
The sequence recalls the pair of deaths in Book 2 (816 ff.); the
deaths of Idmon in Book 2 and of Mospus in Book 4 are very
closely and characteristically related. Both Idmon and Mopsus
are prophets. The opening of this passage, which says that
Mopsus could not escape his fate through prophecy recalls most
strongly the opening of the passage in Book 2 (4. 1502 ff., 2.
815 ff.). The account in Book 2 suits the grandiose opening,
which echoes Hom. *Il.* 2. 859. Idmon is slain by a boar—a type
of death with heroic resonance. Idmon is revenged on the beast
by two of the Argonauts. He dies in the arms of his own friends
(2. 834), χείρεσσι δ᾽ ἑῶν ἐνὶ κάτθαν᾽ ἑταίρων: that weighty and
harmonious close develops poignantly the theme of friendship
and concord (cf. 2. 714 ff.). A magnificent funeral follows.[93]

---

[91] Contrast Call. *H.* 3. 110 f.; the hunger of his son is the motive in Call. fr. 24. The
humour is of a quite different kind in AR 1. 1170 f.: it plays on his zeal.

[92] Cf. Prop. 4. 9 for a depiction of Heracles' imperious thirst.

[93] The statement that the very nymphs of the marshes feared the boar (2. 820 f.) does
not dissolve, or greatly modify, the tendency of the episode: it merely produces a
momentary sense of distance.

Mospus is killed by a snake. The creature is described, sluggish but lethal: less grand than a boar. Intensity is diluted: even Apollo could not heal this snake's bites—if Apollonius may be permitted to say so (4. 1511). The mythological origin of the snake is given, and Perseus' other name is explained with an air of laborious erudition (1514). The bite is not shattering and violent, like the onslaught of the boar (2. 826); it is deceptively painless (4. 1522 ff.). The corpse immediately begins to rot away (1529 ff.), and the burial must be conducted in haste (1533). This episode (which appealed to Lucan) forms a bizarre distortion of the grandeur and pathos of the other. The Argonauts here simply gather round in amazement (1527 f.). But the poet stresses that Medea, and her maids, could contribute nothing either. They flee (1521 f.), in useless female terror.

The following episode combines two stories so as again to have the Argonauts at a loss and again to show mysterious deities.[94] This, however, is a deity masculine and vigorous. When Triton appears to the Argonauts, unable to escape from the Tritonian Lake, he appears as a heroic mortal like themselves (ἥρως 'hero', Euphemus addresses him at 1564). In his dialogue with him, Euphemus mentions, with no immodest purpose, the achievement of carrying the Argo so praised by Apollonius (1568 f.). In his real form Triton pulls the Argo to sea like a man leading a splendid horse (1604 ff.). The simile recalls other uses of the horse to suggest action and vigour;[95] it enhances the manly quality of the episode. We contrast the episode with that of the Nereids; they likewise guided the Argo with their hands. But the episode closes on a bizarre note: Apollonius describes Triton's true form, half man, half fish (1610 ff.), laying weight on its strangeness (1618 f., cf. 1598). The poet also recalls the appearance in Book 1 of the marine god Glaucus:[96] but Triton is weirder.

Medea has been pointedly placed in the background during the Libyan section. It comes as a surprise that in the next episode she should once again be the sole source of victory. The

[94] Triton disguises himself as Eurypylus, on the one hand, in Pind. *Pyth.* 4. 33 ff.; on the other, he shows Jason how to escape the shallows of the Tritonian Lake in Herodot. 4. 179 (cf. Timaeus *FGrH* 566 F 85. 5). See further Vian, iii. 58 ff.

[95] 3. 1259 ff. (Jason), see p. 115; 4. 1365 ff. (the horse from the sea which gives the sign to the Argonauts).

[96] Compare 4. 1602 with 1. 1310, 4. 1609 with 1. 1313 f., 4. 1618 with 1. 1326.

Argonauts are confronted by Talos, a being made entirely of bronze save for a single vein by his ankle. Medea proclaims grandly that she alone can kill him (1654 ff.): δαμάσσειν 'slay' ends the first line of her speech (1654), δαμῆναι 'be slain' the last (1658). We do not forget that Medea is with the Argonauts because of Jason: Jason guides her through the ship, holding her hand; the resonant gesture is marked out by the emphatic expression (1663). The poet plays wittily, as he does in Book 3, with the language of the *Iliad*. But the divergences enhance the power of Medea. Medea says she can kill Talos even if he has a body made all of bronze (παγχάλκεον 1655 f.); in the *Iliad*, Aeneas says that if Achilles were not favoured by heaven he would not beat Aeneas easily, 'not even if he vaunts himself made all of bronze' παγχάλκεος (20. 102). The claims of Medea in effect give literal form to the claims of Aeneas; and Medea fulfils them. Homer often has his heroes 'crash as they fall', δούπησεν δὲ πεσών; the brazen Talos naturally 'fell with a prodigious crash', ἀπείρονι κάππεσε δούπῳ (1688, the close of the episode). But Medea's magic—here particularly sinister—is not treated so straightforwardly as before. The poet bursts out, exclaiming his surprise that magic should be possible, that destruction can be worked at a distance.

Ζεῦ πάτερ, ἦ μέγα δή μοι ἐνὶ φρεσὶ θάμβος ἄηται ...   (1673)

Father Zeus, great is the amazement that moves in my spirit, that ...

The drama is much distanced by the pretended *naïveté* and the actual artificiality of the poet's philosophical and practical alarm at his own narrative. This intrusion does not merely make Medea's weapons strange; it complicates and greatly lightens the effect of the whole passage.[97]

We considered earlier the extravagantly grandiose episode of the darkness from which Apollo rescues the Argonauts (1694 ff.). We considered also the coda with the maids of Medea (1713 ff.), which appears to bring to a light-hearted conclusion the oppositions of male and female in the poem. But

[97] G. Paduano misses the tone, which is surely made evident by the extravagance of 1673 and the laborious simplicity of 1674 f. (*Stud. class. e orientali* 19–20 (1970–1), 60 ff.).

the poet allows himself a brief and final play with sexes in the
dream of Euphemus, which is recounted next. Euphemus
dreams that he lies with a girl who has grown from a clod which
he fed at his breast with his own milk. The poet's language
stresses the bizarre and disquieting fusion of peculiarly male
and peculiarly female actions (1739f.). But the girl declares
that she is not after all his daughter as well as the mother of his
children (1741 f.). She is the daughter of Triton and Libya: the
mysterious metamorphoses of the episode are apt enough.

The last paragraph of the work brings a sudden rise in tone.

ἵλατ', ἀριστῆες, μακάρων γένος· αἵδε δ' ἀοιδαὶ
εἰς ἔτος ἐξ ἔτεος γλυκερώτεραι εἶεν ἀείδειν
ἀνθρώποις. ἤδη γὰρ ἐπὶ κλυτὰ πείραθ' ἱκάνω
ὑμετέρων καμάτων, κτλ.   (1773–6)

Be gracious, heroes, offspring of the gods! May this my
song from year to year grow ever sweeter for mortal men
to sing! I come now to the glorious end of your toils, etc.

We launch into an exalted address. The prayer ἵλατε 'be
gracious' invests the Argonauts with a status almost divine:
they themselves have used it to gods, particularly in the Libyan
section, and so, more archly, has the poet.[98] The valour of the
heroes could not be lauded more lavishly; we feel too a vivid
personal contact between them and the poet. Yet the author
goes on to remind us that they are characters in his work. All
that follows is in form subordinated to the last statement
quoted, so that the narrative is framed and distanced. However, the address continues, and with it the air of splendour.
These still transfigure the final evocation of the passages of
voyaging in the first two books (1779f.), and they transfigure
the Argonauts' arrival on the shores of their own country.

We have now seen in some detail how the large changes
adumbrated take particular shape and move the work, in its
last book, into a sustained and brilliant sequence of complicating and distorting developments, which crowns and unites the
poem. We mentioned earlier how these changes build on
features in the earlier books, and how the thematic structure of
the work is seen in retrospect to inform the first half of the

[98] 2. 693, 4. 1333, 1411, 1600; 2. 708, 4. 984. 4. 1014 does not make against this point
(cf. Livrea's note there); the context here implies a prayer.

poem. At some points we even perceive play with the antitheses
which are to manifest themselves in Book 3. That play is decidedly a play of anticipation only. The Lemnian women are
shown at first paradoxically taking the roles of men and
warriors (1. 627 ff.); but this reversal is soon to disintegrate,
and even now we see them gripped by unmanly terror (638 f.).
In Book 2 we are confronted with the idea of a conflict which
would have occurred between the Argonauts and the warlike
Amazons (985 ff.). The poet presents the Amazons' virile
nature in a prolonged parenthesis before explaining why they
did not in fact encounter the Argonauts. The Amazons have no
actual part in the story, and Apollonius sports with this. The
cloak of Jason is given an extended description (1. 720 ff.),
which is now seen by the reader to have an emblematic significance for the whole poem. It opposes images of force to images of
other means.[99] Particularly striking is the picture of Aphrodite
bearing the shield of Ares (1. 742 ff.). The image has obvious
relevance to Jason's unwarlike dalliance with Hypsipyle, but it
takes on another meaning when the Argonauts make Aphrodite not Ares their helper.[100] The exposure of Aphrodite's
breast gives a sensual piquancy to this exquisite foreshadowing.
The description closes with her reflection, mirrored in the
shield: the touch creates an evocative sense of distance from the
image, itself merely a picture on an artefact in the narrative
proper. The antitheses have yet to enter the narrative in the
fullness of their paradoxical force. Yet these passages prepare,
not only the emergence of the antitheses, but the mutation and
vigorous play they will eventually undergo. The poem again
shows the force of its large movements and the subtlety and
aptness of its cohesion. This is a singularly rewarding work to
read as a sequence and appreciate as a whole. We are fortunate
that it has survived complete.

[99] The essential nature of the passage is seen by Lawall, *YCS* 19 (1966), 154 ff.,
though he unfortunately brings in his notions of didacticism and Jason's education.

[100] 3. 559 f., see p. 111. The image of Aphrodite with the arms of Ares was familiar:
see Gow–Page on Leon. Tar. XXIV, E. Wind, *Pagan Mysteries in the Renaissance*[2] (1968),
91 n. 32, F. Graf, *ZPE* 55 (1984), 250 ff. But as so often Apollonius gives traditional
material new meaning within the thematic texture of his poem.

4

THEOCRITUS

THEOCRITUS has found more favour with ordinary readers of
Greek poetry than Callimachus or Apollonius; but in my conception of all three, their affinities are fundamental. This will
become clear from the discussion of his poems which occupies
most of the chapter. The chapter places its emphasis on characteristic poetic concerns as seen in individual poems; it will also
consider the evidence for his relation with Apollonius and Callimachus, and the possibility that his work as a whole has its
context and significance in literary controversy. This will involve considering some aspects of genre; so too will the preliminary points which follow on the whole corpus of Theocritus'
work.

The poems which deal with cowherds, goatherds, and shepherds have generally been seen as the essential part of Theocritus' œuvre; they are most commonly treated in isolation from the
rest.[1] There are twice as many genuine poems that do not
belong to this group (15 against 7), and they contain twice the
number of lines (1,363 against 689). I include poem 10 in the
group of 'bucolic' poems, although it deals with harvesters, and
I leave out of the reckoning altogether the epigrams, and also
poem 11, which deals with the Cyclops Polyphemus. It certainly uses the profession of this mythological shepherd, but it is
clearly related to poem 13, another account of a mythological
lover, again addressed to Nicias. I think that poem 25 (mythological) is most likely spurious. We may add that at least one
non-bucolic poem has been lost (the *Berenice*, fr. 3 Gow). A view
of the poet which concentrates on one-third of his output is
bound to be distorted.

It is also rash to insist too strongly that the 'bucolic' poems
form a self-contained group. They were not designed by Theo-

---

[1] Against this tendency cf. B. Effe, *RhM* NF 121 (1978) 48 f., Bulloch, in *CHCL* i,
579 f.

critus to stand together as an independent work. The order of
the poems in the papyri and the MSS is too unstable for us to
suppose that the author himself collected, and so ordered, his
poems.[2] The papyri, which all date from the Christian era,
place the 'bucolic' poems together and first, as do the MSS,
roughly speaking; but this is no evidence for Theocritus' conception of his work. The 'bucolic' poems won especial popularity. The stem βουκολ- (from βουκόλος 'cowherd') came to be
used of poems of this kind; Theocritus became known as ὁ τῶν
βουκολικῶν ποιητής 'the author of the bucolic poems'.[3] We are
not entitled to project these terms into Theocritus' time. Theocritus uses the stem of herdsmen's song within his poems.[4] This
made easy a transition to using it of the poems in which such
songs were apt to occur, especially when poem 7 was assumed
to be autobiography (see p. 203). But no such genre is likely to
have existed before Theocritus, and later generations are most
unlikely to have known anything of Theocritus' conceptions
beyond what appears in his text. The later usage and arrangement therefore possess no authority.[5]

It is natural to see as related the poems which deal with
herdsmen. But that is something different from supposing that
we must sort the poems into immutable groups, and that the
chief basis for division must be the presence or absence of rus-

[2] For the facts see Gow, pp. lxvi ff., P. Oxy. L (1983), 100 ff.

[3] *Life of Theocritus*, p. 1 Wendel. For the stem cf. e.g. Artemidorus (i BC), [Theocr.]
Ep. 26 Gow (preface to a collection) βουκολικαὶ Μοῖσαι; [Mosch.] 3.94 f., 120 ᾠδᾶς |
βουκολικᾶς, βουκολιάσδευ, Ovid, *Trist.* 2. 538 'bucolicis ... modis'. Compare on the
whole subject D. M. Halperin, *Before Pastoral* (1983) (of which the negative portions are
the more acceptable).

[4] Note especially 1. 20 τᾶς βουκολικᾶς ... Μοίσας, 7. 36, βουκολιασδώμεσθα (on poem
7 see pp. 204 ff.). Cf. Dover's edn., pp. liv f.

[5] There is no evidence that bucolic poetry was written by Philetas, who is likely to
have been born some time before Theocritus; Theocr. 7. 39–41 makes the supposition
improbable. Asclepiades should not be on all fours there, as a rival, with a poet in the
same supposed genre, indeed its founder. Virgil's 'Syracosio ... versu' (*Ecl.* 6. 1, cf. 4. 1)
suggests that he regarded Theocritus of Syracuse, not Philetas of Cos, as the originator
of his genre. Longus' novel contains a Philetas, widely associated with the poet (see especially R. L. Hunter, *A Study of Daphnis and Chloe* (1983), 76 ff., and E. L. Bowie, *CQ*
NS 35 (1985), 67 ff.). The name could perfectly well have been borrowed from the pages
of Theocritus; the choice of it is adequately justified by the connection with φιλεῖν 'kiss'
which Longus stresses (2. 4. 4, 5. 1, 7. 7, 8. 5, etc.). If Longus and a Latin poet do have
at some point a common source, we must remember how much other post-classical
poetry has been lost, including bucolic poetry later than Theocritus, which is important for Virgil.

tics. We might just as reasonably divide the poems into those primarily concerned with mythological characters and events (6, 11, 13, 18, 22, 24, 26) and the rest. Again these occupy one-third of the numbers of poems and of lines; the same result would occur as to lines if we chose the poems primarily concerned with love (2, 3, 6, 10, 11, 12, 13, 14, 29, 30). All these are important aspects of the poems, and no more. The 'bucolic' poems are united, and separated from the rest, by few features not implicit in the criterion for division, that is, the appearance of herdsmen. Songs occur within other poems (2, 15, 18; note also 11). The bucolic songs, despite their special designation (see above), are not distinguished from the rest of Theocritus' work by unique features of style. Comparisons are taken from the country by the rustic singers (7. 97, 6. 15 f., 10. 30 f.); but so they are by the maidens of ancient Sparta (18. 29 f.), by the singer of Alexandria (15. 121 f.), and, very strikingly, by the poet himself in a love-poem (12. 3 ff., cf. also 13. 12 f.).[6] Rustics may draw comparisons from their environment outside their songs too (1. 1 ff., 7 f.); and the polished city youth Delphis extracts a simile from his own experience in a much less natural fashion (2. 114 f.). The idea of singing-competitions, which appears in poems 5 and 6, and stands in the background of poem 7, was obviously a part of the tradition about herdsmen and their songs; it does not appear in other poems. But the balancing or opposing of songs is found in 10, which does not deal with herdsmen, and also in 2 (from the same singer, Simaetha). The two narratives in 22, on the Dioscuri, yield in formal terms a related design. Formally, indeed, the answering couplets of 5 (Comatas and Lacon) are far removed from the two more extended songs of 6 (on the Cyclops) and 7 (Thalysia). All these phenomena, however, should be associated with Theocritus' wider interest in exploiting frames and the artefacts set in them. To isolate the bucolic exchanges is to obscure the concerns of the poet.

No aspect of the country is ever contrasted explicitly with any aspect of the city, which makes it difficult to see an opposition between them as the essence of the 'bucolic' poems. Beautiful scenery is scarcely a predominant or exclusive feature in

---

[6] Poem 12 is in Ionic, not Doric like the poems with rustics.

these works.[7] In 3 (the *Comos*) and 10 (the Harvesters) it plays very little part; it is only a minor element in the dialogues 4 (18 f., 23–5) and 5 (33 f., 45–9). The sea appears in 6, on the Cyclops (11 f., 35); but the sea hardly counts as the habitat of herdsmen. Scenery is much more important in 1 (on Daphnis) and 7 (Thalysia). The first twenty-three lines of 1, although principally concerned with music, also conjure up the delectable scene from which the speakers draw their comparisons; the end of 7 describes the lovely garden of Phrasidamus (see p. 209). But the description of Amycus' spring in the poem on the Dioscuri (22. 37–43) paints a natural scene with a kindred concentration and beauty; the effect within the poem is striking. The spring is in this narrative the focal point of the action; in the narrative of Apollonius, here Theocritus' chief exemplar, it had not appeared at all.[8] Similarly, the site of Hylas' spring is described in 13. 40–2, with lavish naming of botanical species; Apollonius does not describe the site. Theocritus liked to evoke the beauty of natural objects—but always with a larger effect in view. The use of scenery too must be seen as part of a wider characteristic.

That larger effect is typically one of jarring or piquant juxtaposition. The tranquil and melodious description of the spring in 22 is abruptly succeeded by a description of the man who was sitting there, a hideous and alarming figure: the first thing we learn of his appearance is that he was

δεινὸς ἰδεῖν, σκληρῇσι τεθλασμένος οὔατα πυγμαῖς.   (45)

a terrifying sight, his ears crushed by harsh boxing.

This is Amycus, who will not allow the Dioscuri to drink unless one of them boxes with him. The surprise and the contrast are extremely forceful. Hardly less forceful is the change in 5. 45 ff. to Comatas' beautiful description of his surroundings.

οὐχ ἐριψῶ τηνεί. τουτεὶ δρύες, ὧδε κύπειρος,
ὧδε καλὸν βομβεῦντι ποτὶ σμάνεσσι μέλισσαι,

---

[7] On scenery in Theocritus, see especially W. Elliger, *D. Darstellung d. Landschaft i. d. gr. Dichtung* (1975), 318–64.

[8] Some artistic representations show a man-made fountain: J. D. Beazley, *Etruscan Vase-painting* (1947), 59, 79.

ἔνθ' ὕδατος ψυχρῶ κρᾶναι δύο, ταὶ δ' ἐπὶ δένδρει
ὄρνιχες λαλαγεῦντι, καὶ ἁ σκιὰ οὐδὲν ὁμοία
τᾷ παρὰ τίν.   (46–9)

No, I won't go there for the contest. Here there are oaks,
here galingale; here the bees are buzzing delightfully
about their hives; here there are two springs of chill water;
the birds are twittering on the tree; the shade by you will
not stand comparison with the shade here.

Comatas' acrimonious exchange with Lacon had just reached
its most sordid and brutal point: Comatas had taunted Lacon
with the painful homosexual assault he inflicted on Lacon in
Lacon's youth, and Lacon had retorted with crude ingenuity
(41–3). We reach a great contrast with the radiant simplicity of
the description, but we do not simply abandon the rivalry. The
same repetition of 'here' which lends a lyrical rapture to the description is seen at the end of the speech to be simultaneously
the vehicle for one more expression of superiority. Comatas'
ground is far better than Lacon's. In what follows the place for
the singing-contest is disputed over, though in seemly fashion.
The poet thus achieves, in addition to the contrast in sequence,
a discordant counterpoint within the description between the
beauty and restfulness of the scene and the rancour and heat of
the rivals.
    Poem 1 opens thus:

Θυ. Ἁδύ τι τὸ ψιθύρισμα καὶ ἁ πίτυς, αἰπόλε, τήνα,
      ἁ ποτὶ ταῖς παγαῖσι, μελίσδεται, ἁδὺ δὲ καὶ τὺ
      συρίσδες· μετὰ Πᾶνα τὸ δεύτερον ἆθλον ἀποισῇ.
      αἴ κα τῆνος ἕλῃ κεραὸν τράγον, αἶγα τὺ λαψῇ·
      αἴ κα δ' αἶγα λάβῃ τῆνος γέρας, ἐς τὲ καταρρεῖ
      ἁ χίμαρος—χιμάρῳ δὲ καλὸν κρέας, ἔστε κ' ἀμέλξῃς. (1–6)

(Thyrsis) 'It is a delicious thing, the whispering this pine-
tree gives forth in song, the pine-tree by the springs; just
so, goatherd, your piping is delicious. You will win second
prize to the piping god Pan. If he gets the horned goat you
will take the female; if he takes the female there falls to
you the kid—the meat of a kid is excellent, until the time
comes to milk her.'

The first half of this speech is strikingly attractive, not only in
the beauty of what it describes, but in its richly elaborate order
of words and the courtesy of its praise. The courtesy continues

in what follows, but the content becomes increasingly bizarre. The contest with Pan, presented as a definite possibility, is not like a myth of mortal challenging god: it is an equable competition with prizes. The arrangement of prizes is elaborated with a herdsman's expertise; and the merit of kid's meat is pointed out knowingly, in a prosy appendage. However metaphorical the competition, the development of the conception here would seem grotesque to an educated reader. In fact the reader has little reason to suppose the language remote from the speaker's beliefs. The next speech repeats the structure (with the Muses and singing). After the third speech, which again evokes scenery, the fourth expresses terror of Pan: piping would vex the irascible and jealous deity because he is a piper himself.[9] There is strictly a difference here from the notion of competition; but the essential picture of the god, in its extreme of anthropomorphism, is only maintained and made nervously practical. In the passage quoted, then, the beauty of nature, and of exquisite manners, is set against the bizarre *naïveté* of rustic ideas.

These instances, as it was suggested, belong with a wider, and central, aspect of Theocritus' poetry. It delights to place the beautiful and the passionate in opposition to the grotesque, the unattractive, and the low.[10] It is easy enough to find further examples of such opposition in the first poem itself. Within the shepherd's song, the speech of Priapus (81 ff.) to Daphnis, who is languishing from love, begins with the evocative and emotional image of Daphnis' beloved wandering through every brook and every grove, in her search for him (82–5). Priapus then compares Daphnis to a goatherd in his subjection to unfulfilled passion. The description of the goatherd, by contrast with the preceding lines, is exceedingly crude and unromantic. The goatherd sees he-goats mounting she-goats ($\beta \alpha \tau \epsilon \hat{v} \nu \tau \alpha \iota$) and weeps with overflowing eyes: he wishes

[9] This is the point, not a fear of disturbing the god's repose at midday: singing is permissible, in emphatic contrast to piping (16, 19). The god's attention will not at this time be devoted to the chase (16 f.).

[10] This is something different from the contrast between the ideal and the practical discussed e.g. by J.-H. Kühn, *Hermes* 86 (1958), 56 ff., and especially by U. Ott. *D. Kunst d. Gegensatzes in Theokrits Hirtengedichten* (Spudasmata 22, 1969). The opposition tends, I fear, to be too crudely formulated, and too narrowly centred around the supposed bucolic world; it is not much treated from the point of view of tone and tonal discord. The complexity, the piquancy, and the strangeness of Theocritus rather fail to emerge.

he were a he-goat himself (87 f.). By contrast with this, the description which follows in respect of Daphnis himself is unexpectedly delicate and delightful.

καὶ τὺ δ' ἐπεί κ' ἐσορῇς τὰς παρθένος οἷα γελᾶντι,
τάκεαι ὀφθαλμὼς ὅτι οὐ μετὰ ταῖσι χορεύες.　　　　　(91 f.)

Even so, when you see the laughing of the maidens, you too weep with overflowing eyes because you are not dancing with them.

The non-sexual 'dance' ends the speech, the charming 'laugh' ends the preceding line. The three contrasted images are essentially separated by refrains.[11] Even in Daphnis' own speech, we find such conflict of tone. He makes an assault on his enemy Aphrodite; this includes even the gloating coarseness of

οὐ λέγεται τὰν Κύπριν ὁ βουκόλος;　　　　　(105)

Do they not say that a certain cowherd did something to Aphrodite I won't mention?[12]

The pungency and malice of the spirited rhetoric here (100–13) stand in sharp contrast with the pathos, fantasy, and extravagance of the following part (115–36) and of the surrounding narrative. The force of the song resides in the vigour of these oppositions: it is not mere monochromatic langour.[13]

The poem ends with the goatherd giving the shepherd the two objects he promised him if he sang of Daphnis: a cup and a she-goat. The cup has already received a rich description

---

[11] Usually only the crude element in Priapus' speech is remarked on.

[12] This is far cruder than Hom. *Il.* 3. 406 ff., where Aphrodite is attacked by Helen.

[13] The main points will stand, whatever the story; I take it to be this. Daphnis has vaunted that he could defeat Eros (97, perfectly explicit). Aphrodite afflicts him with passion for a girl, to which he refuses to yield, out of pride: even when he has died, through love (130, cf. 93, 98, 78), his refusal will give pain to Eros. He taunts Aphrodite, whose son is killing him, with her own defeat by passion and by mortals (105 ff.). The notion that Daphnis is killed for vengeance by a nymph or nymphs does not appear in the poem, and is incompatible with 141 and 66; it makes 90 curious. Theocritus avoids the story whereby Daphnis and a nymph are in love so that he can heighten the contrast between god and mortal. For other accounts see R. M. Ogilvie, *JHS* 82 (1962), 106 ff., F. J. Williams, *JHS* 89 (1969), 121 ff. It does not seriously affect my view, but I believe 95 f. to be corrupt, and G. Zuntz's explanation unappealing (*Opusc. Sel.*, 83 ff.).

(27–60); the goat has been mentioned briefly, with the homely detail that the milk she has to spare from her kids will fill two buckets (25 f.). Here the fragrance of the cup is again remarked on (149, cf. 28):

'Ωρᾶν πεπλύσθαι νιν ἐπὶ κράναισι δοκησεῖς.   (150)

You would think it had been rinsed in the springs of the Horae.

The line exquisitely transports homely reality into an enchanting and delicately elevated conception. But we move at once from the remote and beautiful Horae to the she-goat Cissaetha, summoned by her name. The names of herd-animals strike a note of low rusticity in Theocritus. They do this in poem 4, when the mellow and comforting reflections of the cowherd are interrupted by the misdeeds of his cows, and he calls them by their names, with rustic noises and colloquial omission of the verb (4. 45 f.); much the same occurs at 5. 100–4. There can be no mistaking the lowness of the final reference (1. 152) to the sexual activity of the he-goat (the she-goats are not to excite him). The giving of the reward is an important event in the story of the poem, and the end of a poem is a significant point in itself. Here, as at the beginning, we find the juxtaposition of beauty with low or grotesque rustic elements. Clearly the poet is laying weight on the effect.

Yet perhaps the best means of illustrating the importance of this concern in Theocritus is to discuss two of the poems where the very structure depends on a contrast of this kind. Poem 15 deals with a festival of Adonis produced in Alexandria by Queen Arsinoe. The latter third of the poem gives a song sung in honour of Aphrodite and Adonis; it is elevated and lavish in its language and feeling, and depicts the visual beauty and extravagance of the tableau created by the Queen. The rest depicts two women going to the festival (named Praxinoa and Gorgo). Praxinoa in particular, rather the dominant member of the pair, is loquacious, sententious, and by no means agreeable. The poet also conveys through the dialogue the bustle and animation of their getting ready and travelling through the city. Modern readers are fascinated by the depiction of ordinary life in the past; modern scholars are interested by the connections of Theocritus with mime.[14] But the climax of the poem is the song, and a chief purpose of the dialogue is to contrast with this. The poem was clearly intended to exalt the royal festival: the song gives Arsinoe and her mother a prominent place, in lines (106 ff.) which resemble the formal panegyric poem 17 (17. 36 ff., on Berenice); earlier references to the royal family have prepared for this (21-4, 46-50, 51 f., 95). It is probable, therefore, that the song presenting the festival was meant to be the heart of the poem.[15] The festival in the court is the goal of the women throughout, and their effort to enter is marked by the appearance of two fresh speakers (60 ff., 71 ff.). This makes us actually feel the depiction of the festival in the song as the culmination of the work. But it is the division of song from dialogue that matters most.

The movement to and from the song may be considered more closely. The women enter the court, with an injunction to the unfortunate slave Eunoa to push (76) and with a particularly marked form of proverbial utterance (77); the ready use of proverbs has been a great hallmark of Praxinoa's speech. The mood is altered abruptly as Gorgo suddenly calls Praxinoa to look at the beauties of the festival. Praxinoa's response is rapturous. It is evidently the same Praxinoa who speaks. She exclaims on the tapestries:

ἔμψυχ', οὐκ ἐνύφαντα· σοφόν τι χρῆμ' ἄνθρωπος. (83)

The figures are living things and not woven—man is a clever creature.

The colloquial pattern of the first part recalls her ἰλεόν, οὐκ οἴκησιν 'a hole and not a house' (9); the second reminds us of her various sententious expressions. But the subject-matter lifts us away from the trivial and everyday objects we have been encountering, and the style grows warm; it acquires a richness found only in Gorgo's opening description of the crowds for the

[14] The scholia tell us that the poem is modelled on a mime of Sophron (5th c. BC) (Wendel p. 305). One fragment has been assigned to this, a little rashly (fr. 10 Kaibel, Olivieri). Herodas 4 bears resemblances in subject to Theocr. 15. 78-149; but the final invocation by the temple attendant is tiny (83-5), and the opening prayer has none of the poetic atmosphere of this. On mime see further pp. 200 f., 240.

[15] The point is seen by Bulloch, in *CHCL* i. 580. The aspect of praise is emphasized by F. T. Griffiths, *Theocritus at Court* (*Mnemosyne* Supp. 55, 1979), 82 ff. On royal festivals see Rice, *The Grand Procession of Ptolemy Philadelphus*.

festival (5 f.). We feel these changes much more forcefully than the sameness of speaker; but just as it seems we are rising to the festival, we are abruptly brought down again. A man tells the women to stop their chatter—so stressing for us the speakers not the speech. Praxinoa replies at length in the manner we should expect. Even Gorgo now bids her be quiet, for the song is about to begin. This command highlights the break between the women's utterance and the singer's. Yet Gorgo's last words before the song invest even the singer with an air of the every-day: διαχρέμπτεται ἤδη 'she's clearing her throat now'.[16] Then at once we hear the first, extended period of the song, with its movement from grandeur to noble and delicate pathos. The effect of this moment is extremely powerful, and the false start, the interruption, the speech of Gorgo, have all contri-buted to its force.

The end of the song is followed by the words of Gorgo which close the poem:

> ἵλαθι νῦν, φίλ' Ἄδωνι, καὶ ἐς νέωτ'. εὐθυμεύσαις
> καὶ νῦν ἦνθες, Ἄδωνι, καὶ ὅκκ' ἀφίκῃ φίλος ἥξεῖς.
>
> Γο. Πραξινόα, τὸ χρῆμα σοφώτατον ἁ θήλεια·
> ὀλβία ὅσσα ἴσατι, πανολβία ὡς γλυκὺ φωνεῖ.
> ὥρα ὅμως κῆς οἶκον· ἀνάριστος Διοκλείδας,
> χὠνὴρ ὄξος ἅπαν, πεινᾶντι δὲ μηδὲ ποτένθῃς.
> χαῖρε, Ἄδων ἀγαπητέ, καὶ ἐς χαίροντας ἀφικνεῦ.   (143-9)

(Singer) 'Be gracious, dear Adonis, now and at our festi-val next year. We are glad at your coming now, Adonis, and you will be no less dear when you return.' (Gorgo) 'Praxinoa, what a clever creature the woman is! Happy woman to have such skill, thrice happy to sing with such beauty! But it's time I was off home. My husband hasn't had his lunch. That man's temper's pure vinegar, and you'd best not come near him when he's not had his food. Farewell, darling Adonis, and may we be faring well when you return.'

The final speech drives home the structure of the poem incisi-vely. The name of Praxinoa follows sharply on the name of Adonis; but Gorgo is speaking of the song and her words echo

---

[16] It is interesting that Clement should actually find unpleasant τὸ χρέμπτεσθαι βιαιότερον (*Paed.* 2. 60. 1.).

Praxinoa's earlier speech of rapture on the festival (83, above, and note the anaphora in 146, cf. 80 f., 82). We then descend to 'home', the environment in which the poem began, and to the criticism of husbands, which played so large a role in the first part of the dialogue. Gorgo's attitude to her husband stands in marked contrast to the sentiment she feels for the youthful god. Her final words echo the final words of the singer, and associate her with the warmth of the singer's addresses to Adonis (cf. also 136), and with the lavishness of the rhetoric and the ritual. The lines also reinforce the contrast between the prosaic and cantankerous marriages of the two women and the romantic and erotic marriage of Aphrodite and Adonis, ὁ κἢν Ἀχέροντι φιληθείς, Adonis 'loved even in death' (86, spoken by Praxinoa). The idea that Adonis is Aphrodite's husband has been stressed pungently in lines of the song which are strikingly simple in language and physical in conception (129–31). The close of the poem thus juxtaposes once more strange beauty and passion with the mean and trivial, and through Gorgo's speech it lightly complicates the opposition.

The second poem of Theocritus is also divided into two unequal parts. The girl Simaetha announces her purpose of working a charm on Delphis, who had loved her, but has now disappeared. She then sings a song, some of it addressed to Hecate, in which she works her charm (17–63). After that she sings to the Moon a narrative of her affair (64–166). The second song is twice as long as the first, but the two are made parallel by the use of a refrain in each, by Simaetha's opening declaration that she will sing to the Moon and to Hecate (11 f.), and by the salutation of the respective goddesses (χαῖρε) before the start of the first song and at the end of the last (14, 165). In essence, the first song is intended to seem bizarre and to distance us from Simaetha, the second to move us and to involve our sympathies. There is some interpenetration between the two parts which modifies the fundamental contrast, but we must consider the contrast first: that is, we must establish that the first half is indeed bizarre and distancing. Critics usually raise the emotional impact of the first part to much the same level as that attributed to the second.[17]

[17] C. Segal, *QU* 15 (1973), 32 f., stresses the irrationality of the magic, but treats the whole poem as continuously serious and involving.

Romanticism has invested magic with seductive glamour, and some may be reluctant to allow that the magic has not similar qualities here. We may observe, firstly, that although magic, and in particular love-magic, was widely practised in ancient Greece, Greek literature does not often mention it, and finds extended description of magic ritual alien to its dignity and general character.[18] The (relatively short) descriptions in AR 3. 1029 ff., 1199 ff., make weird the devious alternative to valour opened up by the female Medea. Even these are given a certain grandeur; they are made to recall the ritual in Book 11 of the *Odyssey*. The actions are not designed to have an effect on other human beings, but to win the aid of the goddess Hecate. We do not find there the crushing of lizards or the melting of wax that we find in this poem (28, 58). Much more similar to this poem is the description of a magic ritual in a fragment of Sophron, the fifth-century author of mimes (Page, *GLP* no. 73). Theocritus is said by a scholion to have taken the subject of magic (τῶν φαρμάκων) from Sophron (Sch. p. 270 Wendel), with whom the poem has further connections. At least one other mime of Sophron's would seem to have presented magical ceremonies at length.[19] These mimes were a very lowly kind of work, dramatic scenes not even written in verse, and they were intended to amuse (Testim. 5, 6 Kaibel). Magic must have been treated extensively too in certain comedies, the *Goetes* of Aristomenes, the *Triacades* of Epicharmus, probably the *Hecates* of Nicostratus and Diphilus.[20] This suggests that such a pas-

---

[18] I mean magic designed to affect the living, not the summoning up of the dead, which has a grander resonance. Places where magic is mentioned are often interesting. Pind. *Pyth.* 4. 213 ff. gives the mythical origin of the ἴυγξ, an instrument of love-magic used here: the myth lends dignity. The object was clearly familiar, but the only other work to mention it literally is an epigram on one. Euripides, fonder than the other tragedians of introducing piquantly unelevated elements, is more willing to mention ordinary magic: cf. *Hipp.* 509 ff., *Andr.* 32 f., 157 f., *al.* (Medea is of course a special case, magic forming part of her mythical actions). The actual importance of magic is suggested e.g. by the violent polemic in the Hippocratic *De Morbo Sacro*, or the death-penalty passed on all the family of the sorceress in [Dem.] 25. 79.

[19] 'The women who claim they are expelling the goddess' (the 'claim' suggests the attitude of the work). This will probably be different from the mime of the papyrus fragment, where a single person (note l. 11) is commanding slaves who include men. It is uncertain from what mime come frr. 3–9 Kaibel and the fragment adduced by L. Cohn in *Corp. Paroem. Gr.* Suppl. 71.

[20] See further A. Abt, *D. Apologie d. Apuleius* (1908), 170 f.; on Epicharmus cf. Wilamowitz, *Kl. Schr.* iv. 50 f.

sage as the first half of this poem would not seem intrinsically grand and awesome in content, but bizarre and low. And the actual handling of the ritual here confirms this assumption.

The papyrus fragment of Sophron consists of instructions to slaves, and the slave-girl Thestylis plays an important part in the structure of Theocritus' poem; we are told that she was borrowed from Sophron (Sch. p. 269 Wendel). She appears in the first line, and her departure at the end of the ritual marks the change to the second half. 'I am alone now', says Simaetha; 'where shall I begin lamenting my passion?' (64),

νῦν δὴ μώνα ἐοῖσα πόθεν τὸν ἔρωτα δακρύσω;

The ritual begins, and is halted at once.

ἀλλ᾽ ἐπίπασσε,
Θεστυλί.—δειλαία, πεὶ τὰς φρένας ἐκπεπότασαι;
ἦ ῥά γέ θην, μυσαρά, καὶ τὶν ἐπίχαρμα τέτυγμαι;   (18–20)

Come, sprinkle on the barley, Thestylis.—You wretch, where has your mind wandered to? Have I fallen so low that even you, you foul creature, can take pleasure in my misfortunes?

Thestylis has failed to respond, and her look excites the suspicion of her humiliated mistress; the roughness of Simaetha's language stresses crudely the difference of status between them, but suggests the human awkwardness contained in the little moment. The relation between slave and owner is used to disrupt the ceremony which Simaetha treats seriously. This interruption must dissolve the solemnity of the ritual for the reader, at least for the instant. The bathos is the greater in that Simaetha has just prayed for her magic to equal that of mythical witches, Circe and Medea; her own slave-girl now obtrudes. The passage is very heavily echoed at the end of the ritual, in the final instruction to Thestylis (62, cf. 21). Thestylis appears too in another interruption. Simaetha has begun a grandiose invocation to Hecate (33 f.); she breaks off suddenly and addresses Thestylis. She thinks the goddess is coming, and Thestylis must act to prevent the goddess's presence from bringing evil to Simaetha. The effect of the interruption might have been to enhance the grandeur. The chthonic goddess is one potentially awesome element in magic, and in Apollonius

she actually appears (3. 1212 ff.) and confers new elevation on
the ritual. The same seems to be happening here: Simaetha
calls for the goddess's aid (cf. 14, AR 3. 1211); the noise of dogs
appears to signal her advent in response (35 f., cf. AR 3.
1216 f.). But then at once all is silence; the suddenness of the
contrast is marked by Simaetha's ἠνίδε 'listen, *ecce*' (37).
Simaetha's speech turns away from the appearance of the goddess to herself; the silence must be taken, not as a further sign of
the epiphany, but as the reversal of such a sign. Simaetha, we
gather with some puzzlement, was mistaken; the interruption
with Thestylis proves again to have helped disintegrate the seriousness of the rite.

At 48 f. Simaetha's rigid description of her magical acts
yields momentarily to a different form. In an epic manner she
declares 'there is a plant in Arcadia ...'. Yet the result is not
elevation but grotesqueness, for in the startling form is exhibited devious lore about the magical *hippomanes*.[21] Just before,
the tone had risen suddenly with the mention of a legend, that
of Theseus deserting Ariadne (45 f.); these lines turn the grand
into the bizarre. At 55 f. direct passion intrudes:

> αἰαῖ Ἔρως ἀνιαρέ, τί μευ μέλαν ἐκ χροὸς αἷμα
> ἐμφὺς ὡς λιμνᾶτις ἅπαν ἐκ βδέλλα πέπωκας;

> Ah, agonizing Eros, why have you sucked all the dark
> blood from my body, clinging to me like a leech from the
> marshes?

Simaetha apostrophizes Eros; but the comparison of Eros to a
leech of the marshes tinges the passionate utterance with grotesqueness. The bathetic comparison is kept for the second line,
the first ending grandly with the epic μέλαν ... αἷμα 'dark
blood'.[22] The only point where passion is allowed to have
undiluted impact is the very passage where magic falls apart as
Hecate fails to appear (38–41, see above). That passage
mingles two effects, but the counterpoint does not impede the

---

[21] Theocritus' account diverged from the normal tradition of antiquity: see Sch. ad
loc., Abt (n. 20), 166, Pease on Virg. *Aen.* 4. 515.

[22] Blood itself is common in descriptions of the imagined physical effects of passion.
The nearest parallel I recollect to this comparison is Plaut. *Bacch.* 372, where the moral
Lydus says of the sisters 'hominum sorbent sanguinem'; but this depicts them as
monsters.

force of Simaetha's direct expression of her feeling, which anti-cipates both the solitude and the narrative of the second half. The essential character of the first, however, remains clear, and sharply defined.

The second song, on the other hand, shows a greater admixture of modifying elements. The predominant quality of the passage, however, is its emotional power. The sequence of events from Simaetha's first sight of Delphis to the consummation of their mutual passion is intrinsically compelling, and was more so for Greek readers. For them love at first sight and the use of female slaves to establish contact belonged to the inherited pattern of the love-affair, with its own momentum and weight.[23] But the narrative is much enriched by its form. The story is told by Simaetha, so that we feel primarily its impact on her emotions; the story belongs to the past, so that we follow its movement to a happy ending with the consciousness that desertion will follow. The use of the first person is particularly potent in Simaetha's forceful descriptions of her feelings when she first saw Delphis (82 ff.) and when he entered her house (106 ff.). So at the start of the earlier description we have ὥς μοι πυρὶ θυμὸς ἰάφθη | δειλαίας (82 f.) 'My heart was struck with fire, unhappy me'. δειλαίας, 'unhappy me', expressively placed, stresses the identity of speaker and sufferer, and thus intensifies the immediacy of our response. The second aspect, the irony, lends especial pregnancy to Delphis' long speech. The irony is sly when for example Delphis says that his peers all call him ἐλαφρός (124), either 'nimble' or 'fickle' (cf. e.g. Philemon fr. 171. 2). It is terrifyingly direct when he ends his speech by illustrating the power of Eros with an instance of desertion (137 f.). Delphis has just declared that Eros' fire is often fiercer than a volcano's (133 f.); that grandiose comparison—very different from the comparison to a leech—is not deflated by this irony. Rather we apply it in different directions, as the 'often' invites us, to the new passion that afflicts Delphis now (cf. 7), and also to the

---

[23] Both elements appear in the purportedly true story at Lys. 1. 7 ff. For *women* falling in love at sight cf. Medea in Apollonius, Phaedra in Euripides (*Hipp.* 24 ff.) and e.g. Ariadne in Catull. 64. 86 ff. (and cf. Pind. *Pyth* 9. 97 ff., 10. 59); for their sending slaves cf. Eur. *Hipp.* 649 f., *Sthen.* (Page *GLP* 16) 10 ff. It is thus mistaken to think that we should be surprised at Simaetha's falling in love and taking the initiative (F. T. Griffiths, *Arktouros* (Festschrift Knox, 1979), 83, S. F. Walker, *Theocritus* (1980), 96 ff.); Walker's view of her action at 138 f. seems to ignore ἁ ταχυπειθής.

passion that afflicts Simaetha. The image thus enhances the alarming conception of love, destructive and irresistible. In the narrative as a whole the combination of dramatic irony and emotional involvement leaves no room for an essentially detached and distanced reception.

None the less, the poet uses extensively devices which modify, without dissolving, this primary response. The whole narrative is differentiated from the first part by being addressed to the Moon; this device is variously exploited. When Simaetha says that the chests of Delphis and his friend gleamed πολὺ πλέον ἢ τύ, Σελάνα (79) 'much more brightly than you, O Moon', we are a little distanced from the event by the ingenuity with which present and past are connected and by the lover's amusing contravention of piety. More radical is the breach at the very climax of the story. The progress of the love-making is interrupted by the clause

$$\text{ὡς καί τοι μὴ μακρὰ φίλα θρυλέοιμι Σελάνα ...} \qquad (142)$$

I do not wish to chatter on too long to you, dear Moon.

The fact of sexual intercourse is then mentioned in a line. Modesty and brevity at such a moment are natural;[24] and the impact of the climax is not destroyed. Yet we are distanced here by the *naïveté* suggested in the address, and by the light in which the narrative is presented. The goddess might get bored; the narrative is chatter. An insistence on brevity is assuredly conventional in itself; but the language and the situation make this one piquant and intrusive.

A related feature which lends distance is the appearance of trivial and everyday information, naïvely and garrulously relayed. Thus Simaetha explains that when she went to the festival she was wearing Clearista's shawl (74); and she identifies the woman who told her of Delphis' infidelity as 'the mother of Philista my flute-girl and of Melixo too' (145 f.). The latter description is followed at once, in the same sentence, by an elevated picture of the dawn; the contrast is typical of the poet. Even the powerful descriptions of Simaetha's feelings are modified by elements grotesque or low. In 81–6 the potent concep-

---

[24] Cf. e.g. Aesch. fr. 145. 4, Eur. fr. 102. 8 Aust. (neither perhaps with an audience on stage).

tion of physical sickness appears dramatically (85 f.). But after
the refrain this is pushed to a grotesque extreme: all Simaetha's
hair falls out (89). The next two lines mention the visiting of
witches, and so recall the magical concerns of the first part. The
second description, 106–10, moves downward in its imagery,
from snow and dew to the babble of infants, and then to a
doll.[25] The distancing here is much lighter. There are various
links in this half of the poem with the first, the associations of
which have an effect on the tone. The most salient link is provided by the important figure of the go-between. This is Thestylis (95), who so helped to dissolve the seriousness of the ritual.
We think back to Simaetha's accusation that now 'even' that
slave takes pleasure in her calamity (20). Here the irony of the
narrative becomes drier, sharper, and less pathetic.

The two songs, then, are essentially contrasted, but the
second song does not escape being tinged with the atmosphere
of the first, sometimes through direct connection; the reverse
happens once in the first part. The last lines of the poem, somewhat as in poem 15, weave the different parts and colours into a
texture singularly dense. Having arrived back at her present
situation, Simaetha declares she will use further magic to capture Delphis (159), as she had intimated at the end of the first
song (58). She is not assured of its efficacy, it is promptly suggested:

$$αἰ δ' ἔτι κά με$$
λυπῇ τὰν Ἀΐδαο πύλαν, ναὶ Μοίρας, ἀραξεῖ,
τοῖά οἱ ἐν κίστᾳ κακὰ φάρμακα φαμὶ φυλάσσεν,
Ἀσσυρίω, δέσποινα, παρὰ ξείνοιο μαθοῖσα.   (159–62)

> If he still grieves me, it is the door of Death he shall beat
> on, by the Fates! So potent are the evil drugs which I am
> keeping for him, I declare, in my magic chest.—I learned
> about these drugs, Lady Moon, from a foreigner from
> Babylonia.

The suggestions of aggression in the earlier rite are here made
overt and extreme; magic appears in its most sinister aspect,
and our sympathies are cooled. But the appended information
alters the tone. The address to the Moon is the first since the

---

[25] The images of snow and wax are similarly discordant in Call. *H.* 6. 91.

distancing address of 142 (see above), and it reintroduces suddenly the note of naïve loquacity. The Babylonian, in this context, makes magic seem outlandish. With an abrupt switch, the
listening Moon is bid turn her horses to the Ocean and leave
Simaetha (163 f.); the lofty picture recalls the earlier description of Dawn (147 f.). Simaetha now sets herself, a suffering
mortal, against the sublime divinity; the intimacy is broken up,
and we again feel straightforward sympathy for Simaetha. The
poem ends with an ornate couplet addressed to the Moon and
stars; its elevation and calm remove us from human magic and
pain.

In poem 15, the distance between the two parts is increased
by the difference between them in narrative status. The song is
known to be a song by the singer and the characters in the rest
of the poem; the characters in the rest of the poem are unaware
that their part is poetry. Thus the song occupies a special position within the dramatic world of the poem. In poem 2, the
songs are separated by the self-contained character of the songs
as such; the two can be the more pointedly contrasted, as distinct and equivalent entities. In most of the poems with more
than one song in, the songs are separated and balanced by
having different singers; here the device of the refrains subserves the same end.[26] These two qualities of songs, then, their
status within the poem and their self-contained nature, heighten the basic effects Theocritus is pursuing in the two structures. They also sharpen the piquancy of modifying or even
playing with those structures. In the other poems with songs
too they are of great importance. In the greater number of
poems without songs there are analogous or related elements.
By considering from this angle the form of some of the poems
without songs, and then of some of the poems in which songs do
appear, we may come to understand better the general character of Theocritus' poetry.

Poem 26, like poems 2 and 15, consists of two parts one of
which is twice the length of the other. Ll. 1–26 narrate the dis-
memberment of Pentheus by his mother and her sisters under

---

[26] In the only other poem with a refrain, poem 1, the refrain is perhaps intended to
mark off the song from the long description of the cup which precedes it: that description does not possess so distinctive a character and so obvious a narrative status as
dramatic dialogue.

the influence of Dionysus. The form of these lines conveys the horror of the event with lucid elegance. The names of the three relations appear at the beginning of the description of an orderly sacrifice, prompted by Dionysus (1);[27] the three appear again at the destruction of Pentheus (20–3), with 'his mother' substituted for the name of Agave. The account of Pentheus' doom begins with his name (10), and the name recurs twice, again at the beginning of lines (16, 18); but the account closes with a denial of the name. The dismembered Pentheus is πένθημα καὶ οὐ Πενθῆα 'a source of pain, not Pentheus' (26).[28] The women do not think Pentheus to be a lion, as Agave does in the *Bacchae*; on the contrary, Agave herself is compared to a mother lion (21).[29]

The last third of the poem (27–38) commences with the intrusion of the narrator himself. οὐκ ἀλέγω 'I care nothing about Pentheus', declares the poet; he stresses that such indifference is demanded by piety and prudence. Callimachus and Catullus close narratives with two or three lines of mock-nervous prayer, which deprecate for themselves and their friends the doom of the impious man just narrated.[30] But here we have six lines on the theme, after a very short narrative; and the entry of the narrator is far more abrupt. The attitude proclaimed is obviously intended to conflict with the attitudes aroused in the reader by the narrative. These lines themselves emphasize the suffering of Pentheus, and introduce a fresh element of pathos, his youth (29).[31] At the end of the poem Theocritus declares that the women

---

[27] Such, and only such, would be practised by historical maenads: see A. Henrichs, *HSCP* 82 (1978), 147 f. (others dissent).

[28] The two words differ only by one consonant and are applied to the same person: Theocritus thus trumps in neatness Euripides' Πενθεὺς δ' ὅπως μὴ πένθος εἰσοίσει δόμοις (*Bacch.* 367).

[29] Ll. 18 f. appear in order to make it evident that the women see Pentheus as human; cf. B. Effe, *RhM* NF 121 (1978), 72. Paley's deletion in Eur. *Bacch.* 1108 f. seems attractive to me, despite Dodds's defence from psychology.

[30] Call. *H.* 6. 116 f. (cf. Hopkinson ad loc.), Catull. 63. 91–3. Call. *H.* 3. 136 ff. is different, and moves away from the subject of piety.

[31] Pentheus usually has no beard in art (L. D. Caskey and J. D. Beazley, *Athenian Vase Paintings in the Museum of Fine Arts, Boston*, ii (1954), 2; cf. Philostr. *Im.* 1. 18. 2). His beard is just beginning in Euripides (*Bacch.* 1185) and elsewhere (Nonn. *D.* 46. 201, *al.*). The numbers nine and ten in l. 29 lend a grotesque precision; καὶ δεκάτω ἐπιβαίη must mean 'has embarked on his tenth year as well'. αὐτός is contrasted with the subject of μογήσαι and εἴη (Lobel's text should be followed at 27 f.).

τόδε ἔργον ἔρεξαν ὀρίναντος Διονύσω
οὐκ ἐπιμωματόν· μηδεὶς τὰ θεῶν ὀνόσαιτο.   (37 f.)

performed this deed at the impulse of Dionysus, and it
must not be found fault with: let no one disapprove the
doings of the gods.

The ending is abrupt, and affects a curt finality; but in doing so
it introduces explicitly the notion of criticism which it pushes
away so briefly. Again the expression of the narrator's attitude
in itself invites a different evaluation, one prompted by the narrative, to which τόδε ἔργον 'this deed' explicitly looks back. The
treatment of the second part makes it a frame inside which the
narrative is set; the frame is conscious of the narrative, but not
vice versa. The narrative is separated off, and there is piquant
play between the two: narrative and narrator are in discord.

In poem 22, a hymn to the Dioscuri, we have two narratives,
one concerning Polydeuces (27–134), one concerning Castor
(137–213). The narratives are made into distinct entities, and
contrasted. The narrative form is marked out as distinctive in
different ways at either end of the work. The poem begins
ὑμνέομεν 'I hymn' the Dioscuri, 'twice and thrice I hymn'
them (1, 4). It proceeds to describe how they rescue ships, just
as the Homeric Hymn to them does (Hom. *H.* 33), and at much
the same length. But the Homeric Hymn ends there, save for a
final couplet; Theocritus makes a new start, dividing all the
first section from what he now presents as the hymn proper:

Κάστορος ἢ πρώτου Πολυδεύκεος ἄρξομ' ἀείδειν;
ἀμφοτέρους ὑμνέων Πολυδεύκεα πρῶτον ἀείσω.   (25 f.)

Shall I begin my song first from Castor or from Polydeuces? I shall hymn both, but I will sing of Polydeuces
first.

The device bears some relation to the design of the Homeric
Hymn to Apollo as Theocritus knew it.[32] Theocritus' more
surprising arrangement neatly demarcates narrative from
generalized description; at the same moment it separates the
two narratives from each other and sets them in balance.

---

[32] However, the opening section of that work (1–18, possibly not original) is primarily concerned with Leto, before the poet turns to hymn Apollo. In l. 24 Theocritus
recalls the ἄρχομ' ἀείδειν which forms a standard opening in Homeric hymns (2. 1, 11.
1, 22. 1, 25. 1, 26. 1, 28. 1).

In the last section of the poem (214–23) the poet stands apart from what precedes, and so gives what precedes a different status from this frame. The frame presents the rest as poetry, Theocritus' own production (222 f.), parallel to Homer's (218 ff.), capable of fame (214 f.), and valuable to heavenly patrons. The section is much more extended than, say, 24. 171 f., and the arguments of the poet's appeal surprise when addressed to gods. The author thus creates a marked sense of distance between the rest of the poem and this *envoi*. The rest of the poem formally includes the opening description of the Dioscuri; but we are made to think primarily of the narratives by their length and by the fresh start at 23. So we are too by the comparison of the poem to the *Iliad*, which was evoked and exploited in the narratives and is here contemplated, along with Theocritus' hymn, as a source of glory to the Twins and as the artefact of a poet.[33]

The two narratives are separated from each other by the lines in which they are introduced (25 f., quoted above), with the mannered emphasis of question and repeating answer. Between the two narratives Theocritus stresses still more the parallelism and the division:

καὶ σὺ μὲν ὕμνησαί μοι, ἄναξ· σὲ δέ, Κάστορ, ἀείσω,
Τυνδαρίδη ταχύπωλε, δορυσσόε, χαλκεοθώρηξ.   (135 f.)

You, Polydeuces, I have hymned now; it is of you that I shall sing, Castor, son of Tyndareus, Lord with the swift horses and the brazen breastplate, and brandisher of the spear.

Theocritus plays here with the ending of many Homeric hymns, where the first 'you' (σὺ μέν) leads to the actual end of the poem (*Hymns* 1, 3, 4, etc.). This sets the two narratives apart as distinct objects. The string of epithets for Castor in the following line recalls the similar string that appeared in the rapturous address to both brothers when the two narratives

---

[33] ὑμῖν αὖ καὶ ἐγώ (221) takes up ὑμῖν at the start of 218. The Dioscuri are mentioned by Homer at *Il.* 3. 236–44; both are mortals there, and dead. There is a concealed *a fortiori* argument: the gods (and the reader) are to contrast this brief mention in the narrative on the Trojan War (219 f.) with the narratives of Theocritus, devoted to them entirely.

were introduced (24). This heightens the sense of independence here, and of neat design.

In the first narrative Polydeuces boxes with King Amycus; in the second Castor fights with one of the two sons of Aphareus over the daughters of Leucippus. In both there is speech before the combat of the brother and his opponent; the form of the speech differentiates the two sections boldly. The first exhibits a stichomythia of the most saliently tragic type (54 ff.). Not only is each utterance kept strictly to one line, but the whole conduct of the dialogue is very close to Euripides in particular. The most startling divergence from epic is the quasi-dramatic omission of introductions to the utterances—after the epic τὸν πρότερος προσέειπεν (53) 'him Polydeuces addressed first' at the start of the dialogue. The speech is presented directly: the narrative form falls away.[34]

In the second story we have only a single long speech, by one of the sons of Aphareus (145–80).[35] The speech is accommodated into the narration (144), and the central portion of it narrates a similar speech made in the past (154–66). The narrative form is here not dissolved but redoubled. In form, then, the speech of the first story, by contrast with that of the second, surprises in a narrative, especially one of epic type. In content, the speech of the second song surprises in a hymn. In the first story the dialogue sets Amycus very firmly in the wrong; in the second Lynceus' speech sets the Dioscuri at a moral disadvantage.[36] The brothers whose praise is being sung behave in a somewhat disquieting fashion; the first narrative has made us look for morality as well as prowess.

The accounts of the two combats are much less sharply opposed. Boxing occurs in the funeral games of the *Iliad* (23.

---

[34] It certainly seems justified to talk here of a 'contamination of genres' (Rossi, *BICS* 13 (1971), 85; cf. Kroll, *Studien z. Verständnis d. röm. Lit.* 205). On the other hand, to regard the poem as contaminating the hymn with the 'epyllion' seems very dubious. As Rossi realizes, the hymn is a narrative and epic genre (begun supposedly by Homer). Furthermore, such an approach makes too simple and too technical the handling in this work of other poems and other types of poem.

[35] F. T. Griffiths, *GRBS* 17 (1976), 353 ff., rightly disputes Wilamowitz's lacuna after 170, which gives Castor a speech in reply; Κάστωρ in 175 would naturally be changed to Λυγκεύς, cf. Sch. 173 Dübner. But Vossius' ἑός should be received in 173: ὅμαιμος stresses, for the Dioscuri and for us, that the two combatants are related (170) and that kindred blood will be shed (171).

[36] Cf. C. Moulton, *GRBS* 14 (1973), 41 ff.

653 ff.), and Theocritus alludes to that episode (98, cf. *Il.* 23. 697; 129, cf. *Il.* 23. 698); but the subject is not typically Iliadic, like the second combat. Indeed, the episode in Homer plays on the difference from warfare (*Il.* 23. 670f., 675). Theocritus, however, is concerned, in a sense, to narrow that interval: here too one can 'accomplish some mighty deed', ῥέξαι τι ... μέγα ἔργον (118). The chief means of bringing the boxing closer to war and the *Iliad* is the emphasis on blood and physical destruction. Apollonius' account, which is probably Theocritus' source, is not at all gory. We only see Polydeuces strike one blow, the fatal one (2. 95 f.). This is in harmony with the contrast sustained there between Amycus' ugly ferocity and Polydeuces' radiant ease. Theocritus' account is filled with grisly descriptions of Polydeuces' blows (105, 110f., 125 ff.). Theocritus employs the Iliadic ἕλκεα λυγρά 'dire wounds' (100) and μέλαν αἷμα 'dark blood' (125).[37] With an Iliadic question to the Muse (see below) he leads us to think that Amycus will be slain, as in Apollonius: καθεῖλεν (115) is naturally taken by the reader to mean 'killed', until he discovers that it must have meant 'defeated'. For Polydeuces spares his opponent, exacting a promise that he will behave morally in the future (131 ff.). This surprising development reverses the tendency of the account, and our sense of the extremity and bizarreness of that account is heightened by the anti-climax. The continual descriptions of Amycus' face and the injuries it receives are grotesquely ugly as well as fearsome: the first such, of shrinking eyes in a swelling face (101), establishes this note. When in the course of the fighting Polydeuces' body grows larger, and Amycus' small, the effect is grandiose, but so extreme as to disconcert (112–14). The question to the Muse which follows is certainly intended to seem grand.

πῶς γὰρ δὴ Διὸς υἱὸς ἀδηφάγον ἄνδρα καθεῖλεν;
εἰπέ, θεά, σὺ γὰρ οἶσθα· ἐγὼ δ' ἑτέρων ὑποφήτης
φθέγξομαι ὅσσ' ἐθέλεις σὺ καὶ ὅππως τοι φίλον αὐτῇ.   (115–17)

How did the son of Zeus defeat (kill) that greedy hulk?
Tell, goddess, for you know. I will be your interpreter for

---

[37] Compare more particularly with 125 *Il.* 13. 655 = 21. 119. The phrase χερσὶ τιτυσκόμενος in 88 is noteworthy: the verb is used in the *Iliad* of spears, not hands; and so it is used in 187 ἔγχεσι ... τιτυσκόμενοι, to be contrasted with the earlier passage.

others; I will speak all that *you* wish, in accordance with
your desire.

The lines do not show the obvious play found in Callimachus'
and Apollonius' treatment of the device. But the attitudes
struck are deliberately excessive: one notes, for example, the
purposely laboured deference to the goddess. The excess seems
particularly evident in retrospect, when we know the issue (see
above). Even on first reading, however, ἀδηφάγον ἄνδρα 'that
greedy hulk' somewhat diminishes the stature of Amycus and
the greatness of the event which the Muse is asked to tell of. In
this account, then, a striving towards Iliadic heights is united
with a certain sense of the exaggerated and the grotesque. This
is not mere parody, but a finely judged modification of an effect
straightforwardly Iliadic.

Such an effect is actually found in the account of the fight
with Lynceus. There is nothing in these lines to suggest that
they parody a Homeric or pseudo-Homeric style.[38] Such a
view robs of its obvious force the expressive phrase, adapted
from Homer, describing Lynceus' death:

κὰδ δ' ἄρα οἱ βλεφάρων βαρὺς ἔδραμεν ὕπνος.   (204)

Heavy sleep raced down over his eyelids.

It does so too to the following lines on the death of Idas (205 f.),
with their Homeric grimness and pathos and their ironic echoes
of Lynceus' speech (176–81). In the previous combat with
Amycus the unexpected avoidance of death had enhanced the
morality of the brothers who are hymned, and had at the same
time impaired the epic quality of the account. This narrative
again shows a double divergence. Castor's killing of Lynceus is
a disquieting act (he is a kinsman, and the injured party); but
the realization of the deaths gives the narrative epic seriousness
and weight. Idas' breach of the agreement, and Zeus' intervention to kill him, do not detract from the Iliadic quality; they
alter slightly the moral balance.

The detachment and opposition of the two narratives is
related to a conscious and surprising use of Homer and the
hymn, of form and narrative status. To suppose that Theocritus

[38] The contention of F. T. Griffiths (n. 35), based on an unacceptable view of literary factions in this period.

is chiefly concerned to assert a controversial position about literature is to take too crude a view of the poem's tone, especially in the second narrative. To suppose that Theocritus is concerned simply to subvert the mythical tradition and its values is to take too crude a view of the tone in the first narrative and to subordinate arbitrarily the treatment of form.[39] The effect of the poem is much more self-contained, and is created through the complexities of its design.

In poem 30 the poet speaks of his passion for a boy; he then records his speech to his heart dissuading it from this passion (12–23), and the heart's reply (25–32).[40] The two speeches are made distinct and are contrasted in a fashion related to the treatment of songs and narratives in other poems. In short poems delivered in the first person speeches may stand out sharply. Thus poem 28 (the Distaff) is closed by the comment of an external voice (24 f.) which annuls the poetic fictions of the rest. The poet is giving a distaff to the wife of his friend Nicias. The poem is addressed to the distaff, which has been treated almost if it were a person itself; the author plays with its fictitious personality in relation to the real persons of the poem.[41] The other voice treats it as an object, and an insignificant one in itself (contrast line 22); the relationship alone becomes important.

κῆνο γάρ τις ἔρει τὦπος ἰδὼν σ'· "ἦ μεγάλα χάρις
δώρῳ σὺν ὀλίγῳ· πάντα δὲ τίματα τὰ πὰρ φίλων." (24 f.)

When someone sees you, distaff, this is what he will say:

---

[39] For such a view cf. B. Effe, *RhM* NF 121 (1978), 64 ff. (an important article, however).

[40] Gow supposes 12–23 to be a soliloquy. But the idea of the heart as judge in 11 and 24 seems quite implausible, and in 24 requires an object of reproach other than the speaker himself—that would need to be expressed (ταῦτα is an internal accusative). πρὸς ἐμὸν θῦμον will be designed to recall the Homeric πρὸς ὃν μεγαλήτορα θυμόν (it is unlikely to be adverbial). In 12 πόης suits the heart somewhat better than Theocritus, despite ἔρδ' in 15. ἐμαύτω not ἐμαύτῳ should be read in 11 (cf. 9), and on any hypothesis εἰσκαλέσαις should be questioned: possibly δὴ καλ., with καὶ το[retained in 10?

[41] For the treatment of the distaff see especially 3, 10, 17–21. Note ἐκτελέσῃς (10) in relation to the following description of Theugenis, καὶ γάρ τοι πάτρις (17) in relation to 16 and to ἄνδρων δοκίμων in 18, and οἶκον ... ἄνερος (19) in relation to οἰκήσῃς (21); note also the juxtaposition of descriptions in 7 and 8. Nicias is the true addressee of the poem, Theugenis its most important character, but Theocritus' relationship to these real people is conveyed only at one remove.

'In truth, a little gift brings great pleasure: anything that friends give is valued highly.'

In poem 12 the enamoured poet imagines utterances being made in the future on the glory of his love (12–16, 20 f.). These are separated from the poet's utterance by a great interval of time; they are themselves the events to which the poet's sweeping fantasy aspires. But the separation and distinctness of the two speeches in poem 30 is more paradoxical and more pointed.

Addresses to the θυμός ('heart') are common enough in Greek poetry.[42] They are essentially addresses to oneself, often with relation to one's passions; they frequently employ language appropriate to a human being but not to his heart. Even where the heart is presented as being in conflict with the speaker, it is scarcely conceived of as a person itself.[43] In this poem itself Theocritus' speech to his heart appears at first to have the character described. After the opening question most of what Theocritus says fits himself as well as his heart or fits only himself. The reply of the heart comes as a delicious surprise. In the light of that reply were are compelled, I think, to read Theocritus' speech again, and feel a greater sense of distance between the speaker and the second person of his reproaches (12, 13, 16): his tone becomes more censorious. Such rereading is called for in Theocritus not uncommonly. In poem 4 the revelation of Battus' feelings for Amaryllis (38–40, cf. 62 f.) not only explains his remarks about his former rival Aegon, but gives to several of them an altered tone (26–8, 9, 11). In poem 14 the closing revelation that Aeschines is aging (68–70) should make us look again at the rest, and especially at the narrative of his misfortune in love.[44]

At any rate, the heart adopts a quite different manner from Theocritus himself in speaking to Theocritus, who now appears as a separate person, addressed as ὦγαθε 'my good fellow' (29).

---

[42] See F. Leo, *D. Monolog im Drama* (1908), 94 ff., add e.g. Cratinus fr. 171. 63 Kass.–Aust.

[43] For such conflict cf. Eur. *Med.* 1056, by some thought spurious, and also Hom. *Il.* 11. 407, al. τίη μοι ταῦτα φίλος διελέξατο θυμός; in that place of Homer—contrast 'said to his θυμός' of the same words in 403—may inspire the real speech of the θυμός in Theocritus. Observe διελεξάμαν in 11.

[44] Horace's second epode offers an extreme example of such a poem; many particular lines acquire a different tone and sense (e.g. 4, 23 f., 37 f., 49 ff., 61).

The heart's manner is pronouncedly urbane. It does not attack Theocritus directly for his folly in thinking he can overcome Love: it refers to 'whoever thinks ..., that man' (25–7). It stresses, on the other hand, its own weakness, not only in comparison with the gods (also beaten by Love), but absolutely (31 f.). Its general attitude is one of resigned good sense. Theocritus had called for sense (φρονέην, 14) and awareness (καὶ μὰν ἄλλο σε λάθει 'there is something else you do not realize' 16). But in fact the heart possesses more of these qualities than Theocritus. The heart, however, is conventionally associated with passionate emotion, and is here taking the side of infatuation against restraint. There is an exquisite paradox in the union of manner and content; both sides of the paradox are given force by the contrast with the preceding speech. It will be apparent how unexpected are the very existence of a dialogue-form and the degree of distinct personality which that form gives to the heart. In short, the opposition of the speeches and their self-contained nature are fundamental to the effect of the poem.

Speech in the poem is marked out as an individual mode of discourse by the opening section. The poet first tells of his passion in general terms. His picture of the boy suggests both his infatuation and his awareness that he is infatuated: the boy, though delightful, is 'only fairly good-looking' (κάλω μὲν μετρίως, 3). The poet shows both the fluctuation of his passion and his consciousness that it will soon master him entirely (5 f.). We thus see divisions in Theocritus' consciousness, and we see that he possesses the attributes which later in the poem are confined to the personified heart. The section prepares the psychological situation underlying the dialogue, but stands apart from its extraordinary presentation. A short narrative then locates the dialogue in the past (7 ff.), and thus divides it in time and narrative status from the present discourse of the poet's unreported voice. From this division the speech of the heart acquires an impressive finality: its single statement (τοῦτ', 25) is contrasted with the quantity of Theocritus' utterances on the occasion (24, cf. 11). There is also, in the heart's closing picture of itself, an evocative tension between the distance produced by form, personification, and urbanity, and what the picture actually implies, the present feeling and real nature of the poet.

ἔμε μὰν φύλλον ἐπάμερον
σμίκρας δεύμενον αὔρας ὀνέλων ὦκα φόρει ⟨∪ −⟩.   (31 f.)

(Love can master the very gods.) As for me, he lifts me up,
like a leaf that lasts a day and needs only a faint breeze to
raise it, and he bears me along with speed.

The introductory narrative itself produces a much more
straightforward effect: 'As for me, Love seized a tighter hold of
my heart' (9: κραδίας, not θύμω). Again this prepares for the
dialogue but contrasts with its artificiality of conception and its
complexity of tone.

Given that the aspects of form we have been considering are
highly significant in some poems without songs, it would seem
likely that they are no less significant in poems with songs,
where those aspects are as a rule more saliently apparent. In
most of the poems with songs there is a difference of narrative
status between the songs and the rest, and it is strongly marked.
This naturally contributes to, and cannot readily be separated
from, the marking out of the songs as self-contained artefacts.
Where there is no divergence in narrative status, other means
are employed to that end.

At the beginning of poem 18 there is a brief description of the
girls who 'once' (ποκ' ἄρα, 1) sang the wedding-song for Helen
and Menelaus in Sparta; the song itself opens with an address
to Menelaus which stresses that the situation is a present one for
the singers: οὕτω δὴ πρωῒσδὰ κατέδραθες; (9) 'So early as this
you have fallen asleep?'. The difference in narrative status is
self-evident. The sentence before the song begins with ἄειδον
'they started to sing' and ends with ὑμεναίῳ 'wedding-song'; the
song and poem end with the ritual cry by which the wedding-
song is characterized. The first section of poem 11 sets a wide
interval of time between itself and the Cyclops' song. Theocritus addresses his real contemporary Nicias, dwelling on his
actual profession and talents (5 f.); the mythical Cyclops is
ὠρχαῖος Πολύφαμος 'Polyphemus of ancient times' (8). ὁ παρ'
ἀμῖν 'my fellow-Sicilian' (7) only accentuates paradoxically the
distance in time. It is essential to the argument of the poem that
Polyphemus is not merely soliloquizing but singing. The Muses
end the first sentence and begin the third line; the rest of the
frame reinforces the idea of song (6, 13, 18, 81). There are two

songs in poem 6, one supposedly addressed to the Cyclops, one supposedly replying; both are sung by rustic youths. These youths themselves are placed in a narrative addressed to Theocritus' contemporary, an Aratus (2), and set apart in time with the word ποκα 'once' (2). Hence the dramatic situation of the songs is doubly removed from the poet's utterance in the frame. That the songs are songs is emphasized by the close of the poem, in which each singer gives the other a musical instrument as a prize, and they continue with these their music and probably their contest. To this music their very cattle dance (45): the theme of music is startlingly heightened by this fantasy, half lyrical, half comic. The songs of poem 7 are again set in a narrative; the opening phrase marks a separation in time (ἧς χρόνος ἁνίκ' 'there was a time once when'). Even within the dialogue reported by the narrative the songs are not reactions to the situation they are sung in: on the contrary, they were both created earlier, and in a different place (51, 91 ff.). The dialogue, on the other hand, is well aware that the songs are artefacts, devised by the two speakers. The notion is stressed further by the attention given to the younger speaker's aspirations as a poet (37–48, 91–5, 129).

In poems 1, 3, 5, and 10 there is no narrative framework for the songs but a dramatic one. (On poems 2 and 15, see above.) The song in 1 has been sung by Thyrsis before (61, 19). Its nature is driven home by the disjunction between piping and singing which dominates the first 24 lines; by the sombre reflection which precedes the song directly (62 f.); by the words of the refrain in the song itself (referring to the Muses and bucolic song); by the singer's closing prayer to the Muses (144 f.), and the aesthetic pleasure of his listener (148). The device of the refrain marks the song out formally (see p. 160). The songs in poem 10 are similarly marked out by their rigid organization into couplets. The love-song of Bucaeus is seen as an artefact, accorded sarcastic praise (38 f., note ποῶν 'composing'; cf. 22 f.). The harvest-song of Milon was produced by the mythical Lityerses (41). In poem 5 the songs are short matching exchanges between Comatas and Lacon, who have been disputing in the dialogue before. In the songs all the utterances are strictly confined to two lines each; in the dialogue, although there is some tendency to have equal length in pairs, the utter-

ances range freely between two lines and five. The subject of
the singing-contest occupies most of the dialogue (there is an
opening wrangle about a skin and a musical instrument). The
relation between the two men is so hostile and contentious that
it takes them 59 lines to arrange and begin their match (21–
79). Among other things, this amusing protraction gives heavy
weight to the difference of the match from the dialogue as being
conscious art. The different standing of the contest is also
enhanced dramatically: a new character is called in to judge.
That moment is made particularly striking by the division of a
line between speakers (66), the ony such division in the poem.[45]

Even in poem 3, almost all of which is occupied by a song,
the introductory lines (1–5) to some degree mark the song off,
although the speaker is the same. The lines are placed in a different locale from the song. They address a colleague, insistently (3–5), and are thus opposed to the song, the main part of
which addresses the beloved throughout and begins from her
name (ὦ χαρίεσσ᾽ Ἀμαρυλλί 'O lovely Amaryllis' 6). They do
not explicitly describe the song as song, but their first word
κωμάσδω 'I am making a serenade' would indicate to Theocritus' readers that what followed was sung.[46] It may be
allowed, however, that the separation of the song is less striking
and significant here than elsewhere. But in this poem the song
in fact falls into two distinct songs, 6–36 and 40–51, which are
sharply contrasted. The second is sensuous, oblique, and elegant, the first naïvely direct and grotesquely artless.[47] The
less emphatic demarcation of the singing goes with a strong
division inside the singing itself, although it is all executed by
one person and addressed to one person, and all performs a
single object. Thus the divergence in the framing of song
accompanies a divergence in the way song is exploited: it does

---

[45] The same effect is obtained from the only division in poems 4 and 10 (4. 45, the
sudden misbehaviour of the cows; 10. 16, the revelation of who it is that Bucaeus loves).
Unlike those lines, 5. 66 is divided twice. Poems 14 and 15 split lines freely, as do the
Mimiambi of Herodas.

[46] For the singing of the lover in the κῶμος cf. Headlam on Herodas 2. 34–7.

[47] See on the poem Ott (n. 10), 180 ff.; cf. R. Whitaker, *Myth and Personal Experience
in Roman Love-Elegy* (Hypomnemata 76, 1983), 49 ff., and the literature he mentions.
Whitaker is right in what he says of the exempla at p. 49 n. 67; but the treatment of
death in 46–51 is rather more romantic than he suggests, and the contrasts of tone and
level are not properly emphasized.

not damage the notion that the division of songs from their surroundings is in general of particular importance.

Such division is not emphasized by the poet merely to underline an abstract structure in the poem. As we should now expect, the separation is central to the effect which each poem produces. So firm a stratification of the poem makes it possible to exploit the levels in a fashion both elaborate and striking.

We may start from poem 10. The poem is set in the harvest-field. One harvester, Milon, chides another, Bucaeus, for his feebleness at his task. Bucaeus reveals that he is in love, and is encouraged to sing a love-song while he works; this he does. Milon then sings a harvest-song purportedly ancient, and after it declares that this is a more suitable type of song for the occasion. It is obvious that each of the two songs bears a very different relation to the dramatic context and the singer. Bucaeus' love-song is out of place in the scene of harvesting, and expresses his individual emotions, which separate him from others. Milon's song is eminently suitable to the situation; it does not express his private emotions, but deals with the common activity of the harvesters.

Milon only exposes by degrees the unsuitability of the love-song. He at first urges Bucaeus to sing it, as an aid to work, and suggests that Bucaeus is skilled as a singer (23). After the song he bursts out in praise, which we soon learn to be sarcastic; but it is not yet clear what the sarcasm is directed at, save that Bucaeus' merits as an artist are now decried. The point has to wait until after Milon has sung his own song, which he bids Bucaeus consider (41). He then adds:

> ταῦτα χρὴ μοχθέντας ἐν ἁλίῳ ἄνδρας ἀείδεν,
> τόν δὲ τεόν, Βουκαῖε, πρέπει λιμηρὸν ἔρωτα
> μυθίσδεν τᾷ ματρὶ κατ᾽ εὐνὰν ὀρθρευοίσᾳ.   (56–8)

> That is what should be sung by men toiling in the sun;
> your love, a thing of starvation, ought to be spoken of to
> your mother in her bed first thing in the morning.

Bucaeus' love-song is scorned as being unsuitable to the situation, and, by extension, unsuitable to a grown man and to a worker who must make a living. The activity of ἄνδρες 'men' is contrasted with the act of a disturbed child; the allusion to the lover's traditionally starved appearance gains from the whole situation a harsh and practical point.[48] The preceding comment (38–41) now gains fuller force. Milon had pretended to lament that he had 'grown his beard in vain' (40), that is, had reached manhood without acquiring a skill so valuable as Bucaeus', a skill manifested in songs hitherto concealed from Milon and the other reapers (38). Now those songs are seen as being suited to young boys, not to men, and reapers: thus the colourful detail of growing the beard is turned round by the real immaturity of Bucaeus' behaviour.[49] We also see a fresh emphasis in the original exhortation to sing (21–3). Milon is concerned with Bucaeus' work, not his ease. In ἅδιον οὕτως | ἐργαξῇ 'you will work more easily if you do', we now mentally place the stress on ἐργαξῇ 'work' which is invited by the enjambment.[50] By the end we see an obvious relation between the unsuitability of the song to the scene and the unsuitability of love to such men as Milon and Bucaeus. The latter theme was developed in the opening dialogue. But Milon's three sets of remarks produce a design which focuses attention on the songs as songs and on their relation to the setting and the singers. We ought not to view the last two-thirds of the poem (containing the two songs) as simply an extension of the first third (the opening dialogue), and concerned chiefly to reveal the minds of the characters.[51] The poem is not, on the other hand, an abstract or generalizing treatment of song: it develops in a highly concrete fashion the relations between these songs and this particular drama. The development forms the vehicle for the effect of the poem; it does not form its subject.

The first part of the poem provides a vigorously dramatic

[48] The enamoured Cyclops is shown to be childish in a similar fashion (11. 70 f.). For the appearance of the lover cf. 11. 69, Ovid, *Ars Am.* 1. 733, *Am.* 1. 6. 5, etc.

[49] One thinks of the similar play with the beard in Dante, *Purg.* 31. 68 'alza la barba', cf. ibid. 61–7.

[50] The poem begins with Milon's address to Bucaeus as ἐργατίνα Βουκαῖε.

[51] Cf. F. Cairns, *Hermes* 98 (1970), 38 f.; he also sees the second part as repeating the standard sequence of the first (unconvincingly). He maintains that the poem would have no interest if it did not distort a type of poem normally set in the city; and that unless it does so, the reader will feel a lack of sympathy towards Milon that will ruin all its effect. The first point, and in part the second, require us to underplay the part of the songs in the poem. I do not see that the reader does feel strongly unsympathetic to Milon, or that the link with convention would prevent him from so feeling, or that it would be fatal to the poem if he did. This is not to deny that the probing of a lover forms a standard theme in literature; it is to deny that the most important aspect of the poem is its relation to other treatments of the theme.

and consequential dialogue of a type not unknown to the comic stage.[52] The mode of the second part (the songs) is contrasted with the mode of the first, even while it advances its themes. Bucaeus had gladly divulged the fact of his passion, but had not in the least expressed or conveyed it; Milon had made presuppositions about a reaper's activity, but he had not conveyed in words its nature or its ethos. The form of Bucaeus' song is elaborately stylized. The song (we noted) is divided firmly into pairs of lines; there is an opening invocation to the Muses; the address which opens the song proper is repeated at the start of the final couplet. Both artistry and emotional expression are brought into relief by the dialogue: the dialogue has its artistry of arrangement, but the artistry is only Theocritus'. Both elements in the song are joined with *naïveté* of thought in such a way that their impact is transformed into absurdity. Particularly striking are l. 32–5:

αἴθε μοι ἦς ὅσσα Κροῖσόν ποκα φαντὶ πεπᾶσθαι·
  χρύσεοι ἀμφότεροί κ' ἀνεκείμεθα τᾷ Ἀφροδίτᾳ,
τὼς αὐλὼς μὲν ἔχοισα καὶ ἢ ῥόδον ἢ τύγα μᾶλον,
  σχῆμα δ' ἐγὼ καὶ καινὰς ἐπ' ἀμφοτέροισιν ἀμύκλας.

O that I had the wealth which Croesus possessed of old, as they say! Then golden statues of us both would be dedicated to Aphrodite: you would be holding your pipes and a rose or an apple, I should be wearing new clothes and new shoes on both feet.

The first couplet here makes a strong break from the couplet that precedes it. This both continues the strictness of the form and expresses the suddenness with which the lover's emotion catches fire. The syntactical continuity of the second couplet with the first conveys the lover's excited elaboration of his fantasy. The lover's wish is for the fame of the relationship, like the wish of the enamoured poet himself in poem 12 (17 ff., cf. 11 ff.). In poem 12 the expression of the wish combines touching extravagance with purposely distancing erudition and a weird perspective of time. Here the concreteness of the wish, and its oddity in a rustic's mouth, produce a grotesqueness which is finally crystallized in the direct comedy of the last line:

[52] Men. *Her.* 1 ff., Plaut. *Pers.* 16 ff. (slaves in both places).

the rustic in his dreams of opulence stresses that he (in his statue) would have new shoes on both feet. The passion suggested by form and language enhance the bathos.

The last couplet of the song, which follows, displays a more ironic division of form and content. After highly specific comparisons of praise for his love's feet and her voice, Bucaeus ends 'of your character I cannot speak'. The form demands that we should understand him to be closing at the point when the subject-matter surpasses his powers, so that his very silence is an expression of supreme praise and rapture (itself verging on the absurd). However, his illusions about her beauty (see below) suggest very forcibly an undercurrent of meaning: he simply does not know what her character is really like. After all, he has only been in love 'almost eleven days' (12). The blunt conflict of form and elevation with reality matches the play at the beginning of the song; there the words hint that the song will confer on the beloved beauties not her own (25).

Milon's song exactly matches Bucaeus' in its length and in its division into couplets; it too begins with a prefatory invocation to a deity—but prefatory to the harvest rather than to the song as such. The correspondence in form heightens the force of the song as a counterblast; but the division into pairs here conveys not artistry but rather roughness. It is not that the individual couplets are unconnected in subject.[53] But the abrupt transitions from one piece of advice to another, and from one addressee to another, do not express, and are not joined together by, an underlying passion, and suggest instead an unpolished manner. The song does not, like Bucaeus', close by returning to the singer's one preoccupation, but ends with a rough joke against the overseer. The artlessness naturally distances our response to the song as a conscious artefact within the dramatic situation, and suggests that Milon's sarcastic praise of Bucaeus' artistry is not founded on any artistic sensibility of his own. Bucaeus had shown a comic union of artistic and emotional pretension with actual *naïveté*; now we have pretension reversed in homely crudity. The poem juxtaposes two contrasting divergences from successful art: successful, that is, within the world of the singers.

[53] So Gow's description rather suggests (p. 193); but 44–51 give advice, and 51 leads on to the thought of refreshment, which concerns 52–5.

Even in the second we admire the vividness of the poet's evocation.

The first song, it was suggested, shows the isolation of the individual in his passion, the second the singer's involvement in communal action. The theme is prepared, but not actually brought out, in the dialogue of the first part. The languishing Bucaeus has fallen behind the row of reapers; but this is only expressed by saying that he is not reaping at the side of the man next to him (3). Milon's remark in 9 implies that Bucaeus' desire is unsuited to any labourer, but the emphatic ἀλλ' ἐγώ 'but I' with which Bucaeus shortly reveals his love contrasts him with Milon in particular (Milon's ἐγώ 'I' in the following line reinforces this contrast). Bucaeus attempts to riposte to Milon's mockery by warning him that he too could fall in love (19 f.). The dramatic mode, then, concentrates attention on the opposition between the two speakers; the songs encompass a wider range. Bucaeus' song proper begins:

> Βομβύκα χαρίεσσα, Σύραν καλέοντί τυ πάντες,
> ἰσχνάν, ἁλιόκαυστον, ἐγὼ δὲ μόνος μελίχλωρον.   (27 f.)

> Lovely Bombyca, everyone else calls you the Syrian, the
> woman gaunt and scorched by the sun; I alone call you
> one with the shade of honey.

ἐγὼ δέ 'but I' here makes a large contrast; but Bucaeus' isolation here is not touching, as he feels it to be. Rather it is a classic sign of his delusion.[54] It is the contrast with the second song that most brings out Bucaeus' abstraction. After his opening invocation of the Muses, patronesses of his art, he addresses only Bombyca: the encircling of the song with her name reinforces the effect. After the dissociating reference to 'everyone else', the only people he mentions are Bombyca and himself, an emphatic ἐγώ appearing three times in the song. Milon's song is not even of his own composition or time, and the first person singular appears nowhere. Once Demeter has been invoked, injunctions are distributed to cover all participants in all stages of the harvesting. Then, with striking effect, the singer enters heartily into the feelings of his fellows, addressed as παῖδες 'my

---

[54] See Gow's note, adding Hor. *Sat.* 1. 3. 38 ff.; for the same device in flattery see P. Oxy. 2891. Cf. also p. 269.

lads': he makes a homely joke about drink. He then turns (formally) to the overseer, with another jest; this affects to express the general dissatisfaction with the food. At times the song is vigorously involved in the rough ethos of the rustic; at times it presents more aloof advice, mingling arcane country lore with a suggestion of strenuous country life.[55] This is a song directed towards, and belonging to, an unindividualized group of men. The songs, then, as songs, stand in contrasting relations to their singers and to the setting and world of the drama: one is intimately related to the singer and detached from the setting, one intimately related to the setting and detached from the singer as an individual. In this area too the special nature of songs allows further possibilities to the poet exploiting separation and opposition.

The significance of such matters to Theocritus is suggested further by poems 6 and 11. These both deal with the same area of subject-matter, the feelings of Polyphemus the Cyclops for Galatea the nymph, but they differ completely in their form and their handling of song. Both poems take inspiration from a lost dithyramb by Philoxenus of Cythera, an author of the late fifth and early fourth centuries BC. Poem 11 stands especially close, and we may imagine that its form played an important part in making it different from its model. Philoxenus' poem (*PMG* 815–24) treated the familiar story of Odysseus' escape from the Cyclops (frr. 820, 823, 824, 816); but it also presented, before that adventure (821), Polyphemus' song of love for the absent Galatea (821, *al.*), accompanied by the lyre (819).[56] Theocritus 11 presents a song of love addressed by the Cyclops to Galatea (19–79). This ends with Polyphemus dismissing his passion, for the present (72 ff).[57] In the first part of the poem (1–18) Theocritus tells his friend, the poet and doctor Nicias, that the only cure for love is poetry, as the Cyclops shows; he

---

[55] The advice feels no less distant from the reader for the somewhat Hesiodic quality; at the same time the evocation of Hesiod suggests the author's address and literary sophistication.

[56] That the work was a dithyramb, a narrative lyric, is clearly indicated by Aristotle, *Poet.* 1448ᵃ13–16, cf. Aelian, *Var. Hist.* 12. 44; note also fr. 820 (ἐν τῷ ποιήματι appears in Sch. RV, not merely Sch. Junt.; the preceding sentence does not). The paroemiographers (fr. 824) and Tzetzes (fr. 819, last sentence) say that it was a drama, but their testimony bears little weight.

[57] ἐποίμαινεν in 80 suggests that the process is not decisive and unreversed: cf. E. W. Spofford, *AJP* 90 (1969), 35.

then describes the Cyclops' passion and stresses again that he was cured (17); two lines at the end of the poem reinforce the point (80 f.). In Philoxenus Polyphemus bade dolphins tell the sea-nymph that he was curing his love with music (Μούσαις εὐφώνοις ἰᾶσθαι τὸν ἔρωτα, fr. 822). But in Theocritus the metaphor of healing, not striking in itself, is made significant and pointed by the exploitation of Nicias' profession (5, 81); and the notion of song curing passion governs the structure of the whole poem.

However, the end of the song gives the idea a different colour to that given in the first part of the work. The tone of the poet's own voice in the first part seems serious to the reader. The rhetorical vehemence and the personal orientation of the opening statement (1–3) are not undermined by the graceful compliment to Nicias (5 f.). The language used of the Cyclops' 'wound' has the seriousness of conventional expression, and yet it wins force from the physicality and strength of the phrasing:

ἔχθιστον ἔχων ὑποκάρδιον ἕλκος
Κυπρίδος ἐκ μεγάλας τό οἱ ἥπατι πᾶξε βέλεμνον.   (15 f.)

Most terrible was the wound he had beneath his heart:
great Aphrodite's arrow had fixed it in his liver.

We think of the cure in the noble form of the assuaging of emotion through art.[58] The actual alteration of feeling produced by song is much more abrupt and radical than we expected, and the effect is comic. The Cyclops represents himself as awaking from wild delusion (70): much more sensible to get his jobs done (74). The girl he has loved long and unceasingly (25–9, 40) he now cares nothing about.

εὑρησεῖς Γαλάτειαν ἴσως καὶ καλλίον' ἄλλαν.   (76)

You'll find another Galatea [he tells himself], perhaps still more beautiful.[59]

[58] The ideas here obviously resemble Aristotle's theory of tragic κάθαρσις in the *Poetics*, on an orthodox medical interpretation. Whether or not that interpretation is correct, or adequate (see most recently S. Halliwell, *Aristotle's Poetics* (1986), 184 ff.), later readers of the *Poetics* may have made it. Cf. also Philodemus, *De Mus.* 4 col. v 41 ff. Obviously the argument of Theocritus' poem treats poetry, song, and music as the same thing, by a familiar convention.

[59] I take ἴσως with καὶ καλλίον', as this seems to suit better what follows, and probably what precedes. The line recalls Archilochus' dismissal of his shield: ἐξαῦτις κτήσομαι οὐ κακίω (fr. 5. 4); the humour is enhanced by the transference of this attitude from a replaceable object to a beloved individual.

From his earlier shyness about his physical appearance he moves to cheerful confidence in his attractiveness; but he is now laughably deluded, as his own words suggest (77 f.). The unseriousness spills over into the poet's ending.

οὕτω τοι Πολύφαμος ἐποίμαινεν τὸν ἔρωτα
μουσίσδων, ῥᾷον δὲ διᾶγ' ἢ εἰ χρυσὸν ἔδωκεν.   (80 f.)

Thus then would Polyphemus shepherd his love with his music; his state was more comfortable than if he had paid over gold.

ῥᾷον δὲ διᾶγ' 'his state was more comfortable' takes up a phrase from the opening (cf. 7); it is followed by an uncomplimentary allusion to doctors' fees. With mock tact Theocritus refrains from actually mentioning the medical profession to which his friend belongs. The song itself transposes into comedy the thought of the poet's introduction.

There are other divergences between song and introduction which deserve attention, both because they contribute to the contrast between the two parts, and for a further reason, which will emerge. The introduction says nothing of the one-eyed giant's horrible appearance. It may be said that this does not matter: the name automatically conjures up the image. It would be better to say that that image creates for the reader a sense of suppression and of precariousness. This is reinforced by the physical description of the hair newly-grown round Polyphemus' mouth and temples (9). The ostensible purpose is to show us his age; but we feel that there are aspects of the same face no less remarkable. In the song the Cyclops' grotesque appearance is set starkly against what is potentially emotional and beautiful, and it almost dissolves these incipient effects. The Cyclops tells of how his passion began and continues (25–9). His feeling half awakens a response, and his final outburst is both absurdly childish and a litle touching: τὶν δ' οὐ μέλει, οὐ μὰ Δί' οὐδέν (29) 'you don't care, though, not a bit'. But he proceeds at once to a graphic description of his bizarre face (30 ff.). His purpose is persuasive—to show that he is aware of what repels Galatea and to counter this objection; but the purpose only heightens the monstrous effect of his account. He later says that Galatea will enjoy spending the night 'in the cave with me', ἐν τὤντρῳ παρ' ἐμίν (44). The sensual suggestion

causes us to dwell on the 'with me' that makes the assertion
unlikely. Polyphemus proceeds to elaborate on the cave with
lavish rhetoric (45–9); his description impresses us with its
beauty. He finally returns to himself:

αἰ δέ τοι αὐτὸς ἐγὼν δοκέω λασιώτερος ἦμεν,
ἐντὶ δρυὸς ξύλα μοι καὶ ὑπὸ σποδῷ ἀκάματον πῦρ—
καιόμενος δ' ὑπὸ τεῦς καὶ τὰν ψυχὰν ἀνεχοίμαν
καὶ τὸν ἕν' ὀφθαλμόν, τῷ μοι γλυκερώτερον οὐδέν.   (50–3)

And if I myself appear to you rather too shaggy, I have
oaken logs there and unquenchable fire beneath the
ashes—and I could bear to be burned by you, Galatea,
not only in my soul but in my single eye, the dearest thing
I have.

In contrast to his earlier explicitness over his appearance, he is
here amusingly brief and sparing. He moves back at once to the
amenities of the cave;[60] this suggests to his impassioned mind
both an amatory metaphor and an amatory fantasy. The
movement between the literal and the figurative conveys
powerful feeling. The fantasy develops in concrete terms the
common idea of loving someone as much as one's own eyes.[61]
Yet it is in itself gruesomely extravagant, it reminds us of Polyphemus' eventual fate, and above all at the height of passion it
reintroduces and dwells on the grotesque element in his appearance which he has just been glossing over.

In the introduction the sea and the shore are evocatively
employed as the locale for the Cyclops' melancholy complaints.
The Cyclops is shown sitting on a high cliff and looking out to
sea (17 f.), where Galatea dwells. The image suggests in itself a
haunting loneliness and separation from the beloved.[62] The
Cyclops is also said to sing ἐπ' ἀϊόνος ... φυκιοέσσας (14) 'on the
shore strewn with seaweed'. The desolate scene is to be contrasted with the 'green pastures' where he has abandoned his

---

[60] A. Baragazzi, *Hermes*, 103 (1975), 184, rightly objects to Gow's metaphorical
understanding of 51. Even *naïveté* would not express itself thus, and there is surely a
pointed allusion to Hom. *Od.* 9. 375.

[61] Call. *H.* 3. 211, Catull. 104. 2, etc.

[62] Cf. Catull. 63. 48 ff. (Attis addressing his lost country), 64. 126 ff. (Ariadne
deserted by Theseus), Hom. *Od.* 5. 156 ff. (Odysseus kept from Ithaca); cf. also
[Theocr.] 8.55, with Gow's note.

sheep (13).[63] In the song the sea acquires a less romantic aura. First Polyphemus attempts to convince Galatea, with rhetorical facility, that the sea is an unattractive place to live in compared with his cave. The roaring of the sea is presented with disdain by Polyphemus (the poet's language suggests a different aspect, 43); he uses the words 'sea' and 'waves' as if the things were self-evidently uninviting (49). The next section of his song returns to the sea with a lover's fantasy of extreme grotesqueness. He wishes he had been born with gills so that he could dive down to Galatea (54 ff.). The physical bizarreness of the Cyclops is redoubled by this conception. The idea is abandoned in bathos as he talks of learning to swim instead (60). He wants to discover why ever it is (τί ποχ') the nymphs should like to have their home in the deep (62); this last sulky reference removes all the evocative force from the poet's image of the inaccessible sea (17 f.).

In contrast to the sea stands the rustic life of Polyphemus. The reference in the introduction to the forsaken sheep has a tinge of beauty; primarily it subserves the apparently serious depiction of the shepherd's absorption in love. Beauty does appear in the Cyclops' description of his cave (45 ff.), and in his mention of flowers for Galatea (56 f.); but in both cases the beauty is disintegrated by what follows. More important in the song is the Cyclops' unelevated emphasis on his dairy products, not incidentally, but as a prime weapon in his campaign of seduction. Against his undesirable appearance he sets first the abundance of his flocks (which sounds well enough), and then the excellence of his milk and his unfailing supply of cheese (34 ff.). Again, he first bids Galatea become a shepherdess, and then proceeds to milking and then to the precise details of getting cheese to set (65 f.). In the opening address of his song he elaborates on the whiteness of Galatea's skin by claiming it excels a particular type of cheese (20). Cheese seems to dominate this love-song: the low trivia of rusticity help to banish a serious response. It is apt that it should be these trivia which in the end bring the Cyclops himself to abandon his song of love (75 ff.).

In these and other ways the poetry of Polyphemus is made to

---

[63] χλωρᾶς is more striking, and has more sense of lushness, than the English 'green'. There is nothing low about the mention of seaweed: the epithet is Homeric.

frustrate the expectations which the introduction implanted, or affected to implant. Not only does the effect of poetry upon life turn into comedy; the poetry of the Cyclops quite reverses the earlier suggestions of emotional seriousness and artistic excellence. In the introduction poetry is seen both as the work of goddesses (3, 6), and as difficult of attainment (4).[64] The song of the Cyclops, when seen as art produced by him, is ludicrous. He claims to excel all the other Cyclopes in piping, and presents that music as a part of his love-songs (38 ff.): the intended vaunt only enhances the artistic absurdity. This is closely connected with the lack of emotional seriousness in the reader's response to the song, which is heightened by the emotional seriousness that seems to adhere to Theocritus' description of the Cyclops. Correspondingly, we set the convincing poetry of the poet Theocritus against the ridiculous poetry of his creation Polyphemus.[65] The manipulation of the two levels is central to the effect of the poem.

In poem 6 the poet introduces himself principally in order to mark out two different levels of narrative, with different 'status': one the level of the youths who sing, the other the level of Polyphemus. In the first place, the content of the two levels is contrasted. The two youthful herdsmen engage in a singing-contest. Although no judge is mentioned, it is made clear that this is a competition at the beginning (ἐρίσδεν (5) 'had been challenging the other to a contest'); and it is made clear at the end:

νίκη μὲν οὐδάλλος, ἀνήσσατοι δ' ἐγένοντο.

Victory fell to neither; both were undefeated.

That final line, with its emphatic restatement, does not merely register a draw: it marks out an abnormal competition, with no competitive spirit. The other singing-contests in the corpus

---

[64] So I understand οὐ ῥᾴδιόν ἐστι: only this explanation makes 1–6 cohere into an effective and intelligible sequence. Against it see Barigazzi (n. 60), 184 ff.; but he does not appreciate the change of direction in the poem. There is little point in using the opening of Nicias' response (*SH* 566) to support interpretations of Theocritus. Only the context would determine the tone of Nicias' lines; they are perfectly compatible with the view of the poem suggested here.

[65] Compare Spofford (n. 57) 22 ff.; the article is rewarding, despite its conclusions.

show the most vehement desire to worst the opponent;[66] in this poem, after Damoitas has followed Daphnis' song with his own, he kisses Daphnis, and they exchange gifts (42 f.). The kiss need not be erotic; but the surprise of the action increases the surprise of the competitors' delightful goodwill and affection.[67]

If in the outer story rivalry is changed into something strangely soft, in the inner story love is changed into something strangely harsh. Tradition makes us expect to see the Cyclops languishing from passion. The first song, addressed to Polyphemus, suggests that he fails to notice the unexpected advances of the coquettish Galatea: we do not at first imagine that he is no longer in love, despite Galatea's insults (7).[68] This idea is intimated, however, by the last part of the song, which implies that Galatea is making her advances because now Polyphemus does not love her (his indifference causes her passion).[69] The notion that he does not acquires much sharper form in the second song, which is put into the mouth of the Cyclops. He reveals that his actions are fully intended. He even caused his dog to bark at her—whereas 'when I was in love with her', ὅκ᾽ ἤρων, the dog often nestled up to her (29 f.). Now, then, he is not in love; but he says that he will cease his implacable behaviour when she swears an oath that she will sleep with him (32 f.). This final statement, precisely because it surprises, directs us towards an understanding of his emotions. He will naturally be glad to lie with Galatea, but he is not in the grip of love. He treats Galatea so roughly not simply in order to win her but because he exults in his own freedom from ungovernable long-

---

[66] We see this not only in poem 5, where the two competitors detest each other anyway, but also, very forcefully, in poem 8 (most likely not by Theocritus), where we know nothing more of the singers' relationship (5. 142 f., etc., [8]. 6–10, 88–93).

[67] For the erotic interpretation see Cairns, *Generic Composition in Gk. and Lat. Poetry* (1972), 195. The difference of age between the youths is slight, and both have begun to grow hair on their faces (Gow on line 3). Neither point encourages the assumption that the relationship is homosexual (at Plat. *Smp.* 181 c delete with Schütz). For non-sexual kissing cf. Soph. *OC* 1131, Kroll on Catull. 9. 9.

[68] τάλαν τάλαν (8) need not mean that Polyphemus is pitied, but it invites that interpretation as we first read the line. The Cyclops' pipe-playing is compatible with melancholy abstraction.

[69] καὶ οὐ φιλέοντα διώκει | καὶ τὸν ἀπὸ γραμμᾶς κινεῖ λίθον, 17 f. On the comparison with thistledown see J. H. Betts, *CP* 66 (1971), 252 f. The comparison seems so plausible that it is hard to make the passage ironical (thus Ott, *D. Kunst d. Gegensatzes*, 78). The poet may be seen as hypothesizing Galatea's interest and then pursuing Polyphemus' reaction to it.

ing, and in Galatea's subjection to it. When Galatea hears him
say, in pretence, that he is married,

$$\zeta \alpha \lambda o \hat{i} \ \mu', \ \hat{\omega} \ \Pi \alpha \iota \acute{a} \nu, \ \kappa \alpha \grave{i} \ \tau \acute{a} \kappa \epsilon \tau \alpha \iota. \tag{27}$$

She is jealous of me—oh triumph!—and she is consumed
with envy.

A lover's joy would ill suit his persistently complacent tone,
quite apart from l. 29 ('when I was in love'). Rather, he rejoices
at the pain he can inflict on her who once pained him.[70] In
part we relish the characters' reversal of their expected roles;
but the structure of the song makes us think primarily of the
Cyclops. In him we see love replaced by an attitude brutal and
malicious, gloating in superiority. It is not strained to make a
contrast with the outer section. The opposed surprises brought
by the second song (21–40) and by the final narrative (42–6)
inform the whole tone and atmosphere of those parts, and the
contrast is palpable and immediate.[71]

The difference of narrative status is exploited in a complex
manner. The second song is given directly to a character in the
myth. It forms a very specific and complete reply to the first
song, rebutting it at every point. And yet the first song is not
assigned to a mythical character; the second does not mention
it or its speaker.[72] The nature of the voice delivering that first
song remains undefined; this gives the song a pleasing and
evocative sense of distance. On the one hand, the mythical
situation is present to the speaker, and he addresses Polyphemus throughout in the language of lively involvement. At the
same time we feel aware of Daphnis relishing the beauties of his
creation.

[70] A nervous plea for protection from her jealousy is no less out of place: 39 f. are
quite different in tone. Nor would a jocular pretence at alarm suit the uncomplicated
Polyphemus. One may note further that $\zeta \alpha \lambda o \hat{i} \ \mu'$ would most readily be taken as denot-
ing Galatea's envy for Polyphemus' felicity.

[71] Cairns sees that the two levels are related, but wrongly seeks to make the supposed
love-affair of the singers point to real love on the part of Polyphemus, and to the happy
ending of a permanent union. The notion of real love in my opinion clashes with the
text. Their producing children is attested by this date (Timaeus *FGrH* 566 F 69, with
Jacoby's note); but the idea of their later felicity is not particularly wanted here.
Lawall's understanding of the relation between the levels is adequately refuted by
Ott (70).

[72] Note $\hat{\omega} \varsigma \ \mu \epsilon \ \lambda \acute{\epsilon} \gamma o \nu \tau \iota$, not $\lambda \acute{\epsilon} \gamma \epsilon \varsigma$, in 34 (taking up 19).

καὶ τύ νιν οὐ ποθόρησθα, τάλαν τάλαν, ἀλλὰ κάθησαι
ἁδέα συρίσδων. πάλιν ἅδ', ἴδε, τὰν κύνα βάλλει,
ἅ τοι τᾶν ὀΐων ἕπεται σκοπός. ἁ δὲ βαΰσδει
εἰς ἅλα δερκομένα, τὰ δέ νιν καλὰ κύματα φαίνει
ἅσυχα καχλάσδοντος ἐπ' αἰγιαλοῖο θέοισαν.
φράσδεο μὴ τᾶς παιδὸς ἐπὶ κνάμαισιν ὀρούσῃ ...   (8–13)

Yet you do not look at her (ah, you are foolish): you sit
there, piping sweetly. And again, she's pelting the dog,
look! the dog that goes with you to guard your sheep. It
looks into the sea and barks; the lovely waves mirror it
clearly as it runs on the shore with its placid swirl of
waters. Take care the dog does not jump at the girl's legs
...

Here an animated address is followed at once by the image of
the Cyclops at his music. ἁδέα 'sweetly' indicates that Daphnis
wishes the picture to be contemplated: this is not simply a reproach. In the next sentence, ἴδε 'look!' heightens both the
immediacy of the situation to the speaker and his concern for
Polyphemus. But the description of the dog on the shore cannot
all be seen as advice: we are again withdrawn into an image
consciously presented. The reflection of the excited animal in
the peaceful sea distances it with delicacy. We return at once to
direct warning; the action envisaged is graphically unpleasant
and unelevated. This oscillation continues to the end of the
song. The last sentence (18 f.) combines a marked and encour-
aging address to Polyphemus with a formulation amusingly im-
polite:

ἦ γὰρ ἔρωτι
πολλάκις, ὦ Πολύφαμε, τὰ μὴ καλὰ καλὰ πέφανται.   (18 f.)

Truly, to the eye of love, Polyphemus, what is not beautiful often seems so.

It thus forces home the ambivalence of perspective.

The contrast of the second song with the first, and the surprise which it affords, derive much of their vigour from the difference between them in relation to their respective speakers.
In the second song the voice is very clearly defined: unexpectedly, the Cyclops himself issues a rejoinder, full of his own
character. Speaker and subject are brought firmly together;
and this effect is linked with the firm roughness of the utter-

ance. Whereas the first speaker, with his uncertain status, hovered between admonition and the self-conscious evocation of beauty, the second is bluntly practical, and in reinterpreting the material of the first song reduces it to unevocative crudity. The comedy is enhanced by the Cyclops' one expatiation on an object which he thinks beautiful: his own face, mirrored in the sea (35 ff.). The idea of reflection in the sea here turns into grotesqueness; the Cyclops' tone is loudly confident, not poetic. Another level of meaning does appear in the song, but it is entirely separated from the overbearing and unambiguous voice of the Cyclops. So, when he says that he looked beautiful in his own judgement (37), the humour lies in his freedom from doubt as to the validity of this isolated verdict. At the other end of the song, Polyphemus refuses to accept the prophecy of Telemus that he will be blinded (23 f.); in the *Odyssey* Polyphemus speaks of this prophecy when it has come true (*Od.* 9. 507 ff.). The point lies in the folly of the speaker and the unfamiliarity to us of his perspective in time. The opposition between the songs in atmosphere and ethos cannot be separated from their divergence in the handling of dramatic status.

The two aspects of the poem we have been considering interlock. In particular, Damoetas' song (the second) appears to counter Daphnis' and to undermine it; but Damoetas gives his song to a voice (Polyphemus') which is wholly distinct from his own, and the voice is made to excite amusement at its own expense. The handling of the speaker thus dissolves the rivalry suggested by the form. The Cyclops thinks to deflate the speech of his adviser; Damoetas has no such intention with the song of his antagonist.

The separation of song can be shown to have equal significance in the poems not yet discussed. This may be questioned as regards poem 18, which gives the wedding-song sung for Helen and Menelaus. Crucial to that poem, however, is the dramatic irony which results from the singers' position in time, before the seduction of Helen by Paris;[73] the poet's introduction (1–8) underlines the difference in time and correspondingly in narrative status. Also central to the poem is the nature of the singers: Helen's qualities and the change in her life are pre-

[73] Cf. Effe (n. 39), 74 ff.

sented through their relation to the chorus of maidens. The reader both sees the matter through their eyes and observes their world and their attitudes as from a distance. The introduction dwells on the singers' nature: again the effect of the song is conjoined with its status.

We may now look briefly, to end this part, at how Theocritus can infringe the separation he establishes so strongly between songs and their surroundings. The most salient example is provided by poem 5. In ll. 80–137 the two herdsmen, bitterly hostile, begin their contest. This is marked off from the preceding dialogue with particular firmness, as we have seen. At first, the shepherds sing about themselves, but not directly about their present environment or their present actions.[74] The first rupture occurs in 100 f., where Comatas suddenly calls his goats away from an olive-tree. Comatas' next couplet will resume the subject of the one before, that of gifts for the beloved. Accordingly, the reader is obliged to take the call to the animals as showing the intrusion into the context of a present external reality (cf. 4. 44 ff.). We do not see the representation of an imagined event (cf. [8]. 63–70). Yet Lacon follows the couplet of command, as before, with a corresponding couplet, making a parallel address to his sheep. The poet is playing with the artifice and abstraction of the form.

In 110 f. Lacon apostrophizes cicadas as Comatas has just apostrophized locusts; but within this artificial form is placed an explicit and vexing reference by Lacon to the present competition. He stirs up Comatas to effort as the cicadas stir up the reapers. By contrast, the next couplet (112 f.), Comatas', does not touch directly on the rivalry at all. There may be an oblique suggestion of Comatas' dislike for Lacon; but the obliqueness would be the point. Lacon's response is similar. Again by contrast, Comatas' next words (116 f.) address his rival directly, and resume a subject from their earlier dialogue, which had been so strongly divided from the songs. The subject is Comatas' vaunted homosexual conquest of Lacon; this earlier produced a particularly sordid moment (41 f.). Lacon ripostes with equal brutality. Comatas then addresses the judge of the contest:

---

[74] The present tenses in 84–9, one may note, describe things which are not occurring at the time of the song.

ἤδη τις, Μόρσων, πικραίνεται· ἢ οὐχὶ παρῇσθευ;
σκίλλας ἰὼν γραίας ἀπὸ σάματος αὐτίκα τίλλοις. (120 f.)

A certain person is becoming vexed, Morson: did you not
not notice? Pray go, quickly, pluck squills from an old
woman's tomb (i.e. to avert the danger).

The couplet dwells on Lacon's present emotions, as betrayed
by his last couplet. The tone is cool and mocking; but this is
intended as a further irritation to the enemy. The judge had
been used to mark off the contest from the dialogue. Here he
serves both to emphasize the reference to the contest within the
contest, and also to stress that now the songs are not separated
from present reality any more than the dialogue itself. But
Lacon's reply shows the same exactness of correspondence as
before, and his second line, like Comatas', here displays a
deviousness of connection characteristic of songs in Theocritus.
The artistry suits the antagonism, but heightens the strangeness
of its appearance here. The following couplets (124 ff.) with
sudden beauty distance the quarrel; they touch it only through
indirect suggestion. The songs now resume their original character, for the next two pairs of couplets.[75] But the final song,
Comatas', addresses Lacon, refers to the contest, though with a
slight indirectness, and ends with a direct description of
Lacon's character:

τὺ δ', ὦ τάλαν, ἐσσὶ φιλεχθής. (137)

But you, you wretch, love hatred and aggression.

Here the distance of art disappears altogether. The form of the
abuse echoes strikingly the bickering which immediately preceded the contest; from that bickering the opening songs were
divided forcibly.[76] Theocritus can play between the levels so
emphatically divided, for the sake of pungency and amusing
surprise. The effect depends on and presupposes the division; it

[75] Lacon's reference to his flute in 134 f., his last couplet, certainly recalls for us the
beginning of the dialogue, where Lacon's flute formed the principal source of dissen-
sion. It seems unlikely, however, that Lacon intends a reference to the dialogue; it is not
clear even that the recollection occasions Comatas' address to Lacon in the next couplet. G. Giangrande contends (implausibly) that the implausibility of his couplet loses
Lacon the contest (*Mnemosyne*, 4th ser. 29 (1976), 143 ff.).

[76] Cf. 77 τύγα μὰν φιλοκέρτομος ἐσσί (and 75, and 79).

shows in a fresh way how the impact of these poems cannot be detached from their form.

Theocritus uses form, it will now be seen, not only to achieve contrasts in tone as such, but also to mark out, through opposition with the straightforward, modification and distortion of the same; to undo or unsettle the seriousness of a whole poem; to play with art and pretensions to art; to accomplish strange and delicate effects; and in general to create intriguing, piquant, and delectable combinations. The elements of beauty and emotion are vital, but they form part of a whole, whether as one side of an opposition or as something to be distorted or complicated—or to complicate. It will be evident in what sense I see Theocritus as fundamentally related to Apollonius and Callimachus.

The last part of the chapter will consider the more particular evidence for the connection of Theocritus with those two writers. It will thus provide a necessary background to the picture that has emerged, and in various ways further our understanding of Theocritus. We shall take first the question of chronology. Then we shall consider the places where Theocritus imitates or is imitated by one of the other two, in order to see what these passages do and do not suggest about the poets' relations to each other. We shall look next at some possible connections between Theocritus' poems and the literary principles usually attributed to Callimachus. Finally, we shall attempt to interpret poem 7 (Thalysia). This poem has often been viewed as holding the key to comprehending Theocritus, and so a consideration of it will be necessary to complete the argument of this section. But in any case so impressive and so enigmatic a poem demands discussion in a depiction of this author and it will be particularly suitable, for reasons that will appear, to close by reflecting on an individual poem.

The three poets, it has already been said, were probably in a broad sense contemporaries: each could affect, as well as be affected by, the work of the others. (See pp. 5, 88 f.) Theocritus, we shall see, probably drew on Apollonius; Apollonius, we have seen, probably drew on Callimachus; we shall see that Callimachus probably drew on Theocritus. The last case is the least evident, but this matters somewhat less: Theocritus is in any case unlikely to have been very much younger than Callimachus. The only poems of Theocritus of which the approximate date is plain belong to the same ten years as the earliest poems of Callimachus for which the same is true (Theocr. 15 and 17, 279 (276?)–270 BC).[77] Theocritus wrote four poems (at least) which flattered the Alexandrian royal family (14, 15, 17, *Berenice*). They suggest, especially 15, that Theocritus spent some time in Alexandria at a period when Callimachus and possibly Apollonius were there, and working for the same patrons.

About the dating of Theocritus' non-Egyptian poems, save for 16, we know nothing. Yet the ring of imitations suggests that the poets were roughly contemporary, and, if this is so, we shall not want to argue that the poems of the 270s are at any rate very markedly later than the rest of Theocritus' work. It would thus be unwise to suppose that, apart from those poems and from 13 and 22 (which probably draw on Apollonius), Theocritus' poems cannot have been affected by the approach of his fellows to their work. Of course, such influence need not necessarily have begun with Theocritus' sojourn in Alexandria.

Poem 16, the only other poem that might be datable, is addressed to Hieron, who became a king in Theocritus' native Syracuse. It refers to fighting against the Carthaginians, which should belong either to the earlier part of Hieron's domination (from 275 BC?) or to the time of his alliance with Rome (from 264). In the former case it cannot be much earlier than the Egyptian poems; in the latter it will come after them, perhaps by a considerable interval. In my opinion, the earlier fighting is not satisfactorily attested.[78] To connecting the poem with the later fighting the splendour of Theocritus' picture (73 ff.) affords no serious objection (Theocritus wished to praise). Nor

---

[77] Cf. Rice, *The Grand Procession of Ptolemy Philadelphus*, 41, 121 f., Gow ii 265, Fraser, *PA* i. 666 and n., ii 367.

[78] The only evidence for it is Justin's version of Trogus, which claims that Hieron was first made general against the Carthaginians, and soon after made king (23. 4. 1). Justin's account plainly descends from the same source as Polybius' (Timaeus?); yet Justin's formulation cannot easily be reconciled with Polybius' narrative. Polybius in effect makes the Mamertines (called οἱ βάρβαροι) Hieron's first and only target before his kingship: note especially 1. 8. 2, 1. 8. 5 ff. The Latin account is singularly prone to distortion and error, and there is no audacity in supposing that, for example, it has misunderstood οἱ βάρβαροι in its source. For the standard view see H. Berve, *ABAW* ph.-h. Kl. 47 (1959), 8 ff. The approach of B. D. Hoyos to Hieron's reign (*Antichthon* 19 (1985), 32 ff.) would in fact accord well with the view taken here.

does Theocritus' lament that he has no one to pay for his praise, even though this poem would be later than those written for the royal house of Egypt (Theocritus was not aiming to be just to all patrons). The absence of Hieron's earlier deeds from the poem in my view sorts with its whole nature. It is not itself a panegyric, but contemplates the possibility of writing panegyric, and displays the author's ability to do so. The effect is deliberately strange, and the tones play between wry humour, burlesque, and lofty eloquence.

There is no good reason to think the 'bucolic' poems any earlier than the rest. Indeed, poem 11, which is usually made 'bucolic', most likely belongs to the same period as the non-bucolic poem 13. That poem also addresses Nicias on love; and it is probably based on Apollonius.

Both Apollonius (1. 1207 ff.) and Theocritus (13) tell of how, in the course of the Argonauts' expedition, Hylas, a boy in the care of Heracles, was pulled into a spring by a nymph or nymphs; and of how Heracles, searching for him in vain, was lost to the expedition. One of the two accounts clearly draws on the other. Which does so we are unlikely to discover from internal weaknesses. A poet of such skill as Apollonius or Theocritus will hardly have adopted an element without noticing that it sounded unnatural in his own work. On the other hand, he will hardly have perpetrated unawares an improbability (noticed by his successor) which he would otherwise have avoided as spoiling his composition.[79] The important point is that the story of Hylas, like that of Amycus (2. 1 ff., cf. Theocr. 22. 27 ff.), would naturally have appeared in Apollonius' poem in any case. Apollonius ransacked earlier poetry and prose for stories of the Argonauts. On the other hand, the story of Hylas was evidently obscure;[80] and Theocritus has no particular penchant for obscure mythology. To be sure, he can on occasion deploy the local historians for a myth especially apt (most notably that of Comatas the goatherd in 7. 79 ff., cf. *FGrH* 570

---

[79] For such arguments cf. A. Köhnken, *Apollonios Rhodios u. Theokrit* (1965) (note Griffin's review, *CR* NS 16 (1966), 300 ff.); Dover's edn., pp. 179 f. Dover properly stresses the point that follows.

[80] Cf. Dover's discussion. Gow wrongly suggests (ii. 231) that there is evidence for Callimachus' treating the story of Heracles' loss. See Pfeiffer, i. 31, and *Kallimachosstudien*, 80 ff. Such a thing seems indeed positively unlikely in *Aetia* 1.

F 7); and on occasion he can exploit obscurity to achieve an elaborate mixture of erudition and emotion (most notably in 12. 27 ff.). But he does not visibly evoke obscurity here, and unlike Callimachus he has no aversion to retelling at length stories told by celebrated poets. The other poem to Nicias on love draws on Philoxenus' famous *Cyclops*; the second myth in 22, like the myth of 24, had been narrated by Pindar.[81] There is a very considerable presumption that Apollonius came first.

Does Theocritus' reworking of Apollonius convey general statements about literature? There seems little ground for supposing that Theocritus is demonstrating the badness of Apollonius.[82] Apollonius' account is most certainly not devoid of atmosphere (cf. especially 1. 1229 ff.). 'Clumsinesses' have been found at points where he differs from Theocritus; yet in most cases the clumsiness appears only through misapprehension, and Theocritus' divergences are much more naturally explained by Theocritus' concentration on Heracles as a proof of Love's power. (Apollonius' Heracles is not in love with Hylas.) In one point Apollonius may be allowed to be improbable, by the criteria of the real world. He makes the Argonauts forget Heracles at first when they set off (1. 1283), whereas Theocritus' Heracles, through his passion, abandons the expedition himself (13. 67). Yet the sequence of Apollonius' narrative produces contrasts of great force dramatically and poetically; and if Theocritus wished to stress Apollonius' implausibility, it is strange that his own account should seem so confused at this very point (for a realistic narrative).[83]

Should we think that Theocritus is undermining the heroic ideal of tradition, by showing Heracles' subjugation to love; or demonstrating its inadequacy in an erotic situation?[84] If so, the reader is surely to link this with the use of Apollonius, in whose work Heracles forms the supreme exemplar of heroic excellence. However, these notions sort ill with the last line of the

---

[81] It is unlikely that in 22 Theocritus means to couple a well-known myth and an obscure one. The first story was well known enough before Apollonius, and had been told by Epicharmus and Sophocles.

[82] Cf. Gow ii. 231 f.

[83] See Gow on Theocr. 13. 69, Köhnken, 79 f.

[84] Cf. Effe, art. cit. 60 ff., D. J. Mastronarde, *TAPA* 99 (1968), 273 ff. Effe presents Theocritus' activity as destructive, Mastronarde views it as a 'significant response to an important literary and philosophical dilemma' (over the relevance of the hero).

poem. Theocritus, after telling how Heracles abandoned the expedition to Colchis, suddenly divulges:

πεσδᾷ δ' ἐς Κόλχους τε καὶ ἄξενον ἵκετο Φᾶσιν.

(The other Argonauts mocked him because) it was on foot that he arrived at Colchis and the inhospitable Phasis.

He accomplished the journey after all. In most versions (including Apollonius') he did not ever reach Colchis; but to have him both abandon and pursue the expedition is extraordinary.[85] If Theocritus' object is to expose the hero, the choice of this ending is inexplicable. If we say that Theocritus is stressing here that his doubts as to heroism only extend so far, we do not do justice to the startling quality of this reversal. The depiction of Heracles in love had suited the rhetorical purpose of the poem: love could seize even the future god and make him forget his valour. The ending undoes the argument which the poet had seemed to be enforcing in accordance with his address to Nicias (note particularly 66 f.). Somewhat as in 11, the poem eventually subverts the ostensible purpose of the poet, linked with his own voice. In other words, we should think not of philosophy but of play with the reader, and exploitation of the double register of the poem. The poem is not merely a narrative, like the *Argonautica*, but also a disquisition by the poet as lover to his friend. This is what gives pungency to the presentation of Heracles. On the one hand, it is an extraordinary paradox that this mighty figure of myth and epic should be in love, just like Theocritus and Nicias.[86] But on the other hand, Heracles in love is still Heracles. To describe Heracles deprived of Hylas Theocritus uses a heroic and epic comparison to a lion (62 f.); Apollonius had used such an image too, of another

---

[85] For the various accounts see Sch. AR 1. 1289–91a, cf. Sch. Theocr. 13. 75b. Dionysius Scytobrachion had special reasons for making Heracles reach Colchis: see J. S. Rusten, *Dionysius Scytobrachion* (Papyrologica Coloniensia 10, 1980), 96 f. Almost nothing is known of Demaratus (*FGrH* 42).

[86] The first sentence (1–7) in fact stresses this extraordinary connection, even though the 'we' with whom Heracles is contrasted turn out, surprisingly, to be mortals in general rather than simply the poet and addressee. (This is not the normal view of ἁμῖν in 3.) The description of Heracles in 5 f. means that we can hardly avoid thinking of him as a mythological character, not merely a god.

Argonaut searching for Hylas (1. 1243 ff.).[87] Theocritus makes Heracles instruct Hylas in manliness (9 f., 14 f.). Heracles here accords with a familiar ideal of pederasty;[88] but his model is himself (9)—himself, a fit theme for song (ἀοίδιμος). We think of this figure as the subject of high poetry; we think also, wryly, of the poem we are reading.

When Apollonius recounts his nymph's abduction of Hylas, the atmosphere is suffused with love, and powerful sensuality. Into the virile world of heroes, forcefully evoked in the surrounding narrative, love and femininity intrude, with disastrous results. The episode thus subserves the large patterns of Apollonius' work. Theocritus eschews Apollonius' atmosphere. His nymphs are plural; their sight of Hylas is not described (contrast AR 1. 1229 ff.).

> ταὶ δ' ἐν χερὶ πᾶσαι ἔφυσαν·
> πασάων γὰρ ἔρως ἁπαλὰς φρένας ἐξεφόβησεν
> Ἀργείῳ ἐπὶ παιδί.   (47–9)

All the nymphs clung to Hylas' hand: all their soft spirits
had been routed by passion for the Greek boy.

The description of their actions here is deliberately unevocative (contrast AR 1. 1236 ff.); the description of their passion is less evocative than Apollonius' and much less emphatically placed (AR 1. 1232 f.).[89] In both these clauses the stress falls on 'all': all of them were moved to seize Hylas. The collectivity enhances rhetorically the power of love and the beauty of Hylas; simultaneously, it prevents any communication of sensuality to the reader. The picture of the nymphs comforting the tearful child and holding him on their knees (53 f.) pleasingly dissolves the erotic in the maternal. Certainly all this must be

---

[87] The blunt reference to the lion's meal in 63 only heightens the impression of Heracles' wild heroic vehemence. It does not destroy the epic quality, any more than (say) κέλεται δέ ἑ γαστήρ in Hom. *Od.* 6. 133. That simile (like Apollonius') serves to contrast the wild and heroic with the feminine. To make this comparison suggest the predatory brutality of Heracles' intentions on Hylas seems to fit ill with the situation.

[88] Cf. Dover, *Greek Homosexuality* (1978), 202 f.

[89] It should be noted that the important name of Κύπρις in AR 1. 1233 is heightened by the contrast with that of Artemis (1225).

seen as part of Theocritus' concentration on Heracles' love.
The nymphs provide a very subsidiary illustration of love, but
warm devotion and fierce passion are to be shown only in the
case of Heracles. Yet a positive contrast is sought between the
description of Heracles and the description of what happens to
Hylas. Theocritus directly opposes the nymphs dandling Hylas
to Heracles in his alarm (μέν 53, δέ 55). When Heracles shouts
with his full power and Hylas' cries come faintly up from the
water (58–60), we should feel an opposition between the vehemence associated with the narrative about Heracles and the
distanced fantasy of the narrative about the nymphs. Hylas' fall
into the water is likened to the fall of a star into the sea; we are
then given, in direct speech, the cry which a sailor who saw this
would give to his comrades to set sail (50–2). This cry suggests
the Argonauts' coming departure; its air of lively realism is set
against the strange and arresting beauty with which Hylas' fall
is depicted by the image. Heracles, then, who formally exem-
plifies Theocritus and Nicias' emotion, stands both close to and
remote from the frame of the poem and the reader. The abduction by the nymphs, which forms no less impressive a part of the
poem, has much less formal connection with the friends, and
stands remote from frame and reader in a quite different
fashion. It keeps a quite different degree of distance from
emotional intensity and from the real world. The effect of the
poem springs from the divisions of its form.

The treatment of Heracles is enhanced by awareness of his
role in the *Argonautica*. Ignorance would not destroy the effect;
but knowledge of the 'model' gives it edge. It is still more important that the form of that work and its use of narrative are
utterly dissimilar to Theocritus'. In this sense, there is play with
types of poem.[90] But it is, as we have seen, implausible that
the play is intended to communicate general beliefs about literature. The use of Apollonius is pragmatic. Similar conclusions
follow from the discussion of poem 22 (pp. 162 ff.). Once we
grant that Theocritus' account of Hylas comes after Apollonius', it seems perverse to resist the likelihood that Theocritus'

---

[90] This approach seems more satisfactory than making the poem 'contaminate' the
supposed genres of epistle and epyllion (cf. Rossi, *BICS* 13 (1971), 85).

account of Amycus comes after the account in the very next
episode of the *Argonautica*. If Theocritus is reworking a passage
in that epic, the strangeness is sharpened when he inserts stichomythia and when he makes the fight at once Iliadic and grotesque. But it would be odd to extort from this strangeness a
comment about literature (least of all a polemic against Apollonius). In fact, a knowledge of Apollonius is of much less importance to the reader of the poem than a knowledge of Homer:
Homer was by convention the father of the epic and the hymn.

Whereas Theocritus' use of Apollonius appears substantial,
his use of Callimachus, and Callimachus' use of him, appear by
comparison extremely limited.[91] Call. *Ep.* 46 Pf. (III GP)
begins from the Cyclops' curing his love by song. It then adds
that poverty too cures love, so that Callimachus himself, a poor
man and a poet, is doubly secure. The poem is more likely to
draw on Theocritus 11 than on Theocritus' source Philoxenus.
It sustains through both its halves continued reference to the
curing of disease.[92] We saw that Philoxenus is known to have
referred (with little colour) to the curing of love; but that the
idea is central to Theocritus' whole structure—which was
plainly not the case in Philoxenus. The epigram has far more
point if its second part extends the primary conception of its
original, recapitulated in the first part, into a new and unelevated region. It is much less effective if the medical language
appears merely because its addressee Philippus was a doctor.
And in fact the appearance of a doctor with that common name
on a contemporary papyrus gives us very little ground for
thinking that he was one.[93] On the other hand, we do know
that Theocritus' addressee was a doctor, and his profession
explains and gives force to the use of healing in that work. An
epigram, then, is the one place where in my view Callimachus
can be seen to draw extensively on Theocritus, and wishes to be

---

[91] On this question cf. G. Schlatter, *Theokrit u. Kallimachos* (Diss. Zürich 1941).

[92] ἐπαοιδάν, 1, κατισχαίνοντι (a term with medical associations), 3, πανακὲς ...
φάρμακον, 4, ἐκκόπτει ... νόσον, 6, ἐπῳδαὶ ... τραύματος, 9 f. Gow and Page seem to
deny that ἐκκόπτειν is ever used in a medical sense; but it is certainly used later of eradi-
cating a diseased condition (διάθεσις): Galen, *In Hipp. Epid. VI* 2. 9 (CMG v. 10. 2. 2 p.
68. 19, 25), Stephanus, *In Prgn. Hipp.* i. 1 (CMG xi. 1. 2 p. 36. 1 f.). It seems probable
that it had such a flavour at this time too.

[93] P. Mich. Zen. 55. 19, with Edgar's introduction.

seen.[94] Overt references to particular contemporary poets were more congenial to him in that little genre (cf. *Epp.* 27 and 43 Pf.). Here, as in *Ep.* 43, much of the point lies in Callimachus' wry movement away from his original to himself (himself in a conventional pose). To achieve the desired deflation he ignores the deflation in Theocritus. Theocritus' poem is forced to serve simply as Callimachus' foil.

Apart from poem 11 of Theocritus, it is only in his poem 17 that I myself feel any very striking connection with Callimachus. (I suppose poem 25 not to be by Theocritus.) In particular, Theocritus describes there the island of Cos taking the new-born Ptolemy in her arms and asking that he will honour her (58 ff., 64 ff.). In Callimachus' fourth hymn the island of Delos acts similarly with the new-born Apollo, and her speech dwells on the honour she will receive (264 ff.). Theocritus refers explicitly to Apollo's birth of Delos (67) as Callimachus refers earlier in the hymn to Ptolemy's birth on Cos (160 ff.). There are a good many other plausible connections in the poem, not all of which have been noted. In the other poems of Theocritus even possible echoes are infrequent. The treatments of Delos and Cos derive from the model of *Hymn* 4 (the Homeric Hymn to Apollo). This makes it somewhat more natural to suppose that Callimachus here came first. Theocritus would then be adorning this poem to Ptolemy with allusions to one of his poets, and especially to passages involving Ptolemy. Theocritus' use of Callimachus here would not be exceptional by chance.

Callimachus and Theocritus do not normally make sustained allusion to each other, although they knew one another's work and pursued concerns in the writing of poetry which were strongly related. In general, we have seen the three poets using each other's work as suits their own needs; the changes they make accord above all with the nature and form that belongs to the new production and to their own general technique. We

---

[94] General evocation of Theocritus is possible in *Ep.* 22 Pf.; but the metrical pattern remarked by Pfeiffer need not in itself suggest Theocritus, notably not in fr. 27. 1 (*Aetia*), where the anaphora stresses the *aition*, and hence has a very un-Theocritean ring. For the pattern elsewhere in Callimachus cf. e.g. *H.* 3. 44, 5. 45. The use of Theocr. 18. 22 ff. seen by Bulloch in *H.* 5. 23 ff. I do not, I fear, find notable. The single line *H.* 4. 98 may imitate or be imitated by Theocr. 26. 30 (or neither); it does not seem desirable for the reader of Callimachus to recall the force of the line in Theocritus.

have seen little reason for finding in allusion a proclamation of general literary principles. We must now ask more broadly whether Theocritus and Callimachus were in fact united by forthright allegiance to novel theories about literature, and whether their practice is dictated by a common programme. We must consider first whether Theocritus' whole work does not implicitly support what some think one of Callimachus' most revolutionary tenets, the permissibility of mixing genres.

We have seen earlier that the novelty and importance of such mixing in Callimachus' work have been much overstated (pp. 16, 55). In so far as the practice and the conception are significant there, they form part of Callimachus' general variousness and unpredictability. In so far as they are significant in Theocritus, their force can hardly be the same. All Theocritus' poems are written in hexameters, save the Lesbian poems (28–31), which naturally adopt Lesbian metres, and the epigrams, several of which indeed show unusual metres for the genre (17–22 Gow). All probably adopt some kind of Doric colouring, save for the Lesbian poems and, probably, poem 22—a hymn—and poem 12 (a love-poem); of the epigrams, perhaps all have some Doric colour save 19, on the Ionian Hipponax and in choliambics. Hence even 24 (hymn to Heracles), 26 (on Pentheus), and almost certainly 13 (Hylas), 16 (to Hieron), and 17 (encomium of Ptolemy), fail to show the limitations of dialect expected in this metre: the Doric elements in Theocritus cannot be explained everywhere as, say, being broadly appropriate to the locale of the poems or as imitating Sophron the writer of mimes.[95] Such metre and such dialect, then, are not confined to a single type of poem; quite the reverse. Theocritus cannot be displaying the virtuosity and perpetual novelty of a Callimachus. Indeed, it is conceivable that he wished to unify his work in this way: epigrams 17–22 and the Lesbian poems

---

[95] For 13, 24, and 26 the Doric dialect is explicitly attested by papyri (Δωρίδι). Doric features appear in papyri of both 16 and 17; in 17 P. Ant. mingles Ionic and Doric vocalism chaotically (cf. 17. 97 in P. Oxy. 3551). Gow's practice is probably too hesitant, his divisions (lxxii) not unproblematic. See, beside his discussion of the whole question, Dover's edn., pp. xxvii ff., Hopkinson, edn. of Call. *H.* 6, pp. 43 ff., Bulloch, edn. of Call. *H.* 5, pp. 74 ff., C. J. Ruijgh, *Mnemosyne*, 4th ser. 37 (1984), 56 ff. Ruijgh's theory that Theocritus' Doric is the Doric of Alexandria would not answer all our present questions.

would show, if it needed showing, that he might adopt diverse
metres and dialects when he pleased. At any rate, the heteroge-
neity of the poems makes it seem very doubtful whether there is
a single effect of piquancy to be found in the appearance of the
hexameter and of Doric in the individual works.

The standard view of the bucolic genre is that it mixes or
contaminates the epic with the genre of mime (and the sub-
literary genre of bucolic song).[96] We have already questioned
the desirability of viewing bucolic as a distinct genre or even
the 'bucolic' poems of Theocritus as an indivisible entity. That
conception is unhelpful in exploring the relations of Theocritus
to mime. Some of the 'bucolic' poems lack the dramatic form
which is essential to mime (6, 7, 11). Elsewhere—notably in
poem 1—the element of drama and racy life is so small that one
feels very little connection with that genre. The poems which
would seem to have most flavour of the mime are 2, 14 and 15;
two of them are known to recall and draw on mimes by Sophron. None is 'bucolic'. Both 2 and 14 contain a very large narrative element; 15 contains a lofty song. 2 is in part intensely
emotional; even 14 interweaves elevated forms of expression
with its unelevated narrative (32 f., 39 ff.). We may surely suppose that in these poems, and to a lesser degree in others, the
associations with a lowly form of literature on the one hand,
and on the other the dignity which must still attach to the hexameter, will enhance the interplay of the base and sordid with
the grand and the intense.[97] Similarly, the dramatic framework was at the least not the standard one in hexameter verse:
this will have sharpened the exploitation of narrative levels. But
it seems doubtful whether Theocritus' procedure is the same as
Callimachus' in the *Iambi*. Callimachus there mingled different
kinds of poetry, flouting horizontal boundaries. Theocritus
here raises into verse what is not actually a form of poetry at all.
There are difficulties in deciding whether a given text is a
mime; but Sophron's, which have the most undisputed claim to
the title, and which most concern us, were not written in

---

[96] Cf. e.g. Kroll, *Stud. z. Verst. d. röm. Lit.* 203. For dissent, see notably Halperin,
Before Pastoral, ch. 10. For mime cf. p. 151 and H. Wiemken, *D. gr. Mimus* (1972).

[97] On the associations of the hexameter cf. Aristotle, *Poet.* 1459^{b}34 f., Russell on
[Longin.] 39. 4.

verse.[98] Various dramatic or quasi-dramatic papyrus fragments in prose have been associated with the genre, not unrea-
sonably. A lyric monody and a lyric drama, both on amatory
subjects, have also been so associated, but this seems more or
less arbitrary: in the post-classical period, situations involving
love were clearly exploited in a wide range of literary forms
(many little known to us).[99] Theocritus, then, is doing something different in kind from Callimachus; but as with Callimachus, we see a relation to the author's larger concerns.

Such a relation can be seen even in the few places in Theocritus where one could see mixture of a more Callimachean
quality. Poem 22 provides the most striking and perhaps the
only really plausible instance of such mixture; and we saw how
that was linked to characteristic divisions and design.[100] This
does not seem to be an area where affinity between the poets is
most salient. So far, at any rate, we have had little reason to see
Theocritus' work as his contribution to a debate or a crusade.

The only positive evidence for seeing that work in such a
light has been found in some lines of poem 7. The whole poem
has been thought to deal with Theocritus' poetry in
general.[101] It describes how Simichidas encounters Lycidas and
both sing bucolic songs; Simichidas then proceeds to a festival,
with his companions. Simichidas himself is the narrator. He
ends his first speech to Lycidas by dissenting from the view of
all others that he himself is the best of singers and poets (ἀοιδὸν
ἄριστον). In his own judgement he does not yet surpass or equal

---

[98] Aristotle's attitude is quite definite: see fr. 72 Rose and Bywater on Aristotle, *Poet.*
1447[b]10 (and *Suda* Σ 893); the fragments, certainly in prose, do not seem obviously
more rhythmic than Plato.

[99] Prose fragments in G. Manteuffel, *De Opusculis Graecis* (one with a little verse at
special moments); drama, Page *GLP*, no. 79; monody, *CA*, pp. 177 ff. On the monody
see Ed. Fraenkel, *Elementi plautini in Plauto* (1960), 315 ff. Possibly it may be a specimen
of ἱλαρῳδία; but the discussion of that genre in Athenaeus (621 B–C) makes it seem a
very different type of writing from mime. I doubt whether P. Oxy. 3700 radically complicates the question.

[100] See above p. 164 and also n. 90. For other possible instances see Rossi.

[101] A very short bibliography on this poem: J.-H. Kühn, *Hermes*, 86 (1958), 40 ff., M.
Puelma, *MH* 17 (1960), 144 ff., Archibald Cameron in *Miscell. di studi aless. in mem. di
Rostagni* (1963), 291 ff., G. Lohse, *Hermes*, 94 (1966), 413 ff., G. Giangrande, *L'Antiquité
classique* 37 (1968), 491 ff., Ott, *D. Kunst. d. Gegensatzes*, 138 ff., F. Williams, *CQ* NS 21
(1971), 137 ff., C. W. Macleod, *Coll. Essays*, 168 ff., C. Segal, *WS* NF 8 (1974), 20 ff.,
AJP 95 (1974), 128 ff., E. L. Bowie, *CQ* NS 35 (1985), 67 ff., G. B. Walsh, *CP* 80 (1985),
1 ff.

Asclepiades and Philetas, two poets likely to be substantially older than Theocritus (see pp. 264 f.). Lycidas begins his reply:

τάν τοι ... κορύναν δωρύττομαι, οὕνεκεν ἐσσὶ
πᾶν ἐπ᾽ ἀλαθείᾳ πεπλασμένον ἐκ Διὸς ἔρνος.
ὥς μοι καὶ τέκτων μέγ᾽ ἀπέχθεται ὅστις ἐρευνῇ
ἶσον ὄρευς κορυφᾷ τελέσαι δόμον Ὠρομέδοντος,
καὶ Μοισᾶν ὄρνιχες ὅσοι ποτὶ Χῖον ἀοιδὸν
ἀντία κοκκύσδοντες ἐτώσια μοχθίσδοντι.						(43–8)

I give you this club as a gift, since you are a sapling which Zeus has formed entirely for truthfulness. Just as I loathe and detest the builder who seeks to produce a house as high as the peak of Mount Horomedon, so I detest all those birds of the Muses who make their noises in rivalry with Homer the singer of Chios—a vain struggle.

The passage has generally been seen as striking a blow on the side of Callimachus in his supposed battle against the writing of epics. It is taken as primarily a comparison between untraditional poetry and poetry which imitates Homer. The analogy with builders is thought to be aimed at the length of epic poems. These suppositions produce a very strained and implausible dialogue. I find it more satisfactory to see Lycidas as declaring the approval of Simichidas' seeming honesty which moves him to make Simichidas a present. Simichidas has acknowledged in contemporary terms that he is not the best of poets. Lycidas expresses his dislike of the opposite attitude, seen in larger terms. Homer was already conventionally regarded as the best poet of all time: to see this as the point gives the passage proper coherence and tightness.[102] The comparison with builders, to whom poets are so often likened, should picture foolish and hopeless ambition; it does so in the way most obvious for that profession.[103] It is neither necessary nor desirable to

---

[102] For the period leading up to this poem cf. *HE* 2749, *CA*, p. 98. 28, *al.*, and note Theocr. 16. 20. See also A. D. Skiadas, *Homer im gr. Epigramm* (1965). It is obvious that rivalry with the best poet need not be confined to writers of epic; cf. e.g. *FGE*, pp. 157 f. and indeed [Longin.] 13. 4.

[103] It is interesting that at Arist. *Pax* 749 f. the metaphor of making a large building does not apply to the length of comedies. (It applies to artistic status, with some play on μέγας.) The Coan mountain is assuredly what we require here, not a Giant Oromedon or Eurymedon (a familiarizing corruption). See the scholia, with R. Herzog, *APAW* 1928 ph.-h. Kl. 6. 17, S. Sherwin-White, *Ancient Cos* (1978), 303, 549.

see in the passage an attack on contemporary epic. The connections with Callimachus do not seem striking. He is chiefly concerned, in any case, with the brevity and variety of his own
works; and there is little reason to see contemporary emulation
of Homer as something that appals him. The most plausible
area of connection would be grandeur. Callimachus does (misleadingly) deprecate grandeur for himself at fr. 1. 19 f.; what we
have said so far is compatible with grandeur being borne in
mind here. However, the analysis of the poem suggested below
would make it unattractive to give even this stylistic element
any weight. Certainly it would be forced to make the passage a
defence of Callimachus himself.[104] Whether we could make it
a defence of Theocritus' own *œuvre* depends in part on our views
of the whole poem. But prima facie that seems uninviting too.
By contrast with Callimachus' defences, there seems nothing
here to suggest such a reference. The lines are spoken by a character as part of a dramatic situation. Not only are the lines
general in form, but their very generality subserves a particular
function in the dialogue. Their role in the poem is merely subordinate. They do not begin or end a book (contrast Call. *Ia.* 13
(fr. 203) and fr. 1). These lines, then, seem not to make Theocritus into a campaigner for a revolutionary aesthetic.

We must turn now to the poem as a whole. Is its real subject
Theocritus' work in general? The most significant reasons for
thinking that it is are connected with the identity of the narrator Simichidas. The view would obviously become more
attractive if we supposed that this poet is seen to be Theocritus
himself. That identification, which many now reject, had been
made in antiquity, probably at least as early as the first century
BC.[105] But the scholia to this poem record a rival identification, with a historical Simichidas who lived on Cos, where the
poem is set. Circumstantial details are given of this Simichidas'
family's history (Sch. 7. 21a). The existence of this second identification reinforces the probability that the first was not based
on evidence from lost poems but on reading of this—whereas

---

[104] This whether or not the use of Hesiod's encounter with the Muses in 91–3 is later
than, and dependent on, Callimachus' use of it in the *Aetia* (fr. 2, fr. 112. 5 f.).

[105] [Theocr.] *Syrinx* 12, Sch. Theocr. 7. 21, *al.*; Virgil probably derived from scholia
to this poem the play with self-identification at *Ecl.* 5. 85 ff. (cf. ibid. 9. 32 ff.).

the second is clearly based on evidence for a Coan family of the
period. Simichidas is supposed by the first to be an alternative
designation by which Theocritus was known, like Sicelides and
Battiades for Asclepiades and Callimachus. One would naturally expect those alternative designations to derive from the
father's name; but Theocritus' father was called Praxag-
oras.[106] External evidence does nothing to favour a supposition which the internal evidence is not adequate to confirm.
The first-person narrative of course proves nothing: one may
think of Plato's *Republic*, narrated by Socrates.[107] The Aratus
of whose love Simichidas sings need not be the same as the
Aratus whom Theocritus addresses in poem 6. If he is, this
again proves nothing, for other characters mentioned in the
poem must be acquaintances of Theocritus'. In describing at
the end of the poem Phrasidamus and Antigenes' reception of
Simichidas and his companions, Theocritus cannot be sending
thanks to hosts for recent hospitality to himself: the opening ἧς
χρόνος ἁνίκ' 'once' (1) in my view implies a considerable interval of time. He might still be drawing on his own experience,
and intending incidentally to give pleasure to these two men;
but as the poem is likely in any case to involve a large element
of fiction, this supplies no reason to make Simichidas the
author.

The rival account in the scholia places us under some obligation to suppose provisionally that Simichidas belongs to the
family it mentions. He would then match his companions and
hosts, who are very likely to be historical Coans (see below).
Theocritus would be partially transposing a real person into a
situation found in some of his poems, that of herdsmen singing
one another bucolic songs (1, 5, 6; cf. 10). Does this mean that
Theocritus regards the sphere of the 'bucolic' poems as his own
primary sphere as a poet, and that the work is a comment on
his principal kind of poetry? That inference would be precipi-
tate: for it is possible to see the poem as being much more self-
contained. Indeed, such an approach might even seem inviting
when it is recalled that Theocritus' various productions were
probably given no corporate unity by their author. It has

[106] Cf. Gow ii. 128.
[107] Cf. below, n. 120.

further attractions too. But for the present let us merely observe that we should not make Lycidas actually initiate Simichidas into the art of poetry or a branch of it, and in this way seek to confer on the encounter a wider significance. The notion would seem confusing on a straightforward level, as Simichidas claims already to have been so initiated by pastoral deities (91 ff.). Lycidas' present of his goatherd's club is represented as an exchange between two men who are already poets (43–51, 129). The resemblance with the branch of laurel which the Muses pluck for Hesiod (*Theog.* 30 f.) is not in itself overpowering; one connects the present much more readily with the rustic gifts presented to other singers of bucolic songs (1. 23 ff., 146 ff., 6. 43, *al.*). The encounter does not have as such the quality of a mysterious epiphany, in that the two men are not strangers to each other, and the reader is not given sufficient reason to think that Lycidas is Apollo in disguise.[108] If Lycidas is ironically parodying an initiation, one would expect the irony and the parody to emerge more pointedly.

There are three poets involved in the poem, Simichidas, Lycidas, and Theocritus; the use of narrative levels is particularly complex. The song of Simichidas obviously stands on a different plane from his narrative. The song is his poetry, but it would be unnatural so to regard his account of the past: that is Theocritus' poetry only. The narrative is set in his mouth, which distances us even here from contact with Theocritus; but the substantial interval of time marked at the beginning of the poem separates the two types of discourse. An intermediate position is occupied by the speeches of Lycidas and Simichidas to each other, as opposed to their songs. The speeches are not their poetry, but they belong to the past and are strongly imprinted with their natures and their feelings about their art. To a lesser degree, the nature of Lycidas imprints the description of him in 13–20. The whole poem is Theocritus' creation; but it is the outer narratives, above all perhaps the opening lines (1–9) and the description of the festival (131–57), which seem to give us the least indirect and entangled access to his poetic voice. On the other hand, the two songs in the middle of the poem (52–89, 96–127) are not merely the utterances of the

---

[108] Thus F. Williams (n. 101).

poet's characters, but are very forcefully represented by the
dialogue as the utterances of poets with their own ideals, ambi-
tions, reputations, and perhaps limits. It is the broad contrast
between the songs and the rest that really matters. For in any
case the final portion of narrative, essentially the description of
the festival, is the part that will strike the reader most as
belonging to Theocritus alone. By then the characters' remarks
and the songs together have directed our attention to the
special difference of level; and we read the narrative after viewing the chief objects from which it is differentiated, and with
which it is to be compared.

The poem also involves different levels of reality. We cannot
distinguish fully what is historical in the poem and what is not.
There is a considerable likelihood that Theocritus composed
the poem in the first instance for readers with external knowledge of the Coans it mentions. The compliment in 4 ff. to the
two men who held the festival can only be explained plausibly
on this hypothesis. At the same time this passage also indicates
to the uninformed reader at the start of the poem that these
particular people are real. The manner of referring to Amyntas
in 132 similarly suggests to us that Simichidas' companions on
the road are also historical persons. The ignorant reader will
naturally take the festival itself for a historical event, not only
because the people holding and attending it seem real but
because the complimentary allusions in 149 ff. have most force
if they refer to something actual. Presumably it is true in fact
that Phrasidamus celebrated the Thalysia.

This then is one level of reality. It seems almost as clear that
Lycidas is a fiction. Simichidas' first speech ends with the passage mentioned above, where he says that everyone regards
him as the best poet, but he does not think himself equal to two
historical poets (Lycidas is not mentioned). Simichidas begins
by saying that everyone regards Lycidas as far the best player
of the syrinx among the country folk, although he himself
thinks that he equals him (27–31). Now, it is presupposed in
this dialogue, as it is in other poems, that playing the syrinx,
singing, and composing songs are all a single skill (cf. 11. 38 f.,
4. 29 ff., *al.*). Hence there is a contradiction between beginning
and end as to Lycidas' standing as a poet, quite apart from the
pointed—and natural—contradiction between modesty and

immodesty in the young and ambitious Simichidas.[109] We could escape the contradiction regarding Lycidas by stressing that he is only the best of the rustics, not of cultivated poets. But that would produce the most dismal incoherence in this speech; and Lycidas holds strong views on cultivated poetry: he is not presented as a simple rustic singer. Rather, the poet creates a fissure which displays his conjunction of a historical level with an imaginary. It is the figure of Simichidas that joins them.

The exact relation of Simichidas to each of these two levels is obscure; but some mixture there clearly is. He is shown as the companion of real people; of the people he sings of Aristis (99) is likely to be real, and Aratus may be; there is some reason to think he is real himself. On the other hand, he can scarcely have been in reality a bucolic singer. Simichidas might well have been a poet in reality; but we should not see him as a would-be poet flawed fatally by his contact with the city. We are scarcely justified in attributing such importance to that antithesis by Simichidas' use of a wrestling-school as a metaphor (125), by his mention of lying on the beloved's doorstep (122), or by his proceeding to the festival from the city (2).[110] Much more prominent in Simichidas' song is rustic superstition. And pastoral poetry does not appear in poem 7 as one genre of poetry. Rather, poetry appears now in general and actual terms, now in the form of bucolic song which accords with the rustic fiction. Instead, we should see the figure of Simichidas in the poem as conjoining incredibly the friend of aristocrats with the country singer, whom the nymphs taught while he tended his cows on the mountain-side (92). This last assertion by Simichidas is not plausibly seen either as metaphor or as deceit. The real and the fictional are thrust together in this poem with deliberate incongruity and strangeness.

The levels of reality are variously exploited within the two

[109] Simichidas' praise of Aristis' poetry in 100 f. (ὅν οὐδέ κτλ.) does not produce any discrepancy with this speech. On Simichidas' modesty cf. C. Segal, *WS* (n. 101). The verbal similarities between 30 f. and 39 f. and between 26 f. and 37 f. are too striking to ignore. The tension is evident even in 37–41; and Simichidas is immodest again at 93, so that the contradiction is not confined to this passage. (Implausible attempts to understand Ptolemy by 'Zeus' in 93 do not remove the immodesty of expression.)

[110] It is assumed at 5. 78 that the woodcutter Morson will return to the city. Especially with a relatively small city such as Cos, contact with the city need not exclude rusticity.

songs and the final narrative. In Simichidas' song the crudity of rustic beliefs produces grotesque effects, most strikingly in the prayer to Pan (103 ff.). There physical pain is wished on the god if he does not grant the prayer, and the pain is colourfully and spiritedly described:

$$\kappa\alpha\tau\dot{\alpha}\ \mu\dot{\epsilon}\nu\ \chi\rho\acute{o}\alpha\ \pi\acute{\alpha}\nu\tau'\ \grave{o}\nu\acute{\nu}\chi\epsilon\sigma\sigma\iota$$
$$\delta\alpha\kappa\nu\acute{o}\mu\epsilon\nu\sigma\varsigma\ \kappa\nu\acute{\alpha}\sigma\alpha\iota\sigma\ \kappa\alpha\grave{\iota}\ \dot{\epsilon}\nu\ \kappa\nu\acute{\iota}\delta\alpha\iota\sigma\iota\ \kappa\alpha\theta\epsilon\acute{\nu}\delta\sigma\iota\varsigma,\ \kappa\tau\lambda. \qquad (109\,\mathrm{f.})$$

First, may you be bitten by insects and scratch all of your
skin with your nails; may you sleep among nettles, etc.[111]

The bizarreness of this extreme rusticity would be heightened if the persons mentioned near the start of the song are real. The end of the song would confront address to a real person, and prosaically realistic language, with an old woman spitting to avert bad luck (122–5, 126 f.). Now, such grotesqueness is eminently pleasurable when we feel that the poet is conscious of it, and stands distant from the belief while relishing its oddity. Obviously Theocritus is thus conscious; but is Simichidas? When he is presented as a rustic, it is as a thoroughgoing rustic—notably so in the lines which precede the song (92, see above). Hence one would naturally take his rusticity here as genuine, not ironical or contrived. The erudition which is employed to increase the sense of distance it would be especially unattractive to attribute to Simichidas.[112] So while we enjoy the song as part of Theocritus' creation, as Simichidas' creation it seems, much of it, uncouth in thought and crude in tone. And yet Simichidas had proclaimed this as far the best of his excellent and celebrated songs (90 ff.).

Lycidas had introduced his beautiful song with easy detachment and smiling modesty (50 f.). His sense that one should recognize one's limits in art (45 ff., quoted above) matches the feeling of recognized limits in the song itself. In particular, although he belongs (we opined) to a fictional level, that level is strongly separated from the mythological. He describes how at

[111] I prefer to take κατά as a pre-verb in tmesis. I usually feel sceptical about effects of sound in Greek poetry, but the threefold repetition of the group κν in 110 must surely enhance the imprecation. Cf. 22. 12.

[112] 106 ff., which must derive from a local historian of Arcadia; 114, which presumably derives from a geographer (cf. H. Berger, *D. geographischen Fragmente d. Eratosthenes* (1880), 303).

his party (a hypothetical occasion) another will sing of Daphnis the mythical cowherd, lover, and musician, and of Comatas the mythical goatherd and singer. The stories have connections with Lycidas himself.[113] But they are not merely marked off as coming from the past, by the πῦκα 'once, once upon a time' which introduces both stories (73, 78) and by Lycidas' consciously impossible wish that Comatas were alive in his day (86). There is also an unbridgeable interval of excellence between the goatherd singer of myth and the goatherd singer of the present. Comatas was miraculously preserved on account of his powers (80–2), and Lycidas dwells on his felicity (83–5). Lycidas wishes that he could listen to Comatas singing while he himself tended the singer's goats (87–9). The division of roles implies that Lycidas would bear no comparison with the 'god-like Comatas', θεῖε Κομᾶτα (89).[114] It is the more plausible that the outlook of Lycidas' second speech to Simichidas (43–51) should be linked with the moods of his song.

Theocritus' description of the festival (131 ff.) is overwhelming in its beauty. In his evocation of the delicious place and the delicious experience of the travellers, the poet amasses sensuous images in richest profusion. He appeals to all the senses, to sight throughout, but more emphatically to smell (especially 143), to hearing (especially 139–41), to feeling (especially 132–4, 147), to taste (especially 148–55). This lavish fullness is sought also in particularities of language.[115] One desires an account of the poem that will accord with one's response to it, and make this *tour de force* a climax rather than an appendage. One desires also to connect this religious symposium (as it were) with the symposium that dominates the song of Lycidas.[116] If we follow the line of interpretation suggested here, Theocritus is now excelling the poets he has shown us. This may be seen not only in the physical description but in the last part of the passage. There the speaker asks whether the drink he had then did not equal

---

[113] Cf. Macleod (n. 101).

[114] The epithet is often used to convey the matchless excellence of Homer.

[115] Thus πολλαί at 135, ἔχον πόνον at 139, the asyndeton in 140 ff., πάντ' and the anaphora in 143, the chiasmus and the picture in 144, δαψιλέως at 145, καταβρίθοντες at 146.

[116] Note how at the start 132–4 seem to look back to 67 f.; but the similarity is one of occasion, and it is important that similarity of language should be avoided.

wines drunk in myth, and wishes that he may celebrate the festival of Demeter again, with the goddess's favour (148–57).

> Νύμφαι Κασταλίδες, Παρνάσιον αἶπος ἔχοισαι,
> ἆρά γέ πᾳ τοιόνδε Φόλω κατὰ λάϊνον ἄντρον
> κρατῆρ' Ἡρακλῆϊ γέρων ἐστάσατο Χίρων;
> ἆρά γέ πᾳ τῆνον τὸν ποιμένα τόν ποκ' Ἀνάπῳ,
> τὸν κρατερὸν Πολύφαμον, ὃς ὤρεσι ναᾶς ἔβαλλε,
> τοῖον νέκταρ ἔπεισε κατ' αὔλια ποσσὶ χορεῦσαι
> οἷον δὴ τόκα πῶμα διεκρανάσατε, Νύμφαι ...;   (149–54)

You nymphs of Castalia, who possess the heights of Parnassus, was perhaps the bowl of wine like that that old
Chiron set before Hercules in Pholus' cave of rock? Was
the nectar perhaps like that which drove to dance in his
cave that shepherd that once lived by the river Anapus,
mighty Polyphemus, who used to hurl mountains at
ships—was it like the drink which then, nymphs, you
made flow from your spring ...?[117]

The mythology is again divided from the time of the narrative.
The language used of Polyphemus not only brings out rhetorically the power of the wine he drank, but marks the interval
from the world of the present. 'Once' stresses the disjunction
from the familiar which is actually produced by the playfully
ordinary 'shepherd' and 'Anapus'; the difference is marked
more directly with the extravagant evocation of his attack on
Odysseus' fleet, pleasingly extended to a habitual action. Yet
although the event of the narrative is historical, the experience
it brought is made to approach the superlatives of mythology.
The tentative form of the speaker's questions heightens the
boldness of the assimilation, while absolving the poet from
facile extravagance.[118] Thus in the last part of this section of
the poem Theocritus and his scene move towards equality with
myth, when in the last part of Lycidas' song there is felt an insu-
perable inequality. It is true that this sensuous experience is not

---

[117] διεκρανάσατε, Νύμφαι reads most naturally perhaps if the liquid is spring-water.
It would not be surprising that wine should be avoided in connection with the cult of
Demeter. Cf. Th. Wächter, *Reinheitsvorschriften im gr. Kult* (1910), 109 (and note that the
old supplement οἴνου at *LSCG* 151. 60 f. (Cos) was erroneous).

[118] Cf. ἦ πᾳ 4.3. πᾳ alone seems to exclude J. Schmidt's reference of the πῶμα (154)
to accompanying song (*RhM* 45 (1890), 149); the double comparison also makes this
unattractive.

the same thing as song. But the enhancement of physical sensation in the preceding lines, and the emphasis on religion in what follows (154 f.), should prevent us from regarding the subject as trivial. So too should the lyrical intensity and largeness of the rhetorical structure here: the lightness of tone with Polyphemus merely enriches the central effect.

The rural religion of the section associated with reality has a quite different atmosphere from the rustic religion of Simichidas' song, an element associated with fiction. The vehement crudity of Simichidas' elaborate prayer in the song may be contrasted with the quiet rectitude of the simple prayer which ends the poem.

> ἇς ἐπὶ σωρῷ
> αὖτις ἐγὼ πάξαιμι μέγα πτύον, ἁ δὲ γελάσσαι
> δράγματα καὶ μάκωνας ἐν ἀμφοτέραισιν ἔχοισα.

> May I once again fix on Demeter's pile of corn the great winnowing-fan; and may the goddess smile on me in favour, as she holds her sheaves and her poppies in both her hands.

The wish that Demeter may smile is both subdued and warmly concrete, like the traditional picture of her which concludes.[119] The ritual action spoken of has a very different ring to the Arcadian rite which had appeared in the song, that of beating Pan's statue with squills (106 ff.). Assuredly, that rite does not in the song form part of Simichidas' own rustic environment; but the context indicates his acceptance of its theology and its attitudes, and it colours the poetic flavour of the passage—which is what concerns us.

Naturally Theocritus does not dwell on his own role as a poet explicitly: his absence as a character enhances the elegance of the effect I am supposing.[120] There would then be a certain irony in the assignment of the narrative to Simichidas, so eager to proclaim himself a poet. One must in any case feel the sharpest difference between the passages which Simichidas narrates

---

[119] There is no need to refer this to an image on Phrasidamus' farm, and indeed γελάσσαι makes this awkward.

[120] It is possible that for the first 20 lines of the poem Theocritus beguiles the reader into thinking that he is the speaker (cf. E. L. Bowie, *CQ* NS 35 (1985), 67 f.). I cannot, however, accept that throughout the work we shall take Simichidas to be Theocritus turned into fiction.

and the passage which he has composed. However, the address
to the nymphs in 148 delicately emphasizes that the final scene
is poetry. Simichidas claimed to have been taught his songs by
the nymphs (92). When the nymphs of Parnassus and Castalia
are addressed here, the place-names inevitably recall the Muses
and Apollo: they can scarcely have been chosen with any other
purpose, however the nymphs are conceived.[121] The address
indicates that the myths are poetic material; but the very
nature of the comparison means that the same is true of the
scene itself. It also indicates, as an utterance, the poetic character of Theocritus' narrative.

The poem, and its last section, would still have something of
the effect suggested if the reader did not articulate the supremacy of Theocritus so consciously as has been done here. At all
events, the supremacy should essentially be experienced within
the poem, not extrapolated to apply to all the other poems of
the author. That is to say, although the superiority of the writer
here implies his excellence in a general sense, yet the contrasts
between the sections should not be understood to demonstrate
by what particular qualities Theocritus' whole work excels the
work of others; or, more particularly, to show in the last section
what he cultivates and in the songs what he eschews. Plainly
that would bear no relation to the actual nature of his poems.
Still less, however, does the use of a bucolic contest and of a rustic level of fiction show how Theocritus regarded his *œuvre*. He is
exploiting a form and a milieu, used in other poems, which
were uniquely well suited for contrasting poets and for rendering distinct and distinctive the actual, the fictitious, and the
mythological.

I put forward this account of a singularly difficult poem with
more hestitation than my account of the others. But it will be
seen that my account of the others is closely related; so that if
that should be found acceptable, it would confer an additional
advantage on this.

---

[121] It is hard to believe that Νύμφαι Κασταλίδες and the bare Νύμφαι in 154 could
describe the Muses (note also Himerius 48. 37 Colonna, the nymphs of Castalia as play-
fellows of the Muses and Apollo). One might introduce the Muses in 148 by supposing
that Νύμφαι has displaced e.g. κῶραι. If the text is sound, it seems implausible that the
nymphs of Castalia should be identified with the nymphs of the farm. Rather, the two
addresses in the sentence are to related but separate beings; the nymphs are used in 148
for the sake of an elegant movement back to the scene in 154.

One result of this part of the chapter has been to remove the effect of Theocritus' individual poems from a significance conferred by supposed debates of the time, and also from a significance conferred by each other. In this sense, the individual poem is strongly isolated. Unlike Callimachus, Theocritus does not build his short poems into larger structures; he does not comment on his work as a whole. Each poem, within its narrow compass, acquires a vigorous and striking individuality, not least through the production and exploitation of marked differences within the poem in its levels of narrative and its levels of emotion. Theocritus' organization of his poetry, structurally and tonally, constitutes the most important area of connection with his two fellows; no less, it gives his work as a whole its own vigorous individuality and striking cohesion.

5

OTHER POETS

A. ARATUS

WE turn now from the three pre-eminent poets of the time to deal with four others. Only four are considered, since it would sort ill with the objects of this book to treat rapidly a large number of authors about whom little, or little of interest, is known. For the course of its discussion, a fuller treatment of a few writers is more to be desired than completeness of information on the literary activity of the period. The authors have been selected with a view partly to the quantity of their work surviving and partly to their literary interest. After consideration, Asclepiades has been chosen, in preference to a string of epigrams from various hands. His and Callimachus' are much the most attractive epigrams of the time. And by viewing Asclepiades alone we are able to see him more broadly as a poet than we should from the perspective of the established genre, a perspective somewhat limiting and somewhat inappropriate.

We consider first Aratus, whose poetic career overlapped with Callimachus'.[1] The only substantial work of his to survive is the *Phaenomena*. The poem was praised by Callimachus and others for its elegance; it also contains some elevated passages on the gods.[2] We should not allow either fact to limit too greatly our approach to the poem. It does have for its core a poetic version of two exceedingly dry works in prose. The first part, on constellations, draws on the *Phaenomena* of the astronomer Eudoxus (5th–4th cc.); the second, on weather-signs, draws on a work perhaps by the philosopher Theophrastus

---

[1] The only datum on Aratus' life which merits much confidence is that he lived at the court of Antigonus Gonatas (first regnal year 283, died 240/39). See the *Lives* in J. Martin, *Histoire du texte des Phénomènes d'Aratos* (1956), 153, 157, 160 f. The claim in one life that Callimachus μέμνηται ... αὐτοῦ ... ὡς πρεσβυτέρου (fr. 460) deserves little credence: cf. Wilamowitz, *HD* i. 212 n. 1 (for the form note Sch. Nicander, *Ther.* 3).

[2] Praise of his elegance (λεπτ-): Call. *Ep.* 27 Pf., a Ptolemy *FGE*, pp. 84 f., cf. Leon. Tar. CI. For other works of Aratus see *SH* 83 ff., *HE* 760 ff.; didactic poems bulk large.

(4th–3rd cc.). Many sentences of Eudoxus' work survive in quotation; the other work is represented by later adaptations, independent of Aratus, but frequently displaying resemblances in wording.[3] Aratus often paraphrased his originals very closely; but we should not view him as simply imposing on his content neatly patterned versification and style. So contentless a conception of his art we shall see to be unrewarding.[4] For the present we may note that in general even the most conspicuous patterns in his verses serve an expressive end: they highlight the meaning and further the sense of articulate discourse.[5] The prelude on Zeus and the excursus on the goddess of justice use lofty tones and philosophical conceptions. But they should not obscure the lighter and the more complex tones found in much of the rest of the poem; nor should they impose too grave an air on the actual treatment of the subject-matter. Indeed, the treatment of Zeus himself in the poem deliberately and disconcertingly mingles the notions of a benevolent God, a being of mythology, and a synonym for the sky.[6] Thus Zeus' son Perseus, translated to the skies, makes his strides ἐν Διὶ πατρί (253) 'in Zeus his father'. The following lines produce a less strident echo of the bizarre collocation (259 sky, 265 God; cf. 275). The poem is far from monochrome.

One of the work's most salient features is its conjunction of two different areas of subject-matter, taken from two different sources. The transition is smoothly handled, and there are many links between the two parts; but this does not cancel out

[3] The fragments of Eudoxus derive principally from Hipparchus' commentary on Aratus: see for them F. Lassere, *D. Fr. v. Eudoxos v. Knidos* (1966), 39 ff. The principal adaptation of Aratus' other source is 'Theophrastus', περὶ σημείων (Wimmer, *Theophrasti Opera*, iii. 115 ff.); cf. also C. Wessely, *SBAW* 112 (1900), 1 ff. (a papyrus probably of the 2nd c. BC). On the problems involved see O. Regenbogen, *RE* Supp. vii. 1412 ff.

[4] The acrostic λεπτη found in Aratus 783–7 need not show that Aratus was aligning himself with Callimachus in his alleged battle for λεπτότης (J.-M. Jacques, *RÉA* 62 (1960), 48 ff.). The significance seen in the acrostic actually derives from, and can hardly survive without, a dubious view of the literary history and of the word λεπτός as a slogan. (An acrostic πασα appears on the next page.) Even if that significance were present, it could not constrain us to see in the poem nothing but elegance of phrasing.

[5] Thus, to take simple examples, the anaphora at 367 (for the significance cf. 370 ff.) or 458 f., or the position of verbs in 1096.

[6] The name of Zeus, despite its Indo-European origins, is rarely used of the sky itself in Greek. Aratus will be influenced by Stoic identification of Zeus with the aether (Zeno, *SVF* i. 169, Chrysippus, *SVF* ii. 1076. 16, 1077. 5). This provenance heightens the paradox of using 'Zeus' for the sky when it produces phenomena hateful to men (294, 936).

the fundamental sense of change. The conjunction can hardly be explained positively in terms of style, conceived merely as verbal artifice; nor do positive explanations in terms of thought seem very satisfying. For example, the idea of practical utility has not been insignificant in the first part of the poem, so that the second would be needed to bring it in (cf. 287 ff., 413 ff., 463, 559, 266 f., *al.*).[7] We might, perhaps, find a more promising starting-point in the broad contrast between the elevation attaching to the subject-matter in the first part and the lowliness of much of the subject-matter in the second. This contrast between the parts will be developed and much modified in what follows; but we may note here the implausibility of supposing it accidental. To take a particular point, there is no expansive description of storms in the second part, which gives means for predicting them. Such a description, however, appears in the first part, extravagant and forceful (423 ff.); also in the first part appears a sweeping and grimly ironical passage on the perils of the sea (287 ff.). The distribution must surely be associated with the level and colour of each part. Now, the poem clearly presents itself as a kind of imitation of Hesiod's *Works and Days*: hence, for example, its prologue on Zeus recalls Hesiod's, and its lengthy digression (98 ff.) on Dike (Justice) recalls most emphatically Hesiod's Dike and his myth of the Ages of Man (*WD* 212 ff., 256 ff.; 109 ff.). A prime aspect of the *Works and Days* is its broad movement from grand matter to lowly; the movement would have appeared still more striking to the sensibility of Aratus' time than to that of our own (cf. pp. 11 ff. above). The poetic 'model' of the *Phaenomena* makes it the more plausible that differences of level should be fundamental to the poem. In general, it encourages us to see tone and register as important: for it is not only the more grandiose sides of Hesiod that Aratus evokes. We shall consider separately the handling of material in the two parts of the poem.

Aratus' handling of the constellations derives much of its effect from the interplay between their two aspects: the stars to the eye are points of light, but they were conventionally formed into figures, most of them with a place in mythology. The double aspect is inherent in the most prosaic treatment of the

---

[7] Cf. M. Erren, *D. Phain. d. Arat. v. Soloi* (*Hermes* Einzelschr. 19, 1967), 227 ff., etc.

stars: Eudoxus not only uses the names of the constellations but identifies particular stars or groups of stars with physical parts of the imagined figure. But it is only in poetry that this strange union can be exploited and explored.

Aratus emphasizes the splendour of the constellations both as purely visual phenomena and as animated figures. If we consider it as it were in isolation, each type of splendour is straightforward. Thus, as to the splendour of the figures, when the constellations are referred to as μέγας 'great', it is usually in contexts which lay weight on the figures as creatures (as 84, 305, 354, 523). Sometimes the notion is sharpened, as when Pegasus is called πέλωρ 'a prodigious creature' (205) or the Great Bear δεινοῖο πελώρου 'a dreadful monster' (57, cf. 402). Sometimes the word lends grandeur to an image, as in 305 μέγα Τόξον ἀνέλκεται ἐγγύθι κέντρου | Τοξευτής 'it is near to the Scorpion's sting that the Archer (Sagittarius) draws his great Bow'; or as, more dramatically, in 83 ff.:

> ὁ δ' ἐμμενὲς εὖ ἐπαρηρὼς
> ποσσὶν ἐπιθλίβει μέγα θηρίον ἀμφοτέροισιν,
> Σκορπίον, ὀφθαλμοῖς τε καὶ ἐν θώρηκι βεβηκὼς
> ὀρθός.

(Ophiuchus), standing firmly fixed, treads and presses with both feet on a great beast, Scorpion; he stands upright on its eyes and its body.

On the other hand, we find a more simply visual splendour when the word is applied to particular stars in the phrase καλός τε μέγας τε or the like, 'both beautiful and large' (143, 210, 244, 397).[8] The purely visual magnificence of one particularly impressive constellation is dwelt on warmly (Orion, 323–5), like that of the Milky Way (473 ff., see below). That passage is exceptional, however; generally, the visual splendour of the constellations is kept less separate from the figures. It is when the two ways of regarding the stars come together that the complexities arise.

The two aspects can enrich each other and heighten the

---

[8] The phrase, which probably answers to Eudoxus' λαμπρός 'bright' (Eudox. fr. 28, cf. Aratus 143), is taken from Homer. μέγας applied to storms and signs in the second part becomes a much more practical term, with little suggestion of grandeur (1028, 1071, 1086; 1022). It is so used even in 'Theophrastus' (39).

general grandeur. A relatively simple example occurs at 141 ff. The Great Bear has already been described as δεινοῖο πελώρου 'a dreadful monster' (see above); now it is said:

δεινὴ γὰρ κείνη, δεινοὶ δέ οἱ ἐγγύθεν εἰσὶν
ἀστέρες.

Dreadful is she, and dreadful the stars that are near her.

The epithet overflows from the figure to the other stars, where it would not naturally be appropriate.[9] The effect is impressive, though the unexpected transference suggests lightly the fragility of the fiction. The splendour of these stars is then described in more physical terms, before the bleak close: they are all nameless, all 'borne along in namelessness' (ἀνωνυμίῃ φορέονται, 146). The disparity between physical glory and mythological obscurity yields a strange kind of half-pathos for the inanimate in their inanimation.[10] In his treatment of Orion, who is to produce particular grandeur both as a figure and as a visible constellation, Aratus to some degree keeps the two aspects from impinging on one another. At 586 ff., however, the splendour of Orion is conveyed both by Homeric phrases describing the hero and by emphasis on the brightness of particular stars. The lines unite as it were convincingly the heroic figure and the brilliant constellation:

οὐδὲν ἀεικής,
ἀλλ᾽ εὖ μὲν ζώνῃ εὖ δ᾽ ἀμφοτέροισι φαεινὸς
ὤμοις Ὠρίων, ξίφεός γε μὲν ἴφι πεποιθώς ...   (586–8)

That is no unseemly figure: he shines brightly with his belt, brightly with both his shoulders. Orion, who trusts in the might of his sword ...

But the passage goes on:

πάντα φέρων Ποταμὸν κέραος παρατείνεται ἄλλου.   (589)

carries up the whole River (Eridanus) from the other edge of Ocean, and is extended in the sky.

---

[9] Contrast δεινός used of the Dog-star at 330. There the term suits a star traditionally baneful, and introduces a movement from the figure of the Dog (the constellation) to the terrible effect of the star as such upon earth. (More of a disparity between the aspects appears after the grandiose and fantastic description of Sirius' attack on the trees.) δεινός is naturally apt for Arcturus too at 745.

[10] Eudoxus made nothing of their not having a name, fr. 28.

The notion of one constellation leading up another below it here gives to the figure a conception so extreme in its heroism as to touch on the absurd. At the same time παρατείνεται 'is extended' has a technical sound (cf. παρατέταται, Eudox. fr. 15); it ends the grand description with a slightly chilly stress on the astronomical constellation. Even with Orion here the two aspects exercise a little of their modifying power.

Occasionally the poet uses his concern with the figures as a pedantry which dispels the grandeur of describing the visible stars. Thus in 469 ff. a lavish subordinate clause is accumulated, in which the glory of the Milky Way and the rapt amazement of the spectator are richly expressed. If ever the addressee has marvelled at this sight—Γάλα μιν καλέουσιν 'they call it Milk'. The dry clause obtrudes abruptly as if the glory of the heavens were subordinate to this essential information.[11]

Much more often, however, the grandeur of the figures is infringed or modified by emphasis on the stars as objects. Aratus treats together a trio of constellations representing Cepheus and his wife Cassiepeia (who boasted she excelled the sea-nymphs), and their daughter Andromeda (who was consequently chained up for a monster to devour, until Perseus rescued her). He introduces the 'unhappy race' in lofty tones, dwelling on their fame (179 ff.). But he immediately follows the description of Cepheus' striking attitude—he is stretching out both his arms—with an account of the equilateral triangle formed by the stars of his feet and the Little Bear's tail. Here he rephrases Eudoxus (fr. 33) with arch and aloof elaboration.

The description of Cassiepeia begins from her folly and evil fortune (δαιμονίη, 188). But it proceeds at once to describe the feebleness of her stars, and to offer a complicated simile from folding doors in order to indicate the W those stars describe. Similes are rare in the poem. This impersonal and purely visual comparison is followed by an interpretation of the figure in personal terms. Cassiepeia is stretching out her arms from her 'little' shoulders (195 f.); 'you would think she was grieving for her daughter' φαίης κεν ἀνιάζειν ἐπὶ παιδί (196). The description

---

[11] The effect is still to some degree disconcerting if one makes the clause a parenthesis (thus Wilamowitz, *HD* ii. 273); but 477–9 make a much less satisfactory apodosis, and the δή τοι is displeasing after a demonstrative.

of her shoulders makes the union of woman and stars incongruous. The stress on natural inference, in the context of this whole account of her, must play with the artificiality of the identification. The brevity of that last clause heightens the strangeness of the juxtaposition.

The account of Andromeda seems at first to be proceeding in a similar way. The mention of her 'appalling image' is followed by a description of the magnificent constellation. There is no fusion here: the poet stresses the magnificence by stressing the ease with which the reader will find the constellation in the sky (199 f.). But the gap between bright stars and suffering maiden is suddenly turned to the manner of pathos:

> ἀλλ᾽ ἔμπης κἀκεῖθι διωλενίη τετάνυσται,
> δεσμὰ δέ οἱ κεῖται καὶ ἐν οὐρανῷ· αἱ δ᾽ ἀνέχονται
> αὐτοῦ πεπταμέναι πάντ᾽ ἤματα χεῖρες ἐκείνῃ.

> Yet even in heaven the maiden is stretched out with her arms extended: even there her chains are on her. Her outspread arms are there held high for ever.

This elevated conclusion gains force from, and adds to, the mixture of tones in the whole passage.

The various appearances of the family form a thread to be followed through the poem. The other appearances do not weaken the jarring combinations. Particularly striking is the passage 629–59. Here the poet is describing the relation between the rising of the signs of the Zodiac and the rising and the setting of the other constellations. In this section generally, he exploits the possibilities for bizarreness which the astronomy affords if the figures are treated as more than a mode of reference. In 629 ff. he resumes and elaborates a dramatic scene (cf. 353 ff.). The fearful Monster (Cetus) advances against Andromeda; Cepheus makes a warning gesture to her μεγάλη . . . χειρί (631) 'with his mighty hand'. Yet the drama is placed in a context which makes it bizarre: the heads of all the protagonists disappear beneath the horizon.

Aratus now turns to the rise of Scorpio and represents Orion as fleeing from that monster, in accordance with the myth, which he relates in detail (637–46). The narrative and its morality are distanced by the nervous piety affected in the introduction (637). But formally the narrative creates a firm and straightforward picture of the constellations as mythical figures: the world and morality of the myth are satisfyingly traditional.[12] But then we are told that 'all that is left' of Andromeda and the Monster also flees from the Scorpion with all haste (647 ff.). One myth intrudes grotesquely on another, and girl and pursuing beast alike fly from this new monster. At the same time 'all that is left' stresses the physical astronomy, with an effect of bizarre disharmony: the figures are only fragments. The poet proceeds to the sinking of Cepheus, upside-down, to the head. This is presented in markedly astronomical terms, with only a light injection of religious morality and play with other figures. γαῖαν ἐπιξύει 'grazes the earth' sounds decidedly technical, and the specification of the stars has the flavour of Eudoxus.[13]

After this sudden domination of the astronomical, we are still more abruptly confronted with the domination of the mythical. The inversion of Cassiepeia at her setting is presented as a disordered dive into the Ocean:

$$\text{ἐπεὶ οὐκ ἄρ' ἔμελλεν ἐκείνη}$$
$$\text{Δωρίδι καὶ Πανόπῃ μεγάλων ἄτερ ἰσώσασθαι.} \qquad \text{(657 f.)}$$

Thus she was not to escape a heavy punishment when she made herself the equal of Doris and Panope (sea-nymphs).

The gesture is dramatic, though fitted to the myth with conspicuous ingenuity. The reference to the punishment shows the same grim assertion of morality as in the story of Orion, though the allusiveness, and the lowly status of the deities, produces a fresh sense of archness. The concentration on the figure is complicated and slightly modified by the opening of this account (653 f.). There Aratus suggests a different interpretation in terms of figures.

[12] Aratus' particular version of the myth may or may not have seemed unusual; Callimachus deals with the story too (fr. 570, cf. *H.* 3. 265). The theology of divine power is conveyed with archaic grimness and wit in 643 f. (cf. 639): one thinks of Hom. *Il.* 24. 608 f.

[13] For ἐπιξύω cf. Euclid, *Phaen.*, p. 1. 23 Menge ξύοντες τὸν ὁρίζοντα. πόδας καὶ γοῦνα καὶ ἰξύν neatly echoes κεφαλῇ καὶ χειρὶ καὶ ὤμοις of Cepheus at 683.

παιδὸς ἐπείγεται εἰδώλοιο
δειλὴ Κασσιέπεια.

Poor Cassiepeia hurries after the image of her daughter.

With 'poor' and 'image' Aratus removes and affirms the personality of the figures in the same sentence.

Hence this whole passage, which cuts across the formal division of the subject-matter by signs of the Zodiac, produces an elaborate and yet forceful mixture of aspects and tones in the handling of the constellations. The bizarreness does not wholly deflate the grandiosity and the dramatic pathos but incorporates them in a distanced and delectable compound.

The nature of such compounds changes from passage to passage. The grandeur of the figures can be much less radically infringed than in this last passage; but it is always to some extent modified by astronomy. Even when Aratus expands on the myths, the astronomical teaching limits and complicates the effect. Pegasus provides an elaborate example. After listing the stars present in the figure of the Horse, Aratus proceeds οὐδ' ὅ γε τετράπος ἐστίν 'and he is not four-footed' (214). This startling and piquant formulation is followed by a more dignified statement of how 'the sacred Horse' is shaped. There comes next, firmly marked off, the myth of Pegasus' producing the spring Hippocrene (216–21). Thus far, then, the section consists of two passages of different flavour set side by side, the quality of the second insulated from, and heightened by, the contrary qualities of the first. But Aratus returns to the heavens thus:

ἀλλὰ τὸ μὲν πέτρης ἀπολείβεται, οὐδέ ποτ' αὐτὸ
Θεσπιέων ἀνδρῶν ἑκὰς ὄψεαι· αὐτὰρ ὅ γ' Ἵππος
ἐν Διὸς εἰλεῖται καί τοι πάρα θηήσασθαι.   (222–4)

> But the Hippocrene streams from a mere rock: you will never see it if you are far from the region of Thespiae. The Horse moves in Zeus' abode, the sky, and so you are able to look at him.

Ostensibly the impressive matter of the narrative is spurned, to make a foil to the glory of the constellation. It is an extravagant gesture: the spring was on Mount Helicon. But the emphasis on the spectator yields a final clause much weaker than the underlying rhetoric leads us to expect. We close, not with an exaltation of the stars, but with a neat, dry reversion to the pupil whom Aratus instructs. The grandeur of the narrative dissolves in the complexities of the close.

By far the most extended narrative tells of Justice, who became more and more disgusted with mankind, and finally left them to become the constellation Virgo (100–36). The account of her alienation progresses with sombre firmness, and with the exciting suggestion of moral passion in the narrator to match that of Justice. The effect is somewhat modified by the neatness with which we also seem to be progressing towards physical catasterism. In the middle stage Justice addresses mankind on the hills, not down in the city, at evening; she then returns to the mountains, with men gazing after her as she ascends. These physical elements are not merely atmospheric; they also suggest a moment of transition, ingeniously poised.[14] But more disquieting is the close. Justice seems to be withdrawing from the sight of men (128, 122). Yet although she leaves them in detestation (133), she then takes up the position in the sky:

$$ \tilde{\eta}\chi\acute{\iota} \; \pi\epsilon\rho \; \dot{\epsilon}\nu\nu\upsilon\chi\acute{\iota}\eta \; \ddot{\epsilon}\tau\iota \; \phi\alpha\acute{\iota}\nu\epsilon\tau\alpha\iota \; \dot{\alpha}\nu\theta\rho\acute{\omega}\pi o\iota\sigma\iota $$
$$ \Pi\alpha\rho\theta\acute{\epsilon}\nu o\varsigma \; \dot{\epsilon}\gamma\gamma\grave{\upsilon}\varsigma \; \dot{\epsilon}o\tilde{\upsilon}\sigma\alpha \; \pi o\lambda\upsilon\sigma\kappa\acute{\epsilon}\pi\tau o\iota o \; Bo\acute{\omega}\tau\epsilon\omega. \hspace{2cm} (135\,\text{f.}) $$

where to this day she, the Maiden, appears to men at
night, near conspicuous Bootes.

Aratus does not present this appearance to men as a palliating qualification to a grim close. Rather he seems to undo the pessimistic close to which his story appeared to be proceeding so inexorably. To be sure, when Justice had warned earlier that she would no more come to man's view (122), the rare word εἰσωπός 'visible' recalled the use of it forty-three lines earlier to refer to stars, and so pointed to the coming surprise.[15] But that only sharpens the sense of strangeness. The conclusion is too closely attached to the narrative for us to make it Aratus'

[14] As to atmosphere cf. Bulloch, *CHCL* i. 602 f.; 'wistfulness' seems not quite the word we want for 127 f.

[15] The sense 'face to face' would not accord with the Homeric passage from which poets take the word (*Il.* 15. 653). The sense 'visible' proceeds naturally from the interpretation of that passage ἐν ὄψει (Sch. A, see Dindorf (not Erbse) ii. 86); and it is probably found not only in Aratus 79 but in Simonides (*Adesp. El.* 58. 12 West).

contradiction of the story he retails from others.[16] The final detail of Virgo's position recalls the original introduction of the constellation (96 f.). The link has the sense of drawing us back into the pedantic description of phenomena whose relation to myth is problematic. Again the return to the heavens mingles the prosaic with the subversive. The effect of the narrative it distances and disturbs.

At some points, we saw, the interplay between the astronomy and the figures is heightened by exploitation of the addressee. The first part of the poem frequently delivers its instruction to a spectator in the second person. Most often there is little sense of personal communication, but we have here a latent dramatic fiction.[17] In the *Works and Days*, Hesiod very frequently addresses his brother Perses, and creates dramatic situations which involve them both.[18] In the *Phaenomena*, neither poet nor addressee appear as historical persons; but Aratus can suddenly focus our attention on these figures and on the didactic convention, and so enrich the texture and enhance larger effects.

Particularly striking are three passages, connected together. In the first Aratus tells of the severe winds at the summer equinox, and says εὐρεῖαί μοι ἀρέσκοιεν τότε νῆες 'at that time may my pleasure be for broad ships'. The sublunary world is making one of its relatively infrequent appearances in this part. The poet too affects to involve himself in this world and to take a role less distant from personality. We hear in this generalized first person a deliberately mannered echo of Hesiod's emphatically individual advice on a related theme (*WD* 682 f.). The first person is not so used elsewhere in Aratus' poem. The lines which follow begin on a new constellation, but continue the theme of sailing:

εἰ δέ τοι Ἡνίοχόν τε καὶ ἀστέρας Ἡνιόχοιο
σκέπτεσθαι δοκέει, καί τοι φάτις ἤλυθεν Αἰγὸς

---

[16] δῆθεν in 101 expresses Aratus' usual detachment from the truth of his story rather than any actual scepticism. Cf. Call. *SH* 288. 23; Apollonius uses the particle as synonymous with δή.

[17] The term 'Fiktion' is used by W. Ludwig, *Hermes*, 91 (1963), 448, of Aratus' pretence throughout the poem to instruct common farmers and sailors. The nature of the addressee is not at all so firmly defined as this suggests.

[18] Cf. West's edition, pp. 33 ff., 22 ff.

αὐτῆς ἢ Ἐρίφων, οἵτ' εἰν ἁλὶ πορφυρούσῃ
πολλάκις ἐσκέψαντο κεδαιομένους ἀνθρώπους ... (δήεις)

(156–9)

> If it is your wish to view the Charioteer and the stars of the
> Charioteer, and report has reached you of the Goat her-
> self, or the Kids, who have often viewed mortals being
> scattered in the tumult of the sea, (you will find the Char-
> ioteer) ...

In this long conditional structure Aratus elaborates the fiction
of the inquiring addressee, with no less sense of elegant artificiality. The fiction dominates the structure of the sentence. Into
the same condition he introduces an intrinsically elevated confrontation of stars watching in the heavens and violent disaster
on earth. The use of the same verb σκέπτομαι 'view' for the stars
stars and (as often) for the spectator gives a weird sense of reversal which makes piquant the change in tone. In this passage
the two types of immediacy conflict: human life too is made
more remote by the didactic fiction.

At mention of the winter equinox, Aratus turns again to the
sea (and to Hesiod). He presses home a warning to the addressee with a hypothetical picture of him: at that time of year

οὔτ' ἄν τοι νυκτὸς πεφοβημένῳ ἐγγύθεν ἠὼς
ἔλθοι καὶ μάλα πολλὰ βοωμένη.

(290 f.)

> If the night brought you terror (with its storms), the day
> would not come near to you, much indeed though you
> clamoured for it.

The conception is dark, but the grimness has a touch of satirical
humour. The sudden dramatization of the second person is
startling: we are both alarmed and distanced by the velocity of
this movement. The poet then changes to talking of 'the sailor'
and then to talking to 'us', mankind in its foolish eagerness to
sail; the terrors of sailing are elaborated still more vigorously.
After this he returns to the second person, imagining the
addressee 'enduring much at sea'; he ends the sentence with a
witty reversal of Homer.[19] In these lines the intrusion of
human life is marked by violence and power in material and in

---

[19] πεποιθὼς οὐκέτι νυκτί, contrast e.g. *Il.* 7. 282 ἀγαθὸν καὶ νυκτὶ πιθέσθαι. Earlier the
lines quoted most likely give a grimmer reversal of *Il.* 8. 487 αὐτὰρ Ἀχαιοῖς | ἀσπασίη
τρίλλιστος ἐπήλυθε νύξ.

rhetoric. The abrupt alterations of mode both enhance and limit these qualities.

The third and grandest passage on storms at sea changes its sailors in a similar fashion: first mankind (408–12), then the second person (413–17), then simply 'sailors' (418–29), then the second person (429 f.). The notion of signs for storms will form the basis of the second half; it is here greatly stressed (408–12, 418 f., 420, 430, 433). But Aratus confers on it here a kind of sublimity, by making the deified Night create these signs out of pity for men (408, 420, 434). The violence and misery of the terrestrial is conjoined in an impressive compound with the kindness of the heavens: the use of Night stresses the physical sky. The handling of the addressee ought formally to heighten the intensity and the sense of reality: the poet says μή μοι ... εὔχεο (413 f.) 'do not, I beg you, pray that this ominous star should appear clearly'. The personal warmth of this phrasing, not found elsewhere in the poem, is offset by the deviousness of the negative request. The sentence feels obtrusively artificial. Possibly the grim wit of the close at 429 is modified by another play with the idea of the spectator. Those who do not heed the sign given by the sight of the star sometimes die, sometimes, after great suffering, πάλιν ἐσκέψαντο | ἀλλήλους ἐπὶ νηΐ, 'once more they view one another on the ship'—one another not the stars. But in any case the elevation of the passage is only tinged by such elements. It is less affected by them than the second passage, much less than the first. The addressee furnishes a neat return to the description of constellations (436); with the same verb as in the first passage we recommence astronomical instruction.[20]

The ordinary world, then, by no means diminishes the grandeur derived from the heavens. The addressee, however, although he can sometimes heighten, also helps to modify and complicate the grandeur of this half. He does so on the one hand by thrusting on us the artificiality of the didactic fiction. On the other hand, he serves to underline the dryness of the physical astronomy by suggesting a half-dramatized image of tuition. Thus fictional elements descending from the poetic model and real elements derived from the prose source unite to

---

[20] The verb is δήεις 'you will find' (163); it occurs in Aratus only in these two lines.

produce a sense of pedantry and didactic rigour. This sense
contributes to the impact made by the entire first half, that is
by the accumulation of textures. We have an impression of elevation continually made distant, playful, fantastic, or tremu-
lously fanciful. But in its own terms the elevation exists, most
decidedly; in one's impressions this strange grandeur fills a
principal place.

The first half of the poem presents a remote, lofty, and
uniform world, complicated by the interplay of conceptions
and by the affectation of didacticism. The second returns us
gradually to earth, and presents a heterogeneous assemblage of
phenomena, connected by a single significance: they indicate
changes in the weather. The qualities the second half derives
from this arrangement may be considered most conveniently if
we separate the phenomena and the weather.

Certainly we start with a section on heavenly bodies (778–
908), and move, after a paragraph of less uniform level (909–
23), to a passage on sights in the heavens (924–41). But these
parts turn out to increase our general feeling of downward
movement.[21] After them the phenomena for the most part involve familiar creatures and objects, often quite unpoetic in
their associations. Readers then had a much sharper feeling for
'low' material than we have. Such material in similes, as in
metaphors, has a very different resonance from such material
when it is the direct subject of discourse; and even in similes
ancient commentators on Homer found objects 'low' and saw
Homer as concealing their lowness with epithets (thus Sch. *Il.*
13. 589, iii. 513 Erbse).[22] Aratus is naturally aware of an
intrinsic disparity between much of his matter and the dignity
of the epic style; but far from concealing it, he exploits it and
plays with it.

The section 942–72 illustrates well the richness and the prominence of this play. I will mention the more striking instances
only. In 946 f. frogs are denominated μάλα δείλαιαι γενεαί,
ὕδροισιν ὄνειαρ, ... πατέρες ... γυρίνων 'most unhappy race, a

---

[21] This regardless of whether the section on the heavenly bodies came first in Aratus'
source, as 'Theophrastus' makes plausible. Each of his four main sections, arranged by
type of weather, begins with sun, moon (stars): 10 ff., 26 f., 38, 50 f.

[22] They see similar processes within the narrative, for example in his description of a
fire dying down (Sch. *Il.* 9. 212, ii. 444 Erbse). For other material on this general subject see e.g. Kroll, *Stud. z. Verst. d. röm. Lit.* 47 f., 112.

blessing for water-snakes, the fathers of the tadpoles'. The creatures are generally found too lowly to appear in high poetry.[23]
Aratus affects to be dignifying them, with the grandiose γενεαί
'race', the epic ὄνειαρ with dative 'blessing to ...', and the
kenning πατέρες γυρίνων 'fathers of the tadpoles'.[24] But the shift
of viewpoint from eaten to eater is amusingly abrupt, and the
tadpoles, still more lowly than their seniors, turn the aspiring
solemnity into humour. In 958 f. Aratus refers to

σκώληκες
κεῖνοι τοὺς καλέουσι μελαίνης ἔντερα γαίης.

those worms which they call guts of the black earth.

γῆς ἔντερα 'earth's guts' is a title so colloquial that even Aristotle always adds a 'so-called'; 'Theophrastus' does not, and so
confirms its currency. Aratus with pleasing incongruousness
gives an epic epithet to 'earth'. His 'which they call' in fact
highlights the distance of the phrase from epic style. It also provides a degraded form of the recurrent and significant references to mortal names in the first part of the poem.[25] Next hens
are described as

τιθαὶ ὄρνιθες ταὶ ἀλέκτορος ἐξεγένοντο.   (960)

tame she-birds which are born from the cock.

This is a consciously laboured periphrasis; but their action is εὖ
ἐφθειρίσσαντο 'they have been known to pick off well their lice'.
The verb and the notion are strikingly low; the poet's use of
'well' adds a bizarre touch of epic colour.[26] The whole section
ends with a more straightforward and dignified echo of Homer

---

[23] Xenophanes B 40 DK, probably taken from 'On Nature', is obviously a special
case.

[24] For ὄνειαρ cf. especially Hes. *Theog.* 871 θνητοῖς μέγ' ὄνειαρ, with the same apposit-
ional role.

[25] A bare καλέουσι 66, 245, 315, 399, 476. Cf. Hom. *Il.* 5. 306. Worms appear once in
Homer, in a comparison (*Il.* 13. 654 f.). (εὐλαί are different: they form part of the imagery of death.)

[26] εὖ carries little suggestion of excellence. Cf. especially Hom. *Od.* 19. 446 εὖ φρίξας
λοφιήν. Lice (φθεῖρες) do not appear in high poetry; one will disallow an insulting or
humorous phrase of Archilochus' (fr. 236).

(ὀξὺ λεληκώς (972) 'crying shrilly', cf. *Il.* 22. 141). The language and style of the epic afford Aratus his principal vehicle for play with the low. The effect is sharpened by his earlier play with the grand.

This continual play is by no means incompatible with a sense of diversity in the material. Indeed, particularities or qualities which are low and thus striking offer a major resource for investing phenomena with vivid individuality and enhancing a sense of change. It is seldom possible to 'prove' that Aratus intends a contrast between signs or between sections: he seldom calls attention to them explicitly. Conceivably, too, Aratus was bound in detail by the order of his source, although what we can tell of his handling of Eudoxus would assuredly suggest otherwise.[27] Yet even if he were so bound, the flavour which signs acquire in Aratus' poem makes such a feeling of difference an inescapable part of the work. And in fact it would be very implausible to suppose that Aratus was unaware of this. One may consider a single type of contrast, that between large creatures and small. ἀλλὰ γὰρ οὐδὲ μύες (1132) 'but not even mice' (have not been a sign) surely invites the reader to make a contrast at least with the wolf that has immediately preceded them (1124 ff.). The description of the wolf combined the understanding dignity of a Homeric simile with a sense of the strange and unnatural. The skipping of the mice is deliciously playful in effect. One contrasts their 'squeaking more shrilly than usual' (1132) with the wolf's 'howling long' (1124). The intercourse of pigs, sheep, and goats is described in 1069 f. with piquancy and blunt directness.[28] By saying that they indicate a storm 'just as the wasps do', Aratus surely points to a contrast of flavour with the preceding sentence, on those insects. The small creatures in their ubiquitous swirling multitudes arouse a

---

[27] Aratus followed Eudoxus' general arrangement (Hipparchus 1. 2. 17—notably Hipparchus claims no more). But in 480–96 he goes round the circle in the opposite direction to Eudoxus (fr. 66); he interposes stars at 362 ff., cf. Eudox. fr. 52; the differences between 197–247 and Eudox. fr. 34 are probably to the point. There was much more reason to follow Eudoxus in details than the source of the second part.

[28] Aratus uses the prosaic stem ὀχ- for the mounting, lightly distancing the effect, as often, by novel forms (ὀχή for ὀχεία, ὀχέω for ὀχεύω). As often the term is probably taken from the source (cf. [Theophr.] 25); naturally Aratus could have described the matter more decorously had he chosen. βιβαζόμεναι is probable in 1074; certainly the word is alluded to.

wholly different response from the large domesticated animals
with their homely, half-human action.[29]

More direct opposition of size comes without explicit indication in 1028–32.

> οὐδ' ἂν ἔτι ξουθαὶ μεγάλου χειμῶνος ἰόντος
> πρόσσω ποιήσαιντο νομὸν κηροῖο μέλισσαι,
> ἀλλ' αὐτοῦ μέλιτός τε καὶ ἔργων εἰλίσσονται·
> οὐδ' ὑψοῦ γεράνων μακραὶ στίχες αὐτὰ κέλευθα
> τείνονται, στροφάδες δὲ παλιμπετὲς ἀπονέονται.

Nor, if a great storm were coming would the yellow bees
continue to pasture their wax far away: they remain and
swirl round their honey, round their estate; nor do the
long columns of cranes on high then travel along the same
path: they turn round and fly back.

The bees appear as charming miniatures of farm animals and
farmers, with their pasturing and their estate. The 'long' lines
of cranes moving 'on high' convey a larger and more impressive
image of flight. The two signs are made closely parallel and are
coupled in a single sentence. The bulls of 954 f. are followed at
once by ants, centipedes, and earth-worms. The ants carry all
the eggs out from their ant-hill θᾶσσον 'with some speed'
(957)—this detail of speed is not an intrinsic element of the sign
and does not appear in [Theophr.] 22. Their hurried and prodigious activity one may not unnaturally contrast with the
large animals' more static and ponderous behaviour.

> ὕδατος ἐνδίοιο
> οὐρανὸν εἰσανιδόντες ἀπ' αἰθέρος ὠσφρήσαντο.　　　　　(954 f.)

Looking up into the heavens they have caught the smell of
rain in the sky.

Indeed, the Homeric phrase οὐρανὸν εἰσανιδόντες 'looking up
into the heavens' was used before of star-gazing in a grandiose
passage (325), and here glances parodically at that act of con-

---

[29] ἑλίσσεται ... δῖνος (1067) refers to the storm but suggests corresponding behaviour
in the wasps. The recurrence of σφηκ- in this line lays further weight on the change that
follows.

templation.[30] These instances, taken together, may serve to indicate the importance of diversity in the texture of this part.

The diversity is all tightly focused on the single object of foretelling the weather (usually bad). In accordance with the character of this half, there are after the introduction no digressions, and no expansions of any size (the most considerable is 1101–3). There is not even a description of the weather that lasts more than two lines. Certainly, Aratus wished to avoid the repetitive monotony of his source; but that aim alone, it appears, will not explain or exhaust the qualities of this part. Grandeur and power might well attach to the designation of wind, rain, storm, and calm. In the early, and more elevated, portions, some of the phrases do come a little nearer to this character than later. In the introduction storms receive an epic epithet at 744 and, at 760, the heightened reference λαίλαπι πόντου 'tempest of the sea'.[31] In the section on heavenly bodies οὐκ ὀλίγῳ χειμῶνι τότε κλύζονται ἄρουραι (902) 'by no small storm is the earth deluged then' has a certain impressiveness in its movement from litotes to a forceful verb. But in the earlier οὐδ' ... ἄρραντοι γίνονται ἐπ' ἤματι κείνῳ ἄρουραι (868) 'not unwetted is the earth on that day', the language is meant to sound too solemn for its content, the ostensible grimness of manner is to sound arch. ἢ καί που ῥαθάμιγγες ἐπιτροχόωσ᾽ ὑετοῖο (899) 'or indeed, besides wind, sometimes the drops of rain hurry on' uses an epic word for 'drops' and so mingles the distant with the charmingly small and familiar. Finally, the paragraph on signs in the sky employs the sailor's fear for his life to enhance the drama of the storm (935 f., cf. also 763 f.). In the rest of this half, the phrases used to denote the weather do not make even these limited approaches to elevation and force. They are plain and colourless. We feel an increasing sense of division: between the drabness of the unremitting practical instruction we are ostensibly offered, and the colour and variety of the experience in fact presented to the reader's imagination.

---

[30] A prolonged act of looking is suggested by 325 and Homer; the aorist is 'coincident'. οὐρανός occurs elsewhere in this half only at 940, 15 lines before, where reminiscence of the first half is obvious. Apart from the last paragraph of the poem (1151, 1154), αἰθήρ occurs only here in the second half; in the first half cf. 390, 461, 720. The word is by no means expected here. The line is piquantly constructed.

[31] The disjunction seems to require this sense. Cf. Sch. Hom. *Il*. 16. 384.

This sense of division is furthered by the very structures into which Aratus organizes his material. The opening section on the moon, sun, and Manger, markedly homogeneous in its content, eschews excessive repetition. The instruction σκέπτεο 'look at' appeared in the first half (75), but here it is placed at the beginning of five paragraphs, with a heaviness of emphasis foreign to the earlier part. However, the instances are separated by at least twelve lines (778, 799, 832, 880, 892). In retailing here a huge string of what are essentially conditional sentences, Aratus avoids any feeling of insistent sameness in form. But after this section, and before the last one (1044 ff.), large clusters frequently develop in the connection of the signs: six ἤς ('or'), all at the beginning of the line, in 942–53; five καίς ('and') in 954–62; six μηδές ('and do not') in 973–87; seven καίς in 1021–7 (cf. also 999–1003). These accumulations make the sequences of striking images and striking phrases seem richer and more copious. But they also suggest a pressing zeal to inform in the fictional voice of the author. This function emerges most obviously in 973–87, where the addressee is adjured to ignore none of these signs, and a whole further string is added for him to remember (984). The run of μηδές here is particularly reminiscent of the latter part of the *Works and Days* (cf. *WD* 715–19). The whole section ends by playing with the author's expansiveness. 'Why', he exclaims abruptly, 'should I tell you all the signs there are for men?', τί τοι λέγω ὅσσα πέλονται ...; (1036 f.).[32] The sudden arrest piquantly underlines the relentless flow of the preceding account. Aratus continues the play with delicate wryness: the poet proceeds to illustrate the vast number of signs that exist with a few more, for other types of weather.

It might be contended that all this was meant to produce no complexity of effect: that the writer wishes the stress on the quantity of signs merely to redound to the praise of the gods. Their ample provisions were emphasized in the more grandiose introductory passage (732, 771 f.).[33] Such a view of the effect would make very strange the other complexities of this part,

---

[32] The sense 'how', i.e. 'by what means', would be grammatically impossible, despite Sch. Hom. *Il.* 4. 31–2. Cf. Alcman fr. 1. 58 Page.

[33] The gods and Zeus appear after 941 only at 964, in a sentence whose seeming elevation is by no means without mockery.

and would be especially hard to reconcile with the handling of the addressee.

The didactic fiction is not exploited with such drama in this half as in some passages of the first; but we have a more continuous sense of its presence. With flatter but more insistent didacticism, the author presses on the addressee the practical importance of the signs and the need for vigour in observing them.[34] It would be implausible to make this fiction into Aratus' earnest enlightenment of his reader. But once we acknowledge a sense of division and play, a straightforwardly religious interpretation say of the string of μηδές (973 ff.) becomes very difficult to maintain. The passage 819–91 (the sun) often uses remarks to the addressee as a variation for 'it will rain'. We have seen that some of the other variations in this passage contain modifying elements. It would be strange not to find humour in the version at 857. If it has rained in the day and at sunset a cloud overshadows the sun, with broken rays shining all round it, then

ἦ τ' ἂν ἔτ' εἰς ἠῶ σκέπαος κεχρημένος εἴης.

even the next morning you would still be in need of cover.

The swift movement from impressive sights in the sky to the implied discomfort of a soaking derives further force from the immediacy of the second person. In the next sentence the addressee is told that, if such-and-such happens, he 'certainly need not tremble (περιτρομέειν) at rain that night or the next day' (i.e. it will be fine); but he should so tremble if something else occurs (860 ff.). The preceding sentence directs our attention, not to any serious consequences of rain, but to the physical unpleasantness: the idea of terror is to seem inappropriately inflated for this subject.

Later, the poet speaks of the different significations of single and of double parhelia (880 ff.). He accordingly urges the addressee, μηδ' αὔτως σκοπιὴν ταύτην ἀμενηνὰ φυλάσσειν (883) 'do not keep your watch for this with useless feebleness' (i.e. be sure to distinguish them). The vehement phrasing, with its

---

[34] Aratus' source might have had second-person imperatives, like the papyrus treatise, but unlike 'Theophrastus'. But the colourless προσδέχου, προδέχου have none of the life seen in Aratus.

military suggestion, surely feels somewhat exaggerated. Aratus
proceeds to speak of a storm with grandiose language, using the
name of Zeus (886); but the final reference to rain is in the variation with raindrops (889, see above p. 231). The play with
levels there helps to deflate the portentousness of the command.

The play in 1036 f. ('Why should I tell you . . .?') involves the
didactic fiction too. For the remaining signs (1044–137), the
addressee gives place to a series of rustic figures, and the feeling
of the poem changes.[35] The import of the signs is often linked
with the reactions of the ploughman, or the goatherd, and so
forth; these reactions become a prime source of interest. Repetition of the word χαίρει 'is glad' suggests their structural significance (1073, 1075, cf. 1090; 1095 (negative), 1098). At the same
time, vivid detail and unexpected variation remove any sense of
obsession or of dryness. Thus the section begins with an emphatic description of the farmer constantly gazing at certain trees
(1045 f.). The gaze presents his anxiety in dramatic and concrete form. As for variation, at 1075 f. we are told how the
timely ploughman is glad at the timely arrival of the cranes
(ὡραῖος . . . ὥριον). The event, and the emphasis on timeliness,
remind one of Hesiod, and his moralizing depiction of the untimely farmer's horror at the coming of these birds (*WD*
451 ff.). But Aratus unexpectedly dwells on the superior
pleasure of the untimely ploughman when the cranes are late.
Hesiod's unwearying commendation of work is no less pleasingly avoided at 1117. There Aratus speaks of the *aged* ploughman's eager hopes that bad weather will delay his work. Even
apart from this aspect, the section removes us suddenly from
the strident tones of pressing instruction. Not that the poet's ostensible voice is straightforwardly distanced from his material.
The poet utters wishes which suggest a strange involvement in
this third-person context (1049 f., 1086 ff.). He once expands in
the manner of the first part on the lot of 'us mortals' (1101 ff.),
though he then returns with a tinge of pedantry to the signs.
Rather, we feel the division between the didactic and the
imaginative to be much smoothed over and reduced. Those
affected by the signs now themselves become part of the same
humble and colourful tapestry as the signs themselves. The

---

[35] L. 1138–41 are rightly deleted by Martin. They do not affect the point.

voice of the poet bears a different relation to his material: we no longer feel so strongly that his interest, officially, is only in driving home instructions. This is not to say that the didactic sinks from view. Indeed, a particularly delightful exploitation appears in the last paragraph of signs: squeaking, gambolling mice

(οὐκ) ἄσκεπτοι ἐγένοντο παλαιοτέροις ἀνθρώποις.　　(1134)

have not passed unobserved by the men of former times.

The second half of the line is Homeric (*Il.* 23. 788, in a different sense); and the conception recalls the first part (442, *al.*). The pomp here comically set against the lowness of the sign stands far removed from the manner of the preceding section. The whole of the present section (1044–137) shows Aratus, not merely hitting on a new verbal device with which to variegate his exposition, but consciously presenting a marked alteration of tone and poetic quality. The tone and quality of the earlier sections had themselves stood in contrast with those of the first half.

The final paragraph of the work returns us abruptly to the didactic drama. τῶν μηδὲν κατόνοσσο, it begins (1142), 'make light of none of these signs'. The phrasing echoes the τῶν τοι μηδὲν ἀπόβλητον γινέσθω (973) 'ignore none of these things' of the section before the one just ended. The same air of urgent exhortation and emphatic completeness again invades the text. This is reinforced by the final couplet, which makes a large condition, but closes austerely with no large promise.

τῶν ἄμυδις πάντων ἐσκεμμένος εἰς ἐνιαυτόν,
οὐδέποτε σχεδίως κεν ἐπ᾽ αἰθέρι τεκμήραιο.

If you considered all these signs together throughout the year, you would never interpret the skies offhandedly.

The contrast with the section immediately preceding (1044 ff.) sharpens our sense of the divergence of that section; and it marks the divergence as a limited episode, not a decisive change in the poem. Even while the last paragraph reintroduces the heavens, it seals the unity of the second half in tone.

Our discussion has indicated the fundamental importance in Aratus of differing tones and levels, strangely and strikingly juxtaposed and combined. This concern of the poet's does not

merely govern the effect of the individual sequences and paragraphs. It gives each half of the poem its special character, and,
through this, gives the whole work its poetic shape. The affinity
with Callimachus, Apollonius, and Theocritus is clear and
essential. Yet the effects are much more restrained, the movements and combinations much less drastic and disconcerting.
Naturally, this is connected with the whole character of the
poem, which formally sustains an almost continuous didactic
exposition. But it would be implausible to regard such a poet as
the slave of his genre, and in any case the choice of genre forms
part of his intentions. We should enjoy the poem in the terms it
creates for itself; the relative quietness of its play with tone contributes to its air of subtlety and sobriety. The work should be
approached in the same manner as those of the other three
poets; if these pursue their related ends far more boldly and
strongly, that should not obscure either the kinship of Aratus or
the aesthetic coherence and validity of his superb creation.

B. HERODAS

Herodas is much more deeply divided than Aratus from Callimachus, Theocritus, and Apollonius. He uses some of the same
genres and models as Callimachus and Theocritus, and shares
their interest in certain areas of tone and level. But he is not
preoccupied like them with mingling and opposing different
areas to produce complicated textures and complicated poems.
He does not exploit form to enhance these effects. This makes
the impact of his work very different to any reader concerned
with poems and works in the fullness of their force, rather than
with tendencies of the period. He may well belong in time and
place with the three most famous poets of the age; this increases
the interest of his differences.[36] But although these may heighten our impression of his colleagues, we should not allow our
contemplation of Herodas himself to be distracted or distorted,
let alone think the worse of him for aiming at a different kind of
poetry.

---

[36] In my view the praise of Egypt in 1. 28 ff., especially ὁ βασιλεὺς χρηστός (whatever
the text), associates the poet with country and king. He must be writing after 273.
Though 4. 25 f. need not necessarily show that that poem was written before c.265, it
seems the more likely view. See further I. C. Cunningham, *CQ* NS 16 (1966), 117,
Fraser, *PA* ii. 876 ff.

Herodas' poems adopt the metre and dialect of Hipponax, the archaic poet also imitated in Callimachus' *Iambi*. But in Hipponax the poet himself is made to play a dominant and aggressive role, as later tradition emphasized (see p. 49). In Herodas we have by contrast the impersonality of the quasi-dramatic mode. The poet himself is absent, save for the poem which treats of his work. This unusual poem (8) highlights the poet's habitual conventions; and in other ways too provides a profitable line of access.

Poem 8 is spoken by the poet as a dramatic character. Waking from a dream, he calls for his slaves (1–14). To one he narrates his dream: a goat he had was destroyed; he succeeded in a contest at a ritual of Dionysus, but he was harshly challenged by an angry old man (14–65). This dream he interprets to refer to the criticism his poetry will receive and to its eventual triumph (66–79). The poem proclaims loudly the two formal elements in Herodas' work. The poet states explicitly at the end his connection with Hipponax (78), and it is fairly obvious that the old man with whom he disputes the prize is his model.[37] On the other hand, the goat which represents his poetry is a gift from Dionysus (68); the choice of that deity can only really be explained by his role as patron of dramatic poetry (cf. e.g. Call. *Ep.* 8 Pf., LVIII GP). The particular ritual too has various connections with drama.[38]

But Herodas does not merely assert the presence of these two elements. When he makes Hipponax display, with his own words, his vehemence and physical pugnacity (cf. Hipp. frr. 120–1 West), the striking evocation of Herodas' original brings out the different character of his own work. The effect is only

[37] The old man actually quotes from Hipponax' first poem ($\tau\hat{\eta}$ $\beta\alpha\tau\eta\rho\dot{\iota}\eta$ $\kappa o\psi$- 60, Hipp. fr. 20); Herodas is not known to take more than vocabulary from Hipponax elsewhere, if I am not mistaken. For his age here cf. $\dot{o}$ $\pi\rho\dot{\epsilon}\sigma\beta\upsilon\varsigma$ in Alcaeus, *HE* 76. There is nothing strange in the idea of an imitator being seen as rival to his model (e.g. [Longin.] 13), and so of Hipponax contesting Herodas' supremacy. Herodas the writer does not claim to excel Hipponax, as he does the rest; this surely points to the model. The final sentence will scarcely cohere unless one allows this.

[38] The rite was a part of the country Dionysia, at which plays were also performed (L. Deubner, *Attische Feste* (1932), 137 f.). It was said to be performed in a theatre (Sch. Arist. *Wealth* 1130). The occasion was by some connected with the origin of tragedy and comedy (cf. A. W. Pickard-Cambridge, *Dithyramb, Tragedy and Comedy* (1927), 97 ff., Pfeiffer, *HCS* i. 169 n. 2). It would be pedantic to object that the non-dramatic poet Hipponax is present.

made the more delightful by the objectivity of the form at this
very moment. The author himself in this poem as it were sub-
mits to the conventions he has created and appears as a dramatic character. The address to the slaves in the first section,
with its air of bustle and its impatience and ferocity of
language, belongs to a recurring type of passage in these poems,
a type particularly used to establish their quasi-dramatic
nature (see below). It also marks the speaker as typical in his
manner, and (note 12 f.) in his humble status.

> ἢ προσμένεις σὺ μέχρις εὖ ἥλιος θάλψῃ
> τὸ]ν̣ κῦσον ἐσδύς; κῶς, δ᾽, ἄτρυτε, κοὐ κάμνεις
> τὰ πλ]ευρὰ κνώσσους᾽; …
> τ]ο̣ν̣θ̣ρυζε καὶ κνῶ, μέχρις εὖ παραστά[ς σοι
> τὸ] βρέγμα τῷ σκίπωνι μαλθακὸν θῶμα[ι.   (3–5, 8 f.)

Are you waiting, Psylla, till the sun comes and warms
your bottom? How can you not be making your ribs ache
with that ceaseless snoring? ... Go on, mumble and
scratch—till I come and soften your skull with my stick.

We relish this violent concreteness and energy of language and
feeling because, as usual, we feel the author is making us view
it, and is viewing it, from an aloof position: neither he nor the
reader is involved in the emotion and shares the character's
perspective on the action. We probably do not learn until after
this section that the speaker is the poet (for Herodas probably
did not mark his speakers' names). The section produces in
retrospect a sense of extravagant play in the handling of the
poet within the terms of his art.

The sustained narration of the principal section is untypical
of Herodas in its milieu and in its form. Dreams can be
recounted within full-length dramas; but this account is much
more extended than any in tragedy or comedy, and creates its
own world, that of grotesque rural religion. The text of this part
is very poorly preserved in the papyrus; but the action is certainly comic in part, and made remoter by the form of the
reported dream. Yet we are also aware of the figure of the poet
as a poet, with his characteristic passion to excel. These elements, including the layers of the form, are strikingly brought
together in 41–7. Of the men in the contest trying to stand on

the inflated wineskin, some fell on their faces, some on their backs,

> πάντα δ' ἦν, Ἀνν[ᾶ,
> εἰς ἓν γέλως τε κἀνίη [......]ϵντα.
> κἀγὼ δόκευν ...
> ἐπ' οὖν ἀλέσθαι, κἠλάλαξαν ὤνθρωπ[οι
> ὥς μ' εἶδ[ον ..]ως τὴν δο[ρὴ]ν πιεζεῦντα.   (43–7)

The whole scene, Annas, was a mixture of laughter and pain. I myself decided ... to leap on the skin. The others cheered when they saw me pressing it down.

The handling of the poet in this section mingles distance with suggested significance. This significance the final section defines. Here the dramatic form, and the ostensible exegesis of the dream, only lightly veil our sense of contact with the author's own voice. The topics are conventional enough; but the warmth of the language is designed to give the reader an impression of directness and engagement.

> τὰ μέλεα πολλοὶ κάρτα, τοὺς ἐμοὺς μόχθους,
> τιλεῦσιν.   (71 f.)

Many indeed will tear at my songs, at which I have toiled.

The feeling of pain here serves as the foil to exulting confidence in the fame that he will achieve, as he swears by the Muse who inspired him. The oath, with its anaphora, seems to have had both dignity and vehemence. The lines seem to break through the impersonality and the lowness of the poem with calculated abandon.

In these differing treatments of himself Herodas plays with the limitations and the impersonality of his poems, and heightens our awareness that those aspects spring from conscious artifice. The play, and the movement, hardly lead to a sense of tonal complexity or conflict. Nor does the poet use the various layers of discourse to produce an impression of involution or of devious obliqueness, like Callimachus in his *Iambi*; there is no positive ethos to set against Hipponax'.[39] The humour of the poem is more sweeping than Callimachus', its effects more extravagant and more vigorous. They draw on, and emphasize,

---

[39] Indeed, both Hipponax and 'Herodas' threaten to beat people with their stick (9, 60): the action unites the two dramatic figures.

not the subtlety of the other poems but their simplicity—the large features of their single mode and their restricted world.

What connection is there between Herodas and Hipponax, and between Herodas and dramatic poetry? As for dramatic poetry, connections with Athenian comedy are difficult to judge.[40] The subject-matter of New Comedy is both linked to actual society and shared with other genres more or less perished. It is most plausible to associate with New Comedy poem 2, which deals with a πορνοβοσκός, an owner of prostitutes. But our impression of the prominence and the mendacity of this profession in Comedy derives principally from the Romans: even here caution may be in place.[41] In feeling, register, and dramatic organization, Herodas bears little resemblance to New Comedy. One is sometimes reminded of Aristophanes (e.g. in the mother's speech in 3); but again this does not take us far. It is probable that Herodas is much more radically indebted to a non-poetic form of drama or quasi-drama, the mime. Such a view is implied by the title *Mimiambi* given to the poems in quotations (whoever devised the name).[42] In particular, one suspects links with Sophron (p. 155).[43] In any case, commands to slaves for chairs, food, and drink (Hdas. 1. 79 ff., 6. 1 ff., 4 ff.) would be much more at home in the mimes of Sophron (frr. 10, 15, 16, 18, 99 Kaibel) than in the outdoor world of the Attic stage. All this confirms us in thinking that it is the mere fact of dramatic form in poetry which occasions the use in poem 8 of the Attic Dionysia.

There appears to be very little specific connection between Herodas and Hipponax, apart from metre and dialect. They show proximity only in their concern with the low. Their

---

[40] More optimistic is R. G. Ussher, *Hermathena* 131 (1981), 69 ff. I have not seen B. Veneroni, *RIL* 107 (1973).

[41] In Menander cf. *Colax* 120 ff., especially 131 f. (an event related to Battarus' story); see also Hunter on Eubulus' Πορνοβοσκός (frr. 88–9).

[42] For the evidence see Cunningham's edn. p. 1. The resemblances between Herodas 5 and Page, *GLP* no. 77 (anonymous mime) may perfectly well be due to imitation of Herodas.

[43] The particular similarities between Herodas 4, on the women visiting Asclepius' shrine, and Theocritus 15 (said to be modelled on Sophron) invite, but do not demand, the notion that Sophron was the model for Herodas too. Note also the similarities between the beginning of Theocritus 15 (1–10) and Herodas 1 (1–16). Both poets may take from Sophron the oath by the Moirai found only in Hdas. 1. 11, 66, 4. 30 and Theocr. 2. 160 (in a poem based on Sophron); similarly μᾶ (Herodas often; Theocr. 15. 89).

matter and manner differ widely: Herodas is not cheerfully disgusting or lavishly scurrilous, and has little interest in lavator-
ies. But serious poetry in Greek had long been defined by
elevation, and had severely limited the place of lowly persons,
vulgar attitudes, and everyday objects and activities. Given this
general conception the keen relish of both poets for such things,
and their avoidance of the lofty, would give them a definite
though broad affinity. There is much other 'low' Greek literature, and one would not think of Hipponax if Herodas had
written in a different metre. But granted that Hipponax is Herodas' formal model, one will feel here a certain likeness. At all
events, the low and the dramatic are together fundamental to
the effects of Herodas' poems.

More may be said on these two aspects in general. Herodas'
poems are very unlikely to have been intended for dramatic
execution.[44] To take a detail, the speech at 5.55 is probably
not uttered in the same place as the main action (it is implausible that such a speech would be delivered off-stage). More
generally, poem 8 would make a curious drama. The connected
poems 6 (set in a house) and 7 (set a good time later in a shoemaker's shop) would in terms of ancient staging make a curious
sequence.[45] The visible action in 7 (pp. 243 ff.) would also
seem oddly trivial. Indeed, 6, 7, and 8 all encourage the notion
that they formed part of a series in a book. Consequently, the
dramatic elements must be considered in terms of the reader's
perceptions. One will give particular attention to his sense of
striking physical action; of gaps between the surface of speech
and reality; of contrasts, relationships, and interactions
between the characters. It is with action that the reader's (or
listener's) response will differ most from a spectator's. Here the
visual must be evoked by the poet's words. Yet such evocation
will particularly suggest the simulated likeness of actual drama.
We shall give this feature especial consideration. Lowness Herodas brings out by various means, but normally without writing elevated poetry himself and producing a piquant diversity

[44] As is maintained by G. Mastromarco, *The Public of Herodas* (1984); cf. Parsons's
review, *CR* NS 31 (1981), 110.

[45] For the setting of 7 inside the shop cf. 123, and O. Crusius, *Philologus* NF 6 (1893),
519 f. If ἔξω in 5 meant 'outside the shop', Herodas would actually be inconsistent over
the setting of his scene. The vividness of 123 itself, the Press Reader observes, is one
more sign that the poems were not staged.

of poetic levels. These means are for the most part closely connected with the dramatic features we have mentioned. The two aspects are intimately and elaborately related.

We may consider the various poems from these points of view. Poem 2 consists of the oration made by an owner of prostitutes, called Battarus; he is prosecuting one Thales for the alleged abduction of one of his girls by force. The poem differs from 1 and from 3–7 in that it contains no dramatic dialogue, and it represents ostensibly a formal and dignified species of utterance. Particular moments serve to produce a sense of drama and, simultaneously, to deflate the pretensions of the bawd. In the sequence 71–86, Battarus claims with tones of righteous fury that he would have inflicted terrible violence on Thales had he himself been younger. At this Thales laughs (γελᾷς; 'you laugh!' 74). Battarus polemically asserts his manliness, but with admission of his effeminacy and comic confusion of his thought. Then, changing his tone completely, he addresses Thales as it were aside.

> ἐρᾷς σὺ μὲν ἴσω[ς] Μυρτάλης. οὐδὲν δεινόν·
> ἐγὼ δὲ πυρέων· ταῦτα δοὺς ἐκεῖν᾽ ἕξεις.
> ἢ νὴ Δί᾽, εἴ σευ θ[ά]λπεταί τι τῶν ἔνδον,
> ἔμβυσον εἰς τὴν χεῖρα Βατταρίῳ τιμήν,
> καὐτὸς τὰ σαυτοῦ θλῆ λαβὼν ὅκως χρῄζεις. (75–83)

You perhaps passionately desire Myrtale. Nothing extraordinary in that: so do I my food. Give me what I want and you can have what you want. Or if you feel rather on fire inside, stick the price for the girl into old Battarus' hand, and you can take away your own property and bang it as you please.

He now shows complete indifference to the girl and her past or future sufferings, and perfect amiability to Thales, if he will but pay him. The brevity and simplicity of the first few clauses show his businesslike and reasonable approach to an easy matter. The longer final sentence leads up to the brutal monosyllable θλῆ 'bang'. Battarus then loudly resumes his speech. The whole passage presents a colourful interaction between two people, and a dramatically effective rupture of the fabric of speech which is overtly displayed. At the same time it exposes with unexpected explicitness the falsity of Battarus' oration and the depravity of his character.

Immediately before this Battarus had called on the girl to show the jury her naked body: her private parts betray Thales' mistreatment (65 ff.). The physical action that takes place is very striking, and the solidity of the dramatic context is enhanced by Battarus' stress on the girl's reluctance and by his call to the jury to look (ὁρῆτ', ἄνδρες, 68). The moment is also palpably low and indecent. Battarus' titillating description of the outrage (69–71) heightens the impropriety of the sight. It also displays amusingly his audacious mendacity.[46] Another primary legal procedure is used in a related fashion when Battarus calls for a law to be read out. The voice of the scribe who reads it is the only other voice that we hear in this mime: its intrusion thus has a certain force. Not only does the law sound implausible. Barratus' impertinent introduction of this reading, which follows on a vehement close (40), refers to the water-clock timing his speech with a jocular metaphor of vivid obscenity. This sinks the tone and the speaker startingly low.

It is these moments which undermine Battarus and his speech directly and drastically. They give edge to the slyer strokes of the poet, and turn the rhetoric of Battarus into absurdity. For otherwise his speech, though not neatly paragraphed, shows great facility and address with the bold gestures and the scorn and fervour of oratory.[47] The poem is unusual in simulating at points at least the dignity of impassioned prose. But there is no question of the poem hovering or shifting between the lofty and the lowly as regards the reader's responses. The effect is of straightforward burlesque, the grave stançes are a delightful fraud. The low and the dramatic commingle as the fountain-head of the poem's comedy and life.

The seventh poem forms a sequel to the sixth.[48] In the sixth a woman named Metro had learned of a certain shoemaker's skill in making leather substitutes for the virile organ; she was eager to meet him. Here she brings him new female customers,

[46] See Housman, *Classical Papers*, iii. 1056 f., and D. Bain, *LCM* (1982), 7 ff.

[47] General opinion rates him far too low and even couples him with the ludicrously incoherent orator ascribed to Sophron (fr. 109 Kaibel = Demetr. *Eloc.* 153). Most of Lucan's speeches, for example, display no more systematic a construction than this. Poetry has a freer hand.

[48] Cunningham, *CQ* NS 14 (1964), 32 ff., rightly thus far.

and he displays his shoes; he is interrogated on the prices. Cerdon's less respectable wares are probably not mentioned to Metro's friends, however discreetly.[49] But the previous poem has compelled us to expect indications of a more disreputable level beneath the surface of the conversation. The surface itself is far from elevated. The prolonged and vigorous treatment of shoes obviously expatiates on a trivial and everyday topic. The profession of cobblers was despicable in status; the physical appearance of this specimen is probably characteristic and certainly disagreeable.[50] The opening of the poem establishes the lowly level with a depiction of bustling action. After polite and friendly words to Metro, Cerdon yells to his slaves to bring a bench for the women (4 ff.).

> τῆς γυναιξὶν οὐ θήσεις
> τὴν μέζον᾽ ἔξω ϲανίδα; Δριμύλῳ φωνέω.
> πάλιν κατεύδεις; κόπτε, Πίστε, τὸ ῥύγχος
> αὐτοῦ, μέχρις τὸν ὕπνον ἐκχέῃ πάντα.   (4–7)

Come on, bring the bigger bench out for these ladies! Drimylus! Asleep again? Pistus, hit his snout till he pours out all that sleep.

There is much more in this vein. The excited animation one imagines can scarcely be separated from the excited harshness one hears. This seems the more unelevated because Cerdon evidently wishes his conscious zeal to impress the ladies.

The poet teases his reader: the ruptures he expects are delayed until Cerdon's final speech.[51] Metro has just addressed to Cerdon a speech in insulting language (93 ff.); the insults are not serious abuse, but suggest a considerable interval between the two in status. However, in his speech, Cerdon makes a kind of aside or dreamy apostrophe to Metro.

---

[49] In the main I would agree so far with G. Lawall, *CP* 71 (1976), 166 ff., against Cunningham, loc. cit.

[50] For station cf. Headlam–Knox, xlviii f.; note also Teles fr. 4 B. For baldness cf. Plat. *Rep.* 454 C with 495 E (both sedentary occupations). Hdas. 6. 59 (cf. 6. 76) is expanded into repulsive detail at 7. 71 f., which force us to visualize the character.

[51] L. 63, at the end of Cerdon's long first speech, can scarcely be the cobbler's hint to the women: the tone would be quite wrong. In any case there would have to be a possible meaning prima facie. The poet, on the other hand, is probably hinting at the debauchery of women and further tantalizing the reader. The problems associated with the line are discussed by G. Williams, *CR* NS 9 (1959), 92 ff. (his treatment of Aesop 135 Perry is not convincing).

δύ]ναιτό μ' ἐλάσαι σαν[. .] τὸν πίσ[υγγον
ἐόντα λίθινον ἐς θεοὺς ἀναπτῆναι·
ἔχεις γὰρ οὐχὶ γλάσσαν, ἡδονῆς δ' ἠθμόν.
ἆ, θεῶν ἐκεῖνος οὐ μακρὴν ἀπ . . [. . .] . .
ὀτέῳ σὺ χείλεα νύκτα κἠμέρην οἴγ[εις.   (108–12)

... could drive me, the hard old tailor, to fly up to the
gods. Your tongue is no tongue, but a colander of
pleasure. Ah, that man for whom you open your lips day
and night (dwells) not far from the gods themselves.

We find, then, that he is sexually infatuated with her, and that
he has received from her sensuous kisses (110). Earlier passages
have prepared us for the possibility that Metro would bestow
erotic pleasures on the unattractive old shoemaker in return for
his exquisite artefacts.[52] But the actual disclosure startles, so
sudden is the rift in the texture of the dialogue, and so abrupt
the change in Cerdon from voluble salesman to besotted lecher.
His language here makes a striking mixture. The middle line
('Your ... pleasure') is particularly graphic and vulgar; the
couplets on either side show a repellent distortion of the
language of love-poetry. All this renders more piquant the
shock of Metro's concessions. A stark change to fitting shoes returns us to the accustomed level with trivial but vivid physical
action.

Suddenly a woman appears at the door.

αὕτη σύ, δώσεις ἑπτὰ Δαρικοὺς τοῦδε,
ἢ μέζον ἵππου πρὸς θύρην κιχλίζουσα;   (122 f.)

Hey, you, guffawing louder than a horse there at the
door—are you going to give me seven darics for this? .

The intrusion involves an imagined dramatic action; and the
surprise is heightened by Cerdon's rude and irritated manner,
so different from his courtliness to Metro's friends. The intrusion is unexplained, which gives it the greater pregnancy;
but we are bound to suppose that the woman is laughing
because she knows more of Cerdon than Metro's friends do.
After this odd and dramatic disruption, the surface is recovered
by the speaker Cerdon in the final lines of the poem. But the re-

---

[52] 6. 74–9 (Metro's willingness, by implication, so to act); 7. 3 f. (Metro and Cerdon
are now acquainted).

lationship between Cerdon and Metro is underlined deftly at the close.[53]

We do not find in poem 4 the tension between a real level and a level of deceit that we find in poems 2 and 7. Two poor women make offerings in the temple of Asclepius, who has healed them; they admire the works of art they see there. Their viewing of these occupies the main part of the poem (20–78), though it is interrupted in the middle (41–53). Here one of the women harangues a female slave who does not respond to her command. Her vehemence and agitation is extreme: her friend's attempt to calm her highlights the dramatic disturbance. The characters are in the course of changing scene; this heightens the structural and quasi-visual impact of the moment. The abuse and the threats are characteristically colourful and low. The girl is gazing 'like a crab' (καρκίνου μέζον, 44); one day she will scratch her scalp (51)—a vivid, and yet maliciously understated, way of saying she will be branded on the head. The mistress' calling of Asclepius to witness uses the solemnity of religion to bring out the triviality of the matter in hand.[54]

This passage, of familiar type, breaks in on a sequence of different flavour. The description of works of art is in this poem given a form dramatically effective, as in the first chorus of Euripides' *Ion*: the works are spoken of by characters eagerly communicating to each other what they see and feel. The women's remarks concentrate on the proximity of the depictions to real things. One should not find this attitude naïve in itself. Such notions and such criteria were perfectly standard in the commendation of superlative art.[55] The conversation on the works before the interruption is not elevated writing in the least, but there is little comic lowness. One may note only the movement from the names of famous sculptors at the beginning (23 f.) to the names of humble subjects at the end (35 f.).[56] It

[53] On βαίτην κτλ. cf. V. Schmidt, *Sprachliche Untersuchungen zu Herodas* (1968), 117 ff.

[54] τὠσυρές might as well be read in 51; for the error cf. 3. 58. I should somewhat prefer to make 49 a parenthesis.

[55] Note AR 1. 767 ff. (and cf. e.g. Plin. *Nat. Hist.* 35. 65 f., 88 f., 94 f., 121; J. J. Pollitt, *The Ancient View of Greek Art* (1974), 170 ff.). Contrast P. Friedländer, *Johannes v. Gaza u. Paulus Silentarius*, 31; on the other hand, T. Gelzer, *Catalepton* (Festschrift Wyss, 1985), 96 ff., makes the poem too theoretical, as many have done.

[56] The notion may be doubted that the names are intrinsically disreputable.

is a striking change from fine art to the distracted slave. When the conversation resumes, disparities open between the sublime work of art and the grotesque observations of the spectators. The picture they speak of is by Apelles, we eventually learn (73): one of the supreme ancient painters, and distinguished not only for beauty but for grandeur.[57] The women present us with crudely vigorous images.

τὸν παῖδα δὴ ⟨τὸν⟩ γυμνὸν ἦν κνίσω τοῦτον
οὐκ ἕλκος ἕξει, Κύννα;   (59 f.)

Surely this naked boy in the picture will get a wound if I scratch him, Cynna? [So real he seems.]

The eyes of various low persons would pop out if they saw the silver in the picture (62 ff.). As for anyone who fails to admire Appelles,

ποδὸς κρέμαιτ' ἐκεῖνος ἐν γναφέως οἴκῳ.   (78)

Let him be hung up by one foot in the laundry.

The contrast is not between different levels within the poetry: the lowness of the words is set against the splendour of the painting we imagine the speakers seeing.

At the beginning and end religion is the principal concern, and here some of the poetry does take on truly dignified tones, most notably in the opening invocation. Unelevated matter and *naïveté* of conception appear when the woman comes on to speak of the humbleness of her offering—a mere cock, which will serve for the gods' second course (τἀπίδορπα, 13).[58] But here the lowliness has something touching about it, and the description of the healing is almost poignantly expressive:

τὰς ἀπέψησας
ἐπ' ἠπίας σὺ χεῖρας, ὦ ἄναξ, τείνας.   (17 f.)

the diseases which you wiped away from us, Lord Asclepius, stretching your hands over us in gentleness.

---

[57] Plin. *Nat. Hist.* 35. 111 on Nicophanes 'cothurnus et gravitas artis multum a Zeuxide et Apelle abest' (not in Overbeck). The subjects listed in Overbeck, *D. antiken Schriftquellen z. Gschchte. d. bildenden Künste*, 349 ff., are nearly all lofty, and we may surely assume the picture of a sacrifice here was not mean or comic, despite 67.

[58] Pind. *O.* 1. 50 δεύτατα κρεῶν is of course deliberately grotesque and implausible.

These sections make a frame for the rest, and contrast in their feeling.[59]

In poem 3 a boy's mother brings him to his schoolteacher to have him beaten for his avoidance of education.[60] The first half of the poem consists of a single speech, by the mother. In this half the effects are produced by non-dramatic means: Metrotime describes a whole string of picturesque and extravagant signs of her son's attitudes. The lowness of her milieu and the lowness of our outlook are deliciously mingled when she describes her reaction to her son's sitting on the roof of the tenement and leaning over the edge.

> τί μευ δοκεῖς τὰ σπλάγχνα τῆς κάκης πάσχειν
> ἐπεὰν ἴδωμι; κοὐ τόσος λόγος τοῦδε ...
>   τρὶ ἤμαιθα
> κλαοῦσ' ἑκάστου τοῦ πλατύσματος τίνω.
> ἐν γὰρ στόμ' ἐστὶ τῆς συνοικίης πάσης,
> "τοῦ Μητροτίμης ἔργα Κοττάλου ταῦτα."   (42–3, 45–8)

When I see him doing this, you can imagine what agony my heart undergoes thanks to his wicked behaviour. It's not him I'm so concerned about ... I have to pay 1½ obols, weeping, for every tile he breaks. That is because the whole tenement has one thing to say: 'This is the doing of Metrotime's son Cottalus!'

The simple comedy of the shift from love to expense is heightened by the would-be pathos of her crying in the latter connection. The concreteness of roofing, cost, and tenement opinion evoke a world with pungency. However, we are aware throughout the speech of the action that it will lead to; and the contrast in mode and texture enhances the effect of the second half. This begins with swift action as other boys are summoned to help (59 f.). The dramatic force of the whipping is conveyed through the rapid dialogue of three speakers in conflict. The boy pleads for leniency, the mother for ruthlessness, the teacher changes stance in the midst of the dialogue, when he deems that the punishment has been sufficient. The sordidness of the event

---

[59] One's understanding of the latter part of the last section (88–95) is very seriously impeded by corruption. One would suppose that the σκελύδριον for the temple attendant (89) probably does not deflate what has preceded, though it alters the tone.

[60] See for the background to this poem H.-I. Marrou, *Histoire de l'éducation dans l'antiquité* (1965), 229 ff.

is plain enough, but Herodas again employs a species of contrast to lend it further edge. He avails himself of the Muses.

The Muses are patronesses of education, and their images adorn the schoolroom where the drama is set.[61] They are given a prominent place in the poem, appearing in the first line and the last, at the beginning and end of Metrotime's long speech, in the first words of the boy, and elsewhere. The goddesses possess an intrinsic elevation. The uses the poem puts them to are grotesque, and bring out the nature of the action and of the characters. At the end 'the goddesses whom the boy has hated', αἱ πότνιαι ... ἃς ἐμίσησεν, are to look on his punishment, says Metrotime (in the form of their statues). The naughty schoolboy is absurdly tinged with the colours of a wicked mortal scorning a god and receiving vengeance. The boy's first act is to supplicate his teacher:

> μή μ' ἱκετεύω, Λάμπρισκε, πρός σε τῶν Μουσέων
> καὶ τῶν γενείων τῆς τε Κοττίδος ψυχῆς,
> μὴ τῷ με δριμεῖ, τῷ 'τέρῳ δὲ λώβησαι.   (71-3)

I beg you, teacher, by the Muses, by your chin, by the life of Cottis, don't beat me with the sharp whip, beat me with the other one.

The triple plea itself brings the Muses into low company with its third member. (Cottis is probably a woman beloved by Lampriscus, left unidentified with an entertaining suggestion of impropriety.) The actual appeal in which the sentence culminates produces a bizarre association for them and brings out the lowness of the action. To get the whipping to stop the boy swears an oath to be good 'by the dear Muses', τὰς φίλας Μούσας (83). The sincerity of his claim to love them is clearly dubious. But it is still more striking that respect for education should be presented throughout the poem in terms of love or hatred for the Muses, when all revolves about the act of beating a boy. The poem begins with an appeal by Metrotime to the teacher, which invokes 'the dear Muses', αἱ φίλαι Μοῦσαι; she proceeds in the next couplet to ask for the boy to be flayed to within an inch of his life (3 f.). The change is harsh, grotesque,

---

[61] 57, 97. Cf. Headlam–Knox, p. xlii n. 1, see also *HE* 938 ff. (Asclepiades), 1165 ff. (Callimachus).

and splendidly vigorous. Most jarring of all is Metrotime's demand that the boy should receive another twenty strokes

$$\kappa\hat{\eta}\nu\ \mu\epsilon\lambda\lambda\eta$$
$$a\vec{v}\tau\hat{\eta}s\ \ddot{a}\mu\epsilon\iota\nu o\nu\ \tau\hat{\eta}s\ K\lambda\epsilon o\hat{v}s\ \dot{a}\nu a\gamma\nu\hat{\omega}\nu a\iota.$$
(91 f.)

even if he is going to read better than Clio herself.

The idea of the Muse as primarily an exemplar of fluent reading is exquisitely naïve, and underlines the humbleness of the
whole sphere. It will be seen that the handling of this device is
closely connected with the central physical act.

   In poem 5 a physical act stands to the fore throughout. But it
is to take place elsewhere. All the action in the scene leads up to
it, and heightens the effect of its imminence. A mistress has had
one of her slaves as a lover; but he has slept with another
woman, and the mistress, Bitinna, sends him off to be beaten
cruelly. The intercession of a female slave brings her to post-
pone the punishment. The obvious sordidness of the main
situation is given force by the handling of action. Between l. 5
and 53 Bitinna is making another slave strip, bind, and lead off
Gastron, her former lover. The other slave Pyrrhies, is reluctant
to obey, and we have as it were an extended version of the sequence where a slave who acts slowly is hurried on furiously.
The command to the female slave $\theta\lambda\hat{\eta}\ \ldots\ \tau\grave{o}\ \dot{\rho}\acute{v}\gamma\chi os$ (41) 'smash
Pyrrhies' snout' appears in less drastic form at the start of 7
(above p. 244). Here, however, the action wanted is not trivial.
Bitinna's pressing impatience with Pyrrhies is alarming, and
conveys the fierceness of her emotions—as does the opposition
with Pyrrhies' reluctance. Her emotions seem low rather than
terrible because of their social context. She feels not merely
jealousy but humiliation: her self-respect is injured by the slave
who has preferred another woman to her, the owner who loves
him (20 f., 30, *al.*). The emotions are made squalid by the per-
version of social structures which this whole situation entails.
Interwoven with the forcing on of Pyrrhies is the rejection of
Gastron's pleas. The cravenness and mendacity of the slave
bring out further the lowness of the situation, while increasing
the nastiness of the coming event. Bitinna's actual commands
are almost hysterically brutal. 'Saw into his skin as you tie him'
($\ddot{\epsilon}\kappa\pi\rho\iota\sigma o\nu\ \delta\acute{\eta}\sigma as$, 25); he is to receive 'a thousand blows on the
back and a thousand in the stomach' (33 f.). A further com-

mand indicates for the first time the possibility of weakness in
Bitinna:

δώσεις τι, δούλη, τῷ κατηρήτῳ τούτῳ
ῥάκος καλύψαι τὴν ἀνώνυμον κέρκον,
ὡς μὴ δι᾽ ἀγορῆς γυμνὸς ὢν θεωρῆται;   (44–6)

(To Cydilla) Slave, give this accursed wretch a cloth to
hide his unspeakable crutch, so he won't be gazed on
naked as he's led through the market-place.

The sudden change springs from her passion for Gastron. The
harshness of her language does not merely disguise this superficially: it also suggests to us the sordid physicality of this softer
element. And we are strikingly reminded that Gastron is naked
now. At once Bitinna repeats her command for the two thousand blows and threatens Pyrrhies severely. Thus an elaborate
structure of dramatic excitement is built up around the action
witnessed and the action impending.

The yielding of Bitinna in the second part cannot be discussed at length. It must suffice to say that, on the one hand,
she does not yield simply because she loves Cydilla, as she
implies (81 f.), but rather because her passion for Gastron
escapes her control (hence 73 f. and, I think, 53–5). On the
other hand, the thing is so presented that she scarcely redeems
herself at all in the reader's eyes, or raises the level we associate
her with. What is particularly interesting for our present concerns is the speech which Cydilla makes to Pyrrhies when sent
to fetch him and Gastron back (professedly for a further punishment). Cydilla had hitherto been a mere silent extra (9, 41,
44). Thus her forceful speech, made in a different place from
the rest of the action, has a strong dramatic effect. She abuses
Pyrrhies for his handling of Gastron in the most pungent
language and describes the punishment which Pyrrhies himself
will undergo in bitingly colourful and allusive terms: the igno-
minious servile punishment of labouring in chains for some
industrial establishment.

σέ, μᾶ, τούτοις
τοῖς δύο Κύδιλλ᾽ ἐπόψετ᾽ ἡμερέων πέντε
παρ᾽ Ἀντιδώρῳ τὰς Ἀχαϊκὰς κείνας,
ἃς πρῶν ἔθηκας, τοῖς σφυροῖσι τρίβοντα.   (59–62)

You, by heaven, you these two eyes will see within a few

days at Antidorus' place. Your ankles will be rubbing
those Achaean articles—which you only took off two days
ago.

At the same time, the rightness of her feeling and the generosity
of her anger lift us suddenly above the attitudes seen hitherto.[62]
We contrast her both with the more submissive Pyrrhies
and with Bitinna, whose harshness to Pyrrhies has a very different purpose from her own. With a rather moving transmuta-
tion, vigorously low language becomes the vehicle for noble
feeling.

Poem 6 shows Metro's visit to her friend Coritto. She learns,
after pressing inquiry, that it was Cerdon who made the dildo
which she has seen; this Coritto had given to another woman
(Eubule), and she to another (Nossis). The poem begins and
ends with action involving slaves. At the start, there appears
the common type of passage where a slave fails to act promptly,
and is abused by her owner; the girl hurries to get a chair for
Metro. This establishes a lowly level; the passage also brings
out by contrast the secrecy, and thus the impropriety, of the
women's conversation. The slaves are sent angrily away by
Coritto (not Metro) at 15–17; at the summit of indecency in the
poem, where the dildoes are actually compared with the
natural objects, Coritto stresses that they are alone (70, see
below). The conversation is enclosed on the other side by the
brief moment at the end when Metro has left and Coritto tells a
slave to count the hens (98 ff.). Coritto is so shocked that
Eubule should have presented her precious gift to the detested
Nossis that she feels anxious about all her possessions. The theft
of hens has particular resonance as a low subject: Aristophanes
had used it for his parody of Euripides' baroque monodies
(*Frogs* 1331 ff.). At all events, subject and emotion together give
a new and grotesquely comic shade to the whole scene.

The comedy of the conversation itself does not lie simply in
the lewdness of the subject, and hardly at all in the relationship
between the characters as such. It lies rather in the extravagance of the women's feelings about these sordid objects. These

---

[62] The various attempts to make Cydilla sordid too have no basis in the text (Cunningham, pp. 147 ff., and W. G. Arnott, *G&R* 2nd ser. 18 (1971), 127 f., express themselves with some caution). If she were indeed in love with Gastron (Arnott), that would
not necessarily be a sordid motive.

particular dildoes are not regarded as a dismal substitute, but as actually superior to their human models.[63]

τὰ βαλλί᾿ οὕτως ἄνδρες οὐχὶ ποιεῦσι
—αὐταὶ γάρ εἰμεν—ὀρθά.   (69 f.)

Actual men don't make their things—we are alone, so I can say it—so upright.

To gain a second dildo in addition to one's first, both women regard intercourse with an old man as an acceptable price (79–81, where the comedy of extravagance is plain). When Coritto says that she would not give Nossis one dildo if she had a thousand, she prefaces this imaginary condition with a cautious prayer to Nemesis, so huge a felicity does it seem to postulate.

μέζον μὲν ἢ γυνὴ γρύξω,
λάθοιμι δ᾿, Ἀδρήστεια.   (34 f.)

I am about to utter a thought too bold for a mortal woman: do not heed it, Nemesis.[64]

Our impression of this strong feeling is greatly enhanced by the dramatic structure.

The poem is organized around Metro's enquiries, often held up, but never abandoned. Metro has come in order to find out who made the dildo, and makes her plea at once (15–19). Her inquiry is then superseded by the angry inquiry of Coritto into the fate of her gift (22–36). But Metro soothes her humbly (37–41) and presses her question, till Coritto yields; her seriousness contrasts with Coritto's smiles (44–6). Even when the name is given, the dramatic sequence is not ended. There are several persons called Cerdon (48–62). The dialogue drifts naturally to Coritto's dealings with him; but Metro comes back to a question that concerns her own search: how did Cerdon find out about Coritto? The wording of Metro's present appeal links it to the chain. ... φίλη Κοριττοῖ· μηδὲ τοῦτό με ψεύσῃ '... dear Coritto—do not deceive me in this either' (86) takes up her first appeal, μὴ ψεύσῃ, | φίλη Κοριττοῖ 'do not deceive me, dear Coritto' (18), and her second, ... Κοριττί, μή μ᾿ ἐπιψεύσῃ '... Cor-

---

[63] Contrast Arist. *Lys.* 109, fr. 592 Kass.–Aust., Sophr. fr. 24 Kaibel.

[64] So I understand the lines, which are scarcely apt to her postulated refusal of the dildo. There is a variant δίκη γρύζω in the papyrus, which goes less well with the next words.

itto, do not deceive me' (46). When Metro discovers the woman who established the contact, she is off to find her (95 f.). This basic sequence conveys through dramatic tension Metro's firm and eager involvement. Of the two passages which delay the revelations, the first (19 ff.), on Nossis' acquisition of the dildo, uses Coritto's outrage at the discovery to display the intensity of feeling associated with these objects. Here too revelation is employed dramatically, and the effect is heightened by the sudden reversal in the roles of questioner and questioned. The second passage (63 ff.), on Cerdon and Coritto, employs description and narrative, partly laying the ground for poem 7. But its force is much increased by the device of animated communication (cf. poem 4), and still more by Metro's surprise and censure at Coritto's failure to secure the second dildo. Metro returns to the subject even when she knows the name of the female intermediary (91 f.). Thus the crucial combination of vehement emotion and low material makes much of its impact through the drama.

Poem 1 is unusual. It is mostly unelevated, but relatively little emphasis is placed on its lowness. Humour plays no great part in its effect, and this is not (as in 5) through excessive grimness. The poem portrays an old woman's attempt to make a young one, Metriche, forget her absent beloved for a short while and grant her favours to another; but Metriche remains faithful to Mandris. The work begins with a slave being bid see to the door, and ends with a slave being bid serve wine. Both moments give a sense of activity and movement; but in neither do we find the violent abuse that Herodas employs in such passages elsewhere. Metriche is not to be made laughable. Nonetheless, they establish a certain homeliness of atmosphere. This may be reinforced by echoes of Sophron (or Theocritus) at the start. The moments also contrast, as in poem 6, with the privacy of the women's *tête-à-tête*. The old woman, speaking of Metriche's admirer, breaks off her speech to seek assurance that they are alone (48); Metriche marks the end of their discussion by calling for her slave (78 ff., see below). But there is little jarring crudity in Gyllis' speech of persuasion—as there might have been. Indeed, there is some dignity in the praise of Egypt (25 ff.), some power in the old woman's description of the effect of age on beauty (38, 63).

However, lowness and even humour are positively exploited
in the poem, and in ways closely tied to drama. In their first
exchange (8–20), Gyllis has just spoken of her great feebleness
now she is old.

Μη. . . .]ε καὶ μὴ τοῦ χρόνου καταψεύδευ·
    . . . . . .] γάρ, Γυλλί, κἠτέρους ἄγχειν.
Γυ. σίλλ[α]ινε· ταῦτα τῆς νεωτέρης ὑμῖν
    πρόσεστιν.   (17–20)

(Metriche) 'Don't slander your age, Gyllis: (you can)
actually squeeze men still.' (Gyllis) 'Go on, mock me: you
young women would make such jokes.'

Metriche's earthy words prevent her from appearing too elevated a figure; the dialogue further hints for the reader at a less
than respectable milieu. We are also confronted with a dramatic contrast between the old character and the young in
relation to love. It is because the theme is embodied in this dramatic form that it has such force in the poem (cf., after Gyllis'
speech, 67 f., 74 f., 89 f.).[65] The two aspects of lowness and
drama are conjoined in our feeling that the tone and level of the
words imply a distinctive and significant relationship between
these women; elements in this relationship are intimacy, difference of age, and concern with sex.[66]

The most important example of the exploitation of lowness is
provided by Metriche's reply to Gyllis. This is the high point of
the poem in terms of plot, emotional intensity, and the sympathy of the audience.[67] Metriche conveys her feeling not
decorously but roughly. Had any woman but Gyllis spoken
thus, she would have given her a severe beating-up.

[65] 74 f. does not imply that Metriche is not young, or is even contrasting herself with
the immature. The stress falls rather on πρέπει, which surely cannot mean what Cunningham claims. Metriche is presenting in general terms the impropriety of Gyllis'
action.

[66] The situation should presumably be spelt out as follows. Gyllis is a busy procuress,
as the last lines indicate (88–90). Metriche's association with her suggests that she has
once formed part of Gyllis' network (note 19 f.); but she has now formed a permanent
relationship with Mandris. Compare, say, the relationship between Bacchis and Pam-
philus described in Terence, *Hecyra* 58–62 (cf. Apollodorus Car. fr. 8 Kock); note also
Eun. 81–206. Cf. Cunningham, p. 57. Alan Cameron, in H. P. Foley (ed.), *Reflections of
Women in Antiquity* (1981), 296, contends that Metriche is Mandris' wife; but his argument seems curious in the rigid divisions it implies.

[67] Cunningham's belief that only Gyllis matters shows the dangers of concentrating
on the depiction of characters.

256 *Other Poets*

χωλὴν δ' ἀείδειν χώλ' ἂν ἐξεπαίδευσα
καὶ τῆς θύρης τὸν οὐδὸν ἐχθρὸν ἡγεῖσθαι.   (71 f.)

I would have taught her to sing her misshapen song misshapen herself: she would have learned to detest the
threshold of my door.

The grim control of one epigram heightens the sense that
Metriche is speaking in sober earnest. This declaration about
violence has a most undignified ring in a woman's mouth; but
the lowly level gives a homely sincerity and unpretentious
warmth to the nobility of the essential attitude. Metriche ends
her reply:

τὴν Πυθέω δὲ Μητρίχην ἔα θάλπειν
τὸν δίφρον· οὐ γὰρ ἐγγελᾷ τις εἰς Μάνδριν.
   ἀλλ' οὐχὶ τούτων φασὶ τῶν λόγων Γυλλὶς
δεῖται· Θρέϊσσα, τὴν μελαινίδ' ἔκτ[ρ]ιψον...   (76–8)

Leave Metriche daughter of Pytheës to warm her chair indoors. No one is going to flout Mandris. —But it's not a
speech like this, as the saying goes, that Gyllis is in need of.
Threïssa, wipe out the cup ...

Metriche takes up a cajoling phrase of Gyllis' describing her
inactivity (θάλπεις τὸν δίφρον 'you warm your chair', i.e. sit idly
indoors, 37). She converts its pungency into unglamorous fidelity. It interacts with the dignity and seriousness of the names
enclosing the sentence to convey a splendid stance without her-
oical theatricality.[68] She then turns with a friendly movement
and a proverb to the addressee's own name and to domestic
practicalities. She brings the poem down again after the expressive transformation of the low at the dramatic climax of the
poem.[69] The passage provides a particularly notable indication of the poetic awareness with which Herodas exploits the
limits of his manner.

   This section has attempted to follow lines of approach which
will do more justice to the full effect of Herodas' works than will

[68] The device of a speaker's using his own name appears at 5. 17, 60, 7. 53, but without the same resonance.
[69] It seems clear from 7. 49 (cited by Lloyd-Jones *apud* Cunningham) and from
Theocr. 14. 51, *Garl. Phil.* 117, etc., that φασί marks a homely proverb. A jocular reference to Gyllis' reputation for bibulousness would be quite out of keeping with this tactful transition.

a narrow concentration on his drawing of individuals. In particular they allow more importance to his form and his writing. It was suggested that two fundamental elements in his work— the low and the quasi-dramatic—are not unconnected features which appear in the same poems by chance: they are combined, and they interact, in varied and significant associations. So in 2 and 7 drama heightens the sudden exposure of immorality concealed. In poem 4 the interval between the speakers and what they see and speak of again has drama disclosing lowness by means of contrast. In 6 there is a different kind of gap between the speakers' feelings and the subject of their speech; drama is a prime means of exploiting it. In poems 3 and 5 brutal action forms the centre of attention, and through its sordid violence the unexalted attitudes of most of the characters appear. However, in poem 5, and poem 1, we see lowness transfigured in dramatic moments of generous and upright behaviour. A particular type of dramatic event, the movement and the abuse of slaves, again and again establishes or obtrudes a lowly level. In a sense such alliances are natural enough. It accords with ancient approaches to mean and to base material in poetry that the author should present it with vigour, animation, and comic force. The vividness and concreteness of imagined drama was well suited to this purpose. It also served Herodas in the creation of foils, disparities, and contrasts which could help mark out particularly important low material in the poems. As we saw, he eschews, and effectively eschews, the larger aesthetic concerns of his celebrated contemporaries. The species of poem he creates is satisfying and convincing; but its force comes, not through building up complexity and richness, but through establishing strongly the limits within which it moves.

C. LYCOPHRON

Lycophron will be dealt with briefly: only the most scholarly of my readers are likely to persevere, or to have persevered, with so obscure a poem as the *Alexandra*. The poem presents a prophecy by Cassandra which deals principally with the Trojan War and its aftermath. It is as long as an Attic tragedy; its vocabulary brims over with unfamiliar vocables; and in retail-

ing a great quantity of myths, it normally avoids disclosing the
names of the protagonists directly. The date of the work is disputed; but it most likely belongs roughly to the time of Callimachus.[70] However, the differences from the work of the three
greatest contemporary poets are large and instructive; and here
we must allow a decided interval in quality. Lycophron's
monotony of form brings out their imagination and vitality in
this respect; his crudity of tone brings out their subtlety. He
illustrates well how learning and allusiveness as such will not
produce poems like the *Aetia* or the *Argonautica*.

Nevertheless, one gives a very incomplete account of the
poem if one ignores the emotion, the colouring, and the concreteness with which it presents its material. The poem is not
only a series of conundrums. But one cannot simply consider
these aspects as if they had no connection with the devious
words which convey them—words which belong to the poet as
well as the speaker.[71] In most of the poem two salient aspects
help to give flavour and direction to the language. Firstly, in
recounting myth the work is prone to seize on physical details
or conceptions which are both graphic and bizarre. These
make the novelty of presentation startling and harsh. The relation between the concrete and the obscure is here various and
complicated; but the darkness tends to receive a lurid illumina-
tion from the violent and somewhat nightmarish vividness of
peculiar detail. Secondly, the poem insistently denigrates
Greek achievements and emphasizes the Greeks' misfortunes
and ignominies. It exalts the achievements of Trojans and, at
last, their future honour (1126–212). It is in the first 360 lines or
so that Cassandra mainly concentrates her lamentation for
Trojan suffering; and even here the undermining of the Greeks
is prominent. That strain comes to predominate. In consequence, much of the poem is coloured, not only by a relish in
the enemy's pain, but by a destructive animus in the handling

---

[70] This follows from accepting that it is by Lycophron, a tragedian and scholar who
worked for Callimachus' patron Ptolemy Philadelphus (Sch. in Arist. i. 1A Koster pp.
22, 48). Frr. 2–4 (*TrGF* 100) were probably written before the death of the philosopher
Menedemus (*c.*265?). For the dispute over authorship see S. R. West, *JHS* 104 (1984),
127 ff., and the literature she cites. I share her view that the lines on Rome are spurious
(the intelligibility of their diction is much against them).

[71] Note that the messenger's introductory speech shows all Cassandra's obscurity
(16 ff.), thus indicating that the obscurity is not simply a mimesis of prophecy.

of saga. By selection, distortion, and obfuscation, the careers and deeds of heroes are made to seem wretched, wicked, or merely bizarre. The ingenuity acquires a bitter and demeaning quality.

These aspects and their effects may be illustrated by a discussion of two or three passages. A relatively simple handling of physical detail may be seen in the treatment of the death of Agamemnon and his concubine Cassandra (1099–1119): the climactic scene is deliberately made direct and memorable in its impact. Thus Agamemnon, trapped after his bath in the fatal robe, feels to find the holes for head and arms which are not there.

τυφλαῖς ματεύσει χερσὶ κροσσωτοὺς ῥαφάς. (1102)

He will search with unseeing hand the tasselled embroidery.

The vividness of the experience is brought to a grotesque sharpness by the closing phrase 'tasselled embroidery' (κροσσωτός 'tasselled' was a word in everyday use). This conveys trenchantly the physical sensation of Agamemnon and the bizarreness of the happening. Aeschylus, Lycophron's source here, eschews such a description: the strangeness of the robe is to seem terrible (*Ag.* 1116 ff., 1382 f., *Choeph.* 997 ff., etc.).

A more complicated example is supplied by the very opening of Cassandra's speech; this also involves the second aspect we mentioned. Cassandra begins with a cry of lamentation for her country (31). But the immediate pathos is abruptly deflected: the sentence proceeds not only to the earlier sack of Troy by Heracles but to the deed of his which led up to it, and thence, in a vast parenthetical sentence, to a depiction of the hero's life and death. The deed was his slaying of a sea-monster; to achieve this he went inside its body.

ἔμπνους δὲ δαιτρὸς ἡπάτων φλοιδούμενος
τινθῷ λέβητος ἀφλόγοις ἐπ' ἐσχάραις
σμήριγγας ἐστάλαξε κωδείας πέδῳ. (35–7)

Still alive, he was a carver of liver; he was made to seethe by the smoke of that cauldron, on that hearth without a fire, and through the heat the hair dropped out like water from his head on to the ground.

The description focuses on the falling out of Heracles' hair. Obscure words are used for 'hair' and 'head'; this increases the grotesqueness of the striking image, even as it distances its impact.[72] It is in the phrase 'a carver of liver' that the heroic killing is referred to. The phrase is made part of a sequence of images from cookery; the sequence grotesquely distorts the elevated use of metaphor which marks an actual disjunction from normality. The phrase itself mingles the allusive, the vivid, and the bizarre. The succeeding account of Heracles reflects overtly Cassandra's detestation of λυμεὼν ἐμῆς πάτρας (38) 'the destroyer of my country'. She chooses incidents which suggest heinous crime against his own family (38–43). She then sets the futility of his slaying of Scylla—who was promptly resurrected—against the death inflicted decisively on him by the dead Nessus.[73] The deification of Heracles is not touched on.

The speech returns to Troy, but the pathos of lament is again deferred as Cassandra moves to a single future event: the death of the Trojan Paris and his first wife Oenone. The myth is narrated much more fully and straightforwardly than that of Heracles and the sea-monster, and it moves much nearer to arousing emotion. The closing account of Oenone's tragic suicide is rendered both vivid and somewhat grotesque by physical details and images.

$$\text{ξυνὸν ὀγχήσει μόρον}$$
πύργων ἀπ' ἄκρων πρὸς νεόδμητον νέκυν
ῥοιζηδὸν ἐκβράσασα κύμβαχον δέμας.
πόθῳ δὲ τοῦ θανόντος ἠγκιστρωμένη,
ψυχὴν περὶ σπαίροντι φυσήσει νεκρῷ.

(64–8)

She will endure a death shared with Paris; from the top of the tower she will throw her body down head first, with a rushing sound, to the corpse lately slain. Caught on the hook of desire for the dead man, she will pant out her life embracing the quivering corpse.

In the order of the Greek, the details 'head first' and 'with a rushing sound' are saved for the last line of the sentence;

---

[72] It is attested elsewhere that Heracles entered the monster to kill it: see Hellanicus, *FrGH* 4 F 26 (most likely Lycophron's source at this point), F. Brommer, *Herakles*, ii (1984), 61 f. The detail of the hair one would perhaps guess to be Lycophron's own invention.

[73] κτανών (46) is opposed to ἐξηνάριξεν (50), 49 to 50 f.

'caught on the hook' and 'quivering' each modify the effect of
the line that contains them ('caught . . . man', 'she . . . corpse').
ῥοιζηδόν 'with a whizzing, rushing sound' and probably σπαίρω
'quiver' were words in common use.

The fluctuations of this whole opening sequence display the
gusto with which Lycophron manipulates and alters our responses. The affinity with other poets of the time will be
obvious; but the result is scarcely rich, evocative, or elegantly
piquant. The colours are too garish, there is too little sense of
ironic detachment or sensitive involvement from the author—
his presence is felt plainly enough in this extravagantly artificial
utterance. There is, however, a sense of atmosphere and movement which makes this poetry arresting.

The long section on Odysseus (648–819) deals with a Greek
hero on a particularly ample scale.[74] We can touch here only
on certain moments. The opening shows the sweeping passion
with which Cassandra describes her foes' miseries. A lavish rhetorical structure is built up to stress the multitude and extremity of Odysseus' future sufferings (660–75). ποία Χάρυβδις
οὐχὶ δαίσεται νεκρῶν; (668) 'What Charybdis will not feast on
his dead?' begins a vehement series of similar questions. The
form suggests an extravagant multiplication of each single
danger. For impressiveness in this first case the actual name of
Charybdis is permitted to appear.[75] At the end of this treatment of accumulated calamity, the speech moves to elaborate
on Circe's transformation of Odysseus' men into pigs.

> οἱ δὲ δύσμοροι
> στένοντες ἄτας ἐν συφοῖσι φορβάδες
> γίγαρτα χιλῷ συμμεμιγμένα τρυγὸς
> καὶ στεμφύλων βρύξουσιν.   (675–8)

They, unhappy wretches, lamenting this disaster, will feed
in the sty; they will devour grape-pips mixed with the fod-
der of squashed grapes and the wine-dregs from them.

---

[74] The serious textual problems of this episode are discussed by S. R. West, *CQ* NS 33
(1983), 115 ff., *JHS* 104 (1984), 138 ff. Her deletion of 805–11 is very attractive,
though I should incline to retain 688–737. Might one expunge 788?

[75] I know no evidence that Charybdis did kill (or devour) any of Odysseus' men.
Either Lycophron is employing an obscure version, or the rhetoric overrides tradition.
In view of 669, the line can scarcely be spurious, nor Χάρυβδις a reference to something
else.

The sentence begins by dwelling on suffering but it proceeds to a graphic description of their new diet (675 ff.). The words for all these left-overs of grapes are everyday.[76] Both the lamentation and the feeding derive from a sentence in Homer (*Od.* 10. 241–3), but Lycophron has heightened each element. By placing the sentence after the series of questions, he creates a drastic movement from the impassioned and the grandiose to the grotesque and the prosaic.

It is evident enough with what emotions Cassandra regards the suffering of Odysseus, who is Troy's worst enemy (786 f.); but at 766 f. her vengefulness emerges openly. Odysseus has reached Phaeacia at last (from there he returns home safely). But Cassandra reveals that he will not yet have exhausted the Cyclops' curse.

> ἀρὰς τετικὼς τοῦ τυφλωθέντος δάκους
> οὔπω μάλ', οὔπω—μὴ τοσόσδ' ὕπνος λάβοι
> λήθης Μέλανθον ἀγκλιθένθ' ἱππηγέτην.   (765–7)

The curse of the blinded monster he will not yet have expiated, no, not by any means. Let not Melanthus the driver of horses (Poseidon, the Cyclops' father) recline in so heavy a sleep of forgetfulness as to permit that![77]

The savagery of the wish is striking, placed as it is after the long sequence of Odysseus' sufferings, so pungently described. The form of the next lines conveys her keen regret that he will reach his home, and her satisfaction at the devastation he will find there.

The second half of the *Odyssey* displays poignantly the pain and the endurance of Penelope, besieged by suitors, and of Odysseus, disguised as a beggar. Here Penelope is described as σεμνῶς κασωρεύουσα 'playing the whore with a great air of propriety'.[78] The poet's phrase maliciously unites post-Homeric

---

[76] Such food would be provided by farms which made wine (cf. Varro, *R. Rust.* 2. 4. 16). The fare of Homer's pigs has, so to speak, a more generalized quality (*Od.* 10. 242 f.).

[77] The negative οὔπω is deferred for the sake of surprise and vehemence. It is better not to punctuate before it. At Soph. *Phil.* 961 one ought not to punctuate before μήπω. Cf. also for the order e.g. Pind. *Ol.* 7. 48.

[78] Holzinger believes that σεμνῶς opposes the tales of Penelope's unchastity (for these see his n.). But this would be very feeble stylistically, and the notion hardly fits with 792.

accounts of her actual infidelity with the seemly behaviour she shows in the *Odyssey*. This makes the subversion particularly mordant. Odysseus' endurance is emphasized (τλήσεται μέν ... τλήσεται δέ, 775 ff.); but it is turned into an unmanly acceptance of humiliation, and it is ingeniously linked with the whipping he voluntarily endured to enter Troy in disguise. This leads to fresh manifestations of Cassandra's scorn and hatred (784–7). Homer is distorted neatly. The poet enhances the effect by referring to Odysseus with the term μολοβρός ('greedy rogue' (?)). In Homer this word was used to insult Odysseus by those who were ignorant of his true identity. Lycophron omits to mention Odysseus' triumph over the suitors and passes to his death. The whole account closes by driving home the accumulated sequence of his sufferings (812 ff.). It ends:

> ὦ σχέτλι', ὥς σοι κρεῖσσον ἦν μίμνειν πάτρᾳ
> βοηλατοῦντα καὶ τὸν ἐργάτην μύκλον
> κάνθων' ὑπὸ ζευγλαῖσι μεσσαβοῦν ἔτι
> πλασταῖσι λύσσης μηχαναῖς ᾠστρημένον
> ἢ τηλικῶνδε πεῖραν ὀτλῆσαι κακῶν.

> You wretched man! How much better it would have been to remain in your native land, still ploughing with the bull and the hard-working male ass yoked together, and frantic with a feigned and contrived insanity—how much better that than to endure the experience of so many woes!

Lycophron here proceeds to develop the basic idea (better not to have gone to Troy) with the story that Odysseus feigned madness in an attempt to escape the Trojan expedition. The movement produces bizarreness and paradox; Lycophron adroitly makes the final sentence linger on one more demeaning tale.[79] He closes, however, by stressing the series he has built up.

Cassandra in this last sentence apostrophizes Odysseus: this strengthens the sense of climax and conclusion. The handling of the beginning and the end of this episode, and the predominating tone, give a feeling of structure and purpose to the lengthy exposition. The episode is perceived as a whole, and one finds in it a characteristic mixture: harsh passion from the speaker,

---

[79] Cf. the use of Achilles' disguise as a girl and of Protesilaus to end the account of Achilles (275–80).

agile distortion from the poet. We have a union of dark grandeur and cheerless denigration. This sombre atmosphere is in
harmony with the style and language. Extravagant rhetoric,
grotesque vividness, remorseless erudition and obscurity—all
combine to create the distinctive air of blackness, energy, and
excess. In stature there is no comparison; but Lycophron's
poetry comes closer than his contemporaries' to the spirit of
Lucan.

D. ASCLEPIADES

Of Asclepiades' work we essentially possess only some epigrams
preserved in Byzantine anthologies, which draw on an anthology compiled by Meleager (see p. 23). To judge from the
treatment of Posidippus, Callimachus, and Hedylus, Asclepiades will have written decidedly more epigrams than are
transmitted by this channel (cf. also Asclep. XLVII). In all
probability he wrote other sorts of work as well.[80] The majority of the epigrams preserved deal with love.

We must begin with some words on his position in the literary chronology of the time. It will be seen from ch. 1 that this is
a matter of considerable importance for the understanding of
Asclepiades and of Hellenistic poetry. (The account given of
the early epigram there is presupposed here.) None of the epigrams which are probably Asclepiades' offers an indication of
date.[81] Asclepiades shows a good many connections with Callimachus and Posidippus. No connection points to his borrowing
from Callimachus; but the reverse is sometimes probable. Their
poems on love revealed at the symposium are clearly linked
(Asclep. XVIII, Call. XIII (43 Pf.)); but whereas Asclepiades'
would read very strangely as an imitation of Callimachus', it

---

[80] Cf. *SH* 215–19, *HE*, p. 115. *SH* 216, a choliambic line, is unlikely to form part of
an epigram. It is noteworthy that it uses a more overtly scholarly manner with myth
than one finds in the epigrams. *SH* 219 employs an epic adjective.

[81] XLIV, also ascribed to Antipater of Thessalonica, has a concentration of verbal
point, and other features, which make it quite unlike Asclepiades (both ascriptions are
probably false guesses). XXXIX (also ascribed to Posidippus) there is little positive
reason to give to Asclepiades: Posidippus probably uses Doric elsewhere (Posid. VIII,
cf. XVIII), and in any case the statistics are too small for argument. If it were by Asclepiades, XLIV would probably belong before 309; XXXIX would belong before *c*.275
and would associate Asclepiades with Alexandria.

would be eminently plausible that Callimachus should add a sudden twist at the close. So with the two poems on the mask dedicated by a schoolboy (Asclep. XXVII, Call. XXVI (48 Pf.)). Asclepiades' poem if later would make a rather odd reduction of Callimachus' intricate texture of diverse allusion. I see very slight reason for assigning priority to either Asclepiades or Posidippus in regard to the poems which seem more or less plainly connected (Asclep. IV, Posid. II; Asclep. XXV. 11 f., Posid. IV; Asclep. XVII, Posid. V; probably Asclep. XXV, XXVI, Posid. X). It would be least unattractive to suppose that, of the two poems on hetaerae as riders, Asclep. VI inspires Asclep. XXV (also ascribed to Posidippus in the Palatine Anthology). But it is by no means clear that the latter belongs to Posidippus; and at least one of the epigrams ascribed to both is unlikely to be by either.[82]

The external data fit well enough with the notion that Asclepiades' epigrams preceded Callimachus'; the relation between Asclepiades and Posidippus they fail to clarify. A whole number of items show Posidippus active between *c.*280 and 263/2; he lived to be old.[83] The admiring reference to Asclepiades in Theocritus (7. 39) seems to suggest that at some point he and Philetas were both writing and both enjoying pre-eminence; Philetas was probably active from the late fourth century. An inscription from Delphi most likely shows Asclepiades and Posidippus at work in 276/5 or 273/2 (*Fouilles de Delphes*, iii. 3, no. 192). The poet Hedylus, one of whose poems belongs in the region of 270, seems to refer to Asclepiades as a dead classic of symposiastic verse—presumably epigram (VI).[84] Callimachus in his epigrams looks back to Asclepiades, especially in his epigrams on love. He is much influenced by Asclepiades' handling of himself; and he presupposes and exploits familiarity with particular poems and the type of poem. For Asclepiades there existed few firm conventions for

---

[82] Asclep. XXXVI: note 5 f.

[83] Activity: *HE*, pp. 481 f., cf. also *SH* 961; old age: *SH* 705. 5.

[84] Hedylus was probably not older than Callimachus: cf. *SH* 458 and ibid., p. 236. Hedylus and Theocritus name Asclepiades Sicelidas (from Samos), but the identification is hard to escape. Not only is it accepted by Sch. Flor. ad Call. fr. 1, l. 5, and—as one may infer from the contents of his anthology and his preface—by Meleager, *HE* 3971. It is also improbable that we should have no fragments of so famous a poet from this period.

the genre which might shape the expectation of the reader. The epigram at this time would have created few presumptions in his readers as to tone or style. It was probably Asclepiades and Posidippus themselves who first fixed the manner of epigram within the sphere that was to define it. The one set feature of the genre crucial for Asclepiades was brevity. How he managed and used this feature will appear when we have pondered various aspects of his art.

We may start by considering Asclepiades' employment of imagery, of physical language. Asclepiades very commonly gives force to his poems by exploiting the boundary between people and things, and between things of different kinds. The usual praise of Asclepiades' vividness does not fully capture the range and character of these artistic concerns. Let us take first some changes of persons into things.

φείδη παρθενίης· καὶ τί πλέον; οὐ γὰρ ἐς Ἅιδην
ἐλθοῦσ' εὑρήσεις τὸν φιλέοντα, κόρη.
ἐν ζωοῖσι τὰ τερπνὰ τὰ Κύπριδος, ἐν δ' Ἀχέροντι
ὀστέα καὶ σποδιή, παρθένε, κεισόμεθα.   (11)

You husband your maidenhood. Now, what good does this bring? When you go to Hades, girl, you will not find a lover there. [ll. 1–2] It is among the living that the delights of Aphrodite are to be had; in Hades, we shall lie as bones and ash, maiden.

In the last line the poetic idiom dispenses with an 'as, in the form of' (ὄντες, γενόμενοι), and presents the transformation starkly. 'Bones and ash' is a particularly harsh and physical formulation: contrast 'earth and nothing', 'earth and shadow', 'dust and shadow', used of the dead by poets in a similar way.[85] The phrase begins the last line, and its vigour serves to make the poem close effectively. We obviously set the ugliness and reality of the phrase against the delights of Aphrodite and the notion of finding a lover in Hades. But the form of the clause itself is significant. The poet does not brutally confine the change to the girl herself ('you will lie'), as he had confined the negative statement in the first couplet. But the generalizing 'we' and the vocative 'maiden' intimate that this concerns her.

[85] Soph. *El.* 245, Eur. fr. 532 Nauck, Hor. *Odes* 4. 7. 16; note too 'ash and shadow' Soph. *El.* 1159.

The preceding clause ('It is among the living ...') had been more distanced. In consequence, the word παρθένε 'maiden', looking back to παρθενίης 'maidenhood' and contrasting with the address κόρη 'girl', stands in delicate and unobtruded opposition to the ὀστέα καὶ σποδιή 'bones and ash' which it is placed next to: the virgin girl, addressed by a man, in opposition to the lifeless and repellent objects she will become.

With the same vigour, but with quite different tone and effect, Asclepiades calls on the Erotes (Cupids) to kill him if they will not leave him alone. 'Hurl at me not arrows but thunderbolts;

καὶ πάντως τέφρην θέσθε με κἀνθρακιήν.   (XVII. 4)

make me, I pray you, into ash and embers.'

He proceeds from the familiar notion of Erotes armed with lightning to a drastic picture; it is made drastic by the physical transformation it presents, of man into glowing ash.[86] This he actually wishes on himself, conditionally, and then, in the next couplet, unconditionally. Here the force of the phrasing conveys the amusing extravagance of the speaker's emotion. In poem XI Asclepiades, serenading on a tempestuous night, defies Zeus as god of the weather. He ends:

ἕλκει γάρ μ' ὁ κρατῶν καὶ σοῦ θεός, ᾧ ποτε πεισθείς,
Ζεῦ, διὰ χαλκείων χρυσὸς ἔδυς θαλάμων.

The god who draws me on is the one that masters even you: in obedience to him, Zeus, you once came as gold through the bronze of Danae's chamber.

The transformation of the supreme god into gold betokens the astounding power of Love. The name of Zeus appears for the first time in this final line, to heighten the change. ὁ κρατῶν καὶ σοῦ θεός 'the god who masters even you' stresses (paradoxically) Zeus' godhead and power; χαλκείων 'bronze' highlights his conversion into metal. The second-person form of the sentence makes the rhetoric delectably impertinent. But the brash tones of the speaker's voice are placed in counterpoint to the impressive utterance of the poet. The surprise, and the beauty,

---

[86] Erotes with lightning: J. Boardman, *Intaglios and Rings* (1975), pp. 19, 92.

of the description make an independent appeal to the reader's imagination.[87]

Even when handling relations that are formally metaphorical, Asclepiades can make them startle. In his hands the most familiar metaphors can seem violent and striking fusions; and some of his metaphors are far from familiar. In XII Asclepiades, after serenading a boy in vain, hangs his garlands of revelry on the door, a common custom. The whole poem is addressed to the garlands: garlands

> οὓς δακρύοις κατέβρεξα (κάτομβρα γὰρ ὄμματ' ἐρώντων).
> ἀλλ' ὅταν οἰγομένης αὐτὸν ἴδητε θύρης,
> στάξαθ' ὑπὲρ κεφαλῆς ἐμὸν ὑετόν, ὡς ἂν ἐκείνου
> ἡ ξανθή γε κόμη τἀμὰ πίῃ δάκρυα.

> ... which I have drenched with tears (lovers' eyes are full of rain). But when the door opens and you see him, drop my shower of rain over his head, so that his golden hair may drink up my tears.[88]

The image of rain is made surprising, in the first place, by the wording. κάτομβρα 'full of rain' is a prosaic, as well as an unexpected, adjective, and the parenthetic explanation falls curiously in this address. The combination of these things renders the statement slightly bizarre. ἐμὸν ὑετόν 'my shower of rain' is a phrase of arresting strangeness; even 'the shower of my tears' would have sounded bold in Greek, but this phrase makes the image feels extraordinary. On the other hand, the physical sequence has a grotesque and almost comic flavour; indeed, the action of pouring water over someone's head would in itself seem funny.[89] The assimilation of tears to rain heightens both the extravagance of the lover's feeling (so abundantly does he weep) and the grotesqueness of the event (so substantial will be the quantity of water). The weirdness felt in the image keeps

---

[87] D. H. Garrison, *Mild Frenzy* (*Hermes* Einzelschr. 41, 1978), 42 f., seems to deduce from the last couplet an optimism that is hardly to be found there. Rather, the poem reaches a close by moving part of the reader's mind away from the present scene.

[88] Schneidewin's ἐκείνου for ἄμεινον is clearly right; now it is confirmed by P. Oxy. 3724 i 19.

[89] Cf. Arist. *Lys.* 377 ff., Paul. Sil. *AP* 5. 281 (water poured by the girl while the poet hangs his garlands). Asclepiades is of course unlikely to be deliberately vengeful: that would scarcely suit the mood of the lover or the nature of the act, which was intended to move (Ovid, *Ars Am.* 2. 528, etc.; for the mood cf. e.g. Lucr. 4. 1177 ff.).

absurdity uneasily in check. πίῃ 'drink up' in the last line contains a further suggestion of rain; but the direct 'my tears', instead of 'my shower', gives a poignant edge to the close. The notion of beautiful hair being thus infused with tears produces a strange and memorable conjunction of physical things.[90]

Poem V deals with imagery in a more shifting fashion.

> ὀφθαλμοῖς Διδύμη με συνήρπασεν, ὤμοι, ἐγὼ δὲ
> τήκομαι ὡς κηρὸς πὰρ πυρὶ κάλλος ὁρῶν.
> εἰ δὲ μέλαινα, τί τοῦτο; καὶ ἄνθρακες—ἀλλ᾽ ὅτε κείνους
> θάλψωμεν, λάμπουσ᾽ ὡς ῥόδεαι κάλυκες.

Didyme has seized me with her eyes—ah me! I melt like wax set by fire as I look on her beauty. [ll. 1–2]. If she is dark, what of that? So are coals; yet whenever we heat them, they shine brightly as rose-buds.

The language of the first couplet is conventional, including the image of melting wax.[91] The exclamation merely gives the announcement a histrionic air (see pp. 273 f.). The second couplet surprisingly undermines the poet's claim that Didyme is beautiful: dark complexions were archetypally ugly. The surprise is strengthened by the entertaining change from wild transport to abrupt argumentation. The choice of coal to defend beauty makes a fresh surprise; this in turn enhances our astonishment at the close. An utterly unexpected conjunction of objects creates for the imagination an effect of the most exquisite delicacy and radiance. In part this removes us from the scene into the fusion of images. But the oddity of the rhetoric also directs one's view to the first couplet, and the recurrence of fire. The deliberately curious clause 'whenever we heat them' looks for an equivalent in the case of Didyme. The suggestion is insinuated that her ugliness has been transformed by the fire of Asclepiades' passion—transformed, that is, in the eyes of the deluded Asclepiades. Thus the imagery of the poem begins in conscious triteness, but turns to become startlingly imaginative and to subvert slyly the stance of the lover.

---

[90] S. L. Tarán, *The Art of Variation in the Hellenistic Epigram* (1979), 73 ff., makes the poem more straightforward in effect.

[91] Ludwig's contention that the couplet is actually modelled on Pind. fr. 123 Snell–Maehler seems too strong (*Entr. Hardt*, 14, 316). τήκω of the effect of glances appears commonly in lyric.

In the uses of language we have been considering Asclepiades pursues various kinds of poetic surprise. Characteristic
qualities are the imaginative, the strange, the forceful, the extravagant. This last aspect must be spoken of more generally:
the matter is of importance for understanding the whole body
of Asclepiades' poetry. In a sense, extravagance and extremes
are fundamental to love-poetry; but Asclepiades likes to present
the extremes of his emotion in such a way as to dilute the seriousness of their impact with admixtures of absurdity. In this he
has much in common with Anacreon, the late-archaic lyric
poet; and, as with Anacreon, it is important that author and
speaker should be formally identical. With Asclepiades the
humour lies in the interval between the vehemence of the
speaker and the detachment of the writer. Play with extravagance occurs only in poems that are concerned with Asclepiades.[92] One may learn something of both types of poem by
contrasting the use in them of various figures and devices.

Asclepiades twice employs in the poems on his love the lavish
gesture of imperatives which call for violent action against himself. Poem XI, addressed to Zeus as god of the weather (see
above, p. 267), begins with this couplet:

> νεῖφε, χαλαζοβόλει, ποίει σκότος, αἶθε κεραυνούς,
> πάντα τὰ πορφύροντ᾽ ἐν χθονὶ σεῖε νέφη.

Send snow, cast down hail, bring darkness, set your thunderbolts ablaze, drive all your swelling clouds to earth.[93]

'Only if you kill me will I cease', he goes on; 'if you let me live,
even if you treat me worse than this I will continue my serenade
(κωμάσομαι).' The first couplet adopts a grandiose form, with
the resonance of tragedy; only in the last word of the second
couplet (κωμάσομαι) do we learn how far from grandeur the
situation lies.[94] The defiance of the supreme deity relates to
singing and revelry outside a girl's house; the hostility of Zeus is
merely inferred from the appalling weather. The formal pas-

---

[92] The speaker is laughed at in XXV and to some degree in XXVI (both on preparations for a party), but not at all for the wild extravagance of his passion. See on
XXV Alan Cameron (n. 66), 286 f.

[93] αἶθε κεραυνούς is the admirable conjecture of Ludwig, *Entr. Hardt*, 14, 313 n. 1, for
αἶθε, κεραύνου.

[94] For tragic parallels to the first couplet see Tarán, 53 ff., adding Aesch. *PV* 991 ff.

sion and energy of the opening lose all possibility of seriousness for the reader. Instead, one relishes the excess and extravagance poured with such gusto into so unfitting a context.

We looked also above at poem XVII, where Asclepiades bade the Erotes let him live or else kill him, with lightning. He then fixes on this second possibility:

> ναὶ ναί, βάλλετ᾽, Ἔρωτες, ἐνεσκληκὼς γὰρ ἀνίαις
> ἐξ ὑμέων †τούτων ειτετι† βούλομ᾽ ἔχειν.

Yes, yes! Strike me with thunderbolts, you Loves! I have become dried up and shrivelled with pain, and I wish (to meet this fate?) at your hands.

Here the tone is more complicated, for the striking phrase ἐνεσκληκὼς ἀνίαις 'dried up and shrivelled with pain' introduces a surprising touch of reality and pathos. Nonetheless, the ludicrousness of the earlier commands is not lost here. The abandoned movement with ναὶ ναί 'Yes, yes!' seems delectably overdone: the very notion of such action from the Erotes has been presented as the speaker's invention. The plural Cupids (as we shall see) have a particularly frivolous air for agents of annihilation.

Poem XXX is an epigram on a man buried beside the sea. It begins

> ὀκτώ μευ πήχεις ἄπεχε, τρηχεῖα θάλασσα,
> καὶ κύμαινε βόα θ᾽ ἡλίκα σοι δύναμις.

Provided you keep twelve feet away from me, savage sea, swell and clamour to the height of your power. [*Lit.* 'Keep ... and swell ...']

The imperatives in the second line have a largeness and vigour that sets them with those in the poems spoken by Asclepiades. But the imperative in the first line limits them with prosaic smallness and precision. From this contrast there emerges a pleasingly sober and practical tone. We have quite the reverse of language which directs mockery at the wildness of the speaker.

We may take further bearings from poem XIX, essentially

the only poem spoken by someone in love who is not Asclepiades.[95]

πρόσθε μοι Ἀρχεάδης ἐθλίβετο· νῦν δέ, τάλαινα,
    οὐδ' ὅσσον παίζων εἰς ἔμ' ἐπιστρέφεται.
οὐδ' ὁ μελιχρὸς Ἔρως αἰεὶ γλυκύς, ἀλλ' ἀνιήσας
    πολλάκις ἡδίων γίνετ' ἐρῶσι θεός.

Once Archeades used to be oppressed with passion for me;
now, alas, he does not turn to me even in sportive mood.
[ll. 1–2] Not even sweet Love is sweet always; yet often,
after giving pain, the god becomes more pleasant to
lovers.

This girl is not a comic figure, as Asclepiades so often is; nor
does her emotion appear extravagant, as his so often does. The
second couplet shows her controlling her distress with a rather
touching resignation and optimism. This is quite different from
Asclepiades' abject abandonment of indignation in X; indeed,
the absence of indignation here is another touching aspect of
the poem. We are not conscious of the author producing effects
which run contrary to the emotion of the speaker.

The figure of Eros (Love) brings about the movement in this
poem to a generalized wisdom and detachment. In poem
XXIV Eros produces a harmonious union of two individuals;
this is depicted as a wonderful act of felicitous artistry.[96] Poem
XXII conveys the secluded loveliness of a young boy by por-
traying his strange and exquisite friendship with a childish
Eros; it begins with a delicate playfulness, but grows lyrical and
rich.[97] These uses of the god are far removed from the violent
and comic effects achieved in the poems where Asclepiades
speaks. There plural Erotes inflict savage extremes of pain on
Asclepiades, at which he cries out helplessly. ὦρωτες, τί κακὸν

---

[95] One may set apart VI, a dedication by a courtesan who had had many lovers.
XXV and XXVI (preparations for parties) hardly come into consideration.

[96] The two males are probably lovers. The role of Eros is most naturally explained
thus, and πειθοῦς is most naturally taken as erotic. Call. fr. 75. 30 f. strengthens this
view.

[97] Note also the expressive phrase in XLI on a deceased hetaera; ἃς καὶ ἐπὶ ῥυτίδων ὁ
γλυκὺς ἔζετ' Ἔρως. This is a graphic and paradoxical reworking of convention (cf.
Soph. *Ant.* 783 f.); it is not ludicrous or entertaining, and directs no humour against the
mortal.

τοῦτο; τί με φλέγετε; 'Erotes, what is this pain? Why are you burning me?' (XV. 2); οἴχομ', Ἔρωτες, ὄλωλα, διοίχομαι 'O Erotes! I am finished, destroyed, slain utterly' (VIII. 3). In the latter place the Erotes are apostrophized as supernatural cause of the destruction wrought by a woman. Poem XVII (Erotes to use lightning) was spoken of above. In XV the poet sharply deflates the wild remonstrance just cited: he paints the indifference of the Erotes to the fate in which he attempts to interest them. ἢν γὰρ ἐγώ τι πάθω 'if anything should happen to me' (he puts it gingerly), why, his destroyers will still continue with their boyish game of knucklebones. In VIII the outburst is succeeded by a more detached explanation; this turns the whole poem into the ingenious unfolding of a conceit (the hetaera is a venomous serpent).[98] The abandoned cry thus becomes a laughable dramatization of the metaphor. Even in its initial impact, it is made comic by the appearance of the plural Erotes in this quasi-tragic exclamation. Multiplication reduces the impressiveness of these figures, and removes from them the literary resonance of the singular son of Aphrodite.[99] In a lavishly grandiose context they become incongruous. Asclepiades employs a single Eros in Poem XI (above, p. 267), addressed to Zeus, for the sake of pungent and impudent phrasing. Poem XXIII imagines the poet's love as a small Eros still with his mother; it does not present the poet directly. The conception resembles that of XXII (above, p. 272); but obscure as XXIII is, it clearly paints Eros with very different colouring. The god stays at home with his mother reading out spells for love-magic with a childish lisp (τραυλίζει, beginning the final line). The picture is bizarre and comic. In the poems where Asclepiades speaks as a character in a dramatic situation, the Erotes serve to inflate and to deflate the language of the lover.

One further point may be drawn from poem XIX (the rejected girl, p. 272). In poem V (p. 269, on the dark-skinned Didyme), the ejaculation ὤμοι injected a histrionic note into the poet's declaration of his feeling. The cry in itself has rather a grandiose and tragic quality; this gives force to the undermin-

---

[98] See E. K. Borthwick, *CR* NS 17 (1967), 250 ff.

[99] Plural Erotes appear seldom in literature of the classical period, mostly in passages where personification is debatable (as it is at *SH* 352. 2 (4th c.)). They do appear in classical art: see A. Greifenhagen, *Gr. Eroten* (1957).

ing in what follows.[100] In the poem spoken by the girl, τάλαινα literally 'poor me!', has a quite different effect. It stands out from the texture of speech again, but conveys simply and expressively the speaker's pain. This gives force to the rather affecting movement in the second couplet.[101] The last couplet of poem XXXIII, an epitaph, uses ejaculations (φεῦ ... φεῦ ...) to lament the living father and the dead son. Ejaculations appear sometimes in inscriptional, and quite often in literary, epitaphs.[102] The effect here is powerful, for the poem has hitherto addressed the passer-by, and told him of the misfortune; the first line calls his attention with a shout (ἰώ). Now the poem turns away from him in passion and apostrophizes the son with warmth and grief. Here strong feeling is not undercut by the author.

Not all the poems spoken by Asclepiades as a character show the play with extravagance which we have been illustrating. This is sufficiently indicated by poem II, the first we treated. My concern has not been to divide the poems into two quite separate compartments. Rather, I hoped to suggest how, in poems where he can play with himself, Asclepiades may distort, colour, and subvert his characteristic vigour and imagination. One thus sees both contact and contrast with the poems which do not pursue these aims. The poems which do, have a very distinctive flavour. The interplay of extremity and absurdity is attended by a kind of geniality and richness. This springs from the identity of the speaker. Quasi-dramatic poems which played merely with the emotions of invented characters would produce a colder and more aloof sort of humour (cf. e.g. Theocritus 3 or Herodas 6). They would also lack the insistent charm of paradox which hovers round such a treatment of the poet's own passions.

The poems which do not concern Asclepiades form a minority of those extant, and differ widely in subject and mood: one

---

[100] ὤμοι does not appear in Callimachus, nor I think in any 3rd-c. epigram. In Theocritus it conveys an absurd exaggeration of feeling, real or pretended (3. 20, 11. 54; 10. 41). It does occur in Theognis (probably): 527; 891 with West's note, 1107. The assertion on the cry is scarcely damaged by 527.

[101] Cf. for the isolated τάλαινα Soph. *OC* 1683, 318. Brunck's τάλαιναν though possible is unnecessary, and, as Gow feels, a little awkward.

[102] e.g. *GVI* 332. 1 (4th c.); *HE* 2960 (Phalaecus, echoing the mourner), 2631, 2635, 3534; cf. also 1778.

could scarcely view them as a cohesive group in their own right. They are not distinguished, for example, by any Callimachean concern to play with epigraphic conventions.[103] They do, however, exploit the device of a speaker with no less force than the poems where the speaker is Asclepiades. The tonal effects are quite different in these poems, but they show a related interest in dramatic utterance and the potential of the first person. Such interest may be illustrated most strikingly with some poems where the device of a speaker is used unexpectedly. Poem XXII, on Eros' friendship with Damis (p. 272), greatly heightens the impact of its fantasy and the warmth of its close by being placed in the mouth of Eros himself. The reader only discovers this in the last word of the first couplet, and the discovery is a considerable surprise. XXVIII lauds the poem of Erinna, who died young. At the end of the penultimate line, we suddenly learn that it is she who is speaking: she emphasizes strongly the fame which her early death cut short. The effect is startling, and gives impressive force to the pathos and the praise.[104] A related surprise, with wholly different import, may be seen in one of the poems spoken by Asclepiades (VII). The first sentence merely describes with disapproval the lesbianism of two women from Samos, Asclepiades' own island. But at the end of the penultimate line the poet turns to Aphrodite and asks her to punish these fugitives from the heterosexual intercourse she approves. This sudden animation and engagement entertains: the poet, one surmises, has personal and amatory reasons for his indignation.[105] One poem (XVI) uses another speaker to cajole Asclepiades for the excess of his reaction to the trials of love. It only becomes clear as the poem proceeds that Asclepiades is not addressing himself; and the device

[103] XXVII (the mask) does make a pleasing use of personification in the last line, in a fashion which Callimachus was to develop. See Wilamowitz, *HD* ii. 117, and note the forceful placing of πρεσβύτην and παιδαρίων. But in terms of Asclepiades' interests elsewhere, one would see this as another instance of a speaker appearing in mid-poem (see below). παῖδας takes up παῖδας in l. 1.

[104] O. Knauer, *D. Epigramme d. Asklep. v. Samos* (Diss. Tub. 1935) 26 f., supposes that the earlier part is not spoken by Erinna, but this is most implausible. Dioscorides XXVI, which he cites, does nothing to strengthen his case.

[105] Since the reference to the women as 'Samian' may have a point in relation to the poet and the implied fiction, it does not necessarily indicate that Asclepiades is not in Samos when he writes.

is meant to seem strange.[106] The speaker takes from Alcaeus exhortations to sense and merriment which belong conventionally to the poet.[107] The poet himself remains sunk in despair.

In the light of our discussion, we may return to brevity. Asclepiades may be seen to handle the limits of his form with the greatest address. The startling and imaginative use of physical language; the surprising movements; the expressive or incongruous exclamations and addresses; the bold gestures of rhetoric—all these through their force and their unexpectedness bestow vitality and resonance on these short productions. At the same time, it is the shortness of the poems that enables these features to have so primary an impact on the structures that contain them. These features make the reader feel that the poem is not static and monotone. It moves between, or incorporates simultaneously, different tones or different layers of effect. This is particularly exciting in such a short poem: we have a feeling of rich aesthetic experience in two or three sentences. It enhances this experience to feel that it has shape, and that one has reached, so soon, a real ending. We have seen, for example, how surprises at the end can bring a memorable close in sudden emotion or sudden loss of emotion, and how striking phrases can end the brief poem with sonorous or evocative fullness. The richness of effect seen in so narrow a compass has one of its prime sources in the handling of the first person. Asclepiades' own self makes possible energetic and satisfying play with extravagance in a few bold movements. So compelling is the power of the individual poems, and so concentrated their art, that one is surprised to recall what number of lines we possess which are more or less certainly his: barely 160. In these brief works he shows the most impressive complexity and subtlety—that complexity and that subtlety which were to be developed on so much larger a scale by his great admirers.

---

[106] The last couplet, in particular, it would be very unnatural to give to Asclepiades. σχέτλιε, πίνωμεν and μετά τοι χρόνον οὐκέτι πουλύν make it extremely hard to refer ἀναπαυσόμεθα either to Asclepiades alone or to mankind in general. Rather it refers to Asclepiades and his friends. The echo of Alcaeus 346. 1 Voigt in l. 5 greatly deters one from taking πίνωμεν as 'let me drink'; it would in any case be most odd to understand the plural thus, when πίνω would be quite abnormal here grammatically.

[107] Alcaeus fr. 38a Voigt is particularly relevant to the poem, as well as fr. 346. Cf. also frr. 73, 335, etc.

6

ROMAN POETRY

THIS final chapter concerns the relation between Hellenistic poetry and the poetry of the Romans.[1] Our purpose is not simply to establish that one had some effect on the other, but to discern the most significant aspects of the influence, and to observe how the Roman poets used and transformed what they inherited. The picture we have built up of Hellenistic poetry is one where form and tone possess far greater importance than general theories about literature. Even with the influence of Hellenistic poetry, a broadly similar position obtains. Of course, our conception of the Greek poetry is not invalidated if the Romans in fact misunderstood it, if, as is most commonly supposed, they took Callimachean 'doctrines' to be its central and crucial element. But their poems show the impact of a far fuller conception of Hellenistic poetry (whether or not they could have articulated it). The impact of the 'doctrines' on their actual poems is much less evident and ascertainable and much less helpful to the critic. Even the prologue to Callima-

---

[1] The Hellenistic poetry which will concern this chapter is that which has concerned the rest of the book, the poetry of the 3rd c. BC. For the particular purposes of this book and this chapter it is acceptable not to enter into a discussion of Greek poetry at the time of Catullus and Ovid: see p. 298. Historical evidence suggests that some Greek poets had a significant role in intellectual society. Parthenius, who narrated obscure myths and wrote a poem on his dead wife, was brought to Rome by Cinna (*SH* 605(*a*)), probably the poet, and was a friend of Gallus. Philodemus was patronized by an aristocratic enemy of Cicero's (Nisbet, edn. of Cic. *In Pis.*, pp. 183 ff.); his epigrams sometimes suggest the attitudes struck by Horace (*Garl. Phil.* XVIII, XIX, XXI, XXIII; note Hor. *Sat.* 1. 2. 120–3). Links sometimes appear between other Greek epigrammatists of the period and Roman poets, e.g. Antip. Thess. *Garl. Phil.* VII and Ovid, *Am.* 1. 13 (especially 37 f.). But, for the aspects and areas that interest us here, the poverty of our evidence makes it almost impossible to achieve a proper impression of the relation between the two literatures. What is clear is that, save perhaps in epic, the Greek poets essentially wrote in the traditions founded in the 3rd c.

The reader of this chapter is particularly referred to the bibliography: many works are listed there which are not mentioned in the already numerous footnotes—not least works that exemplify the standard approach to the relation between the two poetries which is questioned in this chapter. That approach, encountered perpetually, the footnotes do not seek to document.

chus' *Aetia*, which the poets draw on so often, gains its primary importance from rather different considerations.

It will be remembered that the prologue to the *Aetia* fell into two distinct parts. (In discussing Roman poetry we ought certainly to consider it as a single prologue.) The first defended the poet, presenting his debate with the Telchines and the speech of Apollo to the young Callimachus. The second described his meeting, on Mount Helicon, in a dream, with the Muses, who were to answer his questions about rituals. Callimachus stresses the parallel with their meeting Hesiod there (*Theog.* 22 ff.): Hesiod offers a kind of whimsical model for the poem.[2] Callimachus' pronouncements on poetry in the first part, and in other poems, were considered in ch. 2 (pp. 77 ff.). I should like to mention first some general points with regard to the Roman exploitation of Callimachus' pronouncements, and then to glance at some particular uses of this prologue. The general points are not intended to demonstrate that aesthetic theories had no importance for Latin poetry; they are intended rather to start us looking from a different angle. Catullus, who does strike a somewhat different attitude from his successors, will be mainly dealt with later.

Firstly, then, poets could certainly use some of the devices employed by Callimachus in his prologue without thereby professing allegiance to his supposed theories (against length, grandeur, the epic, in favour of brevity, refinement, lightness). In particular, poets could so use the second part. Cicero used speeches to himself by the Muses in his poem *On My Consulship* (frr. 6–8 Morel). The poem will not have been a straightforward epic, but it seems not utterly remote from the kind of epic deployed by Callimachus as a foil in the first part of his prologue. More important, Ennius at the beginning of his epic *Annales* described a dream relating to his model: Homer's ghost appeared, and said that he was reincarnated in Ennius. The

---

[2] The prologue to the *Theogony* serves to inspire the form of the whole first two books; the idea of Hesiod as πάσης ἥρανον ἱστορίης 'keeper of all information' may also be pertinent (Hermesianax, *CA*, p. 98. 22). However, there is little fuller evocation of Hesiod in the poem, and no particular work of his is set up as an exemplar: note fr. 2. 3 ff. The use of Hesiod is unlikely to make a programmatic point about the use of Homer (see below). If Pindar should have a bearing on the encounter at all (cf. M. van der Weiden, *ZPE* 64 (1986), 15 ff.), that bearing will be altogether secondary.

dream was probably set on a mountain of the Muses.[3] A dream relating to the model might have appeared in post-Callimachean poetry: Herodas' eighth poem too shows something of the kind. But it is unlikely that Ennius was ignorant of Callimachus himself, or was not making use of him here.[4] Ennius' poem was of precisely the kind that Callimachus set in unappealing contrast to his own work. Ennius can be rescued if one makes him defy Callimachus by turning round his form (though the formal reversal is not very pointed as such), or if one makes him circumvent Callimachus by reimbodying not imitating Homer (though there is little sign that the imitation of Homer was a fundamental issue for Callimachus). It is more natural to suppose that Ennius used a famous poet without restricting himself obediently to his supposed doctrines on epic and size. At the end of Propertius 2. 10 the poet links a full initiation on Helicon with an ability to write grandly of Augustus' campaigns. A pointed defiance of Callimachus' values would seem unlikely and inelegant here.[5] These passages together suggest, not that Callimachus' symbols are being turned against him, but that their drama, colour, and artifice are more potent than their place of origin.

A second point concerns elegy in particular. When elegists refer to Callimachus, it is not so much because he is a poet of unique authority and stature absolutely, as because he is a chief exemplar of the genre of elegy. Their rhetorical object is to stress the legitimacy of their own genre. In such passages, despite Callimachus' own work, they seek to depict that genre as

[3] The only definite evidence is Sch. Persius prol. 2: probably it is reliable in essence, though Persius' text may have affected details (such as the name of the mountain, Parnassus).

[4] On the early fame and the wide readership of Callimachus, see pp. 6 f. In the prologue to Book 7 Ennius spoke of ascending the mount of the Muses (208 Skutsch), and lauded his artistry in a fashion by no means without resemblance to Callimachus. *sophiam* (211) probably refers to poetic skill, perhaps with special allusion to Call. fr. 1. 18 (I should favour, however, Fränkel's notions about the dream, and his only). *dicti studiosus* = φιλόλογος (209) seems more likely to mean 'literary' than 'scholarly' in this context; but still it stresses an approach.

[5] *Ascraeos* in 25, with its allusion to Hesiod, makes a point about genre still more awkward. At *Am.* 1. 15. 35 f. Ovid uses language with Callimachean and Ennian associations; but in that poem Callimachus and Ennius are effectively the only poets in a long catalogue about whom Ovid speaks with reserve. Yet the context (31–5) and the design of the whole poem, which defends poetry in general, make the notion of a pointed reversal quite implausible.

defined not merely by the elegiac couplet but by the subject of the poet's love. Outside these poets Callimachus was made the chief writer of elegy.[6] The older poet Philetas was also given a place of distinction. It is notable that the founder of the genre does not predominate: the place of founder was disputed. Mimnermus, however, was a favoured contender.[7] All these poets duly appear in the Roman elegists. Philetas in particular is made one of a pair with Callimachus, although Callimachus himself approves only some of his works.[8] Propertius 1. 9 sets Mimnermus against Homer (11), both as poet of love against poet of war and as the founder of elegy against the founder of epic. The poem lays stress on the practical value of Propertius' genre to the amorous. In 2. 34*b* a poet in love is bid emulate Philetas and Callimachus (31 f.). Again these appear as exemplars of elegy; the mention of Callimachus' stylistic character is subordinate to the argument about love. In 3. 9 Propertius will follow Callimachus and Philetas, not write on epic themes (37 ff.): the reference to metre (44) makes it plain that genre is in question.[9] Ovid, defending the erotic poetry he had written in elegiacs, associates the epic metre with war, the elegiac with love and lasciviousness (*Rem. Am.* 361 ff.). He adroitly but sophistically refers to Cydippe in *Aetia* 3 in order to suggest that the chief writer in the genre was principally concerned with love. Callimachus' stated predilections in poetry do lend a degree of support to the opposition Ovid draws; but those predilections are not presented as having validity outside the genre.[10]

We may note also how Virgil at the start of *Eclogue* 6

[6] Quint. *Inst.* 10. 1. 55; the metrician Hephaestion takes all his examples of the pentameter from him (*Ench.* 15. 14 f., p. 52 Consbr.).

[7] Didymus, pp. 387 f. Schmidt (dispute); Hermesianax, *CA*, p. 99. 35, cf. Alex. Aet., *CA*, p. 125. 4 (Mimnermus). The supposed position of Mimnermus explains Hor. *Epist.* 2. 2. 100 f., though the sequence of 99 f. is also interesting. Callimachus mentions both Philetas and Mimnermus in the first part of his prologue to the elegiac *Aetia*.

[8] Cf. *SH* 675, Hollis, *CQ* NS 28 (1978), 404 ff. Note Statius, *Silv.* 1. 2. 250 ff., where Callimachus and Philetas appear together explicitly as the Greek representatives of elegy.

[9] Cf. also 3. 1. 1 and 3. 52 (below). Genre will be crucial too at 4. 6. 3 f. (note 5, and 69); the link of genre gives more force to 2. 1. 39–42 (read *intonat*, as S. J. Heyworth suggests, *CQ* NS 34 (1984), 399).

[10] The compliment imagined at *Amores* 2. 4. 19 f., that in comparison to Ovid Callimachus is unrefined, has much more point if it is suited especially to the Virgil of elegy (*Rem.* 395 f.), and is not simply the highest praise any poet could be offered.

ingeniously adapts the general pronouncements of Callimachus to a generic form. In Callimachus Apollo addresses the poet as 'poet' and bids him keep his Muse slender, though he should fatten animals for sacrifice as much as possible (fr. 1. 23 f.). Virgil, as pastoral poet, represents himself as a shepherd. Apollo tells him:

> pastorem, Tityre, pinguis
> pascere oportet ovis, deductum dicere carmen. (4 f.)

> The shepherd, Tityrus, though he should feed his sheep so that they grow fat, should sing a song that is contracted.[11]

pastorem 'shepherd' is emphatically placed; it is the pastoral poet who has no business with grand themes like the praise of Varus' martial achievements (6 f.). The fictional assimilation of shepherd and pastoral poet makes the permanence of Virgil's humble role formally more convincing.

Thirdly, after Catullus, brevity and lightness are seldom proclaimed preferable or admirable absolutely. The opening of Propertius' third book contains something of this notion; but the matter becomes more complicated as the prologue develops (see below). In *Satires* 1. 4 Horace condemns the careless loquacity of his predecessor Lucilius, using at one point the Callimachean metaphor of the muddy river (11, cf. Call. *H.* 2. 108 f.). But when he resumes in 1. 10 and recommends brevity, variety, restraint, he is plainly limiting his remarks to this type of poetry. This is so despite a play with Callimachus' prologue (31 ff.). Elsewhere, however, he speaks of the lightness of his work with studied ambivalence: the achievement is professedly humble, but it merits praise (*Odes* 2. 16. 38, *Epist.* 2. 1. 225). Craftsmanship is much more frequently stressed as a great good in Horace; but this is associated with the Greeks in general, not Hellenistic poets in particular.[12]

It is notable that *tenuis* plays so little part as an actual term of

---

[11] Servius' notion that we should hear in *deductum* a metaphor from spinning does not seem attractive. The verb is used of all kinds of diminution (*TLL* v 1. 280 f.), so that we have no special reason to think of spinning, particularly with this phrasing (rather than *deducere carmen*); nor does that metaphor fit particularly well with shepherds or the original.

[12] *Ars Poet.* 335–7 (*esto brevis* 335) is again relative to a particular sort of writing, though not a genre.

literary praise in Latin poetry, although it suggests so well the
λεπτός or λεπταλέος 'slender, light, elegant' used by Callimachus (fr. 1. 10, 16, *Ep.* 27); and indeed it is employed by Cicero
and others as a critical term. *Dulcis* too is very little used,
although it answers to Callimachus' terms of praise γλυκύς and
μελιχρός 'sweet', and is known as a literary term again. This
sorts well with, though it naturally does not prove, the idea that
Callimachus' work is not taken as a great fount of literary doctrine.[13] Roman poets derived from other sources their conceptions and vocabulary of praise and blame for poetry; indeed
they use such words even to praise Callimachus himself. *Doctus,*
one may note, does not really mean 'learned' as a term of
praise, more 'skilled': it is not limited to Hellenistic poets or
poets who could be thought in any sense erudite.[14] *Rusticus* 'of
the country, with country crudity', another significant term,
Ovid uses for the reverse of Callimachus' quality (*Am.* 2. 4.
19 f.). The word (with its relatives) has its connections with
Greek terminology, but the antithesis of rude country and
polished city is particularly characteristic, and suggestive, of
Rome. The notion is found in Plautus and is frequent in Cicero;
Horace uses it in a specifically Roman context (*Epist.* 2. 1.
156–60).[15]

The elegists are particularly fond of words like *mollis* 'soft'
and *blandus* 'alluring, smooth'; these are the terms they like to
employ when contrasting their own poetry with more exalted
kinds. They suggest not only smoothness in versification (not a
thing Callimachus stresses as such), but notions of a sensuous
and seductive ethos.[16] Even Callimachus' own image of pursuing an unfrequented path in his chariot is changed strikingly

---

[13] *lepidus* 'charming, attractive' and *lepos* 'charm', which Catullus often uses to praise
poetry, should not be regarded as a Neoteric rendering of e.g. λεπτός: he and earlier
writers use it as a term of praise in other areas, and Lucretius uses *lepos* for the beauty of
his poetry (1. 28, 934).

[14] e.g. Catull. 35. 16 f. (Sappho, in effect), Cic. *Tusc.* 4. 71 (archaic lyric poets),
Manilius 5. 475 (Menander), Phaedrus 3, prol. 26 (poets, especially himself). Cf. Nisbet and Hubbard on Hor. *Odes* 1. 1. 29.

[15] Virgil's 'Pollio amat nostram, quamvis est rustica, Musam' (*Ecl.* 3. 84) ·
ingeniously conjoins the Roman and the pastoral.

[16] Ovid, *Trist.* 2. 307 (cf. Catull. 16. 4), *Rem.* 765 f., Prop. 1. 7. 19, 2. 34*b*. 42 ff. *ad
mollis membra resolve chorus … dure poeta* (both passages consider poets in high genres
turning to love and elegy), 4. 6. 5, 3. 1. 19 f. (cf. 4. 1. 61 f.), Ovid, *Rem.* 379 f., *Amores* 3.
1. 45 f. Cf. Fedeli on Prop. 1. 7. 19 and 3. 1. 19 f.

into driving on soft meadows.[17] The poets fit Callimachus into their own aesthetic language, and use that language to develop their own conception of their poetry, a conception far richer and more insidious than Callimachus' overt conception of his. Style, genre, mood, ethos, and personality are intermingled even in their most formalized treatments of literature.

These preliminary thoughts may point to a different approach. The poets, in turning so often to Callimachus' prologue and the topoi that gather round it, are not endlessly asserting their allegiance to a general theory of literature. Rather, they value the possibilities which they are given for writing about their own poetry. This is not simply a matter of defending themselves—though some passages come into this category. Nor is it simply a matter of advertising the merits of their poetry—though this is often an element. Many of the treatments are too light-hearted in tone to make a practical purpose plausible. Even if we do see refusals to write martial epic as actually intended to ward off patrons (in public), that purpose scarcely exhausts the literary qualities of the poems or their appeal for the ordinary reader. In genres other than drama and epic, Roman authors talk about themselves with great frequency, and not only in respect of literature. The figures of the poets are a dominating feature of this poetry: much of its effect lies in the poets' manner of speaking about themselves, and in the division and the unity of the dramatic character and the author. Even in epic, Ennius engages in polemic, and tells us, apparently, of his advancing age (401 Skutsch), in a way that would surprise in Apollonius. To poets with such interests the prologue to the *Aetia* offered particular attractions.

The most important was the possibilities it gave for subtlety and complexity of tone in speaking of one's own work. Callimachus himself had combined actual laudation of his poetry with an avoidance of vulgar boasting. Ennius had reintroduced an element of forthright proud assertion; Virgil heightened the element of modesty. The region thus afforded scope for arresting play between modesty and pride. The images of divine encounter allowed either pole to take a particularly dramatic and forceful shape, in an absorbing fiction. The confrontation

[17] Prop. 3. 3. 18 (see below), cf. 4. 6. 10, Ovid, *Pont.* 4. 16. 32 *Callimachi ... molle ... iter* (probably with reference to elegy).

of the poet with a plurality of sons of Envy, and the contrast
between his poetry and that of most, set the poet and his poetry
in compelling isolation. Callimachus' perspective of a lifetime
of poetry permitted the presentation of the poet in a broad, rich
vista, one which suggested the personal reality of a character
with temporal and biographical dimension. The dream and the
speech to the Telchines deployed the relation of the poet to a
model and a genre; Callimachus' forthright opposition of types
of poetry enabled genres to be vividly defined. This too was a
potent and rewarding area to treat. Finally—an especially important aspect—the fictional and dramatic form of Callimachus' prologue allowed elaborate play between extravagant
pretence and the basic reality of the poet's own work. The most
promising way to read the passages that use the prologue is as
subtle and vigorous poetry, which handles the author and the
work with richness and piquancy.

One may consider some particular poems where the prologue is reworked. In Virgil's sixth *Eclogue* the first part of that
prologue (where Apollo addresses Callimachus) is made more
modest and applied to Virgil himself. The second part (where
Callimachus meets the Muses) is made grander and applied to
his contemporary Gallus. The two parts are used at opposite
ends of the poem. Virgil, turned into a shepherd, begins a song
too grand, quite unlike Callimachus, and is unceremoniously
stopped by Apollo, who pulls his ear and puts him in his place.
The drama is here burlesque.[18] Gallus does not dream like
Callimachus: he is led up to Helicon by a Muse, and all the
Muses react to his coming with great respect:

> utque viro Phoebi chorus adsurrexerit omnis.   (66)

> (Silenus told) how Apollo's whole chorus rose up for that
> man.

Drama here gives grandeur and distance. The disjunction is
elaborate in effect. There will probably be a tinge of irony: Virgil's poetry seems far smoother than the chief fragment of Gallus'.[19] None the less, the chief effect is of a delightful humour

[18] The gesture of pulling the ear has here more the air of a tap on the shoulder than
the solemn suggestion of summoning a witness—that would be quite inappropriate.
[19] R. D. Anderson, P. J. Parsons, R. G. M. Nisbet, *JRS* 69 (1979), 125 ff. The fragment is probably later than the *Eclogues*, in my opinion (cf. *ZPE* 41 (1981), 37 ff.).

and self-deprecation in Virgil's handling of himself as a poet. We should miss the crucial play with personalities if we insisted that both parts sustained a stance over theory.

The poem holds further complications. In the rest of the introduction, Virgil comes closer to the real world of patrons and books of poems, and he conveys a modest but passionate desire for success.

> si quis tamen haec quoque, si quis
> captus amore leget ... (9)

> If anyone, if anyone reads even this poetry captured by
> love for it ...[20]

He then gives a narrative introduction, no less playful but charmingly decadent, to the grave and mysterious song of the mythical Silenus: this song contains the initiation of Gallus. There is thus a series of narrative layers, which separate the three singers Virgil, Silenus, Gallus; they are connected, for example, by their relations to Apollo, and to Orpheus.[21] Silenus' song, which originates in circumstances so much more frivolous and playful than Gallus' or even Virgil's, proves the most splendid song of all. But Virgil is not only one in a sequence of poets: he has also produced the whole structure. This is emphasized by the call *pergite, Pierides* 'Muses, proceed', which follows the 'introduction': all that ensues is his poetic design. The Callimachean forms are incorporated into an elaborate construction, in which Virgil plays with his own poetry and sets modesty in treating himself against extravagance in dealing with others. He plays too with reality and fiction, taking as his point of departure Callimachus' fictional treatments of himself. If one attempted to convert the poem into a manifesto on

---

[20] Coleman's rendering in his edn. 'attracted by the subject of love' is banal, and scarcely accounts for the repetition; nor does it seem wholly suitable to this context. *quoque* means 'like other, grander poetry'; Virgil's broad use of *amor* makes the expression entirely acceptable (cf. together *Ecl.* 10. 73, *Georg.* 2. 476, 4. 205). Priscian's *legat* deserves consideration.

[21] With regard to Orpheus, who links Silenus and Gallus, one needs not only to note 30 and 70 f. but to bear in mind how he and Linus (67) formed a pair, with whom cosmogonic poetry was associated. See on Linus, West, *The Orphic Poems* (1983), 62 ff., and note the pairing at *Ecl.* 4. 55–7. Cf. P. J. Hardie, *Virgil's* Aeneid: Cosmos *and* Imperium (1986), 17.

poetics, one would lose the sense of fantasy and strangeness which feels so essential to its nature.

The first poem of Propertius' fourth book uses pride and modesty in a fashion surprising but ultimately simple. At the end of the first section Propertius announces a Roman version of Callimachus' *Aetia* (57 ff.). He begins by regretting the littleness of his poetry and its tones (58); but this rises into pride. He now contrasts himself favourably with Ennius, who wrote a patriotic poem, but one large and rough (61); he exults in the title of Roman Callimachus (64). But with striking inversion his Callimachean plans are abruptly thwarted by a figure who derives from Callimachus' Apollo. The poet suddenly becomes a dramatic character, and his pride is suddenly deflated for the reader by a Babylonian astrologer. At the end of the poem the astrologer recalls the speech which Apollo made to Propertius at the beginning of his career. We have now a less distorted version of the Callimachean original, but one distanced through its narrative level. The implications of this speech for the author's poetry are at first positive. But as it develops, Apollo turns out to be contrasting Propertius' success in poetry with his failure as a lover; by the end it is on this second aspect that the emphasis has fallen.[22] It should be noted how the occasion which in Callimachus is simply related to his commencing as a writer (fr. 1. 21 f.) is here given an ample context in the real times, places, and experiences of Propertius' life (121–32). The poet as a living person comes in Apollo's speech to offset and overshadow the indirect praise of the author. Earlier in the poem direct self-praise by the author had been converted into self-praise by a dramatic character, and then exploded. The poet is playing. Both here and in *Eclogue* 6 the primary and overall effect is not at all to glorify the author, still less to defend and praise his manner of poetry aesthetically. The reader is of course warmly disposed to the poets who can treat themselves so lightly and ironically; but what matters most is the pleasure that arises from this handling of self and tone.

The opening of Propertius' third book is more elusive in its total impact. In poems 1–3 Propertius essentially adopts the

---

[22] This is particularly pointed because elegy in such contexts is generally praised for its utility in love. (Note 139 here; *fallax* 135 prepares this point if sound (*pellax* Heinsius).) Cf. e.g. 3. 3. 49 f., and note Tib. 2. 4. 13–20.

twofold structure of Callimachus' prologue.[23] Poems 1 and 2
belong very closely together, and may be one poem; they
handle Propertius' poetry in a general and non-dramatic
fashion. Poem 3 describes a dream in which Propertius was
shown his proper kind of poetry. It appropriates, not only the
dream with the Muses from the second part of Callimachus'
prologue, but Apollo's speech from the first; the latter is given
the humbling form established by Virgil. This arrangement
means, broadly, that the first part of Propertius' prologue
(poems 1 and 2) shows a pride which the second does not. At
the beginning of poem 1 Propertius invokes Callimachus and
Philetas as models for elegy, and begs to enter their grove. The
request relates to the writing of admirable poetry, but suggests,
in figurative form, an action in a sacred place. This will be
taken up in narrative form in poem 3. Here, however, the tone
is proud (3 f.); and the poet expresses scorn of those who write
on war (7), and he insists on refinement, clearly as a notion of
general validity. He stresses his fame and originality himself
with imagery which Callimachus had given to Apollo. Apollo
had instructed Callimachus to drive, not on the broad roads
already frequented by others, but on new and narrower paths
(the image is cleverly commending the scale of Callimachus'
poetry). Propertius himself tells the rival poets who pursue him
in their chariots that their struggle is in vain:

> non datur ad Musas currere lata via. (14)

> It is not a broad road by which one is granted to run to
> the Muses.

He gives the road a grandiose function, and speaks with assured
and scornful superiority. There are fluctuations and complexities in the rest of poems 1–2; but essentially the poet asserts his
excellence and immortality with growing warmth. 2. 1 f. seem
to mark a return from such grand themes:

> Carminis interea nostri redeamus in orbem.

> But meanwhile let me return to the course which my song
> properly moves on.

---

[23] Poems 4 and 5 should not be made part of the prologue to the book.

Yet the poetry swells out again into the most magnificent self-praise.

Poem 3 moves to a much humbler picture of the poet. We now have, not a passionate discourse by him, but a detached and fictitious narrative of initiation. The initiation at first goes wrong. Propertius attempts to drink from the same spring as Ennius; but Apollo intrudes and warns him against undertaking anything so unsuited to his restricted and lightweight abilities (15 ff.). Smallness becomes something inferior to largeness and greatness; earlier images and words are given new and less favourable connotations.[24] The drama and (1–14) the syntax of the narrative alike present a deflation of the pretentious author. He is directed to a different place, where the Muses initiate him in his proper genre. That genre now acquires more attractive colours, especially at the beginning of the Muse's speech.

> contentus niveis semper vectabere cycnis
>   nec te fortis equi ducet ad arma sonus.   (39 f.)

> You will always be borne by snow-white swans, and you
> will be content with this; the valiant horse will not bring
> you to battle with his resounding hooves.

The image of Venus' swan lyrically removes us from reality; but at the end of her speech the Muse makes clear the lowness and familiarity of the poet's subject-matter (47–50). Her last line tells us, in unelevated language, that this is poetry for the man.

> qui volet austeros arte ferire viros.   (50)

> who wishes to hoodwink strict husbands by trickery and
> art.

At last Propertius is allowed to drink from the spring of his proper models, Callimachus and Philetas. The moment looks back to the beginning of poem 1, but now the spring becomes a

---

[24] The chariot pursuing a new and narrow path becomes a little chariot in a meadow (3. 18); to leave the track of his song (*orbem* 2. 1, *gyros* 3. 21) becomes mere error; *turba* becomes not a contemptible or adoring crowd (1. 12, 21, 2. 10) but the turbulence of the mid-sea which his little barque should avoid (3. 24; the use is deliberately striking, cf. D. R. Shackleton Bailey, *Propertiana* (1956), 140 f.). The *libellus* is not now more lasting than the pyramids (2. 17 ff.), but something to be read in a bedroom (3. 19 f.).

lesser alternative, not artistically the greater. The initiation
now takes place (literally) which was only about to take place
(figuratively) at the start of the prologue.[25] This emphasizes
that, despite its being set in the past, for the reader the second
part of the prologue essentially follows the first, as one would
expect. We cannot read the sequence backwards and take the
first part as elaborating the consequences of the second. The sequence, then, is one in which strident self-praise is followed by
humiliation and by a cooler and more moderate stance towards
the author's poetry. We certainly cannot read the first poem in
isolation as an absolute assertion of the author's beliefs about
literature. Yet the sequence as a whole is not exactly a moral
tale of punctured pretension. When Propertius becomes a dramatic character, he does not totally explode his utterances as
author. (And even in Book 4 the astrologer does not altogether
have the last word.) The second part of the prologue plays with
and mitigates the vaunts of the first, but does not entirely destroy them. The notes of pride are not quite drowned in the
overall effect of the prologue, and we feel a certain sense of a
rich and conflicting compound.

It is in his last book of *Odes* that Horace turns to use directly
the forms and utterances of Callimachus.[26] In Books 1–3 of the
Odes he had avoided such dramatic fiction, and had employed
his own conventions to express the (supposed) inappropriate-
ness of his life and talents to lofty themes. In particular, he had
spoken of his playful Muse: the more transparent Muses are his
patrons throughout, not, save in abnormal contexts, Apollo.[27]
Book 4 contemplates, and deliberately modifies and alters, conventions in Books 1–3. The last poem begins with Apollo's
warning to the poet not to sing of battle; his sails are small (15.
1 ff.). The placing is meant to surprise: the device for opening a
work is used to close one, and the poem follows a particularly
grandiose martial ode. With abrupt and ingenious diversion of
the commonplace, the poet turns to Augustus' achievements of

---

[25] *ingredior* in 3. 1. 3 means primarily 'begin', because of the infinitive; and note 5 f.

[26] *Sat.* 1. 10. 31 ff. had applied the forms of Callimachus and Ennius in a humorous
and unexpected direction (against the employment of Greek words in Roman satire).
Humour, however, is a normal characteristic of such passages.

[27] Apollo is alluded to at the very end (3. 30. 15): more pride is found in the frames.
1. 31. 1 f. are ironically inflated. For the incompatibility of Horace's Muse and grand
subjects see especially the closes of 2. 1 and 3. 3, and 1. 6. 10, 2. 12. 13.

peace. He ends with a picture of himself and other Romans singing, in Horace's usual environment of drink, on military and patriotic subjects.[28] The opening gesture of the isolated poet is changed for a more public pose; there is a feeling that the poet renounces his habitual stance of separated individuality.[29] The quasi-Callimachean attitude, briefly struck, is not maintained.

In poem 3 Horace takes up another element in Callimachus' prologue, the personal. He begins by alluding to Callimachus' lines on the Muses' care for those they look on when young (fr. 1. 37 f., cf. also Hes. *Theog.* 82 f., Callimachus' model). The poem, however, develops unexpectedly. The long opening, and the models, lead us to expect a generalized statement about any poet beloved by the Muse; but Horace moves instead to himself and his own region of Tibur.[30] The individuality derived from Callimachus takes on an intensely concrete quality. At the same time pride and glory appear. Envy, too, has diminished (16)—envy is a popular theme of Callimachus'. The last sentence of the three in the poem develops thus.

> . . . o mutis quoque piscibus
> donatura cycni, si libeat, sonum,
>
> totum muneris hoc tui est
> quod monstror digito praetereuntium
> Romanae fidicen lyrae;
> quod spiro et placeo, si placeo, tuum est.   (19–24)

> . . . O Muse, you who could given even dumb fishes the voice of swans if you were to wish it, it is entirely through your gift that passers-by point me out with their finger as the player of the Roman lyre: that my breath, my inspiration finds favour, if find favour it does, is your doing.

The design of the whole sentence throws the emphasis warmly onto the Muse. At first the poet discusses his own part with lavish modesty and humour. In what follows, however, he seems to be allowing his glory to appear through the rhetoric of renunci-

---

[28] L. 27 goes with l. 28; the participial clause suggests the whole Roman people, but the rest has a particular though unspoken reference to Horace.

[29] 4. 2. 45 ff. involve a related movement, as regards Horace's poetry. 50 ff. are not meant to include Iullus.

[30] Cf. Kiessling–Heinze on l. 10.

ation. But the last line beautifully reasserts humility.[31] The poem moves expressively between pride and modesty, with a quality of particular mellowness. It endears us to the author in his concreteness, warmth, and delicate manipulation of tone. Callimachus' regret at old age itself, which appears in some degree elsewhere in this book, here gives way to content and satisfaction. Hostility and polemic almost disappear. Horace in all his work has constantly involved the reader in the movement of his career, and the progress of his life: we feel a peculiar pregnancy in this moment. It is the poet's utterance about himself that matters.

In Ovid's use of the Callimachean material, both fiction and reality are employed with striking boldness. The *Amores*, in their second edition of three books, have an introduction to each book, and an epilogue to the first and last. The epilogues show proud assertion; the prologues are comic fictions, in which Ovid plays wholly unserious roles. The epilogue to Book 1 presents what is formally a reply to Envy. The conception derives from Callimachus (including *H*. 2. 105 ff.); but Ovid defends himself simply as a poet, not a particular kind of poet, and he includes every sort of genre in his defence. The first poem narrates how Cupid forced the poet to write love-elegy, not epic. But any serious conflict of genres is averted by the presentation of the difference in grotesquely concrete terms. The distinction between elegy and epic is here that every other line in elegy has one less foot; this distinction is used to make absurd both the form of narrative and the poet's commitment to his chosen manner. Cupid 'is said' to have removed, with a laugh, one foot from Ovid's second line (3 f.). The poem ends

> Musa per undenos emodulanda pedes.

> O Muse who must be turned into song in eleven feet at a time.

The narrative comically inverts the standard form and makes not the god but Ovid deliver the long speech (in protest at Cupid's action). His crossness is both fantastic and foolish;

---

[31] *placeo*, though stronger than modern English 'please', is essentially a mild and relatively humble expression; it is here qualified even before all is attributed to the goddess (contrast the prouder statement *Epist*. 1. 20. 23 and even *Sat*. 2. 1. 83 f.). Kiessling–Heinze's note is amiss.

Cupid responds with five words and an arrow. The first person is made to heighten the humour by its formal self-mockery; but we are far even from the suggestion of real artistic modesty.

The first poem in Book 3 shows a dispute between Tragedy and Elegy for the allegiance of Ovid. The basis of the poem stands unusually close to reality. Ovid went on to create tragedy: the epics of Propertius and Horace were never written. But the fiction of the poem is particularly absurd and parodic; and the poet is concentrated on enjoying it. He plays with historicity (8, 33) and self-reference (37 f., etc.), and he relishes the drama, including his own tact within it. As author he goes beyond Callimachus in formal distance, and presents a speech of defence (by Elegy) but does not make one; we are to be interested rather in the handling of the fiction itself. The last poem lauds Ovid very directly; it places him in an actual environment of time and place. The poet, like Callimachus, marks his progress to another sort of writing (fr. 112); but in Ovid it is a grander one, and he reverses Callimachean imagery to describe his action.

> pulsanda est magnis area maior equis.   (19)

> My new horses are large, and must stamp in a larger place.

the final couplet runs

> imbelles elegi, genialis Musa, valete,
>   post mea mansurum fata superstes opus.

> Farewell, my unwarlike elegiacs, merry poetry, a work that will survive and endure after my death.

The first line ('Farewell ... poetry') suggests a wistful affection for the lesser genre; but the final line with a bold movement turns even this to pride.

The first poem of Book 2 presents another narrative of abandoning epic. Aesthetic terminology is used—the thunder of grand styles (cf. Call. fr. 1. 20), the softness of elegy; but the terms are removed from aesthetics and turned into fantasy ludicrously wild and reality obtrusively concrete. Writing about the war of gods and Giants, Ovid held Jove's thunderbolt in his hand; he dropped it at a greater thunderbolt, his girlfriend's closing of her door to him (15 ff., *amica* 17). But the hard doors were softened by elegy.[32] Within the fiction Ovid cuts not a modest figure but an impudent. The treatment of Ovid in these framing poems is not primarily a matter of nice poise and delicate fluctuations. We are struck rather by the audacious vigour of the poses and of the contrasts between them; and so it is with the levels of seriousness and reality.

The *Fasti* as a whole come much closer to Callimachus than do the *Amores*: they are a Roman equivalent of the *Aetia*. However, Ovid presents the work as a paradox and a surprise. Thus in the prologue to Book 2 we hear:

> nunc primum velis, elegi, maioribus itis. (3)
>
> Now for the first time, my elegiacs, you proceed with larger sails.

The imagery is associated with grand works one avoids; yet this poem is an imitation of the *Aetia*.[33] This prologue marks the astounding change in Ovid's elegy from his poems of love; yet he plays on the opposition between epic subject-matter and this poem, genre, and writer (1. 13, 2. 125 f.; 2. 9 ff.). Certainly, Ovid has practical reasons for aspects of his presentation: he wishes to show that he is now reformed. Yet the actual manner of his poetry here involves a large element of play with genre and with himself. This element is greatly strengthened by the prologue to Book 4 (which deals with the festivals of April). Venus is invoked, April being her month; she sports with the poet about his love and his poem.

> 'Quid tibi' ait 'mecum? certe maiora canebas.' (3)
>
> 'What have you to do with me?' she said. 'Certainly you were singing just now of greater things than love.'

The author is elusive on his being in love himself; the character fervently professes undying loyalty to Venus in his poetry.

> tu mihi propositum, tu mihi semper opus. (8)
>
> You are always my subject and my poem.

---

[32] *elegos*, 21; for *lenis* characterizing elegy (22) cf. Prop. 1. 9. 12.

[33] Compare and contrast with 2. 3 *Trist*. 2. 548. The composition of the *Fasti*, and in particular the time of the prologue to 1 and the original place of the prologue to 2, are matters which for our purposes may be left on one side. The whole stands in a form Ovid wished to be read.

At the same time, we learn, this is a grander and more patriotic
work (the poet will turn next to Augustus). Ovid's warmth towards Venus, and the goddess' delicious laughter when he alludes to his love, produce a drama of delectable charm and
lightness. Although the poet refers to his youthful life and
poetry with pointed care, the whole gives no feeling of frantic
self-defence. The encounter with Venus recalls forcefully
encounters in earlier works.[34] The point is not principally
apologetic. The echoes serve chiefly to heighten the sense of
interplay between true biography and poetic fiction, and to
bring out the unusual delicacy and peacefulness of this scene.

The opening of Book 4 takes up the beginning of Book 3,
where Mars is invoked for the book on his month March. The
god of war no less than the goddess of love is made to seem out
of place at first: Venus asks in Book 4 what Ovid has to do with
her; Ovid imagines Mars asking what a poet has to do with
him, 'quid sit cum Marte poetae' (3). The idea that Mars is
naturally alien to poetry and art involves a little sly mischief,
given the existence of epic poetry on war. Ovid makes a point of
his asking Mars to come unarmed; he proceeds to a highly erotic account of Mars' lying—unarmed—with the mother of
Romulus. In 2. 9 ff. Ovid had stressed that he could not carry
arms himself. These connections with the prologues of Book 2
and Book 4 surely suggest a certain play with the nature of his
poetry and of this poem. To make the prologues to 3 and 4 a
pointed and genuine assertion of Callimachean poetics would
be to miss the tone and mood of the passages. And to see Ovid
as attacking epic and martial values would be historically
implausible, when he wishes to conciliate Augustus; we should
also have to tear the poem into sincere and insincere portions or
voices. Rather, our attention is concentrated on Ovid's play
with himself, and we are to enjoy the light-hearted detachment
with which Ovid handles his life and his work.[35]

The relation between convention and reality is made to take
on a particular force in the poems from exile. In his book-
length appeal to Augustus, *Tristia* 2, Ovid looks back on his

---

[34] In verbal detail compare 16 *'coeptum perfice' dixit 'opus'* with Love's *'propositum perfice' dixit 'opus'* (*Rem.* 40) and 15 *mota* with *mota dedit veniam* (*Amores* 3. 1. 69, of Tragedy).

[35] The dialogue that actually takes place with Mars at 3. 167 ff. enhances the sense
of lightness and play.

past failure to write epic (313–44). The perspective of time is
Callimachus' own, and Ovid, like Callimachus, dramatizes his
apologia as an answer to accusation (327). But we find here no
toying with fictions. The section diverges from ordinary poems
on avoiding epic through the notes of 'real' regret heard in the
lines which surround the formalized modesty and courtliness
(315 ff., 341–4). In *Tristia* 4. 10 the poet looks back over his life.
The close has various connections with Callimachus' treatment
in fr. 1 of poetry, the Muses, and the miseries of old age (fr. 1.
31 ff.). Ovid writes of the Muse who consoles him:

> tu nos abducis ab Histro,
> in medioque mihi das Helicone locum.   (119 f.)

You remove me from the Danube and give me a place in
the middle of Helicon.

Here the dream in the *Aetia* (see *AP* 7. 42. 5 f.) is used to make
convention and poetry boldly transcend the pain of reality.[36]

Callimachus' germ continues to produce crops long after
Ovid (the prologue of Nemesianus' *Cynegetica* (3rd c.) gives a
striking example). We have seen enough, however, to confirm
that aesthetic theorizing and aesthetic self-defence are not at all
the primary objects of such passages; that the authors are much
more concerned with manner and effect in writing about themselves, with movements and compounds of tone, with the interaction of fiction and reality, with the use of other speakers and
of narrative levels. This suggests already a strong interest in
tone and form, and invites us to look rather in this area for the
most significant contact between the two groups of poets.

That aspect we shall consider by looking at a few works in
some detail. This approach is to be preferred to the rapid consideration of many works or poets. Our object requires, not a
superficial list of imitations and common features, but an
attempt to explore in more depth the whole character of one or
two large works or groups of works which have clearly been
much influenced by Hellenistic poetry. This will give us an
impression of how the two literatures are related in general

---

[36] By contrast, in *Pont.* 4. 2 Ovid turns into sourness Callimachus' picture of the
Muses' continued love. They are *solacia frigida* (45) 'a chill source of consolation', and
they have treated him ill; his powers fail. The language of initiation is transferred to the
epic poet Severus (47–50); Virgil's pattern too grows poignant.

terms. We shall look at some of the 'long poems' of Catullus, and the *Metamorphoses* of Ovid. We shall also glance very swiftly at the works of Virgil. With Catullus, however, we must first ponder some larger questions concerning literary history and aesthetic principles.

Should we see Catullus and his fellows as inspired by the precepts of Callimachus to bring about a great revolution in Roman poetry? One may begin by speaking of Catullus' own poems on poetry. Two of these associate bad poetry and extreme fertility (22. 3, 95). The *Annales* of Volusius are twice execrated (36, 95): epic poems on historical events were the sort of work Callimachus contrasted with his own (fr. 1. 3 ff.). The end of poem 95 by implication extends the abuse into a larger principle.

> parva mei mihi sint cordi monimenta ⟨∪ – ⏑⟩
>   at populus tumido gaudeat Antimacho.

> May my love be for the little works of my friend Cinna; let
> the mob delight in swelling Antimachus![37]

Even here the general evaluation of small and big is suggested only obliquely; but the final line alludes to Callimachus' dislike for the wordy poet Antimachus (fr. 398). Clearly, then, these poems make use of attitudes derived from Callimachus. Catullus' utterances on poetry do differ from Callimachus' in avoiding generalized statement and argument; attention is more tightly fixed on particular contemporary poets, good and bad. Distinctive also are the great playfulness they often show and the fantastic extravagance of feeling they often affect. Poem 35 creates a girl who is madly in love with a friend of Catullus' because she has read the start of his poem on the Great Mother (a theme not without bizarre connotations). The comic conception springs formally from a play on *venuste* at the end (17). This is a standard term of praise for the poem 'beautifully' begun, but it suggests the name of Venus. Poem 50 amusingly assimilates to erotic infatuation Catullus' own feeling for the poetry of a different colleague.[38] In poem 14 bad poets are spoken of as if they might kill, like poison, Catullus or his friend.

---

[37] Should we possibly read *sunt?* The wish does not seem very natural.
[38] See Macleod, *Coll. Essays*, 171.

Such material is difficult to use historically. The poems themselves seem primarily interested in playful and concrete abuse and praise, more than in theories about poetry as such. Plainly Catullus and his friends were greatly influenced by Hellenistic models; it is a somewhat different question how far they really viewed that influence in terms of their own conformity to a creed, and quite another how adequate such a view would be for describing the actual relationship. What may certainly be doubted, however, is the value of these poems as evidence for a fundamental change in Roman poetry. Catullus clearly thinks well of his friends; but the play with ardent emotion does not enable us to push behind the poems to a mood of revolutionary fervour from which they overflow. We find the same affectation of abandoned feeling—again arising from a pun—when Catullus speaks of bad oratory (poem 44). The poems make no obvious claims for the originality of Catullus and his friends. We are not particularly invited to infer that they stand alone against a world of barbarous poets untouched by Hellenistic poetry. In any case, such an inference would not accord well with the external evidence.

For Roman poetry the first half or so of the first century BC is still more obscure than the fourth century for Greek.[39] We cannot possibly make the negative assertions which would be required to establish that the poetry of Catullus and his colleagues was fundamentally novel. Even the very little that we do know suggests that they shared not a few of their interests with earlier and unallied authors. Earlier writers too seem to have been eager to appear learned and to narrate abstruse stories.[40] Cicero felt little proximity to or sympathy with the poetry of the younger writers Catullus, Calvus, and Cinna.[41] Yet, as is well known, some of his lost poems look distinctly reminiscent of the narrative poems of Cinna and Calvus in

[39] In the second half of the 2nd c. we have numerous fragments, mostly short, from the satirist Lucilius (still active in 123), and a good many from the tragedians Pacuvius (still active 140) and Accius (still active 104). The lyric poet Laevius, represented by 31 fragments, may belong in the region of 143 (cf. L. A. Holford-Strevens, *LCM* 6 (1981), 181 ff.)

[40] Cf. N. B. Crowther, *CP* 66 (1971), 246 ff., *LCM* 5 (1980), 181 ff. The debt of Lucilius to Callimachus has not in my view been well established.

[41] *Att.* 7. 2. 1 (SB 125), *Tusc.* 3. 45; the former passage is discussed by R. O. A. M. Lyne, *CQ* NS 28 (1978), 166 f.

general concern.[42] The Callimachean design of the *De Consu-latu Suo* was pointed out above. Cicero's translation of Aratus, a poet praised by Callimachus, shows an interest later shared by Cinna (fr. 11 Morel, accompanying a copy of Aratus or of a translation by Cinna himself). Not only the extensive fragments of Cicero's rendering, but the considerable fragments of his other poems (about 172 hexameters) show a refinement of metrical technique which matches that in Catullus' longest poem.[43] And indeed, there is no special reason to think that Cicero introduced these elements to Rome himself: he is a life-less poet.[44]

It is impossible, then, to create a satisfactory picture of the literary background to Catullus' poetry: we know so little of his immediate predecessors and his contemporaries, both in Latin and in Greek. We are hampered accordingly in discussing his relation to the poets who have concerned us. But clearly they exercised a strong influence directly; if that influence was strengthened or distorted by other poets, that need not be fatal to our inquiry. For our concern is not so much to recover the working of a historical process as to observe actual relations and differences between the poems. Even without a proper knowledge of the background, this should help to illuminate Catullus' works.

We shall deal here with some of the 'long poems' 61–8, since it is in them that the impact of the Hellenistic poets is most pal-pable. We may note that it would be mistaken even numeri-cally to regard poems 61–8 as a deviation from the main body of the author's work. These poems (1,120 lines) more or less equal the other two divisions of his poems put together (1,167 lines: epigrams 319, short lyric poems ('polymetrics') 848). It

[42] *Alcyones*, fr. 1 Morel = p. 236 Soubiran, cf. *SH* 750 (Nicander fr. 64); *Glaucus* pp. 5 f. Soubiran, though the use of septenarii seems questionable.

[43] See Soubiran, 101 ff. One need not necessarily see such refinement as springing from close imitation of Hellenistic poets. Features which characterize Callimachus are not taken up by Catullus: thus the proportion in 64 of word-end after the fourth spon-dee is extraordinarily high (see Skutsch, *Annals of Ennius*, 47). Respect for Hermann's Bridge ought not to be thought a particularly Callimachean feature, since it is typical of all Greek poetry (Catull. 64 is not long enough to show more than respect). Cicero's 'anticipation' of the Neoterics is usually found something of a puzzle.

[44] It is not on account of his purely poetical merits that he is the only poet we know much about in the first half of the century. (Most of his fragments are quoted by him-self.)

would be arbitrary to decide that these latter divisions present the essential Catullus; and it would be false to oppose the shorter poems as emotional and sincere to the longer as cold and contrived. Catullus' work is much more deeply unified, despite important differences in the types of poem (a word will be said on this unity later). It should be remarked that the long poems themselves present us with different genres: 61 is a lyric hymn, 64 a narrative in hexameters, 68*b* a personal poem in elegiacs, and so on. There seems to me very little positive reason to think that Catullus wished these poems to be seen as a group.[45] But these diverse creations display characteristic concerns in art.

Let us look first at poem 65, which Catullus sent to accompany a translation of Callimachus' *Lock of Berenice*. The Hellenistic influence is not at its most patent here, but the poem forms a good starting-point. Its twenty-four lines carry a single sentence. In an 'although' clause (1–4) Catullus says he is too distressed to write an actual poem; then, in a long parenthesis, he explains this by telling of his brother's death (5–14); finally, he reveals that he is, however, sending the translation, and he dwells in a simile on the embarrassment he would have been caused by forgetting his addressee's request. The structure offers an extreme of artificiality.

Callimachus and Apollonius in particular often complicate their sentences with parentheses, some lively intrusions, some erudite explanations which deliberately hold up the narrative or discourse with arch pedantry. AR 2. 987–992 (on the Amazons) is a particularly extended instance of the second type. Catullus' longer parenthesis is explanatory, but it explains Catullus' grief (4, 15); and it moves into passionate and personal emotion. In the course of it he abandons his address to his correspondent and apostrophizes his beloved brother. The point of interest to us here is not simply the personal reference of this emotional language, but the place of that emotion within the artificial structure of the poem. The startling disruption of the syntax when the parenthesis began was not an expression of passionate feeling. Even within the parenthesis Catullus rises to his impassioned involvement from relatively detached exposi-

---

[45] Even the view that Catullus ordered the whole corpus of his poems (see T. P. Wiseman, *Catullan Questions*, 1 ff., etc.) appears to me to rest on weak arguments.

tion,[46] and he then moves somewhat away from that intensity. This second movement takes place in the following lines.

> numquam ego te, vita frater amabilior,
> aspiciam posthac? at certe semper amabo,
>   semper maesta tua carmina morte canam,
> qualia sub densis ramorum concinit umbris
>   Daulias, absumpti fata gemens Ityli.   (10–14)

Shall I never see you again, my brother, dearer to me than life? No; but assuredly I shall always love you, always sing songs of sadness at your death—such songs as she of Daulis (i.e. the nightingale) sings beneath the branches with their thick shade, as she laments the death of Itylus slain.

With the expressive repetition of 'always', the poet strikingly moves from utterances of passionate simplicity and directness to art (songs) and a simile; this employs, in the second line, recherché and somewhat distancing language.[47] The progression fits into the larger shape of the work. Catullus claims that emotion prevents him from writing poetry—but this is a poem.[48] In it the emotion is made subordinate in structure and syntax to a courteous and controlled exposition. This is not merely a pun on 'subordinate': after the parenthesis the 'although' clause is weightily cast aside, as the address to the correspondent is formally resumed; the sentence, its tensions now resolved, wanders into a second simile, charming and aloof.

A Hellenistic quality has rightly been felt in this simile.[49] Catullus' (potential) embarrassment is compared to that of a girl who has concealed in her bosom a love-token, an apple, from her fiancé. As she leaps up to greet her mother, the apple rolls out. The incident has an air of smiling comedy, and involves a world from which the male poet and addressee stand

---

[46] Note the appearance of geographical lore with *Rhoeteo* in 7; the picture in 6 combines pathos with distance.

[47] The names are in various ways unusual—although the allusions are not nearly so obscure as in Parth. *SH* 646 on the same subject. The simile also alludes to Homer, *Od.* 19. 518 ff.

[48] Such play is frequent in Ovid's poems from exile; cf. also Hor. *Epist.* 1. 1. 10.

[49] Wilamowitz, *HD* ii. 304 f. Most of the examples he quotes from Apollonius are actually more engaged.

detached. The girl is called *miserae* 'unhappy creature' (21) and her blushing face *tristi* 'sorrowful' (24); but the epithets feel inappropriately strong, and mark the actual distance in the poet's voice, and the actual triviality of the misfortune presented now.

We thus have a remarkable interplay in the poem of artifice and emotion. These are here conflicting elements, as the author makes clear, but they are organized into an elaborate whole. They modify and complicate each other: this is thoroughly Hellenistic. But the extremes of artificiality on the one hand and of passion on the other make the poem seem much more lavish and extraordinary, less balanced and poised.

Poem 64 combines extravagant artificiality in structure with extravagant passion and elevation. The poem affects to be a narrative in hexameters; but unlike the hexameter narratives of Calvus (*Io*, frr. 9 ff. Morel) and Cinna (*Smyrna*, frr. 6 f. Morel), it deals ostensibly not with a story but with an incident, the marriage of the mortal Peleus and the immortal Thetis.[50] The first thirty lines explain how the marriage came about; ll. 31–49 describe the people of Thessaly coming to the wedding. In ll. 50–75 Catullus describes the figure depicted on the wedding couch, that of Ariadne just deserted by Theseus. At l. 76 he digresses from describing the artefact (*nam perhibent* 'for they recount that ...') and tells of the relationship before the desertion (Ariadne helped Theseus in his slaying of the Minotaur and escaped with him). Still digressing (116 ff., 124 *illam perhibent* 'they tell how she ...'), he relates the speech Ariadne made when she had been deserted, a little after the scene depicted on the couch. The speech lasts for seventy lines. The digression continues (202–11), soon proceeding to a further digression (*namque ferunt* 'for they say that ...', 212); this gives Theseus' arrangements with his father, through which Ariadne's curse on Theseus was to cause his father's death. It consists mainly of a speech the father had made when Theseus departed (215–37). The whole digression (76–250) is closed briefly, and we return to a second scene on the couch, showing Bacchus coming to marry the forsaken Ariadne (251–64). Thereafter the human guests depart from the wedding of Peleus and Thetis, and the

[50] The Hesiodic *Wedding of Ceyx* presumably had more story: cf. R. Merkelbach and M. L. West, *RhM* NF 108 (1965), 300 ff.

gods arrive (278 ff.). After a brief and peculiar catalogue, we
proceed to a song of prophecy delivered by the Fates at the
wedding; they tell of the deeds of Achilles, the son to be born
from the marriage (323–81). As soon as the song is closed, the
poet contrasts that time, when the gods often mingled with
men, and the present, when sin has driven the gods from our
sight (384–408).

The organization of the poem shows a wilfulness quite without parallel in extant Hellenistic poetry.[51] It takes characteristic devices and employs them in a fantastic manner. The device
of placing a story in a frame occurs in Callimachus' fifth and
sixth *Hymns*, and elsewhere: there a myth is told in a non-
mythical setting. The story of Theseus and Ariadne comes
within another mythical narrative. It seems to a certain degree
the foremost part of the poem: it is given in full, and it alone
seems like a story and engages our responses as such. Yet this
status is infringed by the song of the Fates which occurs after it,
and in particular by the impassioned outbursts of the poet at
the beginning and end, occasioned by the marriage. There are
many central connections between the two stories or parts in
theme; but the uncertainty of subject in concrete terms should
not be anxiously argued away. The framing is not that of a
character telling a tale: that device can give a very plain sense
that the frame is in fact subordinate, despite its narrative
status.[52] Rather, most of the story is told in a digression within an *ecphrasis* (description of a work of art). Apollonius sometimes draws attention to digression (following Pindar); he thus
disrupts immersion in the narrative by calling notice explicitly
to its procedures. But this happens at the end of minor excur-
suses (1. 648 f., 1220). Different is Catullus'

> sed quid ego a primo digressus carmine plura
> commemorem . . .?   (116 f.)

> But why should I still wander from my first song and tell
> more . . .?

This comes only a short way into the digression, which Catullus

---

[51] This would be so even if R. F. Thomas were correct in his (unlikely) conjecture on
the *Victoria Berenices* (ch. 2 n. 41). One must be quite clear that Catull. 64. 50–266 do
not form a continuous description of the couch.

[52] See p. 160 for this term.

then proceeds with, and *primo carmine* 'my first song' suggests primarily, not the tale of Peleus and Thetis, but the interrupted *ecphrasis*. The whole device of digression in fact produces a weird sense of distance and detachment from this prolonged 'explanation'. This particularly strident and frustrated intrusion (116 f.) occurs just before the vast and passionate soliloquy of Ariadne, which seems at the time the emotional climax of the tale. Catullus here takes Medea's indignant and persuasive speech to Jason at AR 4. 355 ff. (p. 125), and produces from it an extreme display and evocation of emotion: our attention is concentrated purely on the speaker's feeling, not on her manipulation of another person. The altering movements of the three sections of the speech give us a sense of extended exploration and experience:[53] Medea's speech is much less mobile. The placing of speech and intrusion brings to a point the sense of strangeness.

There is also the question of the historical status of the narrative. Greek choral lyric sometimes presents a myth narrated in detail with a 'they say' or the like which distances author and reader from the tale.[54] The poet stands much more to the fore in that genre than in narrative poems; and at that earlier period the device carries relatively little suggestion as to truth. Apollonius seldom uses the device save with subordinate digressions or explanations (4. 984, 1. 172, *al.*). Occasionally he employs it in his main narrative, to disrupt and distance, notably at 2. 854 (see p. 93 above). In such places the story becomes a remote tale, recounted by the author, not a narrative of which the truth is accepted within the conventions created by the work. Callimachus' reference to Xenomedes at fr. 75. 53 ff. (see p. 30) has a related effect. The device, however, is not in the least commonplace in poetry before Catullus.[2] The first sentence of poem 64 begins

[53] Note especially the pathos of the first close at 161–3, where Ariadne shows the extreme subservience of wishing to be Theseus' slave, even though assisting, it is hinted, in his marriage to another (cf. Lyne on *Ciris* 443). The second close occurs at 186 f. For the movement of the speech cf. F. Klingner, *Catulls Peleus-Epos* (*SBAW* 1956. 6), 51 ff.

[54] Cf. especially Pind. *Ol.* 7. 54 f. (gods, as at *Isth.* 8. 46).

[55] It is taken over by later Roman poets, perhaps from Catullus; in Virgil, however, a historical significance is apparent (and the device is frequent in historians). It is not found in what we have of Ennius. Even if it was used by earlier poets than Catullus in narrative, the effect in this poem is still striking. On the subject cf. Norden on Virg. *Aen.* 6. 14.

Peliaco quondam prognatae vertice pinus
dicuntur liquidas Neptuni nasse per undas
Phasidos ad fluctus et fines Aeeteos . . .

Pine-trees begotten on the summit of Mount Pelion are
said to have floated once through Neptune's clear waters
to the river Phasis, and the land of King Aeetes.

dicuntur 'are said' is here the main verb of the sentence; the
whole story is emphatically distanced at the start.[56] *quondam*
'once', the second word, probably serves a related function. At
the end of the paragraph, however, the poet plunges into an enthusiastic exaltation of that age. As our summary indicated
above, the device is particularly frequent in the tale of Ariadne:
this is appropriate for a digression, but the tale is distanced still
further. The first *nam perhibent* 'for they recount', accompanied
by *olim* 'once' (76), separates the narrative digression from the
ecphrasis; it is made to follow a passage where the writing shows
an intense involvement with Ariadne. The next *perhibent* (124)
is joined to the open acknowledgement of digression (116).
Again it marks a contrast with the mode of the *ecphrasis*, whose
matter it recalls; it governs a whole string of reported statements, which lead into the great speech of Ariadne. Once more
distance and emotion are confronted. The next 'they tell'
(*ferunt*, 212) again has an *olim* and again marks a digression;
this introduces the particularly moving speech of Theseus'
father Aegeus.

The combination of emotion with artifice and distance is
thus obtruded on our notice. It is not, however, confined to
conflicts of structure and passion or of distancing and emotive
passages juxtaposed. The matter becomes more complicated.
In order to approach these complications, we must start by
considering the narrator's appearance of involvement, which so
greatly promotes the extremity of emotion in the poem. The
most straightforward instances occur with Ariadne. The first
scene on the couch is described with a passion quite abnormal
in such *ecphraseis.* It is deliberately left unclear at first to what
degree this passion (61 f.; 69 f.) simply pictures the passion of
Ariadne; but the suggestion is that the poet too is sympatheti-

[56] AR 1. 18 is not at all the same.

cally involved (note the anaphora at 63–5), and he actually
bursts out at the end of the passage with an exclamation.

> a misera, assiduis quam luctibus externavit
> spinosas Erycina serens in pectore curas ... (71 f.)

> Ah! poor girl, sent wild with unceasing grief by the god-
> dess of Eryx, who sowed thorny distress in her heart ...

The tone is warm and strong, although characteristically the
reference to Venus and the picturesque *spinosas* 'thorny' somewhat mitigate the appearance of involvement.[57] The narrative
digression ensues, as we saw (76 ff.). Before long Catullus
employs in it Apollonius' apostrophe to Eros (4. 445 ff., p. 128).
He heightens the air of personal engagement with three exclamations and his opening:

> heu, misere exagitans immiti corde furores ... (94)

> Alas! you who so wretchedly stir up wild passion with
> your savage heart ...

There follows shortly the place where the narrator pretends to
break off this mere digression (p. 302). Yet that sentence goes
on:

> ut linquens genitoris filia vultum,
> ut consanguineae complexum, ut denique matris,
> quae misera in gnata deperdita laeta⟨batur⟩,
> omnibus his Thesei dulcem praeoptarit amorem ... (117–20)

> (Why should I continue and tell more:) how the daughter
> abandoned the face of her father, the embrace of her sis-
> ter, even the embrace of her mother, who, unhappy
> woman, delighted in her daughter with hopeless infatua-
> tion; how before all these she chose the sweet love of
> Theseus ...

The writing, even as it stresses the syntax of rejected digression,
suggests the poet's emotional concern. (The next sentence does
much the same.) These instances, however, in themselves are
relatively simple, although they help to form an elaborate texture. More complicated are the beginning and end of the poem.
   After the poet has recounted (1 ff.) the antecedents of the

---

[57] Cf. Calvus fr. 9 *a virgo infelix*; but the future makes it possible that the line was not
spoken by the narrator. Note the apostrophe to the heroine, presumably, in Cinna fr. 6
(for *a* cf. also Parth. *SH* 609(a) 12).

marriage, mostly in a style of some detachment, the writing
suddenly swells into rapture with the mention of Peleus' and
Thetis' love and extraordinary marriage (mortal to immortal);
the poet addresses with enthusiasm the heroes of that vanished
time.

> o nimis optato saeclorum tempore nati
> heroes, salvete, deum genus! o bona matrum
> progenies, salvete iter[um
> vos ego saepe meo, vos carmine compellabo,
> teque adeo eximie taedis felicibus aucte,
> Thessaliae columen Peleu, cui Iuppiter ipse,
> ipse suos divum genitor concessit amores.
> tene Thetis tenuit pulcherrima Nereine?
> tene suam Tethys concessit ducere neptem
> Oceanusque, mari totum qui amplectitur orbem?   (22–30)

Hail, heroes, you sons of the gods, born in an age of the
world so greatly to be desired! Hail, I say again, you
splendid offspring of your mothers ... You I shall often
address in my song, and especially you, Peleus the bul-
wark of Thessaly, outstandingly blessed with a felicitous
union; you to whom Jupiter himself, the very father of the
gods, yielded his own beloved. Did Thetis indeed embrace
you, that most lovely Nereid? Did Tethys and Oceanus
permit you to marry their granddaughter, Oceanus whose
waters encompass the whole world?

The distance established in the opening sentence now becomes
something with emotional significance, and something of particular complexity. It makes an essential part of the narrator's
feeling. The mingling of men and gods is for him an extraordinary event, as is stressed by the rhetoric, but yet through its
extraordinary quality it is a cause for delight and rapture. The
poet's address to the Argonauts is borrowed again from Apollonius (4. 1381 ff., 1773 f., pp. 136, 141). Here, however, the role
of poet is not made to run strangely against the tones of engagement through the suggestion of fiction and self-contained art.
The reader is given a more unified sense of the poet's personal
involvement with the remote subjects of his song.[58] The questions at the close both express feeling and convey the distance of

---

[58] Cf. 65. 11 f. (above, p. 300), Call. *H.* 3. 137 ff. (p. 69).

the narrator's world from that happy age (not any historian's doubt). The stress on distance gives the poet's posture an air of contrived magnificence and conscious artifice. The whole passage seems simultaneously direct and lavish on the one hand, yet on the other artificial and mannered.

The end of the poem takes these aspects further. Here another 'for' (*namque*, 384) moves us into a new region. The contrast between present and distant past is prepared in the closing summary of the Fates' song: *quondam* 'once' (382) had been similarly used at the very start of the poem. The mingling of men and gods in the past is rendered in a warm and stately sequence of three descriptions, each introduced by *saepe* 'often' (387, 390, 394). The account of the present describes the wickedness of men now in a huge *postquam* clause ('since the time that ...'); in this clause a general statement about corruption on earth is followed by a monstrous stream of particular evil actions. All this is taken up finally in the main clause:

> omnia fanda nefanda malo permixta furore
> iustificam nobis mentem avertere deorum. (405 f.)

> The wild and evil confusion of all things, right and wrong, together, has alienated from us the righteous mind of the gods.[59]

This structure conveys not only the extremity of wickedness but the passion of the poet. The crimes are formally set in the (post-heroic) past, but they suggest actions very much at home in the modern Rome of moralistic imagination. At any rate, they certainly belong to a world of which the poet feels himself to be part, and his final *nobis* 'us' firmly and poignantly involves him in the age he condemns.[60] Distance of time again becomes the focus of emotion, and it draws with it a sense of distance from the gods. That, however, is only the beginning of the complications.

It is often and rightly stressed that the favourable attitude to

[59] Only this understanding is tolerable. To make *perfudere* etc. the main clause after *postquam* introduces a strange relation between *tellus scelere est imbuta nefando* and the particular crimes: strange in logic and in expression. It also spoils the run of the argument and trivializes the effect of *postquam*. The correct view is taken by Kroll and by Goold.

[60] It does this even if the word itself means 'the human race', without chronological distinction. Contrast the formal detachment of Aratus 100 ff. or of Sallust's preface to the *Catiline*.

the age of myth which is implied in the last section is hard to reconcile with certain features of the earlier part. The most important of these features is the horrifying description in the Fates' song of the slaughter of Polyxena at Achilles' tomb (362–70). This scene comes very shortly before the final section, and its physical power makes it particularly resonant and repulsive. The irony is heightened by the poet's emphasis on the truth of the prophecy: for the certainty of the song is intended to enhance the joyful praise of the future son.[61] The *quare* 'hence' with which the Fates then urge on the union is stridently jarring in effect. Theseus' desertion of Ariadne is disturbing too. Not only is it heartless, it involves the breaking of oaths, and Ariadne calls on the gods' justice to punish it; Jupiter assents (204 ff.). But the killing of Polyxena has more of the primary horror which attaches to appalling acts like those ascribed to the present in the closing section. However, we need to define more closely the effect of this conflict. To regard the rest of the poem as completely subverting the last section seems no more satisfactory than to ignore the dissonance.[62] The vehemence of the depiction of decline resists an ironic reading. Its formulations do not produce pointed and striking ironies in the light of the rest of the poem. The rhetoric does not in itself seem absurd and overdone, extravagant though its pictures are in historical terms. The section fixes our attention on the horrors and the bleakness of the present age; this emphasis does not sort well with an approach which stresses the falsity of the attitude to the past.[63]

Rather, one must look again at the handling of voices and narrative levels. We have seen how the story of Ariadne is distanced. With Achilles the story is presented from a strange perspective: the Parcae narrate as future what belongs for us to the

---

[61] Cf. for the sequence *testis ... testis ... testis* especially Cicero's eulogy of Pompey, *Imp. Pomp.* 30 f.

[62] The former seems in practice to be the view of those who stress the clashes. J. C. Bramble, *PCPS* NS 16 (1970), 41, employs litotes, but appears actually to take this position.

[63] One would find very suspect any claim that Catullus' own moral laxity makes these lines unlikely to be serious. One could scarcely use supposed biographical evidence to undermine the text of this poem, and in fact many of Catullus' other poems require for their effect conventional reactions. Thus incest, treated here, is treated also in 88. There the lavish condemnation in 5 f. is not to be mistaken; it is not infringed by the humour of the close.

past. The device is characteristic of Hellenistic poetry;[64] here it acquires new strangeness, because the distance of the past is so much emphasized in the poem. The account is placed in the mouth of speakers as different as possible from the poet (they are described, 305 ff.). The narrative status of this discourse is marked out by the extraordinary use of a Theocritean refrain:

> currite ducentes subtegmina, currite, fusi.   (327, 333, etc.)

> Run on, you spindles drawing out the thread, run on.

This is a formal song, not the poet's utterance. The last section of the poem begins by making this very song an example of the vanished contact between gods and men. That section marks an unbridgeable division between the distant past and the poet's presence; his own voice now controls the rhetoric. Our attention comes to be concentrated on the present and its grimness; the events so richly evoked become remote and unreachable. In these circumstances, there is not simply a flat and merely puzzling contradiction. Instead, the tones which dominate as we read the last section are those of the poet's voice, in its extravagant and impassioned description of decline. However, one is also conscious of a discordant and disconcerting descant which gives the whole a sense of complexity, disharmony, and weirdness. One must acknowledge also a sense of surprise in the movement taken by the poem, a sense of shifting direction which confuses our overall response, and leaves us uncertain if we should have one, or if we should simply accept what is being offered at the moment.

The poet's signal audacity is not to be proved by the adduction of parallel audacities. But the general character of his proceeding should not surprise us. We shall find instances elsewhere in Catullus of the uneasy conjunction of diverging emotions: such conjunctions play an important role in his work.[65] Unexpected development is also very characteristic of

---

[64] Cf. L. Deubner, *Kl. Schr.* 240 ff. and see pp. 47, 60, 187, etc.

[65] A delicate example occurs in poem 61. The prevailing mood is one of auspiciousness and delight, but this is lightly complicated by discordant suggestions of the bride's pitiable experience. See e.g. 56 ff.; note the deliberately inappropriate consolation of 82 ff.—contrast 66. 15 ff., Claud. *Carm. Min.* 25. 124 f., and in general cf. Catull. 62. *cupidam* in 32 is probably proleptic, *amatis* in 46 f. is a very doubtful conjecture, and *timens* in 54 may well be corrupt. 169 marks a new departure; at 209 a diminutive is applied to the baby, when hitherto diminutives had been reserved for the bride.

the poet: even the tale of Ariadne shows an unexpected change that complicates our reactions. Catullus has ingeniously and forcefully adapted Apollonius' treatment of lovers forgetting (above, p. 128): as Theseus forgets Ariadne, so he will forget his father's commands and thus cause his death.[66] The father's pathetic speech infuses for us an element of crude brutality into the retaliation we had expected to find merely satisfactory.

The strong and disconcerting close has perhaps some affinities with unsettling closes in Plautus and Terence. But the effect is here related to a structure more than Hellenistic in its deviousness, and the effect is of tonal richness and discord rather than of a bold theatrical stroke. Emotion and artifice stand in an elaborate and disquieting relationship.

Poem 63 does not exhibit so extreme a wilfulness of structure as poem 64; but form is of great importance to the effect of the poem, and that effect is more complicated than is usually supposed. The poem describes how Attis, filled by the frenzy associated with the exotic cult of Cybele, left his homeland and came to Phrygia; there he castrated himself. He makes an enthusiastic speech (12–26). The madness presently vanishes; Attis addresses his homeland in despair and contemplates the hideous change in his life (50–73). Cybele hears, and sends one of her lions to drive him into the woods, where he remains for the rest of his days as Cybele's servant. The poet begs the goddess that her madness may not befall him.

There is no reason to think the poem a translation of a Hellenistic work.[67] However, the poem has obvious connections with Hellenistic poetry. Hermesianax, an early Hellenistic poet, told a version of Attis' life (*CA*, pp. 105 f.); meetings of a lion and a Gallus (castrated priest of Cybele) afforded the theme for some notably ambitious epigrams.[68] Callimachus used the galliambic metre, in which Catullus' poem is written: it appears to have

---

[66] Despite Sch. Theocr. 2. 45/46a, it seems implausible that Theseus is presented as literally forgetting Ariadne through divine action. The reader must naturally suppose that heartlessness is in question (for *immemor* thus (58, 123) cf. e.g. 30. 1). Ariadne, who certainly supposes this, takes up the same words (135, etc.), and Jupiter's assent to Ariadne's curse (200 f.) will reinforce the notion.

[67] See D. Mulroy, *Phoenix*, 30 (1976), 61 ff., an important discussion of Hephaestion 12. 3.

[68] See Gow, *JHS* 80 (1960), 88 ff. The cult also inspired a friend of Catullus to project a *tour de force* (Catull. 35).

been used only for poems dealing with this cult. The anonymous galliambic lines Call. fr. 761 are likely to be Hellenistic, for Hephaestion's examples are never known to be post-Hellenistic. The metre was used also by Varro, an older contemporary of Catullus. Catullus' use of the metre is strict, and displays considerable virtuosity. His handling of style within the metre displays elegance even as it evokes hysteria. Already one finds a characteristic union of excess and dramatic force with conspicuous artistry in the poet.

The structure of the poem has much in common with that of Theocritus 26, and may reasonably be associated with Hellenistic influence. Theocritus' poem (above pp. 160 ff.) begins abruptly with a narrative of the scene of Pentheus' destruction; this is followed by the reaction of the professedly pious poet. The narrative does not mention the impiety of Pentheus which led to his madness and occasioned his doom; it is probably alluded to in the closing passage. The agency of Dionysus in Pentheus' death also appears explicitly only at the end. Catullus' narrative too begins from the catastrophe, without explanation.[69] It is only in the third section that Attis' disobedience is mentioned, and that allusively:

> mea libere nimis qui fugere imperia cupit. (80)

> he who with great audacity wishes to escape my commands.[70]

Here too the agency of Cybele appears for the first time openly. The section (74–90) brings about a considerable change in our reactions. Hitherto we have been principally involved in Attis' experience as felt by him; now we are introduced to a different, and remoter, plane of reality with Cybele's brief and incisive

---

[69] P. Fedeli, in *Studi di poesia lat. in on. di Traglia* (1979), i. 149 ff., connects the feature with the supposed genre, the poem being, he says, an 'epyllion'. But he is right to sense Hellenistic connections.

[70] My general argument is not impaired if l. 80 refers to the second speech, not the past. Yet that speech regards Attis' future service as inevitable, so that the language of l. 80 seems out of place even from Cybele's viewpoint. *Imperia* too makes the other approach more attractive; it points us to the tradition of Attis' defying Cybele's ordinance (of chastity) and being punished through his castration of himself (Ovid, *Fasti* 4. 223 ff.; Lucr. 2. 614, allusive like this passage). For the indignant present cf. Catull. 44. 21 (with Kroll); but *cupit* may be a contracted perfect. *Fugere* includes the notion of lasting escape. The companions pose little real obstacle; they are there to enable contrasts between isolation and community.

speech. We view the whole matter from a fresh angle—and our eyes are focused on the lion. The tragic character bewailing his fate by the sea becomes an undignified figure in a grotesque incident. The wild terror and flight of the Gallus does not merely have ludicrous connotations (see the epigrams mentioned, especially Dioscor. XVI): it is inglorious in itself, the more so as we know that the lion is not to harm Attis. Madness (78 f., 89) now reduces itself to physical farce. One must note the placing of the lion's attack, and the arrangement of the section to confront fierce lion and terrified eunuch. The last line of the narrative is stark and final, but in its context uncompassionate: one contrasts Attis' own horrified contemplation ('Shall I now be called a maidservant (*famula*) of Cybele?', 68).

> (ubi ...) teneramque vidit Attin prope marmora pelagi,
> facit impetum. illa demens fugit in nemora fera.
> ibi semper omne vitae spatium famula fuit.   (88–90)

> When the lion saw soft Attis by the glistening sea, he made his attack. She (the emasculated Attis) flees, out of her mind, into the wild forest. There for ever, for all the rest of her life, she was a maidservant.

Thus we are distanced from the central figure and from the action; the story now becomes bizarre, even absurd.

In the earlier part of the poem touches of the bizarre had not been absent; but they had merely tinged a predominantly tragic atmosphere. The sequence of madness, irreversible act, and realization and lament, occurs in several tragedies (*Bacchae, Hercules Furens, Ajax*); it has an intrinsically devastating quality. Attis' first speech is full of the irony of ignorance and illusion.[71] The second speech is especially reminiscent of the high-wrought passion and rhetoric of Roman tragedy.[72] However, it shifts in its impact. The huge anaphora at the end (*ego* 'I', 63–71) takes up and exceeds the extended and wild anaphora at

[71] *Veneris nimio odio*, 17, where *nimio* is ambiguous (for the sense 'excessive' in Catullus cf. e.g. 68. 137); *hilarate erae citatis erroribus animum*, 18, compare the third section, and note the hint at folly in *erroribus*; *decet*, 26, supremely inappropriate; *aliena quae petentes · velut exules loca*, 14, poignant, cf. the second speech.

[72] Cf. with 50 ff. Ennius 81–93 Joc. (Andromache's lament). *dolet ... paenitet* at the end accumulates impersonal verbs of emotion in a fashion characteristic of the tragedians (e.g. Accius 471 Ribb.). In general the *Bacchae* of Accius may be a more important model than the *Bacchae* of Euripides.

the end of the first speech (*ubi* 'where' 21–6, note 72). It is itself no less wild, and pushes the reader perhaps slightly beyond the edge of simple emotional involvement. The passage begins:

> quod enim genus figurae est ego non quod obierim?
> ego mulier, ego adolescens, ego ephebus, ego puer. (62 f.)

> What species of shape have I not encountered? I am a woman, I have been a young man, I have been a youth, I have been a boy.

The need for verbs and tenses in the English destroys the stunning accumulation of identities around the apparently single self. One feels an exhaustive Ovidian ingenuity in the exploration of the paradoxical calamity. No less Ovidian is the later 'ego mei pars' (69) 'I am part of myself'—that is, Attis has lost some of his body and so is now reduced to a mere part of the former whole. The combination of ingenuity and extravagance again moves us away from straightforward sympathy. The poet's use of the feminine gender for Attis after his emasculation produces a particularly weird and piquant effect; *notha mulier* 'counterfeit woman' (27, narrative) presses on the paradox. And after all, the central event is not straightforwardly and obviously tragic, like slaying one's children: it can seem, and is made to seem, bizarre and intriguing.[73]

The final three lines take still further the distancing and disengagement of the third section.

> dea, magna dea, Cybebe, dea domina Dindymi,
> procul a mea tuos sit furor omnis, era, domo.
> alios age incitatos, alios age rabidos. (91–3)

> Goddess, mighty goddess, Cybele, goddess who art mistress of Dindymus, far away from my own house may all thy madness stay, lady. Drive others in wildness, drive others in madness.

Not only has Cybele now emerged into prominence: Catullus shows himself as directly concerned with her, and he removes

---

[73] The treatment of castration in Herodot. 8. 104–6 has a very different flavour.

our attention from the myth to him.[74] The poet's air of nervous concern for his safety and the whole device of the prayer for himself evoke Hellenistic poetry, which cultivated the device, and the *persona* of anxious piety, in order to bring about distance (above, pp. 89, 161, 220; cf. pp. 28 f., 70 f.). This example is certainly not to be taken as more serious in effect than those in the Greek writers. The notion of Catullus' castrating himself in ritual frenzy stands still further from what can be contemplated with seriousness by poet and by reader. The poet's voice bizarrely imitates the manner associated with Attis. The opening address in particular exhibits an extravagance that would be grotesque if intended to make a serious impression. One is also detached by the nervous crudity of the final call. The entry of the poet removes the poem altogether from any straightforward emotional response.

The structure of poem 68*b* shows an extreme of artifice and strangeness: one should not be so eager to reduce it to an orderly object that one hides its puzzling nature. The poem begins, in my opinion, at l. 41, ll. 1–40 being a wholly separate poem.[75] From 41–69 the poet speaks of the aid given him by the addressee, who put his house at the disposal of Catullus and his mistress for their adultery. In 70–2 he describes Lesbia's first coming, and proceeds as in a simile to tell of Laodomia, who lost her young husband Protesilaus in the Trojan War (73–130, fifty-eight lines, as against the first thirty-two). The last thirty lines resume the description of Lesbia, tell of the poet's resignation to her unfaithfulness, and go on to praise the poet's friend once more.

The section on Laodamia puzzles by its length and status. It cannot be regarded as the foremost part of the poem, to which a

---

[74] It distorts the movement of the whole poem to make it into a hymn (cf. Wiseman, *Catullus and his World* (1985), 198 ff.). For this an address or reference to the god would be expected to open the poem. L. 9 is naturally taken as apostrophe, probably too as mimesis of the characters' excitement.

[75] Attempts to unite or even relate them invariably require strained explanations or elaborate stories, and there is little positive reason to do so. It may be noted in passing that the conjecture *mi Alli* in 11 makes an elision at a point in the line where Catullus never has one (first syllable of the sixth foot). No endeavour to have these poems addressed to the same person seems very convincing. Uninviting too are the endeavours to deal with the identity of 20–4 and 92–6; this is readily explained if 68*a* was written just as a letter in poetry, 68*b* as a more permanent work for wider consumption (41 ff., 151 f.).

personal frame gives special force, as in Theocritus 11 and 13, or Callimachus' twelfth *Iambus*.[76] On the other hand, to appreciate it only for the light it throws on Catullus' relationship would be to devalue, for example, the changing roles of the poet within the passage. Indeed, both the distance and the warmth in his tone as narrator suggest to the reader the independence of the section. Its impact cannot be neatly confined to its bearing on the liaison. Its numerous digressions and expansions heighten the constant sense of wilful movement beyond the subject in hand. However, it would not altogether suffice to invoke the example of Pindar, and to suggest that there is nothing awkward in the formal priority of praise and the actual prominence of other matters besides, the praise making only a part of a structure. Pindar himself is wilful, of course; but here Laodamia is accommodated in the form of a simile within a narrative—or rather, of a simile which itself encloses a gigantic digression (77–130). The whole device suggests strong subordination. The use of a fresh narrative as simile within this subordinate narrative (109–16, on Hercules) enhances the sense of perversity. One feels this the more when two fresh similes follow on the same theme, before the whole vast comparison is taken back to Lesbia.[77] As in poem 64, the status of the individual parts appears as one reads not only strange but unclear.

One's feeling of disorientation is increased by the seeming difficulty of explaining formally the comparison between Laodamia and Lesbia. Catullus speaks of Lesbia coming to the house where he awaited her

> coniugis ut quondam flagrans advenit amore
> Protesilaeam Laodamia domum ...   (73 f.)

as once Laodamia, afire with passion for him, came to the house of Protesilaus her husband.

The basic action produces a bare point of comparison—coming

---

[76] Works like Antimachus' *Lyde* (*IEG* ii. 37 ff.), most probably Hermesianax' *Leontion* (*CA*, pp. 96 ff.), and perhaps Phanocles' *Erotes* (*CA*, pp. 106 ff.) would seem to have presented series of narratives within a personal frame. There is no reason to imagine that the relation of frame and narratives was problematic, and indeed it seems unlikely.

[77] *sed tuus* in 117 is taken up by *sed tu* in 129, which is followed directly by the comparison of Laodamia (not, of course, Protesilaus) to Lesbia.

to a house for a first act of love; but style and rhetoric make one look for an expressive purpose too. The picture of Lesbia as she comes should be in some fashion enhanced. It is easy to find unstated contrasts; but the surface of the exposition ought also to be sustained.[78] One thinks at first that the point of comparison is the passion which each feels for her beloved. The passion of Laodamia is stressed at the start, and forms the dominant subject throughout the section. Catullus suppresses entirely the supernatural events of the myth (such as the brief resurrection of Protesilaus). Before the digression on the death of Catullus' brother (91–100), Laodamia's sensual desire is depicted in strong language, though there is only a hint at its exceptional intensity. Protesilaus departed before the winters of one or two years

> noctibus in longis avidum saturasset amorem. (83)

> had sated her greedy passion in the long nights.[79]

longis 'long', *avidum* 'greedy', *saturasset* 'had sated', are placed forcefully together, displaying but not transmitting the voluptuousness. After the digression, the language grows warm and engaged. Catullus now addresses Laodamia throughout. He resumes:

> quo tibi tum casu, pulcherrima Laodamia,
>   ereptum est vita dulcius atque anima
> coniugium. (105–7)

> Through that event, fairest Laodamia, your husband was torn from you then, sweeter to you than life and breath.

He then builds up her passion in a long and extravagant series of comparisons. The extraordinary strength of the feeling emerges forcefully. The sexual element is still prominent, and

---

[78] To have only the bare point of likeness would give an effect quite unlike Catullus. This is a matter of his whole style, but I list for the sake of comparison his other similes (some may well have escaped me): 2*b*, 7. 3 ff., 11. 22 ff., 61. 17 ff., 21 ff., 34 f., 87 ff., (187 f.), 62. 39 ff., 49 ff., 63. 33, 64. 61, 89 f., 105 ff., 239 f., 269 ff., 353 ff., 65. 13 f., 19 ff., 68. 57 ff., 63 ff., 109 ff., 119 ff., 125 ff., 97. 7 f.

[79] So that, the sentence goes on, she might be able to live after his death (84). This addition presumably hints at her eventual suicide. Cf. Jerome, *Jovin.* 1. 45 (probably from Seneca) 'cantatur ... Protesilao noluisse supervivere'. See for the legend Roscher, *Lex. d. Myth.* iii. 3157 ff.; add for Euripides' play P. Oxy. 3214.

still brings with it an element of distance, but the depiction now embraces a lasting and unconquerable attachment to the beloved. It presently becomes clear that passion cannot be the point of likeness with Lesbia. On the one hand Lesbia turns out to exhibit no such attachment, and on the other hand the phrase with which we return to her could not be used in regard to passion when sexuality has been so much emphasized. That phrase—'aut nihil aut paulo cui tum concedere digna' (131), Lesbia 'deserved to yield first place to Laodamia either very little or not at all'—that phrase can only in the circumstances be referred to beauty.[80] Yet Laodamia's beauty has received very little emphasis from the poet (only the address quoted, which is primarily sympathetic). Our expectations are bewilderingly frustrated; and the frustration does not merely tell us something about Lesbia. It also marks how different a degree of involvement the reader experiences in the poem with these two women.

We see Lesbia only as a vivid image of divine and glittering grace, in two brief passages (70–2, 131–4); we see her in motion, before the act of love.

> quo mea se molli candida diva pede
> intulit et trito fulgentem in limine plantam
>   innixa arguta constituit solea ...　　　　　　　　(70–2)

There my white-skinned goddess came with soft motion, placing her gleaming foot on the worn threshold, and leaning her weight as she did so on her sharp-sounding sandal...

molli 'soft' and *candida* 'white-skinned' are deliciously juxtaposed; the picture then grows sharper and more concentrated. In the second passage a white-skinned, gleaming Cupid darts about her. Our primary impression in both passages is of visual beauty; Lesbia's emotion is unstated and, in a sense, absent for the reader. Even after the second depiction of her coming, we learn only the difficult fact of her promiscuity; her actual feelings are not presented. Laodamia has not been seen in these

---

[80] See Fordyce on the order in this phrase; Cic. *Att.* 13. 29. 1 (SB 300) is a good example. Cf. also Ariosto, *Orl. Fur.* 41. 15. 7.

visually striking images. We have been shown her extraordinary emotion and sexual desire, conveyed in the most lavish fashion; we have also felt strong sympathy for her suffering.
The poet addresses her warmly; he does not address Lesbia.
The reader's contact is much more powerful with the mythological woman in the subordinate section. It is right to compare
our reactions here, for one woman is formally supposed to be
there for the sake of the other. This divergence is not of course a
question of mannerism alone: our sense of relative distance
from Lesbia has something disturbing about it, which the
poet's apology for her in fact underlines.

It may be said that, despite all this, Catullus' own emotion is
the important thing in the outer sections, so that the reader
feels his strongest personal contact there. This is true, to a certain degree; but even in the treatment of Catullus there appears
the same tension between formal subordination and actual
effect. The reader is most forcefully and starkly involved with
Catullus' emotion in the digression within the digression, on a
subject unrelated to the main theme of the poem, on the death
of his brother.

> quaene etiam nostro letum miserabile fratri
>   attulit. ei misero frater adempte mihi,
> ei misero fratri iucundum lumen ademptum,
>   tecum una tota est nostra sepulta domus ...   (91–4)

To my brother, too, Troy brought a wretched death. Oh!
Brother taken away from wretched me! Oh! You light and
joy taken away from your wretched brother! With you
our whole house is buried ...

It is an extraordinary stroke, the sudden outburst in l. 92. The
only address in the poem hitherto has been the opening address
to the Muses, full of artifice and convention. Here the mode of
address influences the poetry. For the only time in the poem,
Catullus uses ejaculations. They fire a pattern of strong and
stark lamentation; in this, *fratri* 'brother' and *miserabile*
'wretched, pitiable' from the preceding statement are given a
new power with *frater ... fratri ... misero ... misero*. The pattern
arouses feeling for Catullus very directly and emotively, and
drives home the fundamental bond. The strong repetition in

94–6 of parts of *tu* 'you' stresses the primary significance for Catullus of the person's death and life.[81] The poet, we are intended to feel, is not describing but reacting, giving direct expression to overwhelming feelings. In the first section of the poem, on his experience in love, Catullus describes his feelings in the past (and that past has by the end of the poem been markedly separated from the present). After the second section, on Laodamia, he describes feelings in the present, but not passionate and overwhelming feelings: rather, uneasy and generous restraint. Our sympathies are certainly engaged, but the response is more delicate and less abandoned.

If we do compare the evocation of Catullus' passion in the first section and of Laodamia's in the second, we feel decided resemblances in manner. In both, allusive erudition is forced on us at points, in both similes at once express and remove us from the feeling. These features are still more strongly marked in the second section, above all in the simile which compares Laodamia's deep passion to the deep gulf dug by Hercules in Arcadia (109 ff.). 'quale ferunt Grai' (109) 'a gulf like that which the Greeks say ...' introduces a direct reminder of Hellenistic poetry (presumably) and a pedantic, quasi-Hellenistic obtrusion of lore.[82] The whole subject is bizarre and obscure. When Catullus wanders on to better-known elements of Hercules' story (113 ff.), he becomes devious in expression and full in superfluous detail; the passage has a very Callimachean quality. At the same time, the section on Laodamia conveys the passion with an extravagance and a stress on extremes that dwarf the earlier section on Catullus and his love. Its very size is a measure not only of its artificiality but of its lavishness. The language has also at some points a directness and an emotiveness which have no match in the earlier section. Ll. 106 f., for example, were quoted above; the simile on Hercules itself returns to Laodamia with impressive intensity:

---

[81] 93 and 94–6 appear, more or less identical, as 68*a*. 20 and 22–4. The lines may, or may not, originally have been written for that poem (indeed *cuius* in 68*a*. 25 feels somewhat awkward). This would not imply that Catullus originally wrote 68*b* without them (cf. J. Wohlberg, *CP* 50 (1955), 45 f., etc.). Whatever the history of the lines, Catullus has deliberately placed them here as part of this poem, and we are fully justified in considering their effect within the whole.

[82] Cf. C. J. Tuplin, *CQ* NS 31 (1981), 119–31 on the source, and note 68*a*. 33.

sed tuus altus amor barathro fuit altior illo.   (117)

But your deep passion and love were deeper than that pit.

Also, one may perhaps say, the extremity of Laodamia's experience (the loss of a newly wed husband) involves our sympathies
at a deeper level than the experience of Catullus in love. However, his feelings have primacy in that they are his and they
belong to the material which forms the basis of the poem. Laodamia is a mythical woman, from whom the poet sometimes
distances us. The poem again confuses us, inviting and then
partly resisting an ordering and subordination of its elements.
For the reader, the strongest passion and the most wilful artifice
do to some degree join together, above all in the central section.

Artifice, elaboration, ornament, never vanish from the
poem. Even in the lines on Lesbia's (other) infidelities we have
a startling comparison with Juno (138–40). Those lines, however, give most sense of a reality appearing painfully naked,
with the layers of gorgeous and concealing costume removed.
We proceed from the glorified past of the first union with Lesbia to the unsatisfying conditions of the present, and to the sordid truth of adultery—a subject which can arouse strong moral
reaction even in the poetry of Catullus. But should one see the
passage simply as destroying the illusions of the rest of the
poem? That standard view seems not only excessively straightforward but definitely unsatisfactory. Firstly, it would undermine the personal purpose of the poem; it would be difficult to
think that purpose unhistorical or a matter of irony. If the love-
affair is in reality wretched, the friend's service was no great
benefit; if the meeting should be seen merely as an act of squalid
adultery, the friend's act would be made to appear far from
splendid.[83] This is not merely an abstract inference: the poem
goes on directly after this passage to place the friend with the
antiquis piis (154) 'the pious men of old', and to say that life is
sweet to Catullus while Lesbia lives (160). Besides this, it is difficult to read the poem before the passage as romantic illusion. It
is certainly unattractive to take the middle section, on Laodamia, as representing Catullus' thoughts at the time of his first

---

[83] The *Digest* enjoins that he who lends out a house (or indeed a friend's barn) for
adultery should be treated *quasi adulter* (48. 5. 9 ff.).

union with Lesbia. Catullus in effect begins his narrative digression by introducing that *persona* of nervous piety which was
mentioned as a Hellenistic means to creating distance.[84]

> nil mihi tam valde placeat, Ramnusia virgo,
>   quod temere invitis suscipiatur eris. (77 f.)

> O maid of Rhamnus (Nemesis), may I not so set my heart
> on something rashly undertaken against the will of the
> gods [like the marriage of Laodamia undertaken without
> sacrifice]!

This surely makes it clear to the reader that we have not a
stream of consciousness but an organized artefact. It is no less
awkward to read the poem up to 135 ff. as depicting a writer's
vain attempt to make his experience poetic.[85] The division pro-
posed between that writer and the real author is of an implausible kind, in this poem at least. In fact, the author carefully
avoids committing himself to an idealized view of Lesbia's
character and emotions or of the morality of the affair. It is
much more a question of manipulating and surprising the
reader than of deluding himself. In 135 ff. Catullus shows something more moving than mere self-deceit. He expresses clear
recognitions, but draws them into an attitude which we are
meant to find appealing and poignant. He displays his own
niceness; separates himself from the reaction of anger; and
closes the section with a gesture of appalling pathos.

> quare illud satis est, si nobis is datur unis
>   quem lapide illa diem candidiore notat. (147 f.)

> For this reason it is enough for me if it is only the days that
> she gives to me which she marks as days of happiness.[86]

This section itself should clearly not be read as mere delusion
and pretence; and it does not simply undo what precedes and
follows it. Rather, we have again a discord, a collocation of jarring elements. The affair is wonderful and sordid, Catullus'

---

[84] Above, p. 314; cf. J. Sarkissian, *Catullus 68: An Interpretation* (*Mnemosyne* Supp. 76,
1983), 20. The flavour of such passages surely indicates that Thomas's understanding
of the sacrifice in 75 f. is mistaken (*HSCP* 82 (1978), 175 ff.). *eris* in 78 seems questionable.

[85] Thus Sarkissian.

[86] Contrast *satis est* of Catullus here with *non est contenta* of Lesbia at the beginning of
the passage.

position is happy and pitiable.[87] The last paragraph of the
poem (149–60) makes the discords particularly strident, as
Catullus extravagantly praises his friend and asserts his own
happiness in lavish terms. Again the conflicts in feeling are connected with the complex relation in the poem between artistry
and emotion. Besides this, the poem, we have seen, is not only
about Catullus' affair: the deviousness of the relation extends to
the whole structure and subject of the work. The extremes of
artifice and passion produce a singularly dense and difficult
poem. The range of tone and manner is greater even than in 64;
its richness and complexity give this poem its own kind of
monumentality.

We may end with poem 66, Catullus' translation of Callimachus' 'Lock of Berenice' (fr. 110). That poem was spoken by a
hair which Queen Berenice had promised to dedicate if her
newly wed husband returned from battle alive; the hair was
transformed into a star. The first half of the poem (1 or 9–38 in
Catullus) narrates the human events; the second narrates the
adventures of the hair, giving great space to the hair's expression of its feelings and rhetorical justification of its conduct. We
possess only fragments of the original poem, principally from
the second half. In those parts where we can compare Catullus
with Callimachus, it is evident that he has made his original
more grandiose and extravagant.[88] Naturally, a translation into
verse cannot be literal; but the character of the changes is still
significant. It does not follow that Catullus' poem is grand and
passionate in total effect.[89] In the second half of the poem the
fundamental conception is fantastic and delightful. Extremity
of language and feeling from the hair cannot be received
straightforwardly by the reader; the comedy and the sense of
distance are pushed to a point more abandoned and less elegant than in Callimachus. Callimachus has the hair say:

> οὐ τάδε μοι τοσσῆνδε φέρει χάριν ὅσ[σο]ν ἐκείνης
> ἀ]σχάλλω κορυφῆς οὐκέτι θιξόμεν[ος.   (fr. 110. 75 f.)

---

[87] The conflict between his present happiness, with Lesbia (160), and his present
unhappiness, at his brother's death (95 f.), should be seen as a further complication.

[88] One thinks of Plautus' treatment of Menander in the *Bacchides*, cf. e.g. *Bacch.* 498
'qui dedecorat te, me, amicum atque alios flagitiis suis' with Men. *Dis Exap.* 17 ἅπαντας
αἰσχύνει γὰρ ἡμᾶς τοὺς φίλους.

[89] Contrast W. V. Clausen, *HSCP* 74 (1970), 90 ff.

I am not brought pleasure by my being a star so much as I
am brought distress that I shall not any more touch Berenice's head.

It is distressed because it will be deprived of Berenice's new
unguents. Catullus has it say

> non his tam laetor rebus quam me afore semper,
>   afore me a dominae vertice discrucior.   (75 f.)

I do not rejoice at this so much as I am anguished that I
shall be absent, absent for ever from my mistress' head.

Given not only the basic situation but the hair's motive, the
couplet produces a more burlesque discord between passionate
expression and playful content.

It is likely that near the end of the poem Catullus has added
the ten lines in which the hair enjoins all wives to make an offering of ointment to it before marriage (except for the unchaste).
In the original the hair probably asked Berenice simply to add
some ointment for itself when she sacrificed to Aphrodite, with
whom the hair is associated.[90] It would thus gain some re-
compense for its loss of unguents on the queen's head. Catullus
creates a much more grandiose conception.[91] The strong
moral language used of the unchaste makes the interplay with
the fantasy the more preposterous. However, the warm and
solemn wish addressed to the brides for their happiness (87 f.)
does introduce for an instant a genuinely dignified note. The
tendencies in Catullus' treatment of Callimachus' poem show
in a small way the same desire we saw elsewhere, to produce

[90] On Aphrodite's relation to the catasterism itself cf. S. R. West, *CQ* NS 35 (1985),
61 ff.

[91] In P. Oxy. 2258 (6th–7th c. AD) there is nothing to correspond to ll. 79–88 in
Catullus. The popular explanation is that the papyrus, late though it is, presents an
earlier version of the poem, before it was adapted for its place at the end of the *Aetia* by
the addition of those lines. However, such a ritual would be very implausible, either as
a historical reality in Alexandria, or as a fiction by Callimachus which the poem is to
explain. (There are various possibilities for the actual subject of the *aition*, for past ritual
and play with *aitia* are both possible in Callimachus' work, especially Books 3 and 4.
Most likely it is the imagined addition made to Berenice's offerings to Aphrodite.)
Moreover, the disputed lines destroy an elegant connection, and make the queen's
offering a strange appendage, the final wish an abrupt resumption. For the mixture of
close translation and independent insertion compare the *Aratea* of Germanicus (Gain's
edn., p. 13) to say nothing of Plautus, or Chaucer.

conflicting extremes from Hellenistic devices and materials, and under Hellenistic inspiration.

One can only hint in the curtest fashion here at the connections between these poems and the rest of Catullus' work. There too emotion, structure, and art stand in complicated and often conflicting relations.[92] It is common in the shorter poems to find the most extravagant grandeur and passion of language applied to a trivial or fanciful subject. The resources of the poet's art are lavished on material which prevents a serious response to the emotion that art suggests; it leads instead to exuberant play (cf. e.g. 58*b*, 36. 11 ff., 25. 12 f.). On the other hand, elegant, obtrusive structures can often restrain strong emotion and pull against its straightforward effect, in various ways (cf. e.g. 70, 72, 8, 45).[93] Structure can also display and highlight the conjunction of conflicting tones and emotions in a poem (cf. e.g. 11, 88, 37). The interplay between artistry and emotion is fundamental to Catullus' poetry, and one might even regard the 'long' poems as the most ambitious and extreme realization of Catullus' poetic concerns.

The idea of tension or complexity in the relation of artistry and feeling must surely derive in large measure from the Hellenistic poets, for all the obscurities of the literary background. Catullus did not see in those poets merely erudition and arid elegance. In 64 the speech of Ariadne and the first outburst of the poet are drawn from Apollonius as much as is the explicit play with digression. In 66 the poet responds to Callimachus' use of feeling in an absurd situation, and pushes it further. The Hellenistic devices he takes over for distancing emotion (say at the end of 63) imply that there is an emotional element to be distanced, and Catullus employs them in that light. The use of structure to complicate is very plainly linked with the Hellenistic poets: the nature of the features exploited, and their effect, show such strong connections. But the extremity and extravagance which make Catullus so different might well be thought something Roman, in a sense: one thinks, indeed, of Plautus.

[92] E. Schäfer, *Das Verhältnis v. Erlebnis u. Kunstgestalt bei Catull* (*Hermes* Einzelschr. 18, 1966) approaches the relationship in an almost opposite way.

[93] 70 is inspired by Call. *Ep.* 25 Pf. (XI GP), and literary resonance itself further complicates the impact. The Hellenistic epigram clearly lies at the root of Catullus': see for a discussion O. Hezel, *Catull u. d. gr. Epigramm* (1932).

However, the basic complexities which Catullus magnifies spring in great part, it should be judged, from Hellenistic poetry. That poetry, then, made its impact on Catullus not through a cold and one-sided conception of its qualities but in and through its real complication and richness.

We come now to Virgil. The chapter does not afford room for an adequate treatment of his relation to Hellenistic poetry. I shall merely sketch as briefly as possible the nature of that relation, as I see it, in regard to each of his three works.

In considering the *Eclogues* it would be possible to concentrate on their relationship to Theocritus, the founder of their genre, and especially on the relation of passages in the *Eclogues* to their originals in Theocritus. The reader who came to the *Eclogues* having built up an independent and (in my opinion) a just appreciation of Theocritus would feel primarily that the model had been greatly changed. The elements of grotesqueness and bizarreness have been very much reduced; elements of grandeur and extravagance play a much larger part; we now meet a pastoral world which by turns is contrasted with, and absorbs, the world of contemporary reality (the city, politics, poets).[94] However, when one looks more broadly, one sees poems of which the artistic character has much in common with the poetry of the third century BC. Striking contrasts and strange complexities of tone possess the greatest importance, and these effects are heightened by structure. The effects belong in part to the book as a whole, with its palpable mixture of the relaxed, the lively, and the playful with the magnificent and the nostalgic. But they are no less salient in individual poems and passages. At the end of the prophecy about a child in *Eclogue* 4, Virgil contemplates with rapture the songs he will sing, if he lives, of the child's achievements. The poet would then defeat even Pan in competition (58 f.). What was a motif of crude religion in Theocritus' characters turns into an ex-

[94] To some degree Virgil is inspired by features in post-Theocritean pastoral: for Theocritus is the founder of the genre, not the exclusive source and model. There was certainly more of this poetry than we possess. The clear contrast of town and country in [Theocr.] 20 is obviously significant. The appearance of a long speech by Silenus in Page, *GLP*, no. 123 (Gow, *Bucolici Gr.*, pp. 168 ff.) suggests that the setting of *Ecl.* 6 draws on a tradition. [Mosch.] 3, the epitaph for Bion, will be significant for *Ecl.* 10. Theocritus' non-pastoral poem 16 (note 90 ff.) is probably of significance for the fusion of politics and pastoral in *Ecl.* 4.

travagant and audacious declaration by the poet; it mingles convention with personality.[95] But in what follows the poet suddenly changes tone and mood. He addresses the child with an adult's voice, tender, amused, and affecting to admonish. Strangely mixed in are suggestions of the child's apotheosis, and a bizarre reminder of the queasiness and tedium of pregnancy (61).[96] Play with childhood in this context of deity reminds one of Callimachus (pp. 64 ff.); at any rate, the complexity of tone and the interplay of conventions and of voices have a quality akin to that of Hellenistic poetry.

One might instance further, say, *Ecl.* 1. 31–9. Here we have first a speech from a rustic marked by unelevated Roman realities and by comic play with subjection to women. There follows at once a sentimental and fantastic picture of the effects caused by his brief absence from the country; the picture would surprise in genuine Theocritus. As to structures and their relations to tone, we have spoken already of the sixth *Eclogue* (pp. 284 ff.). The basic organization of *Eclogue* 5 seems grandly simple in force. It boldly confronts two songs, a lavish lament for Daphnis, recalling Theocritus, and an enraptured picture of his apotheosis. The framing complicates the effect of the poem. The poet suggests that the picture of apotheosis is perhaps simply the singer's fiction.[97] The close assimilates the dramatic frame with the singers to the actual poetic activity of Virgil (86 f.): one singer speaks of the second and third *Eclogues* (quoted by their openings) as songs of his own. Such play with reality and narrative status modifies the impact of the second song. The play again recalls Hellenistic poetry, for example the fifth *Hymn* of Callimachus. Everywhere, then, we see un-Theocritean elements and Hellenistic textures and effects.

The *Georgics* is in many ways the most Hellenistic of Virgil's poems. In my own opinion, the poem is not intended to offer a coherent and deeply felt view of life: aesthetic effect is almost

---

[95] Cf. Theocr. 1. 3 ff. (p. 147 above); [Mosch.] 3. 55 f., noted by Coleman, provides an impetus for this alteration.

[96] Cf. on the passage especially Nisbet, *BICS* 25 (1978), 70 f.; the admonishing plural *qui non risere* is meant to sharpen the incongruity, I suppose.

[97] The ambiguity of the repeated *tollemus ad astra* (51 f.) is unmistakable: we must feel the literal 'I shall raise him to heaven' as well as the idiomatic 'I shall exalt him with praise'.

everything.[98] However that may be, changing tones are vital to the poem; and the tonal effects have much in common with those of the great Hellenistic poets—much more than do the didactic poems of Nicander, which come between them and Virgil.[99] The very opening passage of the work handles praise of the ruler (1. 24 ff.) in a fashion reminiscent of Callimachus. The poet moves from grandeur to arch precision, stylized gesture and finally absurd elaboration. In its vastness and extravagant artifice the sentence (1. 24 ff.) makes to outdo the Hellenistic poets.[100]

The poem is pervaded by the contrast and interplay between tones in the poet's voice of warm involvement, wry detachment, stern exhortation, and ruthless pedantry.[101] The latter two in particular belong to the pose of teacher, which is sustained with a persistent sense of posturing and unseriousness. The poet plays too not seldom with his own air of passionate engagement (as in the list of wines, 2. 89 ff.). A couple of examples may illustrate some of Virgil's textures. In 1. 167 ff. the celebrated line 'si te digna manet divini gloria ruris' 'if you are to receive the full glory of the divine countryside' follows a didactic instruction to take forethought and precedes an essentially dry account of how ploughs are made. In 3. 284 ff. the poet, turning to speak of sheep and goats in the second half of the book, writes dramatically and intensely of his passion for this poetry (though already with a lurking hint of play). He proceeds at once to a sentence which begins with pomp and ends with diseases in the feet of sheep (295–9). The interaction of the lavishly poetic and the consciously prosy must be meant to feel strange and partly playful.[102] The first passage (3. 284 ff.) itself follows a piece of bizarre country lore—which closes a passage that is mostly fired by a Lucretian grandeur and sweep.

[98] Thus in my view the poet designs a visible contradiction between 'pater ipse colendi | haud facilem esse viam voluit' (1. 121 f.) and 'fundit humo facilem victum iustissima tellus' (2. 460).

[99] This poem will have had among its models poems like Nicander's *Georgica*; cf. also, perhaps, Page, *GLP* no. 124.

[100] The huge sentence of panegyric at Call. *H.* 4. 171 ff. has less caprice.

[101] The different 'roles' of the speaking poet are discussed by T. Oksala, *Studien zum Verständnis d. Einheit u. d. Bedeutung v. Vergils Georgica* (Comm. Hum. Litt. 60, 1978), 54 ff.

[102] The inclusion of 294, followed at once by 295, makes against any notion of an unintended failure to achieve elevation—a notion in any case unattractive.

In design Virgil strains to the furthest the pretence of impart-
ing information systematically. Aratus and Nicander seem to
follow prose sources closely; the digressions are very limited in
size (and number), save for the conventional myth (Aratus 98–
136, Nicander, *Ther.* 343–58). With Virgil one feels a constant
impulse to digress: all four books close with large digressions,
and the statutory mythical excursus is placed at the end of the
poem proper (4. 315–558). The sequence of the first book is
wildly unpredictable. The book suggests orderly patterns of
exposition and then wanders away from them. It does not at all
give the appearance of a systematic account of cereal farming,
or of a paraphrase of a prose treatise, however miscellaneous.
The didactic fiction is stretched to an extreme of artifice.

The *Aeneid* contains many elements which recall Hellenistic
poetry, but the impact made by the whole is utterly dissimilar.
This is chiefly because the handling of tone is so different. The
continuous endeavour for extremes of ὕψος, of intensity, elevation, sublimity, leaves little room (say) for play between levels
of seriousness.[103] The bizarre and the weird, for example, do
occupy an important part in the poem; but such moments are
generally raised into grandeur and do not involve the element
of detachment which they so often do in Hellenistic poetry.
Thus the metamorphosis of ships into nymphs at 9. 77 ff.—a
subject with which some playfulness would have been expected
in Callimachus or Apollonius—Virgil treats in the grandest
and most portentous fashion. This is not of course to suggest
that the poem lacks life and colour, or to neglect its poignant
moments of soft and langorous beauty. But the ethos of the
poem demands the radical transformation of much that is characteristically Hellenistic. The work forms to that extent an abnormal example of Roman procedures with Hellenistic
material. Apollonius is much used, but that does not make
against its being un-Hellenistic. There is nothing remarkable in
the use of this predecessor: the primary affiliation of the *Aeneid*

---

[103] Some exceptions: the cows in 8. 360 f. follow a treatment of strange perspectives
in time more solemn and more numinous in character (the interest itself is Hellenistic).
At 1. 405 ff. the characteristic frustration of Aeneas' emotions follows and darkens a
scene with a marked element of charm and lightness—particularly in Venus' disguise as
a figure like Diana. In that aspect too there is a Hellenistic quality (cf. AR 1. 742 ff.,
al.). R. Heinze rightly dwells on sublimity, *Virgils epische Technik*, 481 ff.; cf. now
Hardie, *Cosmos and Imperium*, ch. 6.

is to its genre, and Homer has such importance because he is the founder of that genre. Book 4, for which Apollonius is the primary model, brings no lowering in dignity and no intrusion of smiling or distanced ironies. Book 3 too uses Apollonius extensively, so that one cannot divide the Apollonian elements from the Homeric in terms of basic subject.[104] Callimachus will lie behind, for instance, some of the aetiology in the poem; but we can hardly call this a Callimachean epic because it displays such perfection and refinement of technique. These were no monopoly of Callimachus.[105]

The *Aeneid*, then, is a very special case. The essential nature of the poem forces out the effects which characterize Hellenistic poetry. In Virgil's other works we see a use of that poetry which follows something of the same lines as Catullus'. Their impact, however, seems to come a little nearer to that of the Hellenistic poets. Closer still in spirit and artistry come the *Fasti* and *Metamorphoses* of Ovid. It is the *Metamorphoses* that we shall consider here. That is likely to be for most readers the more familiar poem, and its use and adaptation of Hellenistic elements are especially intriguing. I should like to look first at some aspects of the whole work, and then at a particular part of it (the eighth book).

The basic conception of the poem is thoroughly Hellenistic: we have a series of stories which belong together through a recurring structural feature. The stories in Callimachus' *Aetia* (mostly) give rise to ritual practices; the stories in Ovid (mostly) involve a person changing into something else. A number of works had been written, some or all in verse, which collected tales of metamorphosis (*SH* 50, 378A, 636 f. (Parthenius), 749; Nicander, ed. Schneider, pp. 42 ff.). It is in the use of this form that Ovid shows both a deep affinity with the great Hellenistic poets and features more characteristic of their Roman followers.

---

[104] On Book 3 see F. Mehmel, *Virgil u. A. R.: Unters. ü. d. Zeitvorstellung i. d. antiken epischen Erzählung* (Diss. Hamburg 1940); on Book 4, W. W. Briggs, *Aufst. u. Niederg. d. röm. Welt*, ii. 31. 2, 958 ff., with literature. Perhaps writers on *Aen.* 4 should stress more the contrast between Jason's able and suspect handling of Medea at AR 4. 393 ff. (pp. 125 f.) and the honest tactlessness of Aeneas with Dido at *Aen.* 4. 331 ff. (*pietas* is becoming a somewhat limited value).

[105] E. V. George, *Aeneid VIII and the Aetia of Call.* (*Mnemosyne* Supp. 27, 1974) argues for an extensive debt to Callimachus in *Aen.* 8. 1–369; the atmosphere is very different.

It is often said that metamorphosis is not really important in
the poem.[106] This seems difficult to credit. Simply by providing
the structural principle of the work, it can scarcely fail to draw
the attention of anyone reading the whole poem. And it seems
very hard to ignore the prominence of the theme when half the
last book is devoted to a speech that depicts metamorphosis as
an all-pervading element of the universe.[107] The theme is
played with in other ways, particularly when the metamorphosis itself is less closely linked to its episode: the role of the theme
is not at all confined to the actual moments of transformation.
Those moments themselves are made singularly arresting,
either by detailed and vivid presentation of the amazing sight,
or by ingenious and witty exploitation of the differences and
similarities between person and thing. It is said that one cannot
respond with such emotion or sympathy to the metamorphoses
as to the human elements in the story.[108] But they are not less
important for that reason. That would require us to reduce the
poem to a series of straightforward and satisfactory short narratives. However, even in quantitative terms, a great deal of the
poem is not primarily of interest as story-telling (see below). It
certainly seems undesirable to simplify Ovid's manipulation of
narrative into a succession of good yarns when this requires us
to extrude the close, and the structural node, of the individual
story. In terms of the particular episode, the role of metamorphosis is to provide a bizarre and fantastic element which can
allow serious or straightforward elements to be distanced,
modified, or complicated. This cardinal preoccupation Ovid
pursues in many other ways throughout the poem; but the use
of the structural principle itself for such a purpose is eminently
characteristic of the *Aetia* and, in a different way, the *Argonautica*. This object is naturally promoted by the vivid strangeness
and the wit of Ovid's accounts of metamorphosis. But our reactions are also intrinsically different to a human being and to a
thing—especially when the difference is marked by a transformation. Thus Ovid can draw on very basic responses in producing his effects.

[106] e.g. E. J. Kenney in J. W. Binns (ed.), *Ovid* (1973), 145, and *CHCL* ii (1982),
430 ff.
[107] G. K. Galinsky, *Ovid's Met.* (1975), 103 ff., maintains that Pythagoras' speech is
intentionally boring, a very implausible proposition (and a rather superficial reading).
[108] Kenney in Binns, loc. cit. (n. 106).

These effects a pair of episodes will illustrate. Both stories form part of a sequence distanced by being placed on a different narrative level: they are told by the daughters of Minyeus (who are eventually transformed into bats). In Book 4 Leucothoe has been buried alive by her father for lying with the Sun; her secret had been divulged by Clytie, whom the Sun had loved before. The Sun with his rays breaks up the mound above her for her to bring her head up into the air (241 f.). The action is startling and impressive, uniting passion with divine power. It comes too late, however, and the god's vital heat cannot restore Leucothoe. The pattern of the failed rescue has tragic resonance; the divinity of the lover and the humanity of the girl are made to heighten the pathos. But then the god transforms the girl into a frankincense shrub. With the Sun's compressed speech 'tanges tamen aethera' (251) 'but at least you will touch the air', Ovid plays with the mode of death; and he removes the subject from tragedy and horror by laying weight on this artificial consolation.[109] The Sun has scattered nectar on the corpse:

> protinus imbutum caelesti nectare corpus
> delicuit terramque suo madefecit odore;
> virgaque per glaebas sensim radicibus actis
> turea surrexit tumulumque cacumine rupit. (252–5)

Steeped in the heavenly nectar, the body immediately dissolved; it made the ground wet with its fragrance. Roots were sent gradually through the earth, and a twig of the frankincense-bush rose up and broke through the tomb with its tip.

The metamorphosis begins with a beautiful though bizarre conception. But the appearance of the shrub, described with striking physical detail, focuses our attention on a very unhuman subject. There is a note of triumph in the final phrase; but it is a paradoxical one, and it is distanced by the difference between girl and bush.

Clytie the informer is metamorphosed too. The Sun refuses to come near her, and with her agonized grief and desire she

---

[109] The interpretation of Bömer (and others) fits the narrative less tightly and effectively, I feel. For *aether* in this sense see *TLL* i. 1152. 3 ff. The sequence 242–4 indicates that Leucothoe is still buried.

changes into a sunflower, still facing the Sun. There is certainly
something touching in the idea: *mutataque servat amorem* (270)
'even transformed she retains her love'. At the same time we
feel a distancing ingenuity. And the emphasis on *amor* 'love',
which closes and (256) begins the passage, accompanies a depiction of the distress as decidedly erotic and sensual in nature.
Clytie is not moved by remorse. Although the author affects as
it were to plead her cause to the Sun (256 f.), the pain does not
have a really tragic quality. The process of metamorphosis
further complicates the effect. Like many other metamorphoses, this one appears as an extension of the poignant abnor-
malities of grief; yet we feel a decided jolt as we move from the
description of human behaviour to neat and bizarre transformation.[110] The incredibility is heightened by the distancing
ferunt (266) 'men say'; it is taken up in the disbelief of some of
the mythical audience to this tale (272). Finally, the sense here
of one metamorphosis closely succeeding another disrupts the
flow of the story as such: we sense the structure busily intrud-
ing. This is reminiscent of Apollonius' technique with the
women of the Doliones (1. 1057 ff., above, pp. 94 f.). Both
metamorphoses, then, allow an elaborate handling and distortion of emotional elements.

The following story, by contrast, is comic and salacious.[111]
The nymph Salmacis attempts to seduce the boy Hermaphro-
ditus; she embraces him in the water, against his will, and at
her request the gods join them into a single creature, half-man,
half-woman. For all its conjunction of epic parody, strident eroticism, and soft beauty, the episode has until near the end an
atmosphere which feels straightforward.[112] It is the metamorphosis and its prelude which change this. The sexual momentum of the story carries it forward to the heady sensuality of the
naked Salmacis' fondling the naked youth. But with his deter-

---

[110] Cf. e.g. 2. 333 ff. (Heliades)—a more startling and dramatic change between grief and transformation, with grotesque and half-comic effects. 6. 301 ff. (Niobe) modify far more lightly the unusually strong pathos; 310 however marks the completed metamorphosis with a startling action.

[111] Ovid obtains two similar contrasts by placing before the story of Leucothoe and after the largely romantic and quasi-tragic story of Pyramus and Thisbe a brief account of the adultery of Mars and Venus.

[112] See on parody Galinsky, 186 ff., and on eroticism J. Griffin, *Latin Poets and Roman Life* (1985), 102 ff.

mined resistance the mood becomes stranger. Three similes in a row describe the embrace (361 ff.), one violent and epic (eagle and serpent), one with suggestions of amatory poetry (ivy and trees), and one grotesque, the more so for its direct connection with the story (the polypus grasping its foe beneath the waters).[113] In the preceding passage of narrative the frequent similes depicted in exquisite images the beauty of the boy and the desire of the nymph (331 ff. (two), 348 f., 354 f.). Her speech now contrasts with her earlier speech of seduction (320 ff.). Its defiance of the boy, and its harshness of tone, introduce a para-doxical distortion of amatory ideas and language.

> 'pugnes licet, improbe,' dixit,
> non tamen effugies. ita, di, iubeatis ut istum
> nulla dies a me nec me diducat ab isto.'   (370–2)

'Fight though you may, you monster,' she said, 'you shall not escape. You gods, may you command that no day shall ever separate him from me or me from him!'

The description of the coalescence uses the language of sexual intercourse (*mixta duorum | corpora iunguntur*, 373 f.; *coierunt*, 377); but this marks out the evasion of that natural conclusion and the weirdness of the present event. An unalluring simile from tree-grafting heightens the strangeness (375 ff.), and Ovid draws out the paradox of the hermaphrodite (378 f.). A further *aition*, prepared from the beginning, moves us away from the events in their own right, and underlines the bizarreness of the transformation.

Every metamorphosis has a different effect in its context; but these instances may suggest the importance of metamorphosis in disrupting the narrative and making possible complicated and unsettling mixtures of elements. As regards the individual episode, then, metamorphosis serves a function which it is hard not to associate with the great Hellenistic poets. Ovid was witty and humorous so to speak by nature; but the relation to struc-ture, narrative, and fiction is likely to derive from those authors. However, in the conception of the whole poem Ovid

---

[113] The appearance of the polypus in a simile from the *Odyssey* (5. 432 ff.)—itself somewhat bizarre—does not remove the effect. The foe is non-human, cf. D'Arcy Thompson, *A Glossary of Gk. Fishes* (1947), 207.

invests his structural principle with combined extremes, of grandeur, artificiality, and absurdity. Ovid's poem is vast (Nicander's had four or five books). Professedly it encompasses the whole of time, from the creation to the present (1. 3 f., cf. *Trist.* 2. 559 f.—in reality the period between Aeneas and Julius Caesar is swiftly dealt with). One is certainly given an impression that the whole of mythology is being covered, from the angle of metamorphosis, that all major events and characters are being included.[114] It is possible that Ovid's prologue draws attention directly to the difference between his poem and the *Aetia* in continuity and ambition; if so, one should sense not so much a daring paradox in literary doctrine as a grandiose gesture.[115] Furthermore, Pythagoras' great speech in Book 15 presents metamorphosis as an essential principle of the universe; by elevating, superficially, the significance and universality of the subject it appears to elevate those of the poem.

However, the theme as a theme is intended to be absurd. In general by this period metamorphosis seems to have been regarded by most educated people as an utterly fabulous notion.[116] It seems fairly clear that Ovid himself regarded it as such, as appears from the other works: see *Amores* 3. 12. 19 ff., and *Trist.* 2. 64, where the *Metamorphoses* is referred to, with no particular aim, as 'in non credendos corpora versa modos' 'a work on bodies transformed in ways that are not to be believed'. Within the poem itself, Ovid not infrequently makes ironical play with the implausibility of metamorphosis.[117] Thus with the first full tale of metamorphosis—men produced from rocks—Ovid starts his transformation

---

[114] Ovid in fact excludes some of the many obscure tales in Nicander: Nicander, however, did include some well-known stories too.

[115] Cf. especially E. J. Kenney, *PCPS* NS 22 (1976), 46 ff. The most plausible connection is between *perpetuum* (1. 4) and the Telchines' διηνεκές (Call. fr. 1. 3). But one must take *perpetuum* closely with the rest of the sentence (cf. Hollis, edn. of Book 8, xi f.). Even so, some link might be felt, especially as the two poems are of related kinds. If *illa* is read in l. 2, it seems strained to find, and uncharacteristically opaque in Ovid to adumbrate, a scene like that of Call. fr. 1; and this spoils the sense of point. The use of *deduxi* in *Trist.* 2. 560 makes it improbable that *deducite* carries any allusion to slenderness.

[116] Cf. P. Veyne, *Les Grecs ont-ils cru à leurs mythes?* (1983). Pausanias, in 8.2, does unexpectedly profess belief (see Veyne, 105 ff.); but it would appear that he expects this view to surprise.

[117] Cf. G. Rosati, *Narciso e Pigmalione* (1984), 170 f.

saxa (quis hoc credat, nisi sit pro teste vetustas?)
ponere duritiem coepere ... (1. 400 f.)

The rocks (who would believe this, were there not the age
of the story to vouch for it?) began to put off their hard-
ness ...

A familiar line of argument is distorted into parody by the
untramelled author.[118] The parenthesis is wickedly inserted
after the first word. This and similar passages prevent us from
merely accepting metamorphosis as a simple convention of the
world within the poem. The grotesqueness and strangeness of
the conception, which Ovid's descriptions impress on us, makes
this seem a preposterous viewpoint from which to present myth
(the subject-matter of the most elevated literature) and even
the universe itself. If one were to think that the poem in general
actually promoted a view of the world as unstable, one would
be false to the nature of Ovid's style—so unevocative and self-
contained, so unsuggestive of rich half-hinted generalities.
Pythagoras' speech (15. 75–478) certainly reads as if the true
significance of theme and poem were now suddenly being dis-
closed, with a movement into philosophy. The author, however, slily intimates that such a view would be naïve.

The whole speech is a defence of vegetarianism. It expands
into a depiction of universal change and transformation; but all
leads up to the idea that one might be eating a reincarnate relation. Such ideas were mentioned in ancient defences of vegetarianism, though general disbelief seems to be assumed (Sen.
Epist. 108. 19 f., cf. also Plut. *Mor.* 997E f.). But clearly the type
of thought is one which could easily appear implausible and
ridiculous. In introducing the speech Ovid tells us that, learned
though it was, it was not believed, *sed non et credita* (15. 74); and
after it Pythagoras' own pupil proceeds to institute animal sacrifice in Rome (*sacrificos ritus* in 483 must suggest this). The idea
of reincarnation is not treated without malice. Pythagoras says

ipse ego (nam memini) Troiani tempore belli
Panthoides Euphorbus eram. (160 f.)

I myself (I recall it) was at the time of the Trojan War
Euphorbus son of Panthous.

---

[118] Similarly, but with still more palpable scepticism, at *Fasti* 4. 203 f.

The parenthesis gives a patently ludicrous effect, underlining
the incredibility.[119] The impressive treatment of Rome's future
greatness is made to rest in part on Pythagoras' recollection of
prophecies heard when he was a Trojan: 'Helenus spoke thus to
Aeneas, as far as I remember', *quantumque recordor* (436, cf. 451).
The dubiousness of Pythagoras' contentions is suggested in
other ways too. The irony of self-reference is hard to mistake at
282 f. (where Centaurs are in question):

> nisi vatibus omnis
> eripienda fides.

> unless all credit is to be taken away from poets.[120]

The destructive clause forms (as often) an innocent addition to
the basic sentence. Obvious suspicion is aroused by the confident

> siqua fides rebus tamen est addenda probatis.   (361)

> but if proof need be added to a case already demon-
> strated.

The 'but' appears because two lines previously Pythagoras has
admitted that he does not himself believe the story he has
adduced as evidence (*haud equidem credo*, 359).[121]

And yet, although the metaphysical and explanatory pretensions of the speech are undermined, its sweep and grandeur,
though threatened, are not destroyed. We do not find in its
language only parody and foolish inflation. Rather we feel, as
one of the elements in our experience of the speech, a kind of
preposterous magnificence. This is partly subverted by internal
context and sequence, but partly subsists, in an environment
far removed from straightforward seriousness. The aspects of
elevation and passion coalesce strangely with the aspects of
absurdity and humour. The same applies, in a different way, to
the design of the whole poem. The theme itself, as we see it in
the poem, and the angle from which all myth and history are
presented, seem devious and absurd. But the sweeping magnifi-

---

[119] Cf. *Amores* 2. 1. 11, 3. 1. 33, and also *Fasti* 5. 646.

[120] Contrast Pythagoras' scornful *materiem vatum* at 155.

[121] For the position of *tamen* cf. 3. 513, 10. 200: it should not be taken with *probatis*.
Bömer's account of the particle is possible, but in my view less likely.

cence of the conception does not altogether vanish away beneath the dangerous and transforming light of comedy and self-mockery. The poem remains as a whole something grandiose, astonishing, far more than a set of stories which happen to have been collected. The wilful, the imposing, the absurd, meet in a bold union of extremes which defies separation.

Such, I find, is one's impression as one contemplates the work entire after reading it. The essential splendour of the first and last portions of poem and narrative enhance one's sense of complexity (1. 1 ff., 5 ff.; 15. 745 ff., 871 ff.). But no less important is one's sense of the poem in the course of reading it. We may turn to look at the varying exploitation, in a particular portion of the work, of compounds of the serious and the unserious, and that with reference to more than metamorphosis alone. The whole work explores this region of effect incessantly; it is for that reason that it comes especially close to the quality of Callimachus. The portion we shall look at is Book 8: the book is especially well known, and we shall have several opportunities to consider the reuse of particular Hellenistic poems.

First a word or two on some general aspects of the book. The stories are joined together by the person of Theseus. He entered at 7. 404 (his major deeds up to that point were briefly and deviously mentioned in a song at 7. 433 ff.). At 7. 456 the narrative moved to Minos and his wars, and it connects itself to him until 8. 266. The relation to Theseus is that Minos' attack on Athens will lead to the Athenians' giving up youths and girls to the Minotaur. That monster Theseus will slay: it is his most famous deed. This deed finally appears in Book 8, in a subordinate clause; the killing is obliquely ascribed to *tertia sors* (171) 'the third sortition, the third time that lots were drawn'. The action is taken up in retrospect with *Thesea laude* 'to Theseus' glory' in 263. Thereafter Theseus plays a small and undistinguished part in the hunt of the Calydonian boar; on his return he is entertained by Achelous and further stories are told. At 9. 95 *discedunt iuvenes* 'the young men depart', and that is the end of the famous hero's exiguous role. Ovid is displaying an extreme and deliberate wilfulness over his affectation of making his material cohere and of embracing the major figures of mythology. It may certainly be urged that in the earlier part of the book (1–226) Minos and his war become the significant

frame.[122] But here again the actual war with Athens, after vast
preliminaries, is not even mentioned: we have to infer from the
odd phrase that it has taken place (170, 262 f.). Again we see an
extreme of mannerism. Such is the tension between the poet's
pretence to narrate fully and naturally a given series of events
and his preoccupation with tales of metamorphosis. However,
in respect of metamorphosis too there is mannerism. Sometimes
the metamorphosis appears with quite unusual brevity
(145 ff.—with one metamorphosis in brackets in the pluper-
fect); sometimes the metamorphosis seems like an appendage,
added after the substantial narrative has reached its close
(236 ff. (Daedalus), 526 ff. (Meleager), cf. also 843 ff. (Erysichthon)). This sense of structural prestidigitation does not indicate that metamorphosis is unimportant even in this book: its
part is crucial, as will eventually emerge.

The second point one must note is that story-telling is far
from being the predominating concern of the book. Of the five
main stories (outlined below), only that of Daedalus, and perhaps that of Philemon and Baucis, exhibit the primary momentum of narrative that involves us and excites us in the
development of the plot as such. With Scylla, most of the
account is concerned with two speeches; in the hunt of the
Calydonian boar, with burlesque and parody and with a
speech. In the tale of Erysichthon, a sense of involvement and
narrative tension is dissipated by the colourful digression on
Hunger and by the verbal wit with which the fate of Erysichthon is described. In this respect too there is mannerism, of a
Hellenistic kind; though in Ovid as in those poets narrative patterns form an important part of the total effect. Our attention is
partly fixed on Ovid's self-advertising and obtrusive virtuosity
and on his manipulation of literary convention.

We may turn now to the particular episodes. Scylla, the
daughter of King Nisus, falls in love with Minos, who is besieg-
ing her city. She gives him the city by cutting her father's magical lock of purple hair. Minos refuses to marry her, none the
less, and departs; she clings to his ship and is metamorphosed
into a bird, always pursued by her father (also so transformed).
The episode consists of: a description of Scylla's falling in love

    [122] Cf. A. Crabbe, *Aufst. u. Niederg. d. röm. Welt*, ii. 31. 4 (1981), 2277 f., 2302 f.

(11–42); a speech in which she gradually moves towards the resolve to cut Nisus' lock (44–80); an account of her confrontation with Minos (81–103); a speech in which she expresses her anger against Minos (108–42); an account of her metamorphosis (142–51). The two speeches dominate the episode; Ovid presumably chose this version of the story to make possible these types of speeches.[123] Scylla holds no prior discussion with Minos, and so she can arrive at the idea and the decision through her own monstrous speech; Scylla is fled, not punished, by Minos, and so she can deliver a distorted version of the speeches made by deserted heroines. The first speech plays, like several in this part of the *Metamorphoses*, with an intrinsically serious and dramatic motif: a monologue in which the speaker resolves on a dreadful act.[124] But the speech is removed from dramatic seriousness through the neat and extended sequence of steps by which Scylla glides to her shocking decision. The contrasts of passionate utterance and insidious reflection enhance the feeling of near-comedy. So, for example, 55–7:

> nam pereant potius sperata cubilia quam sim
> proditione potens! quamvis saepe utile vinci
> victoris placidi fecit clementia victis.

> Let that bed and my hopes for it perish first! Sooner that than have won it through betraying the city! And yet defeat often proves advantageous to the defeated when a victor shows mildness and mercy.

The second line proceeds from the decisive energy of phrase and feeling in *proditione potens* (expanded as 'have won it through betraying the city') to the paradoxical blandness of *utile vinci* ('defeat proves advantageous'). The reflective *quamvis* 'and yet' makes the involvement comic.[125] The second speech is very definitely a parody of a tragic type of speech. The grandiose topoi of deserted heroines like Catullus' Ariadne are deployed in a situation where sympathy is impossible: a heroine of the greatest wickedness inveighs against the supposed wicked-

---

[123] See on the variations in the story Lyne, *Ciris* (1978), 5 ff., Hollis's edn., pp. 32 ff. Parthenius (*SH* 637) may well be a source; the relation with the *Ciris* can scarcely be determined.

[124] On these cf. Heinze, *Ovids elegische Erzählung* (BSAW 71 (1919–20), ph.-hist. Kl.), 110 ff. Prop. 4. 4. 31 ff. is a primary model for this speech.

[125] Cf. 10. 322 f. (*si tamen*).

ness of an upright hero. The humour is sharpened by ingenious rhetorical play with stories dealing with and related to metamorphosis. (See especially 122 ff., where Scylla affects to disbelieve a story told earlier in the poem.) Such lavish and thoroughgoing parody of literature moves rather beyond the Hellenistic poets; but it marks another relation between the serious and the unserious.

The first piece of narrative (11 ff.) starts in epic manner; but it soon turns into light amatory writing in a tone characteristic of Ovid's earlier poems. By contrast, the central narrative of the meeting (81 ff.) has a strong feeling of elevation: it is abrupt, dramatic, moral, and stands strikingly above the speeches which surround it. The metamorphosis plays an important part in the episode, despite its brevity. Scylla's speech culminates in a bizarre action, as she leaps to seize hold of the receding ship. The narrative becomes weird and fantastic, and issues in her transformation and the *aition* of a certain kind of sea-bird (an etymology closes, 151). The pretence of an involving and tragic human story is now dissolved. Death is averted; the girl becomes a bird and the object of neat erudition. In this episode, then, different sections are placed in different and designedly different relations to seriousness; but we always stand at a very considerable distance from serious and moving poetry.

The next main story is most unlike this. The Athenian Daedalus, confined to Crete by Minos with his son Icarus, makes wings for them both to escape to Athens. Icarus flies too near the sun and melts the wax which joins the feathers; he falls to his death in the sea. This pleases the partridge, metamorphosed from the youth Perdix: Daedalus in jealousy at Perdix' cleverness had pushed him, as he hoped, to his death. This appended tale of Perdix (236–59), formally the goal of the account, modifies the impact of the main story. Daedalus appears in a shameful light, and our sympathy fades. The pathos of the main tale is lost from view with the grotesque picture of the applauding partridge, and with the bizarre and untragic conclusion to his story which the account of his transformation supplies. Throughout the story proper, we have a real and touching pathos lightly modified by play with the idea of metamorphosis. Such play is typical when actual metamorphosis is only appended (cf. e.g. 2. 235 ff.); it difficult in this poem to dismiss

the evocation of metamorphosis and its atmosphere suggested
by the general situation and by such characteristic language as
naturamque novat 'he alters his nature' (189, cf. especially 4. 279),
ignotas . . . alas 'wings unknown before' (209, similarly 188, cf. 1.
88; 13. 944), *mirabile* 'astounding' (199, cf. 611, 4. 271, etc.).[126]
However, this is not a real metamorphosis, as 195 early makes
explicit (Daedalus fashions the wings *ut veras imitetur aves* 'to imitate real birds'). Metamorphosis, as will be emphasized later in
the book, is produced by divine power: this is a vain, though ingenious, attempt by a mortal to contrive a metamorphosis
through skill. The notion of art and skill is prominent in the
account (188, 189–95, 200–9, 215, 234). There is very little
attempt to present the endeavour as an act of irreverent arro-
gance (the *Ars Amatoria* makes more of the possibility, 2. 38 ff.).
Rather, this appears as a strange and exciting distortion of the
central theme, which colours the whole account and is brought
into various relations with the pathos.

In 195 ff., the boy Icarus, *ignarus sua se tractare pericla* 'unaware that what he is handling is his peril', interferes with his
father's labours by his childish play. This behaviour has two
sides, which interact. The child's happy and frivolous games
contrast tragically with his coming fate; yet the playing amuses,
and the physical details of Icarus' naughtiness seem the more
entertaining because they draw the bold invention into so
homely a light. (It is here that *mirabile* 'astounding' occurs). At
209 ff. Daedalus instructs his son in the art of flying and at the
same time fits the wings on. There is something weird in this
combination of practical behaviour and so novel an enterprise.
(It is here that there occurs *ignotas alas* 'wings unknown
before'.) But

> inter opus monitusque genae maduere seniles
> et patriae tremuere manus. (210 f.)

Amid this labour and these instructions, the cheeks of the
old man grew wet, the hands of the father trembled.

Here the pathos surges over the strangeness. After the tense de-

---

[126] For 189 cf. *Ars Am.* 2. 42 and Hollis's note here. Against any idea of metamorphosis see Bömer's edn. of 8–9, p. 70; he gives further bibliography. The version of the story
in the *Ars Amatoria* (2. 21 ff.) makes less use of such language; but it is significant that
Ovid plainly thinks of metamorphosis there too (42).

scription of the anxious flying, the figure is suddenly introduced of an astonished rustic who takes the pair to be gods (217 ff.). The notion of metamorphosis permits a sudden injection here of slightly impudent humour.[127] The impact of the disaster itself is somewhat limited by the intrusion of aetiology. First, Icarus, calling his father's name, is engulfed by the water

> quae nomen traxit ab illo. (230)

> which took its name from him.

Then the father

> devovitque suas artes corpusque sepulcro
> condidit; et tellus a nomine dicta sepulti. (234 f.)

> cûrsed his skills, and laid the body in a tomb; the land was
> called after the name of the one he entombed.

Here *sepulcro* 'tomb' in the tragic action is taken up and distanced by *sepulti* 'the one he entombed'; each is made, elegantly, to close a line. The smooth connections in the two passages, and the double *aition*, give a sense of slightly chilly neatness and abstraction. Latin poets often refer to the naming of the Icarian Sea so as to make archer the effect of referring to his fall.[128] But the treatment here creates a greater sense of tonal complexity, and is specifically designed for the close of a substantial narrative. It is very reminiscent of Apollonius. Here, then, we have a much warmer episode, with much more appeal to emotion; but strange and paradoxical elements delicately complicate the effect.

The following episode is quite different again. Numerous heroes come together to hunt the boar sent by Diana against Calydon. Their attempts to slay it are largely unsuccessful; Atalanta first draws blood, Meleager kills it. Meleager is in love with Atalanta, and his generosity to her over the spoils leads to fighting; in this Meleager kills his mother's brothers. His mother, Althaea, eventually resolves to avenge her brothers by burning a certain log: this the Fates had decreed should exist

---

[127] I do not feel there is real dramatic irony here, despite the imminent death of one of these supposed immortals. The slickness of the syntax and the enjambment seem to make that unlikely.

[128] The references are mostly later than this passage: Hor. *Odes* 4. 2. 3 f. (earlier), Ovid, *Trist.* 1. 1. 90, 3. 4. 22, Seneca (?), *HO* 685, 689 f.

for the same length of time as Meleager. His sisters mourn him and are changed into guinea-fowl.

The elaborate account of the hunt is firmly divided into two parts, as regards the tone.[129] In 269–328, Ovid describes the anger of Diana with forceful curtness, and much evocation of the *Aeneid*; he gives (281–99) an extravagant and grandiose description of the boar; and he presents (299–323) an epic catalogue of the huntsmen, again evoking the *Aeneid* in language. Now, at the end of the catalogue, with Atalanta and with Meleager's love, the poet moves into an amatory vein, and slightly lowers the poetic level; but up to this point the whole section had sustained a marked elevation. One should not see humorous exaggeration in the treatment of the boar: the passage would not in fact become amusing, and the taste for extravagance in such things is very Roman.[130] The close of the section dismisses the amatory matter, as Meleager does.

> nec plura sinit tempusque pudorque
> dicere: maius opus magni certaminis urget. (327 f.)

Time and modesty alike forbid him to say more. He is driven onwards by the greater task of the mighty conflict.

The section is sealed with the reassertion of grandeur: the grandeur springs from the coming hunt, to which the whole first part has been leading.[131]

The second section in some ways undoes the first. The lengthy catalogue which built up the band of heroes is deflated by a lengthy list of their dismal failures. The list abounds in bathetic structures, physical farce, irony, and black humour. However, the boar retains its extremes of grandeur and force: it is the men who let the heroic narrative down. Atalanta is a source of lowness: she helps make the men look absurd or predictable, without achieving anything spectacular herself. She inflicts the merest scratch on the boar (382 f.).[132] Yet when the

---

[129] Cf. Crabbe (n. 122) 2284 n. 63, though I should not want to describe either section quite as she does.

[130] Cf. e.g. Seneca, *Phaedra* 1035 ff., Manilius 5. 579 ff., in neither of which does humour seem plausible; note also AR 4. 127 ff.

[131] The role of *maius opus* is of course strengthened by another echo of Virgil, *maius opus moveo* at *Aen.* 7. 45; there Virgil is marking a new extreme of ὕψος as he comes to the second half of his whole epic.

[132] Contrast Apollod. 1. 8. 2 εἰς τὰ νῶτα ἐτόξευσε.

hunt is over, she is the cause of fighting which shocks and disturbs. In a sense, the same area which mitigated the seriousness of the first section leads to the reappearance of seriousness here (though seriousness of a different kind, having much less of elevation). So far the structure has produced a clear movement away from dignity; the second section is mixed, but one feels no great subtlety or complexity in the mixture.

The section on Althaea is dominated by the speech she makes, as she is torn between love for her son and love for her brothers. One cannot take the speech as intended to arouse in the reader only powerful emotion. It is too stiff with ingenuity, the phrasing is too palpably designed to win our main attention for the author.

> meruisse fatemur
> illum cur pereat; mortis mihi displicet auctor.

> (492 f.)

> I allow that Meleager's actions deserve death; what I dislike is the identity of his killer (i.e. herself).

The organization of the sentence, and the exquisitely weak *mihi displicet* 'I dislike, am offended by', surely exclude any intention to move the reader with these words.[133] It is significant that even before the speech has started, Ovid is revelling in stunning paradox.

> consanguineas ut sanguine leniat umbras,
> impietate pia est.

> To appease the shades of her blood-relations with blood,
> she shows love and duty by denying duty and love.

And yet the speech, while it avoids a straightforward effect of tragedy, does possess a kind of grandiose theatricality in the lavishness of its gestures and in the very density of the artifice unremittingly applied to a conflict potentially tragic. This is a subtle mixture; yet it is made, quite characteristically, from extremes.

The section is notable too for the weirdness of its story. This goes with a difference in atmosphere from the relatively

---

[133] One thinks of Tac. *Hist.* 2. 10 *nec poena criminis sed ultor displicebat*; but that passage only strengthens the point. The judgement is precisely an external one (that of the city), and is not made in such a case as this.

straightforward first half of the episode. The difference is more
or less plainly signalled at 518f. Meleager wishes that he had
died like Ancaeus, fighting the boar, rather than by this form of
death, *ignavo ... et sine sanguine*, bloodless and ignoble (cf. 391–
402, 407). This is a paradoxical and extraordinary kind of
death. One does not at all wish to describe it as a metamorphosis; but one does feel something of the atmosphere that metamorphosis brings with it. As with metamorphosis, we witness a
vivid yet utterly strange event which is decisive and final.
There are neatly stressed and paradoxical resemblances
between two dissimilar things, a burning piece of wood and a
dying man (522–5, 513f., 515–17). In the poem resemblances
are very frequently drawn between people and the quite different objects they are turned into. The element of the bizarre
contributes to the greater complexity of tone in this section.

The mourning of Calydon is painted in lavish colours. Ovid
eventually pushes beyond the point of tragic seriousness by
drawing inappropriate attention to himself in bizarrely developed hyperbole. Not even if heaven gave him a hundred
tongues, not if it gave him a sufficient genius, and the whole of
Helicon, could he tell all the sisters' cries (533–5). In what
follows, the sisters' mourning remains unchangeable, though
first Meleager's body turns into ash and next they have only the
name on the tomb to embrace. But then in a rapid and elegantly economical passage they are transformed, and the grief
is ended; Diana's anger, too, is appeased. Ovid does not mention that the sisters mourned for their brother even as birds, nor
that they were transported to a particular place (contrast
Nicander's account, Ant. Lib. 2. 7).[134] Rather Diana, who
transforms them, merely casts them into the air (*versasque per
aera mittit*, 546). The story is concluded with this light, swift gesture. The potentially tragic emotion is brought to an excessive
extreme, and then dissolved as the characters cease to be
human.

The last two stories of the book are told while Theseus and
his companions feast in the dwelling of Achelous. They are told
in order to prove that the gods can produce metamorphosis.
This is impiously disputed by one of the companions (Pirith-

---

[134] Hollis notes the difference. Nicander must surely be Ovid's source for the metamorphosis itself.

ous). His view seems preposterous within the world of the poem, obvious outside it. The story of Philemon and Baucis is told with suitably strong emphasis on evidence. The narrator Lelex has himself seen the trees into which Philemon and Baucis were transformed (*ipse locum vidi*, 622, cf. 722); he was told the story of their metamorphosis by reliable old men, with no motive to deceive (721 f.). Yet this emphasis makes it obvious how weak the evidence is, at this seemingly crucial point in the work. Stress on evidence, play with truth, exploitation of narrative levels: all are typical of Hellenistic poetry. But Ovid has turned them so that he may toy boisterously with the fragile basis of his narrative structure.

Philemon and Baucis, an old married couple, entertain Jupiter and Mercury when their neighbours have refused the disguised divinities. After a humble meal, the gods manifest themselves. The rest of the vicinity is destroyed by flood; the old people's house is changed into a temple, which they supervise. As they have asked, one does not die before the other: they are metamorphosed together into trees. It seems probable that in his account of the hospitality of Philemon and Baucis Ovid was much indebted to Callimachus' *Hecale*, where Hecale entertained Theseus (see pp. 56 f.).[135] We have only small (though quite numerous) fragments from the scene in Callimachus; but none the less it is possible to discern differences of some interest. On the one hand, Callimachus' meal uses abstruse foods culled from old literature (frr. 248, 249, 250).[136] This sort of devious erudition does not interest Ovid (though the manner of erudition and pedantry sometimes does so). He aims for a piquant effect by making the meal Roman. The double distance of the narrative level enhances the oddness; it is Lelex, not Ovid, who for example makes implicit contrasts with contemporary luxury (672, *al.*).[137] On the other hand, the bitter poverty of Hecale would not suit the ethos of this poem: suffering so hum-

---

[135] See Pfeiffer on fr. 240 for particular connections. I. Cazzaniga, while not denying the link, attempts to reduce its importance, not very successfully (*Parola del Passato* 18 (1963), 23 ff.). For possible subsidiary models see Hollis, pp. 106 f. It is of course a pleasing irony that Theseus is enjoying a luxurious meal while listening to the story (cf. Crabbe, 2289).

[136] Note Pliny's phrasing in the latter two.

[137] The historical sense of the ancients was fairly strong in such matters.

drum would spoil its harmonies.[138] The Hellenistic poets are much interested in poverty for the bizarreness and harshness it makes possible in the poetry. Callimachus can also make it appeal to pity, though often with wry humour. The poverty of Philemon and Baucis is painted in the mild and attractive colours that appealed to philosophical rejection of society and Roman nostalgia for the past.[139] The whole episode has in consequence a homely warmth, and a relaxed geniality of humour, that would not suit the sharper and drier manner of the Hellenistic poets.

Yet it is important to see that the force of this episode resides in the conflict of contrasting levels, embodied in the contrasting pairs of characters. Indeed, the contrast is still more extreme than between Hecale and Theseus or even between Molorchus and Heracles (p. 46): the unknown guests are gods. The comedy of the human beings' awkward poverty and bustling old age is set against the gods' intrinsic awesomeness. Even when the gods enter, it is said

> ubi caelicolae parvos tetigere penates.

> when the dwellers in heaven touched the little home (*lit.* household gods).

The play enhances their majesty and stresses that they are out of place. Directly before the grotesquely ordinary comedy of propping up the table, we have the pregnant phrase, expressively ordered, *accubuere dei* (660) 'the gods reclined in their place', almost 'they drew up their chairs, the Gods'.[140] When the couple attempt to catch a goose to sacrifice, we have farce, though already the farce plays elaborately with the presence of the gods. It is followed directly by the gods' curt and incisive speech. *di sumus*, they say, 'we are gods' (689); and they reveal with brevity their momentous purposes.[141]

---

[138] Hyrceus' poverty is a little more sordid (*Fasti* 5. 499 ff.).

[139] One should not lay too much stress on 'Augustanism'. Sallust and Seneca are much concerned by wealth, and Horace's Roman *Odes* are not a blueprint of Augustus' policies. In general, Augustus is perhaps less important for Roman poetry than is usually supposed.

[140] *accubo* and *accumbo* in this sense have a homely flavour, and are relatively uncommon in elevated poetry. The use at Virg. *Aen.* 6. 606 is grimly ironic.

[141] Note that they reserve expressions of approval until later, and that they do not (as would be conventional) disclose which gods they are. Ovid's gods often gain force from brevity of speech. Cf. 279 f. (Diana) and e.g. 3. 192 f., 6. 43.

At the end of the story the contrast is blurred softly: the metamorphosed couple seem to be becoming not only trees but gods (722–4). Other ingredients of the earlier section are also altered in metamorphosis. The humble dwelling is metamorphosed into a wealthy temple (699–702); this undoes the scene of not unattractive poverty. The couple themselves have touched us by their fidelity. The story moves to the warm and homely scene of them talking over their experience, when, suddenly, they do not die (despite 712 and 709 f.), but start sprouting foliage. A splendid sentence converts the potentially tragic scene of the last parting into a bizarre spectacle; it sets words of intrinsic pathos against the ludicrous sight.[142]

> iamque super geminos crescente cacumine vultus
> mutua, dum licuit, reddebant dicta, 'vale,'que
> 'o coniunx' dixere simul, simul abdita texit
> ora frutex. (716–19)

> While the foliage was already growing over their two faces, they gave their last words to each other, while they could, and said 'Farewell, my partner'—but while they said it, leaves and branches hid their faces from view and covered them over.

The first two lines are boldly separated from each other in content; the third is boldly divided.

The episode, then, rests for the most part on a juxtaposition of strongly differing levels. But the juxtaposition is not harsh and discordant, rather it creates its own easy mixture to produce a benignant humour. The tonal compound is broken up, and more bizarre and jarring combinations introduced, with the arrival of metamorphosis.

The final story tells of Erysichthon. He cut down knowingly a tree sacred to Demeter, and was punished with insatiable hunger. In the end he could supply his needs only by giving away his daughter Mestra as a slave; she was able to transform herself and escape. When Erysichthon knew of her power, he sold her to one owner after another (she could escape from each). Finally his hunger drove him to eat himself.

---

[142] For other pictures of a couple's last parting cf. e.g. Hom. *Il.* 24. 743 ff., *CIL* 6. 6593, *Met.* 7. 845–62; Tib. 1. 1. 60. A related scene to ours is handled more harshly and less elegantly at 2. 363.

The greater part of the episode shows a striking compound of grandeur and unseriousness; again, however, the compound feels eminently satisfying and in a sense straightforward, on its own terms. Ovid spends most time on Erysichthon's sin and punishment, not on Mestra. With Erysichthon he takes for his source the sixth *Hymn* of Callimachus. The differences are very marked: naturally Ovid wishes to display them. One feels much more strongly that Ovid's narrative has qualities uncharacteristic of Callimachus than that Callimachus' has qualities uncharacteristic of Ovid. The crucial feature of Callimachus' narrative is the shift in tone and atmosphere that occurs when the punishment begins. After the grandeur and moral force of sin, warning, and divine epiphany, there takes over the low theme of eating. Callimachus deftly trivializes the world and conventions of heroic poetry. He imagines, with exquisitely undignified shrewdness, the embarrassment of the parents at their sons's behaviour in feasts. A whole series of their excuses is given; they mostly involve activities characteristic of the epic world (*H.* 6. 76 ff.—beginning with the homely οὐκ ἔνδοι 'He isn't in').[143] Erysichthon's father makes an impassioned prayer to his own father Poseidon; but he closes it with the animals Erysichthon has eaten, last of all the cat (or mongoose), which used to terrify the little beasts (110). We end with the sordid picture of the king's son begging on the public road. The sordidness and social triviality would again not be very well suited to the ethos of the *Metamorphoses*. Yet Ovid does not make the minimum of change necessary: rather he assays a spectacular triumph over Callimachus' compelling structure.

He does not merely render the first part of the story more grandiose still, but contrives to sustain and increase the grandiosity in what follows. Ceres (Demeter) does not now warn Erysichthon in person (disguised); but this is to keep her as an elevated and remote divinity, whom the nymphs of the forest must approach. Hence after the scene on earth we can ascend to Olympus and a still grander scene. Ovid concentrates on the felling of one huge tree, as does Callimachus; but he describes that tree in the most lavish and extravagant conceits. It was *una nemus* (744) 'a grove by itself'; it stood as much above the other

---

[143] Cf. Theocr. 15. 1, Arist. *Ach.* 395, Men. *Dysc.* 464 f.

trees as the other trees stood above the grass (749 f.). Callimachus is grandiose but brief, μέγα δένδρεον αἰθέρι κῦρον (*H.* 6. 37)
'a great tree reaching the sky'. At the death of the tree Callimachus uses lightly human language: κακὸν μέλος ἴαχεν ἄλλαις (39)
'it screamed out to the other trees, as it was cut, a terrible song'.
In Ovid this turns into a baroque scene of horror and pain,
with blood flowing through the bark, and a speech from the
dying nymph of the tree. Before that speech Erysichthon de-
capitates a servant who protests, using the same explicit and
appalling impiety of language which he had shown (755 f.)
when attacking the tree.

> 'mentis'que 'piae cape praemia' dixit.   (767)
>
> 'Here is the reward for your piety', he said.

The mannered extremity of this utterance may be contrasted
with the blunt simplicity of Erysichthon's threat in Callimachus to the seeming priestess:

> "χάζευ," ἔφα, "μή τοι πέλεκυν μέγαν ἐν χροΐ πάξω. . . . ."
>
>   (53)
>
> 'Move away,' he said, 'or I will fix my great axe in your
> body . . . .'

The extravagant and violent scene is closed with the massive
fall of the tree (not in Callimachus).

The notion of eating and an insatiable appetite Ovid affects
to raise into sublimity by bringing on a full-dress allegorical
figure of Hunger. Hunger dwells in a remote and appalling
region; she herself presents hunger in its most extravagant and
fearful form. And yet there is also grotesqueness and the suggestion of comedy in this account: the eating does not lose its lowness through this elevation but mingles absurdity with the
extravagance. Before the ghastly appearance of Hunger is described, we see her tearing up the sparse blades of grass with
nails and teeth (799 f.): the extremity becomes grotesque. At
the end of the scene, so great is the force of Hunger that even
the nymph sent with Ceres' commands, though she stands at a
distance, feels a certain hunger and flies off in her chariot
(812 f.). The motif which rhetorically is intended to enhance introduces an absurdly familiar sensation.

Hunger breathes into the sleeping Erysichthon. Callimachus

raises the onset of hunger with some degree of elevation in language, for the first two lines (66 f.). Ovid turns the onset into a horrifying and grandiose scene of divine invasion and possession, rich with epic resonance (compare Allecto with the sleeping Turnus in Virg. *Aen.* 7. 408–66). Yet the grotesqueness of eating naturally obtrudes. When Hunger has gone, Erysichthon dreams he is eating and moves his mouth: once more the extremity is ludicrous. When he wakes, *furit ardor edendi* (828) 'a passion for eating rages in him'. The grandeur of this language heightens the incongruousness, the more so when one compares the corresponding phrase in *Aeneid* 7, *saevit amor ferri* (461) 'a desire for the sword rages in him'. But Ovid sweeps up higher: Erysichthon demands the produce of earth, air, and sea, he needs more than would suffice cities and a whole people. Ovid's imagery is likewise grand and lavish (835 ff.); Callimachus' was much less so (89–92), despite a reference to the sea. The epigram seems until the very end of the section (841 f.) to be simply a sharpening of the extravagance. We cannot take the account seriously, and we are aware of the absurdity of the treatment; but such are its gusto, energy, and rhetorical fire that the effect is not that of parody. One feels a novel and exhilarating union of the grandiose and the unserious; this seems to explain itself, to stand in its own sphere as obvious and undisquieting. It is only with the final portion of the episode that we feel a stranger and more complicated texture.

As regards the shape of the narrative, Erysichthon's is the primary story. However, the fate of Mestra plays an important role in producing for the last part a more elaborate texture and weirder poetry. One would certainly not want to regard the scene of her first escape as a mere intrusion—though its intrusiveness does heighten its force. Mestra's metamorphoses provide not only the justification for the appearance of the story in the poem, but the value of the story for the teller within the poem: to the metamorphoses the goddess's punishment of impiety is rhetorically subordinate. The transformation is indeed made dramatic and exciting. Mestra is to be sold into slavery, not marriage (as in Hesiod, fr. 43a). She does not yet have her power of metamorphosis, but wins it only by prayer to Neptune in her desperate need (850 f.). The teller stresses that we should sympathize with her as we should not with Erysichthon (847,

848, cf. 782 f.). Mestra is transformed into a fisherman, and we
have sudden calm and relaxed wit as she and her cheated
owner converse. The strange poised stillness contrasts with her
impassioned prayer, and with the hectic energy of the surrounding narrative on Erysichthon. The metamorphosis is
unusual in being reversed directly afterwards and in being
repeatable indefinitely and at will: this was the point that was
stressed in introducing the story (728 ff.). We contrast the
resistless and decisive power of hunger over Erysichthon, which
leads to his savagely grotesque and paradoxical demise.

> ipse suos artus lacerans divellere morsu
> coepit, et infelix minuendo corpus alebat.   (877 f.)

> He started to rend and tear apart his own limbs with his
> teeth: unhappy wretch, he was increasing his body by
> diminishing it.

The description of the act has a disturbing and repellent
quality we have not encountered before.[144] The paradox has a
new wildness and weirdness; the apparently compassionate
infelix 'unhappy wretch' in fact marks the piquant detachment
of the poet's ingenuity. It would be quite wrong to suggest that
Erysichthon's affliction and autophagy make a kind of metamorphosis, or even played with the notion of it. We do, however, now feel something of the atmosphere and manner
associated with end by transformation. The juxtaposition with
a real but abnormal metamorphosis adds to the strangeness
and complication of tone in this final section as a whole.

Ovid pursues very Hellenistic ends in the book: he seeks, as a
primary object, to cultivate and display different combinations
of the emotional and the amusing, the grand and the low. We
have seen the importance of internal structure in creating these
combinations within the episode; we have seen too Ovid's
Roman interest in the lavish and the extreme. The grand and
the serious are always modified, but the combinations tend to
avoid the weirdness so often sought by Hellenistic poets. However, metamorphosis, and elements which are made to share
something of its atmosphere, enable movement to stranger mixtures and tones. This aspect again is closely related to structure.

---

[144] Contrast *divellere* here with *vellentem* 800 of Hunger and grass.

We may summarize swiftly the general picture which emerges from these particular discussions. The Hellenistic poets had a most important effect on Roman poetry for the greater part of the first century BC: but the effect lay in the impulse to complicate the straightforward and the emotional, to make conflicts and contrasts of tone, to exploit structure so as to heighten the sense of complexity and richness. The Roman poets have a very different quality, above all perhaps through their relative extravagance—an extravagance seen not solely in emotive and grandiose writing, but also in the extremities to which artifice can be pushed. One has, in short, a stronger feeling of tension, less sense of a certain poise. It may seem contrived to use a single term for tendencies which seem to be opposites connected only by divergence from a Hellenistic norm. But it appears less like this if one views the tension as something real and attractive, and if one sees how often the Roman poets themselves play with emotional and rhetorical extravagance, in its potential for modifying seriousness. They themselves (one is to feel) exult in the energy of the conflicting work. The Romans, then, seized with vigour on the central features (as I conceive them) of Hellenistic poetry.

I have not been attempting to write a history of Hellenistic influence on Roman poetry. But the reader may still ask whether that influence did not extend beyond Ovid. I have restricted my horizons, not because I think later Roman poetry less important, but because after Ovid the subject becomes difficult to write about. Clearly the Hellenistic poets did not cease to be read and used. Thus Lucan uses Apollonius' sequence in the desert for his own; Statius uses Callimachus' account of Coroebus.[145] Apollonius' *Argonautica* provides the foundation for Valerius Flaccus'. But more fundamental influence it is hard to establish, in isolation from the influence of Roman works influenced by Hellenistic poetry, above all the *Metamorphoses* of Ovid. Ovid had there come particularly close to the quality of those authors, and his epic had particular import-

---

[145] Lucan 9. 294–949, cf. AR 4. 1223–619; Statius, *Theb.* 1. 557–668, cf. Call. fr. 26–31 + 31a. Lucan's borrowing is indisputable; with Statius the verbal links and the poet's use of Callimachus elsewhere suffice to make the borrowing extremely probable. Lucan employs a mythological reference to make the connection clear early on (9. 357 ff.). So perhaps when he echoes Apollonius at the beginning of Book 3 (1–7, cf. AR 1. 533–5), he signals this by a mythological reference at the end of Book 2 (715 ff.)

ance for later poets, not least for Seneca, whose work is so important to Lucan, and for Lucan, whose work is so important to the poets that follow. Yet modifications of seriousness, and the interplay of different tones, are (in my view) fundamental to the work of poets after Ovid.[146] The means to produce such textures—for instance a verbal ingenuity and wit—have often a character more Imperial than Hellenistic. But the basic conception of such poetry, derived principally from Roman poets, had in turn been derived from the Greek poets of the third century BC. Thus those poets were at a remove responsible for determining in some of the most important aspects the regions in which most Roman poetry was concerned to move.

The Hellenistic poets were to a very considerable degree understood by their Roman successors, and their influence was closely related to the true nature of their work. None the less, the Roman poets do not at all provide a justification, or an improved replacement, for the work of their predecessors. Those earlier poets have, each of them, their own beauty and their own life: nothing can replace the pleasure which they alone can offer us. To have aroused in its reader an interest, or a sharpened interest, in experiencing that pleasure, is the great ambition of this book.

---

[146] At present critics seem generally to ignore this aspect, laying too exclusive an emphasis on thought, or attributing deliberate modifications of tragic or epic seriousness to 'lapses of taste', decline, declamation, etc. To take for instance the first act of Seneca's *Phaedra*, it is difficult to reconcile, say, l. 243 with an intention to sustain dramatic seriousness; Phaedra's first speech closes with a paragraph of ingenious mythological play which surely modifies its impact (note 119, 114); the Nurse's first speech closes in a distancing surprise (177—note the design of the sentence and the verse).

BIBLIOGRAPHY

THE humble purpose of what follows is to provide a small selection of material that will help the reader to study the seven Greek authors dealt with in the book, and to obtain some notion of modern work on them, particularly in regard to literary criticism. It does not list all that I think worth reading; nor does it mention everything referred to in the footnotes of this book. In accordance with the aim in view, the general section has been made exceedingly brief. The section added on Roman poetry is very brief indeed in relation to the possible material, and inevitably somewhat arbitrary. (The subject of Hellenistic influence recurs in a prodigious quantity of scholarship; but truly novel approaches to it are infrequent.)

GENERAL. Indispensable collections of texts are provided by J. U. Powell, *Collectanea Alexandrina* (Oxford 1925), A. S. F. Gow and D. L. Page, *The Greek Anthology, Hellenistic Epigrams* (Cambridge 1965), and, above all, H. Lloyd-Jones and P. J. Parsons, *Supplementum Hellenisticum* (Texte und Kommentare I, Berlin 1983). U. von Wilamowitz-Moellendorff, *Hellenistiche Dichtung in der Zeit des Kallimachos* (Berlin 1924), offers a fundamental treatment of the period; it is especially valuable, however, for its discussions of particular works and passages, and repays dipping. A. W. Bulloch's sympathetic sketch contains interesting ideas (in *The Cambridge History of Classical Literature*, I. *Greek Literature*, ed. P. E. Easterling and B. M. W. Knox (Cambridge 1985), 541 ff.); the portion on Theocritus seems to me the best. An anthology with notes is forthcoming by N. Hopkinson. Some other works which discuss the literature in general: K. J. Dover, *Theocritus* (London 1971), lxvi ff.; H. Lloyd-Jones, 'A Hellenistic Miscellany', *SIFC* 3rd ser. 2 (1984), 52 ff.; L. E. Rossi, 'I generi letterari e le loro leggi scritte e non scritte nelle letterature classiche', *BICS* 18 (1971), 69 ff.; K. Ziegler, *Das hellenistiche Epos: ein vergessenes Kapitel der griechischen Dichtung* (2nd edn., Leipzig 1966). Works on the background cannot be mentioned here; but one cannot manage without R. Pfeiffer, *History of Classical Scholarship: From the Beginnings to the End of the Hellenistic Age* (Oxford 1968) or P. M. Fraser, *Ptolemaic Alexandria* (Oxford 1972); the latter is most useful, for these purposes, in its discussions of chronology.

Works on relations between two authors: E. Eichgrün, *Kallimachos und Apollonios Rhodios* (Diss. Berlin 1961); G. Schlatter, *Theokrit und Kallimachos* (Diss. Zürich 1941); A. Köhnken, *Apollonios und Theokrit* (Hypomnemata 12, Göttingen 1965). Cf. also M. R. Lefkowitz, *Lives of the Greek Poets* (London 1981), ch. 11.

CALLIMACHUS. The basic edition is the superb work of R. Pfeiffer, i. *Fragmenta* (Oxford 1949), ii. *Hymni et Epigrammata* (Oxford 1953). The latter volume includes an *index verborum*, and testimonia on the poet and scholia on the *Hymns*; its text of the *Hymns* does not raise quite enough questions. Fragments more recently discovered in *SH*. Commentaries on the *Hymns*: 1, G. R. McLennan (Testi e commenti 2, London 1977); 2, F. J. Williams (Oxford 1978); 3, F. Bornmann (Florence 1968); 4, W. H. Mineur (*Mnemosyne* Supp. 83, 1984); 5, A. W. Bulloch (Cambridge 1985); 6, N. Hopkinson (Cambridge 1984). The last two are especially helpful. Translations in the Loeb edition, *Hymns* and *Epigrams* by A. W. Mair (in a volume with Lycophron and Aratus, London and New York 1921, 2nd edn. London and Cambridge, Mass. 1955), fragments by C. Trypanis (London and Cambridge, Mass. 1958; repr. with Musaeus 1975).

General or on several works: H. Herter, *RE* Supp. xiii (1973), 154 ff.; R. Pfeiffer, *Ausgewählte Schriften* (Munich 1960); E. Reitzenstein, 'Zur Stiltheorie des Kallimachos', *Festschrift R. Reitzenstein* (Leipzig and Berlin 1931), 25 ff.; N. J. Richardson, 'Pindar and Literary Criticism in Antiquity', *Papers of the Liverpool Latin Seminar*, 5 (1985), 383 ff. (391 ff.); P. Veyne, *L'Élégie érotique romaine* (Paris 1983), ch. 2 (general picture); various articles are reprinted in *Kallimachos*, ed. A. Skiadas (Wege der Forschung 296, 1978).

Aetia: P. E. Knox, 'The epilogue to the *Aetia*', *GRBS* 26 (1985), 59 ff.; E. Livrea, 'Der Liller Kallimachos und die Mausefallen', *ZPE* 34 (1979), 37 ff.; P. J. Parsons, 'Callimachus: Victoria Berenices', *ZPE* 25 (1977), 1 ff. (essential); R. Pfeiffer, *Kallimachosstudien. Untersuchungen zur Arsinoe und zu den Aitia des Kallimachos* (Munich 1922); id., '*ΒΕΡΕΝΙΚΗΣ ΠΛΟΚΑΜΟΣ*', *Philologus*, 87 (1932), 179 ff.; R. F. Thomas, 'Callimachus, the *Victoria Berenices*, and Roman poetry', *CQ* NS 33 (1983), 92 ff.; S. R. West, 'Venus Observed? A Note on Callimachus, fr. 110', *CQ* NS (1985), 61 ff.; J. E. G. Zetzel, 'On the Opening of Callimachus, Aetia II', *ZPE* 42 (1981), 31 ff. *Iambi*: W. Bühler, 'Archilochus und Kallimachos', in *Archilochus* (Entretiens de la Fondation Hardt 10, 1964), 224 ff.; D. L. Clayman, *Callimachus' Iambi* (*Mnemosyne* Supp. 59, 1980); C. M. Dawson, 'The Iambi of Callimachus. A Hellenistic Poet's Experimental Laboratory', *YCS* 11 (1950), 1 ff. *Hecale*: edition by A. S. Hollis (forthcoming); K. J. Gutzwiller, *Studies in the Hellenistic Epyllion* (Beiträge zur klassischen Philologie 114, Meisenheim am Glan 1981), 49 ff.; A. S. Hollis, 'Some Fragments of Callimachus' *Hecale*', *CR* NS 15 (1965), 259 f.; id., 'Notes on

Callimachus' *Hecale*', *CQ* ns 32 (1982), 469 ff.; H. Lloyd-Jones and J. Rea, 'Callimachus Fragments 260–261', *HSCP* 72 (1968), 126 ff. (essential); G. Zanker, 'Callimachus' Hecale: A New Kind of Epic Hero?', *Antichthon* 11 (1977), 68 ff. *Hymns*: A. W. Bulloch, 'The Future of a Hellenistic Illusion: Some Observations on Callimachus and Religion', *MH* 41 (1984), 209 ff.; E. L. Bundy, 'The Quarrel between Kallimachos and Apollonius: Part 1. The Epilogue of Kallimachos's Hymn to Apollo', *CSCA* 5 (1972), 39 ff.; H. Herter, 'Kallimachos und Homer: Ein Beitrag zur Interpretation des Hymnos auf Artemis', *Kleine Schriften* (Munich 1975), 377 ff.; N. Hopkinson, 'Callimachus' Hymn to Zeus', *CQ* ns 34 (1984), 139 ff.; H. Kleinknecht, '*ΛΟΥΤΡΑ ΤΗΣ ΠΑΛΛΑΔΟΣ*', *Hermes* 74 (1939), 301 ff.; K. J. McKay, *The Poet at Play* (*Mnemosyne* Supp. 6, 1962); id., *Erysichthon: A Callimachean Comedy* (*Mnemosyne* Supp. 7, 1962). *Epigrams*: G. Kaibel, 'Zu den Epigrammen des Kallimachos', *Hermes* 31 (1896), 264 ff.

APOLLONIUS. F. Vian provides the standard edition, i (1974, Books 1–2), ii (1980, Book 3), iii (1981, Book 4; all Budé, Paris); this contains very valuable notes. The more adventurous text of H. Fränkel (Oxford 1961) should be consulted regularly: Vian's text does not really meet the challenge it presents. Vian's notes make the best commentary; see also G. W. Mooney's commentary on the whole (Dublin 1912); M. M. Gillies's on Book 3 (Oxford 1928), and Vian's separate commentary on it (Paris 1961); E. Livrea's on Book 4 (Florence 1973); and H. Fränkel, *Noten zu den Argonautika des Apollonios* (Munich 1968); M. Campbell, *Echoes and Imitations of Early Epic in Apollonius Rhodius* (*Mnemosyne* Supp. 72, 1981). The scholia (ed. C. Wendel, Berlin 1935) are fundamental for an understanding of the mythological tradition. Index: M. Campbell (Hildesheim 1983). Translations: E. Delage in Vian's Budé (French); R. C. Seaton (Loeb, London and New York 1912).

Studies: C. R. Beye, 'Jason as Love-hero in Apollonios' *Argonautika*', *GRBS* 10 (1969), 31 ff.; M. Campbell, *Studies in the Third Book of Apollonius Rhodius' Argonautica* (Altertumswissenschaftliche Texte und Studien IX, Hildesheim 1983); id., 'Apollonian and Homeric Book Division', *Mnemosyne* Ser. 4, 36 (1983), 154 f.; H. Faerber, *Zur dichterischen Kunst in Apollonios Rhodios' Argonautika* (Diss. Berlin 1928); H. Fränkel, 'Ein Don Quijote unter den Argonauten des Apollonios', *MH* 17 (1960), 1 ff.; M. Fusillo, *Il tempo delle Argonautiche: Un'analisi del racconto in Apollonio Rodio* (Rome 1985) (a stimulating book); M. W. Haslam, 'Apollonius Rhodius and the Papyri', *ICS* 3 (1978), 47 ff.; H. Herter, *RE* Supp. xiii (1973), 15 ff.; id., 'Hera spricht mit Thetis: Eine Szene des Apollonios von Rhodos', *Kleine Schriften* (Munich 1975), 439 ff.; R. L. Hunter, 'Apollo and the Argonauts. Two Notes on Ap. Rhod. 2, 669–719', *MH* 43 (1986), 56 ff.; A. Hurst, *Apollonios de Rhodes: manière et cohérence* (Rome 1967); T. M. Klein, 'Apollonius' Jason: Hero and Scoundrel', *QU* 13 (1983), 115 ff.; G. Lawall, 'Apollonius' *Argonautika*: Jason as Anti-hero', *YCS* 19 (1966), 119 ff.; P. G. Lennox, 'Apollonius, Argonautica 3, 1 ff. and Homer', *Hermes* 108 (1980), 45 ff.; D. N. Levin, *Apollonius' Argonautica Re-Examined, 1. The Neglected First and Second Books* (*Mnemosyne* Supp. 13, 1971); id., 'Apollonius' Herakles', *CJ* 67 (1971–2), 22 ff.; F. Vian, "*IHΛΩN AMHXANOΣ*", in E. Livrea and G. Privitera (eds.), *Studi in onore di A. Ardizzoni* (Rome 1978), ii. 1023 ff.; G. Zanker, 'The Love Theme in Apollonius Rhodius' Argonautica', *WS* NF 13 (1979), 52 ff.

THEOCRITUS. Standard text: A. S. F. Gow, with commentary (2nd edn., Cambridge 1952) or in *Bucolici Graeci* (Oxford 1952); rather a cautious text. Gow's commentary is extremely helpful at the level of verbal interpretation, and also gives a great deal of material; K. J. Dover's commentary should also be consulted (London 1971). Scholia: ed. C. Wendel (Leipzig 1914). Lexicon: J. Rumpel (Leipzig 1879). Translation: Gow, in commentary.

General or on several poems: F. Cairns, *Generic Composition in Greek and Latin Literature* (Edinburgh 1972); B. Effe, 'Die Destruktion der Tradition: Theokrits mythologische Gedichte', *RhM* NF 121 (1948), 48 ff.; W. Elliger, *Die Darstellung der Landschaft in der griechischen Dichtung* (Berlin 1975), 318 ff.; G. Fabiano, 'Fluctuation in Theocritus' style', *GRBS* 12 (1971), 517 ff.; F. T. Griffiths, *Theocritus at Court* (*Mnemosyne* Supp. 55, 1979); D. M. Halperin, *Before Pastoral* (California 1983) (rather wild); A. E.-A. Horstmann, *Ironie und Humor bei Theokrit* (Beiträge zur klassischen Philologie 67, Meisenheim am Glan 1976); U. Ott, *Die Kunst des Gegensatzes in Theokrits Hirtengedichten* (Spudasmata 22, Hildesheim 1969) (a rewarding book); T. G. Rosenmeyer, *The Green Cabinet: Theocritus and the European Pastoral Lyric* (California 1969) (not in my own view very helpful to the student of Theocritus); C. J. Ruijgh, 'Le dorien de Théocrite: dialecte cyrénien d'Alexandrie et d'Égypte', *Mnemosyne*, 4th ser. 37 (1984), 56 ff.; U. von Wilamowitz-Moellendorff, *Die Textgeschichte der griechischen Bukoliker* (Berlin 1906).

Individual poems: R. M. Ogilvie, 'The Song of Thyrsis', *JHS* 82 (1962), 106 ff.; F. J. Williams, 'Theocritus, Idyll i 81–91', *JHS* 89 (1969), 121 ff.; F. T. Griffiths, 'Poetry as *pharmakon* in Theocritus *Idyll* 2', *Arktouros: Hellenic Studies Presented to Bernard M. W. Knox*, ed. G. W. Bowersock, al. (Berlin 1979), 81 ff.; R. Whitaker, *Myth and Personal Experience in Roman Love-Elegy* (Hypomnemata 76, Göttingen 1983), 49 ff. (on poem 3); G. Giangrande, 'Victory and Defeat in Theocritus' Idyll V', *Mnemosyne*, 4th ser. 29 (1976), 143 ff.; on poem 7 see p. 201 n. 101; F. Cairns, 'Theocritus Idyll 10', *Hermes* 98 (1970), 38 ff.; A. Barigazzi, 'Una presunta aporia nel c. 11 di Teocrito', *Hermes* 103

(1977), 179 ff.; E. W. Spofford, 'Theocritus and Polyphemus', *AJP* 90 (1969), 22 ff.; G. Giangrande, 'Theocritus' Twelfth and Fourth Idylls: A Study in Hellenistic Irony', *QU* 12 (1971), 95 ff.; D. J. Mastronarde, 'Theocritus' Idyll 13: Love and the Hero', *TAPA* 99 (1968), 273 ff.; J. Stern, 'Theocritus' *Idyll* 14', *GRBS* 16 (1975), 5 ff.; F. T. Griffiths, 'Theocritus' Silent Dioscuri', *GRBS* 17 (1976), 353 ff.; C. Moulton, 'Theocritus and the Dioscuri', *GRBS* 14 (1973), 41 ff.; J. Stern, 'Theocritus' *Idyll* 24', *AJP* 95 (1974), 348 ff.; F. Cairns, 'The Distaff of Theugenis—Theocritus *Idyll* 28', *Papers of the Liverpool Latin Seminar*, 1 (1976), 293 ff.

ARATUS. There is no really satisfactory text: one should consult both E. Maass (Berlin 1893, with index) and J. Martin (Florence 1956). Scholia: ed. J. Martin (Stuttgart 1974). Translations: J. Martin, at back of edition (French); the translation by G. R. Mair in the Loeb edition of Callimachus, Lycophron, and Aratus (A. W. and G. R. Mair, London and New York 1921) is prone to inaccuracy. Studies: B. Effe, *Dichtung und Lehre: Untersuchungen zur Typologie des antiken Lehrgedichts* (Zetemata 69, Munich 1977), 40 ff.; M. Erren, *Die Phainomena des Aratos von Soloi: Untersuchungen zum Sach- und Sinnverständnis* (*Hermes* Einzelschriften 19, 1967); J.-M. Jacques, 'Sur un acrostiche d'Aratos (*Phén.*, 783–787)', *RÉA* 62 (1960), 48 ff.; G. Kaibel, 'Aratea', *Hermes*, 29 (1894), 82 ff.; W. Ludwig, 'Die Phainomena Arats als hellenistische Dichtung', *Hermes* 91 (1963), 425 ff. (the best introduction); id., *RE* Supp. x (1965), 26 ff.

HERODAS. Standard text: I. C. Cunningham (Oxford 1971). Cunningham's commentary is restricted in scope; there is a great deal of matter in the edition of W. Headlam and A. D. Knox (Cambridge 1922, with translation). Studies: W. G. Arnott, 'Herodas and the Kitchen Sink', *G&R* 2nd ser. 18 (1971), 121 ff.; I. C. Cunningham, 'Herodas 6 and 7', *CQ* NS 14 (1964), 32 ff.; id., 'Herodas 4', *CQ* NS 16 (1966), 113 ff.; T. Gelzer, 'Zur Kunsttheorie des Herodas', *Catalepton: Festschrift für Bernard Wyss*, ed. C. Schäublin (Hemsbach 1985), 96 ff.; R. G. Ussher, 'The Mimiamboi of Herodas', *Hermathena* 131 (1981), 65 ff.; B. Veneroni, 'Divagazioni sul quinto mimiambo di Eroda', *RÉG* 85 (1971), 319 ff.

LYCOPHRON. Standard text in edition of E. Scheer (Berlin 1881–1908), which includes an index, and the scholia; the latter are essential to understanding. Commentary: C. von Holzinger (Leipzig 1895). Translation: A. W. Mair, in Loeb edition of Callimachus, Lycophron, and Aratus (London and New York 1921); S. Josifović, *RE* Supp. xi (1968), 888 ff.; S. R. West, 'Notes on the Text of Lycophron', *CQ* NS 33 (1983), 114 ff.; id., 'Lycophron Italicised?', *JHS* 104 (1984), 127 ff.; K. Ziegler, *RE* xiii (1927), 2316 ff.

ASCLEPIADES. Standard text: *HE* (with commentary); see also D. L.

Page, *Epigrammata Graeca* (Oxford 1975), which differs on some matters. Notes too in O. Knauer, *Die Epigramme des Asklepiades von Samos* (Diss. Tübingen 1935). Translation: W. R. Paton, in Loeb edition of Greek Anthology (London and New York 1916–18). Studies: Alan Cameron, 'Women in the Epigrams of Asclepiades of Samos', *Reflections of Women in Antiquity*, ed. H. P. Foley (New York 1981), 275 ff.; D. H. Garrison, *Mild Frenzy: A Reading of the Hellenistic Love Epigram* (*Hermes* Einzelschriften 41, 1978), 48 ff.; S. L. Tarán, *The Art of Variation in the Hellenistic Epigram* (Columbia Studies in the Classical Tradition IX, Leiden 1979).

INFLUENCE ON ROMAN POETRY. Much useful material is assembled in commentaries: note particularly W. Kroll on Catullus, 2nd edn. (Berlin and Leipzig 1929); R. G. M. Nisbet and M. Hubbard on Horace, *Odes*, Books 1 and 2 (Oxford 1970, 1978); A. S. Hollis on Ovid, *Metamorphoses*, Book 8 (Oxford 1970; with addenda, 1983); cf. also P. Fedeli on Propertius, Books 1 and 3 (Florence 1980, 1983). Other works: W. W. Briggs, Jr., 'Virgil and the Hellenistic Epic', *Aufstieg und Niedergang der römischen Welt*, ii 31. 2 (1981), 948 ff.; A. W. Bulloch, 'Tibullus and the Alexandrians', *PCPS* NS 19 (1973), 85 ff.; F. Cairns, *Tibullus: A Hellenistic Poet at Rome* (Cambridge 1979); *The Cambridge History of Classical Literature*, ii: *Latin Literature*, ed. E. J. Kenney and W. V. Clausen (Cambridge 1982), especially 66 ff. (Gratwick on Ennius), 178 ff., with 832 (Clausen on Neoterics); W. V. Clausen, 'Callimachus and Latin Poetry', *GRBS* 5 (1964), 181 ff. (often cited); id., 'Catullus and Callimachus', *HSCP* 74 (1970), 85 ff.; N. B. Crowther, 'Catullus and the Traditions of Latin Poetry', *CP* 66 (1971), 246 ff.; id., 'Parthenius, Laevius and Cicero: Hexameter Poetry and Euphorionic Myth', *LCM* 5 (1980), 181 ff.; E. V. George, *Aeneid VIII and the Aetia of Callimachus* (*Mnemosyne* Supp. 27, 1974); J. Griffin, *Latin Poets and Roman Life* (Oxford 1985); O. Hezel, *Catull und das griechische Epigramm* (Tübinger Beiträge zur Altertumswissenschaft 17, Stuttgart 1932); M. E. Hubbard, *Propertius* (London 1974); A. Kambylis, *Die Dichterweihe und ihre Symbolik: Untersuchungen zu Hesiodos, Kallimachos, Properz und Ennius* (Heidelberg 1965); E. J. Kenney, 'Ovidius prooemians', *PCPS* NS 22 (1976), 46 ff.; W. Kroll, *Studien zum Verständnis der römischen Literatur* (Stuttgart 1924); R. O. A. M. Lyne, 'The Neoteric Poets', *CQ* NS 28 (1978), 167 ff.; C. W. Macleod, 'Propertius 4, 1', *Collected Essays* (Oxford 1983), 202 ff.; F. Mehmel, *Virgil und Apollonius Rhodius: Untersuchungen über die Zeitvorstellung in der antiken epischen Erzählung* (Diss. Hamburg 1940); J. K. Newman, *Augustus and the New Poetry* (Collection Latomus, 68, Brussels 1967), especially ch. 2; H. E. Pillinger, 'Some Callimachean Influences on Propertius, Book 4', *HSCP* 73 (1969), 171 ff.; S. Posch, *Beobachtungen zur Theokritnachwirkung bei Vergil* (Commentationes Aenipontanae 19,

1969); M. Puelma-Piwonka, *Lucilius und Kallimachos. Zur Geschichte einer Gattung der hellenistisch-römischen Poesie* (Frankfurt 1949); M. S. Santirocco, *Unity and Design in Horace's* Odes (Chapel Hill, NC, and London 1986); O. Skutsch, edition of Ennius, *Annales* (Oxford 1985), 147 ff.; R. F. Thomas, 'Callimachus, the *Victoria Berenices*, and Roman poetry', *CQ* NS 33 (1983), 92 ff.; P. Veyne, *L'Élégie érotique romaine* (Paris 1983), ch. 2; F. Wehrli, 'Horaz und Kallimachos', *MH* 1 (1944), 69 ff.; R. Whitaker, *Myth and Personal Experience in Roman Love-Elegy* (Hypomnemata 76, Göttingen 1983); W. Wimmel, *Kallimachos in Rom: die Nachfolge seines apologetischen Dichtens in der Augusteerzeit* (*Hermes* Einzelschriften 16, 1960) (the fullest treatment; a little dull); T. P. Wiseman, *Cinna the Poet and Other Roman Essays* (Leicester 1974), ch. 2; note also in General section the works by Wilamowitz (ii, ch. 8, Catullus) and Ziegler (pp. 53 ff., Ennius).

I GENERAL INDEX

II INDEX OF PASSAGES AND WORKS DISCUSSED